JAPANESE POLITIC
MEIJI R

RICHARD SIMS

Japanese Political History since the Meiji Renovation 1868-2000

palgrave

JAPANESE POLITICAL HISTORY SINCE THE MEIJI RENOVATION 1868-2000

PALGRAVE, 175 Fifth Avenue, New York, N.Y. 10010

First published by PALGRAVE, 175 Fifth Avenue, New York, NY 10010.
Companies and representatives throughout the world. PALGRAVE is the new global imprint of St. Martin's Press LLC Scholarly and Reference Division and Palgrave Publishers Ltd. (formerly Macmillan Press Ltd.)

Printed in Malaysia

ISBNs: 0-312-23914-9 (cloth)
      0-312-23915-7 (paper)

Library of Congress Cataloging-in-Publication Data
Sims, R.L. (Richard L.)
    Japanese political history since the Meiji renovation, 1868-2000 / Richard Sims.
       p. cm.
    Includes bibliographical references and index.
    ISBN 0-312-23914-9 -- ISBN 0-312-23915-7 (pbk.)
    1. Japan--Politics and government·-- 1868- I. Title.

DS881.91. S5665 2001
952.03'3--dc21

                                                        00-051474

ACKNOWLEDGEMENTS

I must first acknowledge my gratitude to my publishers in London for inviting me to update and extend the earlier version of this book, which appeared in 1991 under the imprint of the Vikas Publishing House in New Delhi. Because that version was part of a series which was intended to include a separate volume on recent Japanese politics, it was not appropriate for me to cover the post-1952 period in detail. I am therefore pleased to have had the chance to make the work more complete (although I am all too well aware that it is impossible to cover every aspect of modern Japanese political history in one volume).

In addition to the historians whose works are listed in the bibliography, this book owes a great deal, directly or indirectly, to a considerable number of scholars who have personally helped to shape my understanding of Japanese history over the past four decades. First among these is Bill Beasley, who guided me initially as a research supervisor and later as a colleague and fellow teacher and to whom I owe an incalculable debt. Among the various Japanese historians who have aided and encouraged me, particular mention must be made of Oka Yoshitake and Mitani Taichiro, both of whom went out of their way, despite their many other commitments, to make my periods of research at Tokyo University rewarding, and of Sakai Yukichi, who provided me with an invaluable introduction to local political history, notably during a trip to collect politicians' records in Akita in 1972. It is a pleasure to express gratitude also to Uchikawa Yoshimi, Miyachi Masato, Miyake Masaki, Banno Junji, Emura Eiichi, Matsuo Takayoshi and Taguchi Shoichiro, with all of whom I have had informative discussions. Needless to say, they bear no responsibility for the ways in which I have incorporated their ideas in this book. In some places, indeed, several of them would almost certainly strike a different balance or emphasise other factors. It is natural, however, that some aspects of Japanese history should be seen through a different perspective from outside Japan.

Apart from colleagues and other scholars I must also acknowledge the contribution of my students at the School of Oriental and African Studies in the University of London. They have provided a testing-ground for the interpretations which appear in the following pages, and have not infrequently forced me to refine or qualify my arguments or to seek further support for them. I hope that their successors will derive some benefit from their critical efforts.

Last but not least, I wish to thank my wife Denise who has laboured long and, on the whole, uncomplainingly in typing not only the present book but also two earlier versions.

London, August 2000   R. S.

CONTENTS

ILLUSTRATIONS

between pages 36 and 37

PREFACE

For much of the last forty years the foreign image of Japan has been overwhelmingly dominated by a mixture of admiration for, envy of, and apprehension about that country's extraordinary economic growth, and at least until the 1990s businessmen and economists alike sought to learn from Japan's success. In stark contrast the Japanese political system and its evolution have impinged only slightly on outside perceptions. Many foreigners are unaware that Japan is a constitutional democracy, and, even among the better informed, few, if any, would advocate the adoption of Japanese political practices or hold Japanese politicians up as models to be emulated. No Japanese political leader has ever attracted anything approaching the fascination aroused by Mao Tse-tung or the admiration felt for Jawaharlal Nehru. Nor does this surprise the Japanese themselves, for even within Japan there is little inclination to boast about the conduct of Japanese politics. Still less is any pride taken in Japan's modern political heritage. Indeed, many Japanese would maintain that between 1868 and 1945 Japan's development was distorted by the ruling élite's propagation of an authoritarian 'Emperor-system', while some would go so far as to claim that the introduction of unequivocally democratic institutions after the Second World War was, and has remained, largely a nominal change which had only a limited effect on basic attitudes and practices.[1]

It would be impossible to deny the validity of much of the criticism of Japan's modern political record. Before 1945, certainly, repression and government indoctrination always existed to a greater or lesser extent, together with a reluctance on the part of the ruling élite to concede full political rights even to the male

[1] One important contemporary politician who has expressed such view is Ozawa Ichiro. In an article published in October 1993, he described Japan's parliamentary democracy as a peculiarly Japanese style of politics and not the real thing. Ozawa Ichiro and Fukuda Kazuya, 'Turing Japan into a Self-Reliant Nation', *Japan Echo*, vol 20, no. 4 (winter 1993), p. 22.

population. It is also the case that the political system which evolved in the early twentieth century out of the earlier oligarchic style of government proved ineffective in terms of providing rational, coordinated decision-making, especially in foreign policy, and clearly contributed to Japan's blundering into disastrous international conflict in the 1930s and early '40s. Moreover, both before and after the Pacific War the management of Japanese politics was tainted by corruption and the use of financial inducements (the latter on a scale rarely matched elsewhere), with general principles and issues playing a relatively minor role in elections.

However justified such criticism is, a political history of modern Japan which sought only to emphasise and condemn failure would be unacceptably one-sided. The fact that Japan has proved able to combine a high degree of political stability with virtually unlimited freedom of political and intellectual expression over the last half-century suggests that its pre-war political experience may not have been entirely unconstructive. Nor is modern Japanese political tradition wholly authoritarian. It also contains a significant anti-Establishment strand which emerged alongside the oligarchic construction of a modern state in the 1870s and was more broadly based than is often supposed. Similarly, although modern Japan has become increasingly centralised, localism has remained strong. Even now, for instance, it would be extremely difficult for a politician to be elected to represent an area in which he was an outsider; and if he did not attend to local interests in general and constituents' requests in particular, his chances of re-election would be negligible. Furthermore, although nationalism was an extremely potent force between the mid-nineteenth and mid-twentieth centuries, it did not completely prevent the development of liberal attitudes; and neither education nor religion nor the law were wholly subjected to the purposes of the state, even when calls for national unity reached a peak in the decade and half preceding 1945.

In an overview of Japan's modern political record one further aspect merits attention. Although conflict has not been uncommon in Japanese politics, and has sometimes taken a violent form, it is generally agreed that among élite groups (including political parties) a propensity to compromise has been far more pronounced than the tendency to stand absolutely firm on principles or policies or to push differences to an extreme. This tendency, which may well owe much to the exceptional racial homogeneity of the Japanese and (despite considerable religious diversity) the absence of bitter sectarianism, has customarily been regarded by idealistic Japanese historians in an essentially negative light – as an obstacle to the achievement of democratic government by political parties through the mobilisation of popular forces and the threat of force. It is, however, not unlikely that a more confrontational style of politics would have led to a strengthening of authoritarianism rather than constitutionalism; and if it is acknowledged that political modernisation presents formidable problems, the development of a 'politics of compromise' may be seen as less deserving of condemnation. A willingness to accommodate different interests and to exercise restraint in the pursuit of power may have played a key role in the evolution of a viable political system which, for all its faults, allowed an increasing measure of popular participation while remaining basically stable. In this respect, at least, Japanese politics may offer a useful lesson.

GLOSSARY

Asahi Shimbun   A major Japanese newspaper.

Bakufu   The administrative organisation (originally a military headquarters) of a Shogun before 1868. Though responsible for national affairs, it ruled directly over less than a half of Japan.

Bungei Shunju   A major Japanese monthly periodical.

buraku   A hamlet, after 1888 part of an administrative village (*mura*).

burakumin   Inhabitants of ghetto-like communities, who continued to suffer discrimination after they were given legal equality in 1871. Also known as *eta* ('full of filth'), they were traditionally associated with professions which involved the taking of life.

bushido   The 'way of the warrior', the idealised ethical code of the samurai (*bushi*) class of feudal Japan. It emphasised total dedication by a warrior to his lord.

Choshu   A feudal domain which played a major role in the Meiji Ishin.

Daido Danketsu   The anti-government alliance which brought together the different wings of the political opposition in the late 1880s.

daimyo   The ruler of a feudal domain in Tokugawa Japan. Many *daimyo* left decision-making to retainers, however, and were little more than figureheads in 1868. Until 1862 they spent every other year at the Tokugawa capital, Edo.

Dajokan   The Council of Government in Japan between 1869 and 1885, when it was replaced by a modern cabinet system.

genro	The select group of Meiji leaders who were recognised as elder statesmen from the 1890s and continued to advise the Emperor on important political matters, usually determining the prime ministerial succession. Until his death in 1922 Yamagata Aritomo was the leading *genro*. The last (and from 1924 the only) *genro* was Saionji Kimmochi.
Genro-in	A high-level advisory body on legislation, 1875–90.
gun	A traditional administrative district which from 1878 to 1923 functioned as a sub-prefectural unit with an officially appointed head.
haihan chiken	The abolition of feudal domains and their replacement by a centralised prefectural system (29 August 1871).
han	Autonomous or semi-autonomous feudal domains, of which there were about 270 in 1868, ranging in size from small fiefs which produced only 10,000 *koku* of rice a year to a few very large ones, like Kaga, Satsuma and Choshu, which produced close to 1,000,000 *koku*. They were subjected to occasional levies by the Bakufu, but not regular taxation.
hanbatsu	Cliques based on particular *han*.
hanseki hokan	The return of *han* registers to the Emperor in 1869, an important step towards the ending of feudal autonomy.
harakiri	The ritual cutting open of the belly, a form of suicide chosen (originally by samurai) to avoid disgrace or make a public protest or gesture. Also known as *seppuku*.
jiban	The political base of established support, usually depending on lower-level assembly members and *yuryokusha*, on which politicians depended to secure most of their votes. They were, and to some extent still are, based mainly on a particular geographical area within a constituency.
jushin	The elder statesmen, mostly ex-Prime Ministers, who were sometimes consulted between 1934

	and 1945 on the choice of a new Prime Minister and other important matters.
Kanto	The region of eastern Japan which includes Tokyo.
kazoku kokka	'Family State', a late-Meiji ideological concept intended to denote the special relationship between Emperor and people and the unique character of the *kokutai*.
Keidanren	Federation of Economic Organisations, the major big business association.
Kizoku-in	The House of Peers, the upper chamber in the Japanese Diet, 1890-1947.
kobun	Literally 'child role', the protégé, henchman or disciple of an influential personage, boss or teacher (*oyabun* or *oyakata*).
Kochi	The name of the prefecture which replaced the *han* of Tosa (and also its main city).
kocho	The mayor of a village or group of villages, 1871-89.
Kodoha	The 'Imperial Way faction', a group of army officers in the 1930s associated in particular with Generals Araki and Mazaki.
koenkai	The support organisation of a politician.
koku	Unit of measurement for rice, approximately 4.96 bushels (roughly 300 lbs).
Kokugaku	'National Learning', a school of thought in late Tokugawa Japan which emphasised the nation's indigenous (non-Chinese) tradition and the supposed divine descent of the reigning imperial dynasty.
kokutai	'National polity (or structure)', a word which implied that the Japanese state possessed a unique (almost tribalistic) character based on the special position of the Emperor and an unbroken imperial line.
Meiji	The name given (from 1868) to the reign of Mutsuhito, the Emperor who succeeded to the throne in 1867 and died in 1912. The Emperor himself is usually referred to by his reign-period name, the use of his personal name being con-

	sidered disrespectful.
Nohonshugi	The ideological tradition which stressed the essential importance of agriculture as the foundation of society and encouraged village cooperation and self-help. It was sometimes linked with hostility towards capitalism, industrialisation and urbanisation.
Rengo	The major labour union federation after its formation in the late 1980s.
Sa-in	The 'Left Board', the legislative advisory body in the *Dajokan*. It was replaced by the *Genro-in* in 1875.
Sangi	State Councillor in the *Dajokan* system of government, 1869–85.
sangyo kumiai	Producers' cooperatives, government-encouraged mutual assistance groups which spread rapidly through Japanese villages in the early decades of the twentieth century.
Sat-Cho	Abbreviation of Satsuma and Choshu.
Satsuma	A feudal domain which played a major role in the Meiji Ishin. After the abolition of the *han* in 1871 it became Kagoshima prefecture.
Sei-in	From 1871 until its abolition in 1877 the highest decision-making body in the Meiji government. Its members, mainly *Sangi*, also laid down general policy guidelines.
Shinto	The indigenous religion of Japan which, as well as its popular side involving fertility and purity rites and reverence for exceptional natural phenomena, also embraced the officially-sponsored belief in the divine origins of the Japanese imperial family and the Japanese islands.
shishi	Patriotic activists (literally 'spirited samurai') who engaged in anti-Bakufu or anti-foreign activities in the 1860s. Sometimes referred to as 'men of high purpose'.
shizoku	'Gentry families', the general name applied to all samurai after *hanseki hokan* in 1869. It de-emphasised the many differences of status within the samurai class.

Shogun	The title, meaning 'general', given to military rulers who controlled Japan in the name of the Emperor.
Showa	The name given to the reign period of Hirohito, Emperor from 1926 to 1989.
Shugi-in	The title of the elected Lower House of the Diet under both the Meiji constitution and the 1946 constitution, and of the assembly of samurai representatives of *han* which met occasionally between 1869 and 1871.
Sodomei	The main labour union federation in Japan in the inter-war and early post-war periods.
Soka Gakkai	The largest and, through the Komeito party, most politically involved of Japan's 'new religions'.
Sohyo	The largest labour union federation from the 1950s to the late '80s.
Taisho	The name given to the reign period 1912-26.
Tokugawa	The family which held the shogunal power from 1603 to 1868.
Tosa	A feudal domain which played an important part in the Meiji Ishin.
U-in	The 'Right Board', which from 1871 until its abolition in 1875 comprised the ministers and vice-ministers of government departments and discussed problems of administration. From 1873 it was not convoked regularly.
yen	The main unit of currency in Japan after the Meiji government took full control of, and unified, the nation's finances in 1872. For the changes in its value in relation to the dollar, see the appended table.
yuryokusha	Local men with political influence.
zaibatsu	The relatively small number of very large financial and industrial combines, each originally under the control of a single family, which in the course of Japan's economic modernisation, and often with the aid of special government subsidies or other favours, came to dominate Japanese banking and industry. Some, such as Mitsui and Mitsubishi, owned or controlled many

companies and were important in almost every sector. They were partly broken up in the early stages of the post-1945 Occupation.

zaikai A term referring to big business and especially the main big business organisations, Keidanren and Nikkeiren.

zoku Literally 'tribe', but in the political context referring to those Diet members (mainly, but not exclusively, from the Liberal Democratic Party) who were recognised as possessing specialised knowledge of an area of government and influence over the ministry administering it.

zoku giin A Diet member belonging to a *zoku*.

A NOTE ON JAPANESE NAMES

All Japanese personal names are written with the family name preceding the given name, as is customary in Japan. In a few cases an alternative reading of a given name is given in brackets when a person is first mentioned. This is because the Chinese ideographs used in Japanese are normally susceptible to being read in more than one way in Japan, and the alternative renderings of some Japanese given names are almost equally common. Hara Takashi, for instance, is very often known as Hara Kei.

It should also be noted that Japanese does not normally distinguish between singular and plural. Whether words such as *daimyo* or *genro* denote one person or more than one, therefore, depends on the context.

Readers may be puzzled by the fact that Japanese political parties are at times referred to by their (sometimes abbreviated) Japanese title and at others by their English translation. For the period before 1952 I have been consistent in using the Japanese title, both because most other books do so and because the translations of some of the very numerous parties would be the same in English, though different in Japanese. Kaishinto and Shimpoto, for instance, would both be rendered as Progressive Party. The post-1952 situation is rather different. Most Western writers tend to use an abbreviated form of the translated title, especially in the case of the long-dominant Liberal Democratic Party (LDP), which in Japanese is normally referred to as the Jiminto, although its full name is Jiyuminshuto. In certain cases, however, where the conventional English rendering is either not literal (as in the case of Komeito/Clean Government Party) or unfamiliar (as with Sakigake/Harbinger Party), the Japanese title is usually employed. In order to minimise confusion I have used whichever title is most commonly found in English-language books.

THE CHANGING VALUE OF THE YEN

	US dollars per 100 Yen		US dollars per 100 Yen
1874	101.6	1921	48.2
1877	96.1	1923	48.9
1879	88.7	1924	42.1
1882	91.3	1925	40.9
1884	88.9	1926	46.1
1886	78.9	1929	46.1
1888	74.2	1930	49.4
1890	82.1	1931	48.8
1891	78.0	1932	28.1
1892	69.8	1933	25.2
1893	62.1	1934	29.5
1894	50.8	1938	28.5
1900	49.4	1939	25.9
1910	49.5	1940	23.4
1920	49.8		

After the Pacific War, Japan experienced hyper-inflation. When the yen-dollar rate was stabilised in 1949, 100 yen were worth approximately 28 cents and this remained the case until 1971. Thereafter the exchange rate varied as follows:

	Yen per dollar		Yen per dollar
1972	302	1987	122
1973	280	1988	126
1974	300	1989	143
1976	293	1990	135
1977	240	1991	125
1978	195	1992	125
1979	240	1993	112
1980	227 *	1994	100
1982	249 *	1995	103
1985	239 *	1996	116
1986	160	1997	130

* Indicates average for year (the other postwar figures refer to the end of the year).

1

THE MEIJI RENOVATION

The year 1868 marks a turning-point in Japanese history comparable with 1789 in France or 1917 in Russia. On 3 January 1868 a
handful of ambitious samurai from *han* (feudal domains) in south-
west Japan carried out a bold *coup d'état* by seizing control of the
Imperial Palace in the ancient capital of Kyoto. With the backing
of some sympathetic court nobles and samurai from a few other
han, they ousted the Bakufu (the regime headed by a Shogun from
the Tokugawa family which had held sway over the country for
over two and a half centuries) and proclaimed the restoration of
power to the imperial dynasty which had reigned over Japan for
well over a thousand years but had for more than five centuries
been excluded from any role in government, save that of conferring legitimacy on whichever feudal leader achieved supremacy.

This was to be far more than a dynastic restoration, however.
In contrast with most contemporary expectations the change of
regime was to lead directly to the epoch-making transformation
known in Japanese as the Meiji Ishin.[1] Within four years *han* autonomy was to give way to a centralised system of prefectures, and
the four-class system of samurai, peasant, artisan and merchant – in
which the samurai, the Japanese hereditary military élite, enjoyed
special status – was jettisoned. These momentous changes were
followed by the ending of the traditional samurai monopoly of
military service in 1873, the abolition of their time-honoured right

---

[1] Meiji Ishin is traditionally translated as Meiji Restoration, a term which lays
stress on the formal return of power to the Emperor (at this time the fifteen-year-
old Mutsuhito), whose close advisers were, towards the end of 1868, to introduce
a new year-period with the name Meiji ('enlightened government'). This translation, however, reflects the bias of pre-1945 official historiography, and is both less
accurate and less appropriate than Meiji Renovation. It should be noted that in
contrast with previous practice, whereby a new year-period name was adopted
whenever it was considered appropriate (often after no more than three or four
years), the name since 1868 has remained the same for the whole of an Emperor's
reign.

to wear swords in 1876, and finally, in the same year, the conversion of their annual stipends into government bonds. Together with these major political and social changes came a policy of 'civilisation and enlightenment' which encouraged the study of the West and involved the introduction of Western-style institutions and systems, notably a modern elementary education system in 1872. Two years before this a Ministry of Public Works was established to promote Western technology and in the same year a loan was floated in Britain for the building of Japan's first railway – from Yokohama to Tokyo. Such changes and innovations were just the most obvious features of the initial stages of Japan's dramatic transformation into a modern nation-state dedicated to the cause of catching up with the leading Western powers.

Japan in the mid-nineteenth century

The rapidity of the change which occurred in Japan from the 1860s was remarkable by any standards; it appears even more striking when set against the static character of Japanese institutional life during the preceding two centuries. Perhaps the most distinctive aspect of Japan's resistance to change was its conscious self-isolation from the West. Following an initial period of intense interest in European culture and military technology (developed in the sixteenth and early seventeenth centuries, principally through contacts with Portuguese missionaries and merchant-adventurers) the early Tokugawa rulers had gradually restricted intercourse with Westerners in order to eliminate the danger of political and ideological disruption. After 1640 the only European foothold in Japan was on the artificial islet of Deshima in Nagasaki harbour, where a handful of Dutch traders, tolerated because of their lack of connection with missionary activities and because they provided a channel for books and information, were kept under close supervision. In 1854 the American Commodore Perry did secure a very limited relaxation of restrictions on visits by Western ships, and in 1858, in the face of a threatening British expedition headed by Lord Elgin, fresh from triumph over the Chinese in the Arrow War, the Tokugawa Bakufu broke more significantly with its traditional policy of seclusion by allowing trade in Yokohama and a few other ports; but ten years later xenophobic attitudes remained strong and foreigners still needed to be wary of attack by fanatical samurai. Christianity, which had been rigorously proscribed after gaining over half a million adherents out of a population of about 18 million in the early seventeenth century, continued to be strictly forbidden to the Japanese; even after 1868, several thousand Japanese Christians whose families had secretly preserved their religious identity until 1865 were subjected to severe punishment for several years.

As part of its policy of suppression of Christianity the Bakufu had compelled all Japanese to register with Buddhist temples. However this form of official patronage did little, if anything, to restore the declining intellectual vitality of the various Buddhist sects in Japan. Nor did it allow them to play any sort of political role. From the eighth to the sixteenth century Buddhist temples had been major landholders and had exercised considerable influence, while the newer Amidhist sects, which sprang up in the twelfth and thirteenth centuries promising salvation in the Pure Land, had attracted such wide support that they became a force to be reckoned with in the endemic civil warfare which wracked Japan in the sixteenth century. But both temples and sects had seen their power savagely emasculated by Oda Nobunaga, the first of the three feudal chieftains who brought unity to Japan between 1560 and 1615; and in a society so tightly controlled by its feudal rulers as that established by Ieyasu, the first Tokugawa Shogun, there was no room for political activity by religious institutions. Even if they had nurtured such ambitions, they no longer commanded the same resources as before. Moreover, religion had ceased to exercise the same influence on the minds of the samurai class. The consolidation of Tokugawa hegemony over rival feudal lords had been accompanied by the official encouragement of Confucian learning, which was seen as a valuable supplement to the traditional bases of feudal loyalty, and in the more stable era which followed the ending of feudal warfare the rational secular approach of Chinese Neo-Confucianism held a much greater appeal than Buddhism to samurai scholars. Under the patronage of Bakufu and *daimyo* (domain lords) Confucian values were intensively propagated in the academies which a growing number of samurai attended.

Confucianism was undoubtedly an important ingredient of the political stability which characterised Tokugawa Japan. At the same time, however, the debates between different scholars and different schools were an indication that intellectual life was by no means stagnant. Moreover, from the late eighteenth century the domi-

nance of Confucian learning began to be challenged from two quite
different directions – on the one hand by the gradual acquisition of
Western knowledge, known as 'Dutch Learning' (*Rangaku*), the
superiority of which in science, especially medicine, and military
matters was appreciated by a small but growing number of open-
minded samurai, and on the other hand by 'National Learning'
(*Kokugaku*), which represented a nativist reaction in favour of Japan's
pre-Confucian traditions and attracted particular interest among
Shinto (Japan's indigenous religion) priests and wealthy peasants.
Even in the field of religion the situation was not entirely static.
During the nineteenth century new sects with roots in popular
religious beliefs such as shamanism were spreading in rural areas. At
the same time education was becoming more widespread. By 1850
there were about 10,000 schools (often one-teacher village schools)
in Japan, and nearly half of all Japanese males (and about one in
seven females) were literate.

Such intellectual and social developments did not pose any
immediate threat to the political system. But feudal government,
with its heavy dependence on agricultural taxes, found it difficult
to adjust to the growth of a vigorous commercial economy. Ironically, one of the main stimuli of urban commercialism was the
policy of feudal control known as *sankin-kotai* (alternate attendance),
whereby the Shogun compelled *daimyo* to spend every other year
in Edo. The large establishments which the near 300 *daimyo* were
obliged to maintain in the capital helped to make it probably the
largest city in the world by 1700 with at least 1 million inhabitants;
while Osaka, the port from which produce from the most eco-
nomically advanced region of Japan was supplied to Edo by sea,
grew to almost half the latter's size. Towns which lay on the routes
to Edo taken by *daimyo* retinues also flourished, as indeed did many
other towns, for like the Shogun most *daimyo* in the early seventeenth century sought to reduce the danger of rebellion (hitherto
not uncommon) by compelling vassals to give up their independent local bases and move to the *han* castle-town, where they would
receive a stipend from the *daimyo's* warehouse. One effect of sev-
enteenth-century urbanisation was to undermine the samurai ethic
of frugality, for in the towns and cities there were opportunities for
consumption which had not existed in the countryside. These not
only included different foods and styles of dress but also new forms
of entertainment, such as the (*kabuki*) theatre, *sumo* wrestling, teahouses,

geisha (skilled female entertainers), books (including cheap novels), and woodblock prints. Since the Tokugawa era was also one of unprecedented peace, it was inevitable that martial qualities would be less emphasised and less tested in practice. Because of these changes it gradually became more difficult for rulers to maintain a tight control over the peasantry, and even though crop yields rose as a result of the dissemination of improved seed-strains, techniques and tools, it proved impossible to meet the expanded needs of the urban-based ruling class by increasing the land tax. Similar difficulties arose when domain governments attempted to establish monopolistic controls over the new forms of commercial production, such as paper-making or soya sauce brewing, which wealthy peasants, especially in the nineteenth century, were developing. All too often the outcome was organised peasant protest, which increasingly tended to end in concession or retreat by the feudal authorities.

Beneath the surface, therefore, Japanese society had changed significantly by the mid-nineteenth century. Even so, the overall appearance of stability was remarkable, and in one important respect in particular that stability was genuine. After a period of rapid increase during the seventeenth century, Japan's population rose only from about 31 million in 1720 to roughly 33 million in 1850. Such a slow growth rate contrasts strikingly with the experience of other countries during the same period. How and why such population control was achieved is still a matter of debate, although it is clear that it owed nothing to official policy and much to conscious family choice. The absence of population pressure, however, may have been a crucial factor in the long duration of the Tokugawa system of government.

The causes of the Meiji Ishin

Since the Meiji Ishin marked the real beginning of modern Japanese political history, it is essential to consider its nature and try to identify the forces which produced it, though this is by no means an easy task. One fundamental problem results from the unusually decentralised political structure of Japan before 1868. The fact that the Tokugawa Bakufu held directly less than a third of the national territory, and that many of the *daimyo* still retained some measure of independence in their own domains, meant that significant political activity took place not just in the Tokugawa capital of Edo but in the various castle-towns where conservatives, reformers and moderates manoeuvred for influence. Moreover, the continued existence of the imperial dynasty and court in Kyoto provided another focus for political machination and agitation in 1858, when the Bakufu's authority was undermined by its inability to resist the Western powers' demands for the opening of Japan and an unstable situation developed in which Bakufu, reformist *daimyo* and radical xenophobic samurai all competed for the support of the Emperor and the court.

Another problem of interpretation stems from the fact that the Meiji Ishin had both internal and external causes. For many years it was the Western impact which was stressed – on the one hand the disruptive challenge to the traditional policy of isolation (which had come to be regarded as sacrosanct), on the other the attraction of the Western model. Eventually approaches which treated major historical developments as the result of internal economic and social changes gained a hold and from the 1920s there was a tendency to regard external factors more as a catalyst than as a main cause. Non-Japanese historians have rarely been willing, however, to play down the latter to such an extent, and in Japan too historians have become more inclined to see similarities with nationalist revolutions against imperialistic pressure or colonialism in other non-Western societies. Nevertheless, wide variations in the evaluation of the relative importance of domestic issues and outside influence still remain.

Nor is any consensus to be found with regard to the nature of internal causes. All historians accept that behind the façade of political stability presented by the apparently unchanging feudal system lurked forces which were undermining or threatening the established order. But which of these forces were most significant and how immediate was the threat has provoked much disagreement. One older view emphasised the growth of a wealthy urban merchant class in Tokugawa Japan. Closer study, however, revealed that the urban merchants were mostly not involved in the overthrow of the Bakufu. Their interests, it is now held, were bound up with feudal rulers to whom most of them were creditors; and if *daimyo* and Bakufu were often slow to repay loans, the Meiji government soon went further by formally repudiating most of the debts incurred before 1868. Moreover, the urban merchants' lack of interest in freeing themselves from feudal restraints was shown by their slowness to engage in modern industry or foreign trade, when this was encouraged by the new regime. Marxist scholars of the *Rono* (Workers and Peasants) school still maintained that the Meiji Ishin was a bourgeois revolution, but the claim was based either on the fact that Japan's incorporation into the world economy resulted in the rapid growth of Japanese capitalism or on the significance of economic growth in the late Tokugawa period at a more local level, particularly among wealthy peasants around cities and towns in central Japan.

Another Marxist school of interpretation – the Kozaha (Lectures Faction) – criticised the view that the Meiji Ishin was a bourgeois revolution by stressing the strong feudal legacy which carried over to the post-1868 period and which, it was argued, accounted for the reactionary militarism which characterised the 1930s. The key political aspect of the Meiji Ishin, according to these very influential historians, was the emergence of an absolutist government based on an alliance between lower-ranking samurai and the wealthy peasantry. The latter normally served as local officials and controlled the villages, but as the chief producers of commercial crops and domestic goods they were most affected by the monopolistic restrictions which *han* governments were often tempted to impose on the marketing of such produce, and it was not unknown for them to participate in the numerous peasant uprisings which occurred in late Tokugawa Japan. In the last resort, however, their anti-feudal feelings were outweighed, it is maintained, by their fear of the increasingly rebellious poorer peasants, who often turned against them during the uprisings. In consequence, the village leaders' concern for law and order led them to support reformist elements in the samurai class in the creation of a new absolutist system which would guarantee their vested interests as landlords and moneylenders. Thus the Meiji Ishin is seen as basically counter-revolutionary – a revolution 'from above' which pre-empted a potential revolution 'from below'.

The Kozaha emphasis on the absolutist character of the Meiji government has an obvious advantage over the 'bourgeois revolution' view in that it does not have to explain away the fact that most of the leaders of the movement which overthrew the Tokugawa were in fact samurai. However, it is open to a number of questions and criticisms. How great, for instance, really was the threat from below? Peasant uprisings were certainly increasing in number, but

their growth pattern was cyclical and there had been almost as many
in the 1830s, when there was a succession of bad harvests, as there
were in the 1860s. They had, indeed, in the earlier decade given
rise to some reforms, both in the Bakufu and many *han*, and there
were some signs that in certain areas lower-ranking samurai reformers and peasant leaders shared a common hostility towards the
han government and *han* monopolies. But there is no clear evidence that peasant uprisings caused wealthy peasants more than
temporary alarm. Moreover, it implies extraordinary prescience on
the part of the peasant élite to suggest that it was able to foresee the
creation of a stronger form of government. Had the Bakufu forces
resisted the *coup d'état* more strongly and the civil war of 1868
lasted longer or proved inconclusive, as might well have happened,
the threat to order and property would have been far greater than
before. Even as it was, the number of uprisings actually increased to
their highest peak in 1868-9. Only hindsight makes the eventual
outcome of a more stable regime seem predictable. Furthermore,
the two south-western *han* which played by far the most decisive
role in the Ishin – Choshu and Satsuma – were areas where village
society was relatively stable and peasant uprisings were extremely
uncommon.

To raise doubts about the counter-revolutionary attitude of the
wealthy peasants is not to deny the existence of a peasant factor in
the Meiji Ishin. There is some documentary evidence that Bakufu
and *han* leaders were disturbed by the breakdown of order caused
by peasant uprisings (especially those of 1866) and feared their spread.
But they were most common in or around land held by the Bakufu
rather than in the domains which supported the restoration of power
to the Emperor, and their main effect may have been to undermine
Tokugawa finances and morale rather than stimulate an anti-
Bakufu alliance. After 1868 wealthy peasants may well have supported the Meiji government's creation of a centralised state, but
there are no grounds for supposing that there were direct links
before 1868 between the peasantry in Tokugawa territories and
samurai from south-western domains.

Whatever disagreement there may be about the place of the
peasantry, no-one would deny the vital role of the samurai. Samurai were still very much in control in the 1860s and their relatively
large numbers (about 6 per cent of the population, a legacy of the
large armies needed in the fierce warfare of the sixteenth century)

made it impossible for other classes to challenge the established system of government directly. Many samurai, however, had cause for discontent by the mid-nineteenth century. The financial difficulties with which all Japanese feudal rulers had to grapple as their revenues failed to keep pace with the increase in opportunities for consumption and with the costs of maintaining large establishments in Edo frequently led them to economise by cutting the hereditary stipends. For samurai at the top levels of the highly-stratified, pyramidic vassal structure, such cuts were hardly more than an inconvenience, but some middle-ranking vassals, and many of the far more numerous lower samurai, may have been forced to seek some form of supplementary employment. Their sense of grievance may have been inhibited by the ideal of loyalty with which samurai were imbued, but when lower-ranking men of ability saw the major positions in the *han* government monopolised by vassals of high hereditary rank but no special competence, resentment was natural. It was only when the political system seemed to have no answer to the Western threat in the 1850s and '60s, though, that open samurai dissidence emerged. Inspired by ideas drawn mainly from *Mitogaku* (a form of Confucianism developed by scholars in Mito *han* which emphasised the primary position of the Emperor as the source of political authority) and from *Kokugaku*, samurai patriotic activists (*shishi*) thronged to Edo and Kyoto, calling for *sonno-joi* (reverence for the Emperor, expulsion of the barbarians) and not infrequently attacking Bakufu officials and foreigners, sometimes with fatal results. In their own domains, however, these mostly low-ranking *sonno-joi* samurai were generally less successful, and even in Edo and Kyoto their agitation was curtailed after 1863-4.

The actual overthrow of the Tokugawa Bakufu was not achieved by terrorist tactics but was carried out by those samurai, principally in Satsuma, Choshu, and Tosa (another south-western *han*), who were able to mobilise the full force of their domains behind their campaign. Some of them were *shishi* who had become more realistic; others were *han* reformers or men who were concerned to improve their *han's* national standing. They were not always natural allies, but from 1864 Tokugawa actions increasingly drove them towards a common cause. In that year the Bakufu leadership abandoned a brief experiment in close cooperation with the major *daimyo* and embarked upon an attempt to recover its former hegemony by seeking help from France; and in 1866 it went so far as to mount an attack on Choshu (after an earlier reassertion of its authority over that particularly defiant domain, in 1864, had proved to have only a short-lived effect). This move proved disastrous. Choshu had not only strengthened its forces by recruiting non-samurai but had imported a substantial quantity of modern rifles, and it was easily able to repulse the Tokugawa forces. This unprecedented setback paved the way for a challenge to the Bakufu's position. In November 1867, after much manoeuvring between representatives of Satsuma and Choshu and a few court nobles, an edict calling for the deposing of the Shogun was issued under the seal of the Emperor. It was this which gave a cloak of legitimacy to the *coup d'état* in January.

The fact that almost all the leaders of the anti-Tokugawa movement were samurai is unquestionable, but its essential character still remains a matter of dispute. The Kozaha emphasis on its counter-revolutionary nature derives some support from the speed with which a more effective system of centralised government was introduced after 1868, but if the primary concern of those who worked for the overthrow of the Bakufu was the control of popular unrest, it is hard to explain their willingness to embark upon a civil war of which the outcome was highly uncertain. Those who argue, by contrast, that the attack on the Tokugawa was part of a broader movement of lower samurai hostility towards feudal privilege can point to the levelling character of the post-1868 *han* reforms. It is doubtful, however, whether many samurai would have wished to go so far as the Meiji government was to do in eliminating feudal institutions, including the samurai's special status, and it should not be overlooked that many lower samurai, notably in Choshu and Satsuma, were to rebel against the new Meiji government.

A rather different approach, which emphasises vertical divisions in society rather than class interests, identifies loyalty to domain (or '*han* nationalism') as the main samurai motivation. This offers probably the most satisfactory explanation of the readiness of the powerful south-western *han* to challenge the Bakufu, but it is not easy to reconcile with the fact that the men who led the way in doing so were to be responsible for the abolition of those selfsame domains within a very few years.

One further approach to the Meiji Ishin, which fits what happened before and after 1868, is that which treats it as a nationalist revolution. From this standpoint the fall of the Bakufu was basically due to general dissatisfaction with its inability to withstand foreign pressure, while the reforms of the new government are seen as primarily motivated by a desire to regain Japan's full national rights and establish Japanese prestige. Many of the conditions for the development of nationalism certainly existed in late Tokugawa Japan, and the samurai, as a military class, were especially sensitive to Western technological superiority (which both Satsuma and Choshu experienced at first hand in 1863-4 when, in turn, they suffered reprisals from Western gunboats for attacks on foreigners). The frequency of references to the Western threat in the letters of politically active samurai certainly attests to the great importance of this factor.

Nevertheless, it may be possible to attribute too much to nationalism. On some occasions the national cause may have been invoked to disguise less idealistic motives or to improve an activist's image of himself. Moreover, the 'nationalist revolution' interpretation, like the 'pre-emptive counter-revolution' one, tends to assume that the swift transformation of Japan into a modern national state was inevitable and predictable. At the time, however, Satsuma and Choshu, in challenging the numerically superior forces of the Bakufu, could not, and did not, assume that the latter would collapse as quickly as it did; and had the civil war been prolonged, the Western powers might well have been offered an opportunity to intervene in Japanese affairs. Indeed, it might be argued that the most obvious way to safeguard Japanese independence would have been to support rather than attack the Tokugawa Shogunate. In fact, however, the south-western *han* became determined to work for the latter's destruction after 1865, when the Bakufu leaders had rejected cooperation and power-sharing with the major *daimyo* and were undertaking serious reforms, including military reorganisation. Hence, the anti-Bakufu forces can be viewed as being motivated as much by concern for the position of their own *han* as by considerations of national independence. Finally, it may also be suggested that the foreign threat to Japan was not so great as is sometimes implied. The formidable reputation of the samurai and the absence of any image of Japan as a rich commercial prize militated against any major intervention in so distant a country, and when the British Foreign Secretary, Lord Palmerston, specifically considered sending such an expedition in 1864, he quickly rejected the idea. By 1865, when the xenophobic nationalists had suffered severe setbacks and the pragmatic Bakufu had lifted the trade restrictions which had exasperated foreigners, the time of greatest danger had passed. Naturally the Japanese themselves could not feel confident enough to relax their guard; but the fact that leading samurai from the south-western domains from 1866 had friendly contacts with British diplomats such as Ernest Satow suggests that fear of foreigners may have been less than in the early 1860s.

The conclusion to be drawn from this consideration of general interpretations of the Meiji Ishin is that no simple explanation can do justice to the complexity of its causes. What is clear is that once the mould of Tokugawa hegemony was broken, Japan was likely to experience major change. Given the contradictory nature of some of the motives and pressures for change, however, it was by no means certain what the outcome would be. Probably the most common expectation was that there would be a struggle for dominance between Satsuma and Choshu, whose relations had generally been antagonistic in the early 1860s and whose leaders still regarded each other with some suspicion. An alternative possibility, which had considerable support in Tosa (the major domain on the island of Shikoku) and some other *han*, was a *daimyo* federation. A less conservative, but inherently more reactionary prospect was a revival of the influence of the old imperial court. Court nobles traditionally controlled access to the Emperor, and their influence was far from negligible since the initial stage of the Meiji Ishin took the form of a restoration of rule to the Emperor (*osei-fukko*). The establishment of a new governmental structure in January 1868 based on the archaic organisation adopted (from a Chinese model) in the eighth century nominally, at least, turned the clock back to the distant past when their ancestors had governed in the Emperor's name.

The establishment and consolidation of the Meiji government

In 1868 Japan's future was uncertain, and much depended on the attitudes, abilities, and ambitions of the activists who were rewarded with influential positions in the new central government. More quickly in some cases than others, most came to perceive that a hybrid system, in which prestige and authority were nominally centred on the Emperor while military power continued to reside in the *han*, would inevitably be unstable. The survival of the new Meiji government – and their own political position – would be in continual jeopardy, as would the nation's independence and social order. The only hope of real stability lay in the abolition of feudal separatism, but formidable obstacles confronted the samurai reformers if they were identified too clearly with the central government or if their ultimate intentions were made too obvious. As it was, they risked losing their local bases of support by their prolonged absence from their *han*; and the continuation of intense xenophobia among ordinary samurai meant that the reformers put their very lives in danger when, in order to improve relations with the West, they not only abandoned the idea of expelling foreigners but also punished with death samurai troops from Tosa and Bizen who attacked and killed foreigners in early 1868. Their own differences of temperament, mutual suspicion, and disagreements over the pace of change and the precise details of reform sometimes made it difficult to maintain cooperation even among themselves. Without an extraordinary combination of determination, flexibility, talent for political manipulation and some luck they would have had little chance of achieving their aims.

Determination and luck were particularly important at the beginning of 1868, for the *coup d'état* of 3 January was an immense gamble. In the first place the military forces which Satsuma, Choshu and their few allies could mobilise were inferior in number to those which the Bakufu could marshal. On top of this their coalition was a fragile one. Some of its members, including the influential *daimyo* of Tosa and Echizen, had come to favour a compromise settlement with the last Shogun, Tokugawa Yoshinobu (involving his membership of a baronial council), after he had, at their persuasion, offered his resignation on 19 November 1867. Others, however, among them the Satsuma samurai leader, Okubo Toshimichi, pressed for the elimination of Tokugawa power. Even among the nobles who had, on 9 November, helped to secure the imperial edict calling for the overthrow of the Bakufu, there were doubts as to whether such a drastic step was really appropriate. At this juncture, as on various later occasions, the determination of Okubo and his close ally, the court noble Iwakura Tomomi, proved decisive. Not only did they insist on going ahead with the planned seizure of the imperial palace, but in its aftermath, when Yoshinobu gave encouragement to the elements favouring compromise by offering to discuss a settlement and by withdrawing to Osaka, Okubo refused to agree to anything short of the surrender of all the land directly held by the Shogun.

Given time this extreme demand would probably have had to be reduced or even abandoned, but on 26 January the more militant Tokugawa vassals in Osaka, angered by the rioting which Satsuma agents were provoking in Edo, began to move troops towards Kyoto, possibly without Yoshinobu's approval. On 27 January these forces were blocked by Satsuma and Choshu troops at Toba and Fushimi, and for three days bitter fighting took place. In the end the smaller, but better-armed and more resolute Sat-Cho units emerged victorious. On 31 January Yoshinobu departed for Edo and in early February Osaka Castle, the Tokugawa stronghold in central Japan, surrendered.

The effects of the battle of Toba-Fushimi were out of all proportion to its scale. Bakufu morale was enormously weakened, and the chance of regaining control of the young Emperor disappeared completely. Many *han* which had up to this point remained neutral now declared themselves supporters of the new government and agreed to provide it with military support. But perhaps the most significant result politically was the eclipse of the elements within the new imperial government which had favoured compromise. The ill-considered Tokugawa attempt to regain control made it impossible for Yoshinobu not to be treated as an enemy of the court, and the influence of the hard-line group headed by Okubo, his Choshu counterpart, Kido Koin (Takayoshi), the Satsuma military leader, Saigo Takamori, Iwakura Tomomi, and a younger but higher-ranking court noble, Sanjo Sanetomi, rose sharply . Although the samurai members of this group were barred by their low rank from holding the highest positions (which were reserved for court nobles and *daimyo* from various important *han*) it was now their proposals which increasingly determined policy.

Evidence of the growth in the influence of the imperial reformers was rapidly forthcoming: on 2 February, Sanjo and Iwakura were elevated to become the deputies to Prince Arisugawa, a neutral figurehead who held the highest position in government. However, the first clear indication that the restoration of the Emperor was to mean a great deal more than a mere shift in the location of power from one centre and one feudal coalition to another, did not come until 6 April (the same day that Yoshinobu agreed to the surrender of his castle, warships and arms in return for a truce). On that date an important assembly of nobles and officials witnessed the reading of a major imperial pronouncement, the *Gokajo no*

Goseimon (Five Articles Oath, also known as the Charter Oath).[2]
This document has tended to be regarded as a rather abstract, even
cosmetic, statement of principle designed mainly to reassure national opinion that the new regime did not intend to behave in an
arbitrary, despotic or reactionary manner, but such a view may
well underestimate its importance, for on numerous occasions it
was referred to by central government officials or by their local
supporters to persuade *han* governments that radical reforms were
expected by the throne. Moreover, not only did the Emperor make
the pledge, but court nobles, officials and *daimyo* were also required
to promise to respect it. Indeed, the latter were not allowed to
return to their domains until they had done so. Significantly, the
ceremony was repeated twenty-six times during the following three
years.

Although the strategy of the government reformers was to make
use of the court to undermine feudal conservatism, they could not
ignore the danger that the emphasis on imperial authority might
encourage a reactionary tendency among the court nobles. It was
to weaken the possibility of this happening that after much debate
and manoeuvring they secured the visit of the Emperor to Osaka
from 14 April to 29 May. Such an imperial excursion out of Kyoto
was almost unprecedented, and even after its initial approval it was
postponed several times. The fundamental reason for court resistance was the same as Okubo's reason for proposing it: it would
lead to the Emperor's ceasing to be a secluded figure hidden away

---

[2] There are minor differences in the various translations of the Oath into English.
That of Hane Mikiso, *Modern Japan*, p. 85, reads:

1. Deliberative assemblies shall be widely established and all state affairs decided by public opinion.
2. All classes, high and low, shall unite in actively carrying out the administration of affairs of state.
3. The common people, no less than the civil and military officials, shall be
allowed to pursue whatever calling they choose so that public apathy may not
beset the land.
4. The evil customs of the past shall be abandoned and everything based on the
just laws of Heaven and Earth.
5. Knowledge shall be sought throughout the world so as to invigorate the
foundations of Imperial rule.

For a persuasive reassessment of the Oath's significance, see Haraguchi Kiyoshi,
'Meiji Shonen no Kokka Kenryoku' in Nakamura Masanori (ed.), *Taikei Nihon
Kokka Shi,* vol. 4.

in the imperial palace where he was always liable to be manipulated or unduly influenced by his traditional advisers and personal attendants. Okubo's first plan, indeed, was to make Osaka the new capital. Such an idea, however, was too ambitious in early 1868, when the court nobles were still indispensable not only as a balance against the *daimyo* but also to avoid the appearance of a Satsuma-Choshu Bakufu. Nevertheless, even a temporary absence from the capital furthered Okubo, Iwakura and Sanjo's aim of associating the Emperor with the government more directly and positively. It not only marked a break with tradition, but also brought the Emperor into direct contact with new influences, including that of Okubo himself, who was given the great honour (for a samurai) of an imperial audience on 1 May.

Behind this important defeat for the court lay its awareness that its revived status owed everything to the Sat-Cho leaders, and that, with the new regime still precarious, nobles and samurai reformers were mutually dependent. In this situation the greater political experience and ability of the latter worked to their advantage, and they also benefited from the fact that the Emperor himself was only fifteen at the time of the coup and therefore malleable. Not that it was anything new for Japanese emperors to confine themselves to the role of simply conferring legitimacy on those who actually wielded power and to eschew any personal involvement in decision-making. But to have as monarch someone who, although apparently not entirely free from vanity (and also more interested in horsemanship than politics, according to one of his more critical advisers in 1879), was willing to preside over a drastic break with Japanese political, social and cultural tradition, was of enormous help to Okubo, Kido and Iwakura.

During the imperial visit to Osaka, Iwakura joined Okubo, Kido and Sanjo there to plan the way forward, and it was decided that the Emperor should return to Kyoto to promulgate a quasi-constitutional document (the *Seitaisho*) on 6 June. In terms of organisational structure the alterations made by the *Seitaisho* were not particularly remarkable. Admittedly, the eight departments of state were reduced to five – for Shinto religion, justice, finance, and military and foreign affairs – but the deliberative assembly of samurai who represented their *han* in Kyoto underwent only slight modification (and certainly no increase in its purely consultative powers). At other levels, however, the changes were more significant. The number of *Gijo* and *Sanyo* (senior and junior councillors), among whom were to be found most of the influential figures in the government, was drastically reduced, thus concentrating the leadership into fewer hands, and the number of *han* from which samurai councillors were drawn was also diminished. Many upper samurai, chosen originally because of their status, were now dispensed with. At the very highest level, the *Sosai*, whose responsibility for 'directing state affairs and deciding all official matters' was not strictly compatible with the theory of direct imperial rule, was replaced by two *Hosho* (Iwakura and Sanjo), whose title clearly showed that their function was to assist the Emperor. No less significant were the restrictions which were imposed upon the *han*. The latter were no longer permitted to coin money or make alliances, and their right to hire foreigners was made subject to government approval. Strict enforcement of these restrictions was not yet possible, but their introduction was an indication that the Meiji government intended to limit *han* autonomy and exercise genuine national power.

In mid-1868, though, that objective was still distant. Indeed, as yet even the civil war had not been won. Although Edo castle had been surrendered on 3 May, a pocket of Tokugawa resistance continued to cause trouble there, and no sooner had this been suppressed on 4 July than the government army was confronted by a much more serious challenge from an alliance of more than 30 northern *han*. The struggle for control of northern Japan involved less danger for the Meiji government than the battle of Toba-Fushimi, but the scale of military action was far greater, and it was not until December that the pacification of the north-east was proclaimed. In the main northern island, Hokkaido, Tokugawa forces even held out until June 1869. Well before then, however, the imperial reformers had taken another important step to undermine reactionary tendencies by announcing in August 1868 that the capital would be moved to Edo (renamed Tokyo [Eastern Capital] on 3 September). Although the Emperor was not yet to move to Tokyo permanently, he did remain in that city from October to December; and from May 1869 he was normally resident there, far from the majority of court nobles and much more open to modern influences. Nor was this all. As part of the process of simultaneously widening his horizons and publicly identifying him with the government, his new advisers also had the Emperor make seventeen tours or official visits during 1868, eight of them outside Tokyo.

Such visits were to be a regular feature of the Emperor's schedule over the next two decades and contributed towards the creation of a more modern image.

The main objective of the imperial reformers, however, was to increase the power of the government *vis-à-vis* the *han*. Some junior members of the government, especially the younger samurai with Western knowledge or experience, such as Ito Hirobumi and Inoue Kaoru from Choshu, Terajima Munenori from Satsuma and Okuma Shigenobu from Hizen, were eager to advance rapidly along this path. Among the councillors Kido sympathised with their aims, but Okubo was inclined to give priority to improving the administrative efficiency of the government, which was encountering difficulties in controlling the territories which it had by the end of the year taken over from the Tokugawa and northern *han*. For the time being, therefore, further encroachment on *han* autonomy was limited to a government directive of 11 December which required the separation of *han* administration from the *daimyo's* personal affairs and sought to encourage reform and efficiency by insisting on the employment of men of ability.

By early 1869, an awareness of widespread and growing disenchantment with the new regime prompted a more dramatic step. On 2 March government members from Satsuma, Choshu, Tosa and Hizen presented a memorial in the names of their *daimyo* offering the return of their lands to the Emperor. The language of the memorial was ambiguous, however, and when the issue of converting *han* into prefectures governed by imperial officials was put both to an assembly of notables, including *daimyo,* and to the assembly of samurai representatives from all the *han*, the opinions expressed were generally in favour of the continuation of the existing system. That the whole proposal should have been in danger of fizzling out in this way seems to have been due in part to the absence of Kido, Iwakura and Okubo. When the two latter returned to Tokyo on 4 June, momentum was restored. On 9 July an inner group of reformist leaders agreed to a proposal by Iwakura that *daimyo* should be renamed *chihanji* (governors) to clarify their theoretical status as imperial officials, and that they should retain a tenth of their formal revenues for their household expenses; and on the following day the danger of opposition was diminished by the announcement of substantial stipendiary rewards for military services not only to individual samurai but also, and on a much larger scale, to important *daimyo*. Finally, on 25 July, all *daimyo* who had not yet offered to return their *han* registers (*hanseki hokan*) were ordered to do so. Although this development was less far-reaching than some reformers wished, it was a significant step towards the ultimate abolition of the *han*. As a result of Kido's strong opposition the position of *chihanji* (the term *hanchiji* was also used) was not recognised as hereditary; and the formal incorporation of the *daimyo*, together with the court nobles, into a new class of higher nobility, the *kazoku*, while samurai were officially entitled *shizoku* (gentry), meant that the previous lord-vassal relationship was weakened.

The *hanseki hokan* episode had another important consequence. In May, while Iwakura, Okubo, and Kido were away from Tokyo, they had agreed upon the mobilisation of further military contingents from Satsuma, Choshu, and possibly Tosa, for the purpose of protecting the Emperor and maintaining law and order in Tokyo. Although the ostensible purpose of these reinforcements was to deal with dissident samurai extremists, the show of support from the south-western *han* would also have helped to persuade the assembly of notables to accept the government's proposals. When Okubo and Iwakura returned to Tokyo, however, they found that their plan for a new force was not accepted by the rest of the government. This setback appears to have provoked them into carrying out a further refining of the leadership. Utilising a previously ignored article of the *Seitaisho* which provided for the election of councillors by government officials who possessed the three highest Court ranks, they successfully organised a combined renewal and reduction of the top policy-making group. However it was managed, the results of this unique selection procedure (which took place on 22 June 1869 and was never repeated) certainly worked out to the advantage of the reformers. Sanjo was confirmed as the (now sole) *Hosho*, the four *Gijo* included Sanjo (again) and Iwakura, while of the six *Sanyo* five were progressive samurai – Okubo, Kido, Soejima Taneomi (from Hizen in Kyushu), and Itagaki Taisuke and Goto Shojiro from Tosa.

This rearrangement proved to be very short-lived, for on 15 August 1869 the government structure was substantially changed yet again. Nevertheless, the dominance of the imperial reformers passed over into the new *Dajokan* system – so-called because of the greater emphasis placed on the Council of State (*Dajokan*), which was given full formal control over the departments of government. These latter now numbered six, with the addition of the *Mimbusho* (Ministry of Civil Affairs). The *Dajokan* itself was headed by Sanjo as *Udaijin* (Minister of the Right), advised by *Dainagon* and *Sangi* (the new names for senior and junior councillors). One of the two *Dainagon* was Iwakura, while the *Sangi* were all reformist samurai. The need for some representation of feudal interests was recognised by the continuation of a deliberative assembly (renamed the *Shugi-in*); and the Court was placated by the granting to the *Jingikan* (Office of Shinto Religion) of nominally higher status than the *Dajokan* itself. But these features did not in practice threaten the hold of the imperial reformers on the central government. The real question now was how far they could extend that power to the more than two-thirds of the country which still enjoyed a large measure of practical autonomy.

Obstacles to centralising reform

The main obstacle to complete centralisation after mid-1869 came not so much from the *chihanji* as from the strength of domain loyalty among the samurai. *Han* nationalism had inevitably carried over from the final years of the Tokugawa, pre-eminently, of course, within those domains which had played a major role in the overthrow of the Bakufu. This situation was acknowledged by Iwakura in June 1869, when he complained to Sir Harry Parkes, the British minister in Japan, that every daimyo 'is a little Mikado in his own right'. From what the Japanese leader told him, Parkes concluded that 'it is easier to talk of controlling such men than to do it', significantly adding: 'More difficult to control than the Daimyos are their *kerais* or armed followers, who compel the Daimios to act according to their wishes'.[3] In similar vein Kido Koin earlier in the year wrote (to Iwakura and Sanjo) that 'since the time of the old Bakufu the pride (of the *han*) has greatly increased'.[4] In the autumn of 1870 he was still lamenting, in his diary, that 'the *han* who played meritorious parts in the restoration of imperial rule, are, by contrast, not satisfactory today'.[5] There can be little doubt that it was

[3] Public Record Office, London. F.O.391 (Hammond Papers), xv, Parkes to Sir Edmund Hammond, 7 June 1869. I owe this reference, and that in note 10, to Mrs Fauziah Fathil.

[4] Quoted by Tanaka Akira, 'Meiji Hansei Kaikaku to Ishin Kanryo' in Inada Masatsugu (ed.), *Meiji Kokkai Keisei Katei no Kenkyu*, p.118.

[5] *Ibid.* p.146.

the actions of Satsuma which provoked Kido's comment, for it was in September 1870 that a further move by the Meiji government to limit *han* autonomy led to the sudden departure from Tokyo of the Satsuma representative, Ijichi Masaharu, and the simultaneous recall to Kagoshima of the Satsuma troops employed in the protection of the capital. Not only did these actions give rise to concern that Satsuma might ignore the new *han* regulations which were about to be approved, but there were even rumours that Saigo Takamori might lead a force against Tokyo and attempt another *coup d'état*.

Such fears were exaggerated, but they were not groundless. Since the end of the civil war there had been a growing alienation between Satsuma and the central government which was reflected in the estrangement of Okubo and Saigo, former boyhood friends and co-conspirators. The difficulties between them began in March 1869 when Okubo was recalled to Kagoshima to settle the dispute between the ruling Shimazu family and the Satsuma military forces which had returned triumphant from the civil war. According to a memorial submitted by the *chihanji's* father, Shimazu Hisamitsu, the young samurai soldiers 'regard lineage and pedigree as useless luxuries and call for their abolition, and their rampant violence knows no bounds'.[6] The leader they most respected, Saigo Takamori, declined Shimazu Hisamitsu's appeals to use his influence to control them; and when Okubo devised a compromise plan, the military leaders rejected it and forced through a more sweeping purge of officials than he had proposed. With the appointment to high *han* office of several young commanders the way was now open for Saigo to assume a position of leadership and carry out radical reforms. In September 1869 the stipends of the upper samurai were sharply cut, from a total value of 202,376 *koku* of rice to 26,103 *koku*, while those of samurai who received 200 *koku* or less remained unchanged.[7] Then, in early 1870, a reorganisation of the Satsuma military system resulted in the formation of a standing army, 13,257 strong (and soon to be expanded). This was a force which the Meiji government could not have risked challenging, and it consisted largely of men who were hostile to Western influences and were ready to condemn the (by their standards) lavish lifestyles of the government leaders in Tokyo. Okubo was not

[6] Quoted by Toyama Shigeki, 'Yushi Sensei no Seiritsu' in Horie Hideichi and Toyama Shigeki (eds), *Jiyuminken-ki no Kenkyu*, vol. 1, p. 17.

[7] A *koku* was equivalent to 4.96 bushels (about 300 lb).

exempted from their criticism, and when in February 1870 he again returned to Kagoshima, this time in the hope of persuading Saigo and Shimazu Hisamitsu to support reform by joining the Tokyo government, both refused.

This rebuff was a considerable setback for Okubo, the more so because it compared unfavourably with the results of a parallel mission by Kido to Choshu. In contrast with his Satsuma counterpart, Kido's relations with both his *daimyo* and the *han* leaders remained good after 1868. Indeed, together with Hirozawa Saneomi and Inoue Kaoru, two other officials from Choshu, he was able to link *han* nationalism with central government policy: when Choshu carried out its first major reform since the civil war, the document which announced it on 16 December 1868 proclaimed both that 'unless we now, at the head of the various *han*, develop trade, we will lose our advantages to other areas' and that 'in accordance with the government's plan, we must establish a national policy which will allow us not to feel shame towards foreign countries in years to come'.[8] The idea that Choshu would gain prestige by taking the lead in carrying out the government's intentions was particularly stressed by Hirozawa until he was assassinated by an extremist in early 1871.

In view of Kido's and Hirozawa's influence it is not surprising that Choshu's reforms differed from Satsuma's in certain important respects. Not only was economic development encouraged but the importance of public opinion in political decision-making was expressly referred to by the *daimyo*, Mori Yoshichika. The reduction of samurai stipends (on 6 October 1869) was even more drastic than in Satsuma, with only those below 100 *koku* remaining immune, while those above 1000 *koku* were cut to a tenth and those below 1000 *koku* were reduced to 100. Samurai were also encouraged to return to agriculture or go into commerce, and by 1872 as many as 868 had done so. The most significant difference from Satsuma, however, related to the way in which the military forces were reorganised and reduced in late December 1869. As when 2000 Choshu troops had earlier been offered to the Meiji government (which accepted only 1500 of them), a major motive was to lighten the *han's* financial burden. But the decision was also prompted by the continuation of strong anti-establishment attitudes in the

[8] Quoted by Tanaka, *op. cit.,* p. 123.

irregular military units (*shotai*). One such group in particular, the *Yugekitai*, in mid-December, castigated its upper-samurai commander, and also advocated village reforms and material aid for the indigent. Its radicalism alarmed the *han* authorities, who deliberately excluded its members from the 2250 *shotai* recruits incorporated in their new regular army. Whatever the long-term gains, the *han* action provoked immediate armed opposition by the *shotai*, and the situation was exacerbated by simultaneous peasant uprisings. By March 1870 the Meiji government was so concerned that it mobilised forces in various neighbouring areas to prevent the spread of the disturbances. However, within a month the outbreak had been suppressed by Choshu forces themselves.

The effect of the Choshu uprisings was to increase the difference between Choshu and Satsuma. In the former the element which was opposed to established authority had been defeated; in the latter it was in partial control. Against this background Satsuma obstreperousness increasingly emerged in 1870 as the major potential threat to the Meiji government, and the relationship between Okubo and Kido, whose characters and life-styles were very different, became more tense. From his visits to Satsuma Okubo appreciated that behind his own *han's* distrust of the central government lay suspicion of the radical young reformists in the Finance Ministry, which had become the most important and active of the government departments, especially since its takeover of the Ministry of Civil Affairs in September 1869. Many of its officials had either studied or travelled abroad and the ethos of 'Westernism' which prevailed among them had already incurred criticism from the *Jingikan* and other bastions of the reactionary nobility. Their efforts to control the sometimes capricious actions of the civil war heroes (many of them from Satsuma) who had been sent to govern the newly-established prefectures in old Tokugawa territories made the ministry further enemies among samurai from the south-western *han*. When Okubo began to attack the ministry too, he inevitably aroused suspicions of acting on Satsuma's behalf. Nor was it only Okubo's apparent encouragement of reaction and conservatism which disturbed Kido. At another level their partial alienation also reflected to some degree a struggle for influence, since the most influential reformers in the Finance Ministry, such as Okuma Shigenobu, Ito Hirobumi, and Inoue Kaoru, were among Kido's closest allies.

From April 1870 Okubo and his supporters manoeuvred to reduce the power of the Finance Ministry, finally succeeding on 6 August, when the Ministry of Civil Affairs was again detached and placed under the control of Okubo's ally, Oki Takato (of Hizen). But Kido's group remained influential. Okuma became a *Sangi* on 26 September, and on 12 December, on his advice and with the approval of Sanjo (who, unlike Iwakura, was closer to Choshu than Satsuma) the Ministry of Public Works was set up. Not only was this contrary to the wishes of Okubo, who had proposed that it should be a department within the Ministry of Civil Affairs, it was also put under the effective control of Goto Shojiro whom Okubo disliked. Meanwhile, cuts in government expenditure showed no signs of materialising.

Given this friction among the samurai leaders within the government and their uncomfortable awareness of Satsuma opposition, it is hardly surprising that 1870 saw a slowing in the pace of centralisation. Not until June was any real effort made to encroach further upon *han* administration, and even then the government proceeded with extreme caution. For the first time it allowed extended debate on its proposals in the *Shugi-in*, and when, on 4 October, it eventually promulgated new regulations, it took some account of the views expressed. In particular, it modified its original demand that the *han* should contribute one-fifth of their revenue towards central government military expenditure. Although 127 *han* agreed to this, almost as many suggested a lesser proportion, and among them were Choshu, Tosa, and Satsuma. In the face of this powerful opposition the government moderated its demand to one-tenth, but this still did not prevent Satsuma's representative from departing from Tokyo in high dudgeon.

This episode made the national leaders more conscious of the desirability of getting rid of the *han* completely, but at the same time it rendered the prospect of doing so rather more remote. At this stage no-one had any concrete alternative to a gradualist approach. Okubo was the most forceful advocate of reform, but only a limited reform of the central government and not, as yet, the abolition of the *han*; and while seeking greater unity of purpose within the government, he also supported Satsuma demands for a reduction of government personnel and salaries. His awareness of Satsuma strength and feeling led him to urge strongly upon Iwakura and Sanjo the necessity of having Satsuma on the government's side; and on 7 January 1871 his approach received a major boost from Saigo Takamori's younger brother, Tsugumichi (who had been sent to Kagoshima in October after returning from Europe and who is believed to have given the Satsuma leadership some idea of Okubo's intentions). The younger Saigo reported that both his elder brother and Shimazu Tadayoshi, the *chihanji*, were now prepared to join the Tokyo government. No time was lost in seizing this opportunity. On 7 February Iwakura arrived in Kagoshima accompanied by Okubo, Kido and Itagaki. After ten days of successful talks there they moved on to Choshu and then to Tosa, where they received similar promises of support. On 4 April Saigo Takamori, Okubo, Kido and Itagaki, all now in Tokyo, agreed that a 10,000-strong imperial guard should be raised from their own *han*, and by 29 July the promised troops had been sent to Tokyo. As a result the Meiji government was stronger than it had been at any time in its existence. One month later it abandoned the gradualist approach and abolished the *han* by imperial decree.

The abolition of feudal domains

In view of the importance of Saigo's role in this outcome, it is natural to ask why he changed his mind so abruptly about supporting the government – a decision which is made even more enigmatic by the fact that six years later his life ended in rebellion. The most plausible explanation is that he hoped to put his imprint on the reshaping of government that was being proposed in late 1870. He was confident enough to present Iwakura with his own ideas about basic reform in early 1871, and the remarks about the government leaders' modes of life which he made to his compatriots when he returned in April 1871 to arrange the Satsuma contingent for the imperial guard show that his critical attitude had not disappeared. In one important respect he seems to have been successful in influencing government policy. It was he who proposed the establishment of an imperial guard made up of selected samurai, and it is likely that part of the price of his cooperation was the tacit abandonment (for the time being at least) of a plan for conscription which had been approved just before Iwakura's mission to Satsuma. The survival of the samurai as a distinctive class was certainly one of Saigo's abiding concerns, and the establishment of the imperial guard carried the incidental bonus of relieving Satsuma of the financial burden of providing for several thousands of them.

Notwithstanding these reasons, it is still difficult to explain Saigo's action in early 1871 if it is assumed, as it often is, that the agenda already included abolition of the *han*. Such may not, however, have been the case. The reform discussions which were taking place at the beginning of the year centred upon Okubo's proposal for administrative reorganisation, and that remained so until the summer. Indeed, it has been argued that the decision to abolish the *han* was taken as early as it was mainly because agreement could not be reached on the more limited reform.[9] One reason for the opposition to Okubo's scheme was that it aimed at putting the Finance Ministry under tighter control. But there was also a major difference between Okubo and Kido over how best to achieve government unity. Both recognised that one of the chief problems was the lack of control by the top policy-makers over governmental administration, but whereas Okubo sought to solve it by having *Sangi* act also as ministers, Kido held that the answer was to regulate more closely the functions of ministries and the procedures to be followed by departmental officials, while the councillors concentrated wholly on policy-making. This difference of approach towards the problem of governmental organisation was to be resolved by a compromise in September (although it was to recur in various forms in later years). Before the compromise emerged, however, the whole issue had more than once bogged down, and although Kido successfully insisted on the establishment of a high-level committee in August to examine his ideas on reorganisation, the prospect of agreement seemed slight. Indeed, the committee was virtually boycotted by Okubo and his supporters after its first meeting on 20 August and was adjourned on 25 August.

The difficulty of resolving the dispute over administrative reform may have made the main Sat-Cho leaders more receptive to the suggestion of a group of younger samurai from Choshu – among them Inoue Kaoru and Yamagata Aritomo – that it was time to move forward to the greater matter of abolition of the *han*, on which there was broad agreement in principle. These bolder reformers had been discussing the issue since 15 August, and on 20 August Yamagata, as a fellow military specialist, was delegated to ascertain Saigo's views. When the latter responded with unexpected positiveness, it was relatively easy to overcome the hesitation of the

[9] Notably by Haraguchi, *op. cit.*, and Masumi Junnosuke, *Nihon Seito Shiron,* vol.1, ch. 1.

other top leaders. *Haihan chiken* (the abolition of the *han* and the establishment of *ken* – prefectures) was proclaimed on 29 August and immediately followed by the summoning of the ex-*daimyo* to Tokyo and their replacement by appointed governors, mostly samurai from other areas. Significantly, Iwakura informed the British diplomat, Ernest Satow, two months later that 'the change of *han* into *ken* had not at first seemed possible for 500 years at least, but events had worked in such a way that the Government thought they had better take advantage of the tide at the flood. They had expected bloodshed, of course, but had been agreeably disappointed'.[10]

It is even more difficult to explain Saigo's readiness to agree to *haihan chiken* than his previous assumption of office in the central government, since he is said, when he left Kagoshima, to have assured Shimazu Hisamitsu that he had no such intention. One of his biographers has described his involvement as 'the tragedy of a politician who was lacking in intellectual capacity', and has suggested that the leaders in Tokyo took advantage of the capacity for human feeling and emotional responsiveness which made him so admired by his Satsuma followers.[11] At a different level, it has also been argued that as one of the two *Sangi* (with Kido) after 11 August, Saigo was bound to see things differently from before and that 'the basic reason which led Saigo to switch to the side of abolition of the *han* was probably the understanding which he had gained through the petitions and reports from various *chihanji* of the extent of the breakdown of the whole feudal system, of which he could not have been aware while in Satsuma'.[12]

This comment points not only to the difference in the Tokyo perspective, but also to the importance of deeper causes of this momentous change. It is widely held by Japanese historians that the ease with which the abolition of the domains was effected was due to the fact that the old structure was about to collapse in any case. They point out that thirteen *chihanji* had already requested that their *han* be made prefectures, that ten had decided to force all their samurai to return to agriculture or enter commerce, and that seventeen more had compelled some of their retainers to abandon their samurai status. The immediate cause of *han* difficulties was

---

[10] Public Record Office, London. P.R.O. 30/33/154 (Satow Diary), 24 October 1871.

[11] Tamamuro Taijo, *Saigo Takamori*, p. 121.

[12] Haraguchi, *op. cit.*, p. 115.

financial. Even the cutting of *shizoku* stipends did not prevent *han* debts from increasing, on average, by over 200 per cent from 1868. In 1871 no fewer than 210 out of 274 *han* had debts larger than their annual revenue. Of the major *han*, Choshu, Tosa and Hizen all owed more than twice their revenue; Satsuma's debts, at 89 per cent, were relatively small.

The significance of *han* debts lies not just in their size but also in the reasons for their sharp rise after 1868. To many historians the crucial factor is the increase in peasant uprisings. These, it is argued, were now so formidable that the *han* authorities were forced on the defensive, and could not exploit the population as effectively as before. The promises of tax reduction made by the imperial forces during the civil war had weakened their position, as had subsequent encroachments by the new government on *han* authority. What particularly showed up the rottenness of the feudal system was the series of about forty uprisings which disturbed western Japan during the winter of 1870-1. These proved difficult to suppress and were especially alarming because they were sometimes led by discontented *shizoku*. Only a fully centralised state, it is suggested, could maintain social order in this new situation.

This argument has to be taken seriously, but it is possible to regard it as overstated. To begin with, only a small minority of *han* actually sought self-extinction, and even if the new imperial guard did not have to be used to enforce the government's will, the fact that the decision to act was not taken until this force had been formed suggests that the government did not expect abolition to be welcomed. Indeed, in Satsuma's case emissaries had to be sent back by Saigo to allay discontent. Nor do the timing and pattern of peasant uprisings fit the argument exactly, for in general the statistics show a downward trend after 1869.[13] Moreover, in the first three years of the Meiji regime a disproportionately large number

---

[13] The standard work by Aoki Koji, *Meiji Nomin Sojo no Nenjiteki Kenkyu*, p. 36, gives figures of 86 peasant uprisings in 1868, 110 in 1869, 65 in 1870, 52 in 1871 and 30 in 1872, while a more recent assessment by Matsuda Yukitoshi in Sasaki Junnosuke (ed.), *Yonaoshi*, p. 337, estimates the number as 108 in 1868, 97 in 1869, 61 in 1870, 47 in 1871 and 27 in 1872. If only the uprisings which were directed against the state or the *han* (*tai-kenryoku ikki*) are taken to be relevant, the picture presented by Aoki is slightly different – 49 in 1868, 51 in 1869, 29 in 1870, 32 in 1871 and 17 in 1872 – but the trend is still basically downward after 1869. The position is still more uncertain if one looks at the geographical scale of the uprisings, but even here the peak was reached in 1869 when the total number

occurred in the territories directly controlled by the new government – which would explain the latter's eagerness to increase its power and effectiveness but weakens the argument that the *han* were under irresistible pressure. It is worth noting, too, that several peasant uprisings after 1871 actually called for the restoration of the *daimyo* and the old system.

The causes of peasant uprisings also have to be considered when attempting to assess whether the feudal system was on the point of collapse or not. One major, but exceptional, factor was the disruption brought about by the civil war of 1868 (and the hopes of tax reduction which it temporarily raised). Another was the bad harvest of 1869. A further cause, which is frequently ignored, was the widespread anticipation of a new civil war, with Satsuma and Choshu as the probable principal antagonists. That such a prospect was taken seriously can be seen from Tosa's establishment of an alliance of all the *han* on the island of Shikoku in 1870 and from its simultaneous pursuit of a military understanding with Satsuma. In such an atmosphere *han* inevitably sought to borrow or to increase their revenues so as to buy more up-to-date weapons, and the consequent resurrection of economic controls and *han* monopolies, together with the circulation of false money, did much to provoke peasant discontent. Undoubtedly most *han* faced serious problems, but in view of the fact that some of the causes of peasant uprisings were of a temporary character, the assumption that the feudal order was bound to crumble under their pressure must be questionable.

The issue is further complicated by the fact that the *han* were also coming under pressure from central government. A considerable number of regulations had already been brought in before August 1871 which made administration difficult. On repeated occasions from 1868 onwards the *han* were forbidden to coin or print new money, and although these orders were not always obeyed, awareness that the government sometimes punished contraventions with death was bound to constrain domain leaders to some extent. The new principles governing *han* administration which were introduced in October 1870 went even further by ordering the *han* to repay their debts and to withdraw their existing currencies. With

---

of villages and towns involved was respectively 1,341 and eleven, compared with 528 and nine in 1868, 1,062 and four in 1870 and 477 and five in 1871. It should be noted, incidentally, that in 1872 no fewer than 1,222 villages and one town were involved. See Emura Eiichi, *Jiyu Minken Kakumei no Kenkyu*, p. 14.

the pending addition of the contentious military levy it was obvious that the *han* were about to enter a period of enormous financial strain, regardless of whether there were peasant uprisings or not. Even if the inducement offered to the *chihanji* of one-tenth of the old *han* revenue as a permanent stipend had been less generous, the fact that their old autonomy had already been undermined reduced the likelihood that they would object to abolition.

A few further points also need to be made. Some *han*, notably the ones which had overthrown the Tokugawa, were clearly not on the point of collapse. Torio Koyata, one of the young Choshu military officers who pressed for abolition of the *han* in August 1871, later wrote: 'Various feudal lords were suspicious of the imperial government, and each of them increased their military power and showed signs, in secret, of consolidating their local bases, and this all reached its extreme in the year the *han* were abolished'.[14] Given such a situation, it is not unreasonable to suppose that fear of another civil war if Japan remained divided might have been one further reason why the majority of the *han* accepted their dissolution submissively. At another, and perhaps the most fundamental, level the continuation of feudal division ran counter to the nationalistic and utilitarian spirit of the age epitomised by the often encountered phrase *fukoku-kyohei* (enrich the country, strengthen the military); and both observation of Western civilisation and repeated foreign advice confirmed the growing belief of the most thoughtful Japanese that greater unity was essential for national strength. These factors obviously affected most strongly the Finance Ministry bureaucrats and military officials like Yamagata and Saigo Tsugumichi who had just returned from study abroad, but few Japanese leaders could remain immune to their influence.

The acceleration of modernisation

The successful implementation of *haihan chiken* opened the way to agreement on the much-discussed organisational reform. The new responsibilities of the central government made it imperative that there should be strong administrative control over the three *fu* (Tokyo, Kyoto and Osaka) and 302 *ken* (prefectures) which now existed (although they were soon to be reduced in number to seventy and ultimately forty-three). It was probably in part to ensure that the

[14] Quoted by Shinobu Seizaburo, *Nihon Seiji Shi*, vol. 2, p. 229.

newly-appointed governors (*kenrei*) did not attempt to act independently that the Ministry of Civil Affairs was again, on 11 September, absorbed by the Finance Ministry. Since 13 August the latter department had been headed by Okubo (the first minister of samurai origin), and with his own position consolidated, he was evidently less inclined to object to Kido's ideas. On 13 September the *Dajokan* was divided into three Boards – the *Sa-in* (Left Board), which was theoretically invested with legislative functions but was in practice an advisory body; the *U-in* (Right Board), which was composed of the departmental ministers and vice-ministers and dealt with problems of administration; and the *Sei-in* (Central Board), which was presided over by Sanjo as *Dajodaijin* (Chief Minister of State) and determined general policy and other important matters. The *Sei-in* represented Kido's inner or supreme council, its membership consisting only of Sanjo and the *Sangi*, who now, with Saigo and Kido being joined by Itagaki and Okuma, numbered four. In practice, however, the new structure did not function in the way Kido had hoped, and within two years the principle of the separation of councillors and ministers was to be set aside.

Before long the Meiji government took another bold step. In December 1871 Iwakura, Okubo, and Kido, accompanied by many junior leaders and students, departed on a goodwill and observation mission to America and Europe which for most of its members lasted at least one and a half years. That several key figures should leave Japan so soon after the abolition of the *han* can only be explained in terms of the enormous importance of the West for the Meiji leaders and their great desire to see conditions there for themselves. Not surprisingly, there were doubts about the wisdom of having the three men who had been most responsible for steering Japan on the course of reform since 1868 away for so long a time, and to ensure stability the 'caretaker' government was made to promise not to introduce further reforms unless they were unavoidable and, above all, not to effect major personnel changes.

This agreement notwithstanding, the pace of reform accelerated rather than slackened while the Iwakura mission was away. Much was admittedly in line with previous government planning. The introduction of military conscription in January 1873, for instance, had been anticipated in the unenforced regulations of December 1870. This did not mean that there was no opposition to its form, for Yamagata, the Army Vice-Minister, raised the hackles of more traditionally-minded military leaders by his insistence on the equal liability for military service of men of all classes. Nevertheless, with Saigo's acquiescence, Yamagata's proposals were accepted. The existence of a mainly conscript army, 30,000-strong, which was not closely identified with the old *han*, was soon to make possible the further diminution of samurai privileges and was crucial to the stability of the Meiji state.

Another reform of comparable importance – the revision of the land tax – was also promulgated during the period of caretaker government (in July 1873), although the process of implementation took nine years to complete. The main promoter of the reform was the Finance Ministry, which needed to have an assured source of revenue that did not fluctuate with the price of rice and therefore had to be established on a monetary base. Despite their wish to improve the government's financial position, however, Finance Ministry bureaucrats were conscious that the land tax had provoked peasant uprisings and initially they hoped to reduce its comparatively high level. This idea was abandoned, however, when foreign governments proved unwilling to allow Japan to raise the low import tariffs accepted by the Tokugawa Bakufu, and thus eliminated the option of increasing the only other means of funding which could, at this stage, have supplied the government's needs. Consequently, although the level of the tax was theoretically standardised at 3 per cent of the value of the land, the government commissioners who determined land values took care to ensure that the total revenue from this source did not drop. Some adjustment between different areas took place but the really significant change was that the form of payment was converted from crop to cash. This change may have pushed many small – and middle – range peasants into debt, and led to a substantial increase in tenancy and landlordism over the next decade. The view that this result was intentional, however, and that it proves the existence of an alliance between a lower samurai-dominated government and the landlord class, is implausible. Indeed, landlords were among the foremost protesters against the commissioners' procedures, which sometimes appeared arbitrary; and in areas where the land tax had previously been low, landlords would certainly have suffered. It is not surprising, therefore, that peasant uprisings were a conspicuous feature of the mid-1870s. Nevertheless, as with conscription (which also aroused peasant discontent), the short-term difficulties caused by land-tax revision were far outweighed for the government by its contribution to long-term stability.

The other notable reform during the period of the Iwakura mission – the introduction in 1872 of a scheme for four years' compulsory elementary education for both sexes – also did not unduly alarm the absent leaders. Nor did they object to the incorporation of the Department of Shinto (which had already been downgraded in September 1871) into a new ministry, the Kyobusho (Department of Religion). But side by side with these major changes were a host of smaller ones, such as the switch to the Gregorian calendar on 2 December 1872 (cutting out the last twenty-eight days of that year) and the attempt to impose a seven-day week in place of the customary ten-day *jun*, which even a reformer like Kido regarded as unnecessary or over-hasty.

Political division and the 1873 governmental crisis

The most serious breaches of the compact, however, were the appointment of new *Sangi* and the decision to seek a military conflict with Korea. The first of these sprang from the persistent problem of departmental coordination and control, further complicated by the continuation of *han* rivalries. As before, controversy centred on the Finance Ministry, the running of which had been left, in Okubo's absence, to the Vice-Minister, Inoue Kaoru. His reputation had been somewhat tarnished by suspicions of favouritism towards his businessman friends, but towards other ministries he was distinctly ungenerous. In particular, the swingeing cuts which he demanded in the proposed budgets of the Justice and Education Ministries aroused the indignation of their heads, Eto Shimpei and Oki Takato. Feelings ran so high that Sanjo wrote to Iwakura requesting his colleagues' immediate return. Meanwhile, with the intention of curbing the Finance Ministry, Eto and Oki were moved up to become *Sangi* (together with Goto Shojiro) on 19 April, and on 2 May new government regulations strengthened the *Sei-in's* control over the various ministries. Inoue's resignation soon followed, and control of the Finance Ministry passed into the hands of Okuma Shigenobu, who had helped to undermine Inoue's position by giving a more favourable interpretation of the government's financial situation.

This breach of the original compact by the caretaker government might well have led to a clash with the Iwakura mission had a more urgent issue not confronted its members as they returned home at intervals during the summer of 1873. Ever since Korea had adopted a unfavourable attitude towards the new Meiji regime in 1869, Japanese-Korean relations had been bad, and during 1872-3 some members of the caretaker government sought to make an issue of Korean discourtesy. Itagaki and Foreign Minister Soejima may have hoped to find a pretext for invasion, believing that such a venture would raise Japanese international prestige, improve Japan's defensive position against Russia, and provide demoralised ex-samurai with a revived sense of purpose. Others may have had more limited objectives. The latter group seems to have included Saigo Takamori, even though the fact that there was a government decision on 17 August to send him to Korea is usually interpreted as a move designed to lead to a complete rupture in relations and open the way to a military expedition. Even if this was not the case, however, the leaders who were now returning from the West with an acute awareness of Japan's backwardness were not prepared to take any chances. As they saw it, invasion of Korea would be financially hazardous and might provoke further Western intervention in East Asian affairs. It also ran the risk of reviving reactionary forces within Japan. After complicated manoeuvring and threats of resignation, Okubo, Iwakura and Kido, backed by Okuma, Ito, Inoue and Yamagata, eventually won the day on 23 October. The struggle was a bitter one, however, and the defeat of those who advocated invasion could not be disguised by any semblance of compromise. All of them chose to resign – the biggest split in the ranks of the leadership since the inception of the Meiji government.

In the long run this split may have been politically advantageous to the group which had triumphed, for it resulted in a more united and homogeneous leadership. In the short term, however, it was a source of great danger. Had the dissident leaders combined, they could have constituted a real threat to the government. Saigo, however, withdrew to Satsuma, where he soon established great influence over the local government. Itagaki, Goto, Eto and Soejima did briefly come together to issue a manifesto on 17 January 1874 calling for the establishment of representative government, but thereafter their paths diverged. Eto captured Saga castle with a force of discontented Hizen *shizoku* but finding few supporters in other areas his rebellion was swiftly crushed and he himself was executed in April. Itagaki, although suspected by the government, followed the very different line of forming a local political association. Thus a combination of local particularism and different strategies of opposition by its opponents helped the Meiji regime to ride out the crisis.

The ascendancy of Okubo

In the defeat of the advocates of a Korean invasion the greatest part had been played by Okubo, and in the aftermath of the split he emerged as the dominant figure in the government. On 29 November, just over a month after the Korean issue was decided, he assumed control of the new Home Ministry (*Naimusho*), which was established partly to counteract the tendency toward Finance Ministry domination. In his hands the Home Ministry became a major force in government, not only taking over from the Justice Ministry responsibility for maintaining law and order but also sharing with the Ministry of Public Works the role of encouraging economic development and, with the Finance Ministry, the implementation of the new land tax. Furthermore, Okubo's ideas about governmental organisation were effectively put into practice in the critical months of late 1873 when vacancies suddenly appeared in the highest ranks of government and unity of purpose became crucial. Not only did he become a minister while also holding the position of *Sangi*, but four other men also combined the roles of councillor and minister, among them Okuma and Ito, both of whom were now closer politically to Okubo than to Kido. That the balance of influence within the government had shifted was demonstrated by Kido's failure in 1874 to prevent a military expedition to eastern Taiwan, where sailors from the Japanese-controlled Ryukyu islands had been murdered by natives. His objections were overruled by Okubo, and he resigned in May.

Kido's withdrawal was a considerable loss to the Meiji government, which apart from its other problems was increasingly being criticised as despotic by a vigorous young press. In order to secure the ex-Choshu leader's return, Okubo met him in Osaka in early 1875 and accepted his twin demands for the restoration to office of Itagaki (of whose support Kido was hopeful) and another reshaping of the government's structure. As before, Kido sought the separation of councillors and ministers, but he also went much further by obtaining agreement that in due course a proper constitution should be established. More immediately he secured the setting up of a supreme court (*Taishin-in*), to strengthen the principle of judicial independence, and the replacement of the *Sa-in* by a senate-like body named the *Genro-in*, which at once became the focus of a struggle for power as Itagaki and other critics of Okubo gained control of it and sought to have all new laws submitted to it for sanction. Kido, however, felt that the Tosa leader was acting rashly, and without the former's support the key element of Itagaki's proposal was rejected. Itagaki then turned for support to the arch-conservative Shimazu Hisamitsu (Minister of the Left since 1874), but their joint effort to oust Sanjo as Chief Minister in October 1875 also failed, and both men resigned. Kido, disillusioned and in poor health (he was to die in 1877), went into semi-retirement as a *Sei-in* adviser, his hope of separating councillors and ministers and strengthening his own political position effectively abandoned. Okubo's conciliatory tactics had thus paid off.

The disestablishment of the samurai and the Satsuma rebellion

The avoidance of a rift between Satsuma and Choshu was important for the government, for it was encountering a new and growing wave of protest. By conceding a one-sixth reduction in the land tax in January 1877 the Meiji leaders were able to defuse most of the peasant unrest. A much more serious threat, however, came from the series of *shizoku* rebellions which erupted from the autumn of 1876. They sprang partly from lingering resentment over the Korean issue but much more from the ban on the wearing of swords in March 1876 and the forced commutation of stipends in August. The latter step – a logical follow-up to the abolition of the *han* and the introduction of general conscription – had been strongly pressed for by the Finance Ministry, since even though stipends had been cut they remained the major obstacle in the way of paying off government debts, withdrawing paper currency issued by the *han*, and encouraging economic modernisation. In 1873 a scheme had been devised under which stipends of less than 100 *koku* could be exchanged for six times their annual value – half in cash and half in interest-bearing government bonds – but this was voluntary. In 1876 choice gave way to compulsion. All hereditary

Above Some of the
key figures in the Meiji
Renovation, photo-
graphed in San
Francisco in January
1872 during their 18-
month tour of West-
ern countries. From
right to left they are
Okubo Toshimichi, Ito
Hirobumi, Iwakura
Tomomi, Yamaguchi
Naoyoshi, and Kido
Takayoshi.
Left Iwakura Tomomi,
the most important
court noble in the
Meiji Renovation.

Okubo Toshimichi (*left*) and Kido Takayoshi (*right*), the principal samurai leaders from, respectively, the domains of Satsuma and Choshu during the Meiji Renovation. Their cooperation was crucial to its success but was sometimes strained, partly because of the difference in their personalities, Okubo being less outgoing than Kido.

Yamagata Aritomo (*left*) and Ito Hirobumi (*right*), the two leaders who exerted the greatest influence on the development of Japanese constitutional politics from the early 1880s. Although both were from Choshu, Yamagata was the more conservative and their approaches often differed.

stipends were from the following year commuted into government bonds capitalised at from five to fourteen times their annual value and bearing from 5 to 7 per cent interest (except for ex-samurai from Satsuma who were favoured with a special rate of 10 per cent). Although the immediate drop in the income of the lowest strata was not great, since their stipends were commuted at the higher rates of capitalisation and interest, their long-term prospects were bleak, for after five years the government was to begin to hold annual lotteries to choose bonds for redemption. By 1906 all bonds would be amortised.

In these circumstances it was hardly surprising that samurai frustration could no longer be contained. The most fanatical (albeit small-scale) incident was the *Shimpuren* (Divine Wind League) attack on the Kumamoto garrison on 24-5 October. A much larger one, involving possibly over 5,000 men, occurred in Choshu – but it was put down fairly easily. The rebellion which broke out in Satsuma in January 1877, however, was quite another matter. Triggered by the central authorities' attempt to remove arms from Kagoshima and by the hot-headed reaction of Saigo's followers, this uprising threatened not only the government's control of western Japan, but its very existence. Saigo's forces numbered about 30,000, including 10,000 non-samurai recruited in the latter stages of the rebellion under coercion, and the rebellion took nine months to suppress. Its failure, however, showed that no future revolt could hope to topple the Meiji government. In that sense it can be said to mark the culmination of the Meiji Ishin, a culmination accentuated by the deaths of Saigo by *harakiri* in September, and of Okubo by assassination the following year.

During the ten preceding years Japan had undergone extraordinarily rapid and momentous political changes. Decentralised feudalism, which in one form or another had existed for nearly seven centuries, had been forced to make way for a unified national government, and a huge ruling class had been effectively disestablished. It is true that most of the top positions in the new governmental system were filled by men of samurai background, but already by 1874 only 14,279 out of more than 400,000 *shizoku* were employed in either national or local administration. Admittedly, many other ex-samurai found worthwhile occupations in such professions as the police force, the army and teaching. Some embarked on careers in banking, commerce and industry. Others assisted in the colonisation of the undeveloped northern island of Hokkaido. A large number, however, failed to make a successful adjustment to the new age, and the phrase '*shizoku* business methods' was often used to pour scorn on their inexperience and inappropriate approach.

The character of the Meiji government

That such a fate was meted out by a leadership composed mainly of samurai is a paradox which can only be explained in terms of the imperative demands of nationalism, the clearly anachronistic nature of the old *han* system, and the transformation of a number of local leaders into an essentially national ruling élite. The top members of this élite were mostly still in their thirties or forties, and they owed their position to their active involvement in the anti-Tokugawa movement. Almost all of them had run great risks. Indeed they were fortunate to have survived, for many of their fellow-activists had been killed before 1868. Those who came through the eventful first Meiji decade required exceptional qualities: a commitment to modernisation; a capacity for cooperation (or at least for compromise) in the interests of government unity; sufficient tough-mindedness to override their emotional commitment to their native province; and enough flexibility, patience, and ability to dissimulate in the pursuit of fundamental objectives not to provoke insuperable opposition at any particular point. Possession of these qualities enabled the Meiji leaders to effect more radical change, probably, than an explicitly revolutionary approach could have achieved.

One other, almost essential, condition of membership of the ruling group was that they should come from one or other of the important south-western *han*; and it was the control of government by men from Satsuma, Choshu, and, to a lesser extent, Tosa and Hizen, which was to allow its political enemies to rally opposition with the accusation of '*hanbatsu seifu*' (government by *han* cliques). In terms of the very highest leaders the accusation was justified, and for many years continued to be so. At other levels, however, *hanbatsu* dominance was far less marked. If one compares the local origins of the highest-ranking government servants (*chokunin*) in 1874, men from Satsuma accounted for twenty-two top officials, Choshu eighteen, Tosa eight, and Hizen nine, out of a total of seventy. However, Tokyo and Shizuoka came close behind with seven and five respectively, showing that the new regime did not disdain to use the talents of specialised ex-Bakufu officials. At the next level down (*sonin*), Tokyo had already taken the lead with 120 officials out of a total of 2,605 as against 108 from Satsuma, 102 from Choshu, sixty-one from Tosa, fifty-nine from Hizen, and seventy-one from Shizuoka. The lowest category (*hannin*) saw an even greater Tokyo superiority, with 1,725 out of 14,209 bureaucratic employees emanating from there, compared with 601 from Satsuma, 875 from Choshu, 382 from Tosa, 297 from Hizen, and 830 from Shizuoka. Three other prefectures, incidentally, provided more than 300 officials, and a further nine over 200.

These are all global figures which conceal interesting differences. If one looks at the top levels of officials in 1877, it is easy to see that Satsuma was particularly strong in the Home Ministry, and Choshu men held an even more dominant position in the Ministry of Works. But in the Justice Ministry Hizen had prime place, while in the Finance Ministry both Tokyo and Hizen were better represented than either Satsuma or Choshu. To some extent, therefore, Okubo's and Kido's legacy was indeed a *hanbatsu* government, but not one which was uniformly dominated by Satsuma and Choshu. Moreover, the fact that other areas had already been drawn into it, and already had strong representation in it at the middle and lower levels, meant that it had a much better chance of surviving the new challenge about to be presented to it by the developing political consciousness of the Japanese people.

2

THE CONSOLIDATION OF THE
MEIJI STATE AND THE GROWTH
OF POLITICAL OPPOSITION,
1878-90

By 1878 the Meiji government had achieved many of its initial objectives. At home it had destroyed local autonomy, rid itself of the burden of an obsolete military class, established (and successfully tested) a new-style army, introduced a more dependable tax system, and weathered the storms which its actions had stirred up. In its relations with foreign countries it had repudiated the xenophobic attitudes of many of its original samurai supporters and had avoided further foreign intervention. The only risk it took was to continue the harsh treatment of the several thousand indigenous Christians near Nagasaki who had in 1865 been discovered to have preserved much of their faith since the seventeenth century. The Franco-Prussian war, however, removed any danger that France might respond to the Catholic missionaries' appeals, and in 1873 the anti-Christian placards were removed. Although formal religious toleration was not granted until the next decade, the persecution was effectively ended.

If the Meiji leaders were successful in avoiding further foreign encroachment, they were less so in their first efforts to persuade the powers to agree to revise the unequal treaties of 1858. Western diplomats took the line that their nationals should not be subjected to the rigours of the Japanese judicial system, and they were not prepared to abandon low tariffs on their imports without compensation. Not until the mid-1890s were they to concede Japan's demands and then only after seemingly interminable negotiations. By contrast, Japan had little difficulty, despite both local and Chinese objections, in establishing firm control over the peripheral Ryukyu islands to the south; while in the almost uncharted north a compromise was reached which gave Japan the Kurile islands in return for accepting Russian possession of Sakhalien. In 1882 and 1884-5 the possibility of military involvement in Korea again loomed, but peaceful counsels prevailed. As a result, between 1874 and 1894 Japan was less distracted by conflicts with foreign countries than it had been either immediately before or after this period, and the Meiji leaders were able to give their full attention to the consolidation of the Meiji state and their own position within it.

The consolidation of the Meiji state

The governmental apparatus which had been built up by 1878 was effective but still rudimentary. Coordination of the growing bureaucracy by the *Dajokan* councillors (the *Sei-in* having been abolished in 1877) remained rather loose, while weaknesses in the organisation and command structure of the army had been revealed in the campaign against Saigo. A remedy for the latter was sought by establishing, along German lines, a General Staff, independent of the Army Ministry, in 1878 – a move which in the twentieth century would make political control of the military more difficult. This innovation still left other problems, however. For example, popular objections to conscription were so great that 82 per cent of twenty year-olds took advantage of the various means of gaining exemption in 1876.

Until the late 1870s, the army's main function had been to suppress uprisings, generally with the aid of *ad hoc* local *shizoku* units raised by the prefectural governor. The newly-organised police were inadequate for this task and functioned mainly in the urban areas prior to the 1880s. In the countryside the everyday maintenance of law and order was left largely to the peasants themselves, with neighbours being responsible (through the traditional *goningumi* system) for each other's behaviour. From 1871 the central government attempted to assert its authority at the sub-prefectural level, by the creation of *ku* (districts), whose heads, in some prefectures at least, were *shizoku*. Under them, however, the villages usually remained in the charge of their ex-headman, drawn, as before, from one of the longest-established families, though now with the new official title of *kocho*.

The *ku* represented too great a break with tradition, and in 1878 they were replaced, except in the cities, by another sub-prefectural division, the *gun*, which unlike the *ku* was based on an older unit of local government and had genuine local significance. In real terms, however, what mattered most to the population was not the ad-

ministrative structure but the character and approach of the prefectural governor. The latter could be a petty tyrant, bent on extorting
the maximum in tax and suppressing all dissent, but some governors were relatively enlightened believers in progress and cooperation,
and by 1875 over half of them had instituted or recognised advisory prefectural or district assemblies, generally composed of local
officials but sometimes including elected representatives as well.

In 1875 the question of local assemblies came to the fore nationally when it was debated, with much accompanying publicity, by
the second conference of prefectural governors. The governors
favoured such assemblies but voted – by thirty-nine to twenty-one
– that they should be composed of local officials, not elected members. In practice, however, there was a gradual movement away
from official nomination towards a hybrid system and even, in some
areas, to elections only. Kochi (the former Tosa), Kumamoto and
Hamamatsu went so far as to dispense with any wealth qualification
for electors. The ground was already prepared, therefore, for the
government's nation-wide establishment in 1878 of prefectural assemblies, elected by men paying at least five yen in tax annually
(which meant that electors needed to own about six *tan* of land –
roughly one and a half acres). To be eligible for election an annual
tax payment of ten yen was required. The reasons for the assemblies' introduction may have included, as some critical historians
have suggested, the aims of integrating wealthy peasants into the
governmental system (separating them from the discontented
shizoku) or, alternatively, of diverting and limiting popular dissatisfaction with taxes to the arena of the prefectural assembly. Whatever
the motive, the regular conflict which developed between many
assemblies and the governors in the 1880s undoubtedly stimulated
popular consciousness at the local level, while assembly elections
prompted the organisation of local political societies. These results
would have a significant bearing on the first election for a national
assembly in 1890.

As the introduction of prefectural assemblies indicates, the Meiji
government did not resort only to crude repression, but also hoped
to steer public opinion towards acceptance, or even support, of its
policies. For men like Kido and Ito the great danger in the 1870s
was a reactionary backlash. In consequence it was natural for them
to encourage *bummei kaika* (civilisation and enlightenment) by such
means as introducing Western scholars into Tokyo University,

recruiting into government intellectuals who had studied in the West, and even, between 1871 and 1873, setting up newspapers. Kido financed one newspaper himself, but several others were established by prefectural offices. Some prefectures provided rooms for reading newspapers, while one went so far as to order regular public readings for the benefit of villagers.

Such an attitude also led many of the Meiji leaders to consider favourably the introduction of a constitutional system. Their interest in constitutionalism was not just a case of imitating the most advanced Western countries or even of trying to impress them in the hope of achieving a recognition of equality and revision of the unequal treaties. There were, too, other advantages to be gained by such a step. Opposition to government could be channelled into less violent forms, while government itself would be less prone to incite violence by acting despotically. The existence of formal constitutional procedures would also reduce the danger that privileged Court advisers or royal favourites might take advantage of the throne's prestige and encourage the Emperor to act in accordance with his whims (or their special pleading). Though the Meiji Emperor had not sought to rule directly, the spectre of imperial interference in government was raised in 1879 when, in approving the recommendation of his Confucian teacher, Motoda Eifu, that the primary focus of education should again be on morality and ethics, he overruled Home Minister Ito Hirobumi. It may have been partly to prevent such occurrences, as well as for the more respectable reason of raising the Emperor above public criticism, that the constitution which was eventually produced under Ito's direction in 1889 was to require all the monarch's official actions to be countersigned by the appropriate minister. Similarly, the inclusion in the constitutional system of an elected national chamber, rather than an assembly of notables, would be likely to provide a progressive counter-balance to reactionary influences in high places. In addition, their Confucian ethical background predisposed Ito and other leaders to expect social harmony as long as government policies were righteous and appropriate and properly explained to the people. In this, however, they were to prove unduly optimistic.

Ito's supervision of the drafting of the Meiji constitution was to be carried out during the 1880s, but already in the early 1870s a number of plans or suggestions of a constitution were being put forward within official circles, and in September 1876 the head of the *Genro-in*, Prince Arisugawa, was entrusted with an imperial commission to draft a constitution. His committee's work, however, was not completed until June 1878, and was then sent back for revision because it gave the proposed legislature too much power and was considered to have borrowed provisions from Western constitutions without sufficient concern for the special nature of Japanese tradition. A further draft was not submitted until July 1880. Such lack of urgency suggests that, despite the general acceptance of constitutionalism in principle among government leaders, several more years might have passed before the time was considered ripe to confront the practical difficulties of introducing such a system. That the decision was taken in 1881 undoubtedly owed a good deal to the pressure of the burgeoning *Jiyuminken* (Liberty and People's Rights) movement.

The People's Rights movement

The growth of the People's Rights movement in the late 1870s and early '80s was a remarkable phenomenon, the extent of which has been made much clearer by the studies in local history which have been carried out by Japanese historians during the last forty years. Their work, like that on peasant uprisings, has made it difficult to sustain, without considerable modification, the older view of the Japanese as traditionally submissive and ready to accept authority unquestioningly. The starting point of the People's Rights movement, it is true, is still located in the *shizoku* opposition to the Meiji government – more specifically, in the petition which Itagaki Taisuke, Goto Shojiro, Eto Shimpei, Soejima Taneomi, Yuri Kimimasa and three slightly less prominent ex-members of the government presented to the *Sa-in* on 17 January 1874. Advocating the immediate establishment of a representative assembly to limit the arbitrary nature of the regime, they argued that by uniting government and people this would produce greater stability and national strength. Historians have often charged that this petition already contained the seeds of a commitment to nationalism which was to prove unconducive to the healthy growth of individual rights and pluralist values; and they have further noted that in an open letter to one of their critics Itagaki and his fellow petitioners sought voting rights initially only for the *shizoku* and the wealthy peasants and merchants who, it was claimed, had helped to make the Meiji Ishin. Leaving aside the fact that appeals to nationalism were by no means peculiar to Japan and that Itagaki could hardly be indifferent to the problem of strengthening the country, it should be noted that the underlying implications of the petition were more democratic than the immediate franchise suggestions, for the petitioners stated that those who paid taxes were thereby entitled to participate in government. That the extension of voting rights in due course was envisaged was strongly implied in their further argument that 'among the foremost benefits of free government is that education of the intelligence and the sentiments, which is carried down to the very lowest ranks of the people when they are enabled to take part in national concerns'.[1] Nor was this petition just a convenient weapon of opposition for Itagaki. As early as 1871 he had endeavoured to persuade Kido of the merits of a representative assembly, and he never wavered from this stand even when he rejoined the government in 1875.

Although the 1874 petition was rejected by the government, it was a landmark in the growth of the People's Rights movement in that it provoked the first public debate about constitutionalism in the press and among intellectuals. Moreover, five days before the submission of the petition, another landmark had been established by the same group of discontented samurai with the formation in Tokyo of Japan's first political society, the Aikokukoto (Public Patriotic Party). Only a few months later, however, its two main leaders, Itagaki and Goto, decided that a national party was not yet practicable and returned to Tosa where they could enlist support from their demoralised fellow *shizoku*, who had lost much of their traditional status and income. This was a major reason for the founding of the Risshisha (Self-Help Society) in April 1874 , as it was also of the Jijosha (Self-Aid Society) which was organised in August in neighbouring Tokushima and had over 2,000 members. Such groups could hope to influence prefectural governments, but their general political activities remained limited, and when, in February 1875, their leaders attempted to broaden their sphere by combining with representatives from other parts of western Japan, the Aikokusha (Patriotic Society), as the new organisation was called, collapsed within a month. In part its demise was due to

[1] W.W. McLaren, *Japanese Government Documents* (*Transactions of the Asiatic Society of Japan*, XLII, part 1, 1914), p. 466.

the strength of localism, but, until the failure of the Satsuma rebellion showed the futility of such action, the appeal of a wider political movement was also limited by the counter-attraction of recourse to arms.

It was during the Satsuma rebellion that the Risshisha again took up the call for a representative assembly. By this time more *shizoku* political societies had come into being, and their participation made possible the re-establishment of the Aikokusha in Osaka in September 1878. The success of the national campaign which the Aikokusha then took over from the Risshisha would, however, have been far less had not numerous non-*shizoku* societies begun to develop, notably among the peasantry and particularly in eastern Japan. These societies, which were mainly led by men of wealthy peasant or rural samurai background like Kono Hironaka and Sugita Teiichi, often had a primarily educational purpose initially or had been set up to improve agricultural or commercial production and cooperation, as was the Kounsha (Farming Society), which was established in Kumamoto as early as 1873. The implementation of the land tax reform, however, tended to politicise them, and when the Aikokusha sent out emissaries from November 1879 onwards to encourage them to press the government for a national assembly, they responded enthusiastically. By November 1880, when of the sixty-four delegates to the second convention of the Kokkai Kisei Domeikai (League for the establishment of a National Assembly – the new name for the Aikokusha) fifty-three per cent were commoners (compared with thirty-four per cent at the first convention in March), they had become the largest element in the People's Rights movement.

The People's Rights movement reached its peak in 1880. Out of an estimated 130 petitions or memorials with 319,311 signatures which between 1874 and 1881 called on the government to establish a national assembly, no fewer than 85 were produced in that year – including a massive one submitted in November to the Kokkai Kisei Domeikai convention which secured some 135,000 signatures through the efforts of at least 149 political societies in thirty-nine prefectures. Even these figures did not convey the full extent of political organisation, however, for, according to another estimate, based on Kanagawa prefecture (where there were sixty societies) and Niigata prefecture (where there were thirty-five), the total number of peasant-based societies by 1881 was probably more than a thousand.[2] Nor were such societies always content to limit their role to petitioning the government. A few of them vied with urban intellectuals in drawing up their own detailed plans for a Japanese constitution, thus helping to account for the production of almost thirty drafts (including one which bore little evidence of foreign influence) between 1879 and 1883.

This remarkable awakening of political consciousness requires explanation. At one level it is likely that the rapid development of communications and social mobility played a crucial role. In particular, the growth of a press increasingly critical of the government (with ex-Bakufu officials and samurai from the less favoured prefectures often becoming editors) allowed, for the first time in Japan, informed public debate of national affairs. Even though a considerable number of editors were imprisoned or fined for advocating violence or for using offensive language, press censorship tended to be unsystematic, except where the position of the imperial family was concerned; and it was possible for fundamental issues such as natural rights or the best form of government to be extensively discussed in print. In character the newspapers of the late 1870s more resembled the organs of political clubs than their highly commercial successors of the post-World War I era. By 1878 no fewer than 225 existed, with a total yearly circulation of 37 million copies. Through them, and through the speech-making tours made by the leaders of the political societies and by liberal lawyers and journalists, the third strand of the People's Rights movement – the urban intellectuals – made its impact on the country at large.

Newspapers and speech-making tours were not the only ways in which the urban intellectuals influenced the rural areas. A more specific stimulus to the formation of local political groups was the return from Tokyo of young men, often of wealthy peasant background, who, having gone there to study, had come under the spell of the advocates of natural rights and political participation. One such was Shibata Asagoro, who founded the Akita Risshikai in August 1880 after spending four years in Tokyo and Kochi. Many of its members were peasants with middle-sized or small

---

[2] See Emura Eiichi, 'Kokkai Kaisetsu Undo to Jiyuto Kessei' in Fujiwara Akira *et al.* (ed.), *Kindai Nihon Shi no Kiso Ishiki*, p. 92. In Emura Eiichi and Nakamura Masanori (eds), *Kokken to Minken no Sokoku*, p. 141, Emura suggests that among the societies which sprouted in the villages those which were specifically political in orientation probably numbered several hundred.

holdings, and they talked much in their meetings of *onarashi* (levelling). They seem to have believed that a constitution would bring equality, but somewhat contradictorily one of their slogans was 'return to feudalism'. At least one member revered Itagaki and was convinced that trust in him would lead to the end of all poverty. In preparation for an uprising, however, they engaged in two robberies, killing one of their victims, and the plot came to a speedy end when the police arrested twenty-eight Risshikai members on 9 June 1881.

This 'Akita Incident' is of particular interest because it possessed some of the characteristics of a *yo naoshi ikki* (world-renewal uprising), in which the participants sought not just the remedy of temporary economic grievances but a more general reform – in particular a return to the time when tenancy did not exist and the village was a less unequal community. Such uprisings had been notable features of the late Tokugawa and very early Meiji periods, and the fact that peasant-based political societies were numerous in areas where peasant uprisings had been especially frequent suggests that there was a link between the two phenomena. Under the influence of the People's Rights propagandists, of course, and also as a result of learning from the failure of uncoordinated local opposition to land tax revision, the focus of peasant protest in most areas shifted to the higher objective of a national assembly. The Akita Incident may therefore exemplify the process of transition from old methods and aims to those more appropriate to the new age.

If there was an element of continuity with late Tokugawa tradition in Meiji political activism, however, the importance of the Meiji break with the past should also not be ignored. The dismantling of feudal institutions and the elimination of the traditional ruling class must have reduced the customary deference to authority and made the idea of institutional change less unthinkable. Moreover, the process of centralisation itself often led those who clung to local autonomy to engage in political activity. In the words of one Japanese historian, 'assertions of freedom and people's rights often went hand in hand with advocacy of decentralisation of authority to localities'.[3] Nor was it only administrative changes which affected people's lives. In many areas the influx of Western manufactures had serious repercussions on local handicrafts and

[3] Nagai Hideo, 'Toitsu Kokka no Seiritsu' in *Iwanami Koza Nihon Rekishi*, vol. 14, p. 160.

traditional industry, while in others the Western demand for silk stimulated unprecedented expansion of production. The Meiji government also initially tried to promote Japan's native religion, Shinto, by separating it from its centuries-old link with Buddhism, a policy which resulted in attacks on Buddhist temple property in some areas and was bound to have an unsettling effect, since Buddhism was an integral part of Japanese village life. That such dislocation may have had a substantial impact on the peasant mentality is indicated by the remarkable growth of new sects such as Tenrikyo, Konkokyo, Kurozumikyo and Maruyamakyo, which tended to combine traditional religious beliefs with a more fervent faith in their founder's special religious powers. Unlike the far fewer Japanese converts to Christianity, many of whom were dispossessed *shizoku*, the supporters of these popular religious sects, who mostly came from the lowest strata of the peasantry and were not regarded as progressive by the People's Rights groups, did not usually involve themselves in political activities. Nevertheless, their very large numbers (over a million in several cases) further attest to the existence of a general climate of unease about modernisation and distrust of authority which helps to explain the emergence of a popular political movement.

   In addition to these general influences there were specific government policies which gave an unintended stimulus to the People's Rights movement in the late 1870s and early '80s. One such was the introduction of prefectural assemblies, most of which were first elected in 1879. Although these had a quiet start they soon gave rise to conflict, since assemblies usually opposed any local tax increases introduced by the governor, even if these were for such worthy purposes as additional educational expenditure or the establishment of a relief fund for coping with natural disasters. Another contributory factor was the inflationary printing of large amounts of paper currency to finance the suppression of the Satsuma rebellion. The resulting rise in the price of rice effectively reduced the real tax burden and especially benefited the landlords who could afford to retain the rice they received and sell it when the market was most favourable. Many members of this class were quite well educated and the unexpected improvement in their financial situation provided them with the wherewithal to engage in politics. Some of them probably did so not just for ideological reasons but also to maintain, or stake a claim to, local preeminence.

Such men became known as *meiboka* (local notables) and were to dominate politics at the prefectural, *gun*, and town and village levels for over half a century. Like the village headmen of the Tokugawa era, whose successors they often were and whose role of representing their community they partly inherited, their attitudes contained a measure of ambivalence in that their criticism of the government was likely to be tempered by concern that lower peasant discontent should not endanger law and order. The very fact, however, that they represented the clearly non-revolutionary village élite meant that their activities were less likely to invite suspicion and suppression by the authorities than were those of discontented samurai or poorer peasants.

By November 1880 the campaign for a national assembly had brought together the various strands of the People's Rights movement, but their objectives had not yet been achieved and there was a variety of different views about future strategy. The movement's solidarity was also limited by the primarily local orientation of most political societies, and the further danger existed that future coordination would be made impossible by the restrictive April 1880 Regulations for Public Meetings and Associations. To overcome these difficulties a unified organisation was required, and during the November congress Kono Hironaka, Ueki Emori, Yamagiwa Shichishi, Matsuda Masahisa and others sought to move in this direction by calling for the formation of a national party. Subsequent discussions by the representatives of four leading groups – the Omeisha (a society composed of Tokyo intellectuals associated with Fukuzawa Yukichi's Keio Academy), the Tohoku Yushikai (which represented organisations in northern Japan), the Tokyo Jiyu Shimbun faction (journalists and others from the Kanto region around Tokyo associated with a planned new radical newspaper) and the Tosa-based Risshisha – led to a decision to establish a party on 12 December 1880. The drawing up of rules followed on 15 December, and in 1881 a committee and an office were set up. Relations among the participants were not harmonious, however, and although they adopted the name 'Jiyuto' (Liberty Party), they lacked a genuinely national organisation and are recognised by historians only as a Jiyuto preparation group. Moreover, a different road to unification was being simultaneously followed in the provinces by the consolidation of various smaller societies into 'local Jiyuto'. Whether such organisational efforts would, by themselves, have produced a national party is a question which must remain unanswered, however, for although a new Jiyuto was indeed formed in October 1881, the political situation had by then been transformed by the most serious governmental split since 1873.

The 1881 political crisis

The 1881 political crisis was caused by the conjunction of two major issues. One was the constitutional question, on which all the *Sangi* had been asked for their views in 1879. Almost the last to comply with this request was Okuma Shigenobu, and when he did so, in March 1881, he particularly requested Prince Arisugawa not to reveal his recommendations to other government leaders. This request was not surprising, for Okuma's proposals were closer to the British than to the Prussian system and thus out of line with his colleagues'. In particular he called for the establishment of an elected national assembly as early as 1883 and acceptance of the principle that the cabinet should be formed by the leader of the party with most seats in the assembly. These suggestions, which owed much to two of Okuma's progressive supporters, Ono Azusa and Yano Fumio, appeared to be so radical that Arisugawa felt impelled to disclose them to Iwakura and Sanjo. In late June they were also made known to Ito Hirobumi.

Ito's response was an extreme one: he offered his resignation. To understand his irritation it is necessary to appreciate the ambivalent nature of his relationship with Okuma. Both men had been protégés of Okubo after 1871, and both stood on the progressive side of the government. Indeed both had been involved in private discussions on how to bring into existence a constitution which would not be too strongly marked by reactionary or ultra-conservative influences. Part of Ito's hostile reaction may have stemmed from annoyance that their informal alliance had been undermined. At a deeper level, however, Ito seems to have suspected that Okuma was seeking to achieve a position of future supremacy within the government by making a bid for popular support.

Such a suspicion may not have been misplaced. When Okubo had been assassinated in 1878, Satsuma was left with no outstanding political leader and Okuma and Ito had emerged as the two central members of the government, holding not only a general policy-making function as *Sangi* but also the major administrative positions of Finance Minister and Home Minister respectively. Okuma had a slight edge in seniority, and he could also look for some support from Satsuma leaders anxious to counteract any trend towards Choshu superiority; but these advantages were outweighed by the fact that Ito could rely on Choshu support, whereas Hizen, Okuma's home province, was not noted for its solidarity. This weakness was evident in March 1880 when, overriding Okuma's opposition, Ito insisted that administrative and policy-making positions should (once more) be separated. In doing so Ito was clearly less motivated by any commitment to Kido's cherished principle – in October 1881 he was largely responsible for a wholesale reversion to the previous system of combining both functions – than by the desire to reduce Okuma's influence by forcing him out of the Finance Ministry. Although Okuma retained a supervisory role over financial matters as a councillor, it was a role which he now shared with Ito; and when, in May 1880, Okuma proposed the raising of 50 million yen from abroad by a flotation of government bonds, it was Ito's objections which prevailed.

In view of the relative decline in Okuma's influence it is possible that he may have hoped to use the constitutional issue to restore his position. It is also conceivable, however, that he was borne along by the enthusiasm of his young supporters, fresh from their studies of foreign countries and eager to put their theories to the test. Such a relationship between leader and followers has not been uncommon in modern Japanese history and is more compatible with the fact that Okuma tried to keep his proposal secret than is the argument that he was making a bid for leadership. Whatever the true reason may have been, Okuma's action was not seen as a direct challenge by all members of the government. Even the conservative Iwakura thought it possible to restore harmony, and his efforts seemed to have been successful when, on 8 July, Ito returned to his duties. Within a month, however, a new issue had arisen which further exacerbated relations between Okuma and his colleagues and allowed Ito to engineer the ousting of his rival.

The second major issue of 1881 arose from the government's decision the previous year to abolish the Hokkaido Colonisation Commission. On 30 July 1881, after very strong pressure from its hot-tempered chief, Kuroda Kiyotaka, the government announced that the Commission's properties, which had cost over 14 million yen, would be sold for 387,082 yen, payable over thirty years without interest. The chief beneficiary was to be Godai Tomoatsu, a 'political merchant' who, like Kuroda, came from Satsuma. Even before the announcement, the decision was criticised by the *To-kyo-Yokohama Mainichi* newspaper, which may have learned of the plan from officials in the Finance Ministry. In August the attack on what was regarded as a blatant example of *hanbatsu* favouritism at the nation's expense widened to other newspapers and was intensified by the holding of rallies. The vigour of the campaign surprised and disturbed most of the government leaders, who attributed it mainly to the elements associated with Okuma. Their suspicions were not unjustified. There is little doubt that Iwasaki Yataro, the ex-samurai from Tosa who had founded the Mitsubishi company and had enjoyed valuable support and encouragement from Okuma when the latter was Finance Minister, provided backing for the public opponents of the sale. Moreover, many of the leading campaigners were associated with Fukuzawa Yukichi or his Keio Academy, from which a considerable number of graduates had joined Mitsubishi while others had become supporters of Okuma within the government. It was certainly the case that Fukuzawa, Okuma's friend, played a major role in orchestrating the public campaign, and that the press praised Okuma as an opponent of the sale.

Okuma's identification with the People's Rights movement on both of the main issues of 1881 was to result in his expulsion from the government on 11 October. He himself blamed his ousting on the Satsuma reactionaries, but although they certainly pressed for his removal, and Kuroda claimed in letters to Iwakura in October that this would 'cut away the source of the infection', it is now believed that the operation was masterminded by Ito. The latter, it is maintained, deliberately magnified, and possibly even instigated, the rumours of Okuma's complicity with the opponents of the Hokkaido assets sale. Having thus driven a wedge between Okuma and the Satsuma elements, Ito was able to persuade the latter not only to join in the attack on his rival but also to agree to the cancellation of the sale and to the announcement of the future establishment of a national assembly. Thus, at one stroke, he eliminated his main rival, undercut popular opposition, and overcame conservative misgivings about the introduction of constitutional government.

There seems no reason to dispute this picture of Ito's skillful opportunism, even though the evidence for it is mostly circumstantial. However, by ignoring one important aspect of the political situation it does not wholly convey the complexity and seriousness of the governmental crisis and makes it difficult to appreciate fully the significance of its outcome. What also needs to be noted is the existence of another camp within the Meiji government which was not only opposed to Okuma – indeed, one of its members expressed the fear that his flirtation with popular groups might 'lead to something like the French Revolution' – but also sought to reduce Sat-Cho power. A loose coalition of elements united mainly by shared resentment and suspicion, the most important of its constituent parts was the Chotei-ha (Court faction), a group of men who had been *Jiho* (Attendant Advisers to the Emperor). Led by Sasaki Takayuki and Motoda Eifu, they had earlier, in 1879, asserted that popular opposition to the government was largely due to the fact that it was controlled by *hanbatsu* cliques, and that the way to overcome this was to restore genuine imperial rule and make full use of the Emperor's virtue. Their proposal, which took the form of an ultimatum, was rejected by Ito and his colleagues, and the position of *Jiho* itself was abolished. Most of them found influential positions within such government bodies as the *Genro-in*, however, and when the government appeared to be in difficulty in September 1881 their hopes of governmental changes were reawakened. Not only did they press for the abolition of the *Sangi* and the strengthening of the *Genro-in*, but they also sought the immediate promulgation of a constitution in the form of an imperial gift. Nor did they refrain from criticising the Hokkaido assets sale, and in this they were joined by four generals who, although not representative of the military establishment, may well have reflected the feeling of junior officers. Further support came from a number of conservative *Genro-in* officials known as the Seigi-ha (Righteousness faction), and from various progressive younger officials who were opposed to both the Okuma faction and *hanbatsu* politics. After voicing their objections to the sale in separate petitions and individual approaches to senior ministers all the groups came together to form a Chuseito (Impartial Party) on 28 September.

The impact of the Chuseito is difficult to assess. It was rather a motley coalition with no proven leaders, but it nonetheless represented a a fairly broad band of discontent with the *hanbatsu* system, and quickly received support from newly-formed groups in Kochi and Kumamoto. In the view of Japanese historian Umetani Noboru, the threat it posed played an important part in enabling Ito and his fellow plotters to overcome both Kuroda's hostility to the abandonment of the Hokkaido sale (on 5 October) and Iwakura's reluctance to sacrifice Okuma (on 7 October).[4] As evidence for this claim, Umetani quotes a letter to Iwakura from Inoue Kowashi, a *Dajokan* secretary and influential aide to both Iwakura and Ito. In it Inoue urged the issuing of a rescript promising the establishment of a national assembly as a means of bringing what he called the 'neutral party' (Churitsuto) into line. If Inoue's warning was, as Umetani believes, related to the activities of the Chuseito, it would help to account for the speed with which the dominant Sat-Cho group acted to safeguard their position. On the evening of 11 October, the very day that the Emperor returned to Tokyo from a ten-week tour of northern Japan (during which he had been accompanied by Okuma), the three Ministers of State and seven of the nine *Sangi* met in the Emperor's presence and secured his approval for the simultaneous cancellation of the Hokkaido sale, dismissal of Okuma and issue of an imperial rescript promising that a national assembly would be established in 1890. Some time after midnight Okuma was visited by Ito and Saigo Tsugumichi and told he must resign. He did so on the following day, having been refused an imperial audience, and the other two decisions were announced on 12 October.

The crisis of 1881 was a further landmark in the consolidation of *hanbatsu* dominance. The challenge from the People's Rights movement, the Okuma faction, and the Chuseito, far from weakening the Sat-Cho leaders, brought them into closer alliance. In the reorganisation of government which followed on 21 October, the Chotei-ha's demands were pushed aside and, instead of being abolished, the councillors were increased to twelve, five of whom were from Satsuma and four from Choshu. Sasaki Takayuki was effectively bought off by being made both a *Sangi* and Minister of Industry. Of the other departmental ministers four were Satsuma men and two Choshu. Numerically, Satsuma emerged with a marginal superiority, but there was no doubt that the central figure in

---

[4] Umetani Noboru, *Meiji Zenki Seiji Shi no Kenkyu*, pp. 243-66.

the reconstructed government was Ito, and his preeminence was shown by his appointment as head of the *Sanji-in*, a newly-established legislative and consultative organ which was placed directly above the troublesome *Genro-in* and also entrusted with supervision of the administrative departments. When in 1885 (two years after Iwakura's death) the *Sangi* actually were abolished and the *Dajokan* was replaced by a simple cabinet system, it was natural that Ito should become the first Prime Minister.

The first national political parties

It is an irony of history that whereas the 1881 crisis first threatened but then strengthened the government, its effect on the People's Rights movement was almost exactly the reverse, for while it accelerated the emergence of a fully-fledged Jiyuto, it was also partly responsible for the fact that this first national party was less broadly based than it might have been. At the height of the ferment over the Hokkaido scandal, Itagaki arrived in Tokyo from Kochi, and on 23 September he met with representatives of various societies and stressed the importance of a national party. Many of the participants opposed this, however, arguing that they should put all their effort into the Hokkaido campaign, and when the delegates who duly assembled for the next convention on 1 October 1881 agreed to a Tosa proposal to change the convention's name the following day to Dai Nihon Jiyu Seito Kesseikai (Great Japan Liberty Party Formation Association), the Omeisha and other pro-Okuma groups did not attend. Their absence did not deter the delegates from proceeding to approve a platform and party rules and electing a president (Itagaki), a vice-president, and both a party board and standing committee; but regional and personal rivalries soon led important elements from Kyushu and Tohoku to withdraw from the convention. In the end no fewer than seven of the eleven elected party positions were filled by Tosa men, hardly a promising basis for a genuinely national organisation.

A major reason for the falling away of support for the Jiyuto so soon after its inauguration was the ousting of Okuma, which unexpectedly provided an alternative rallying-point for opposition to *hanbatsu* government. In contrast to the more emotional appeal of Itagaki, Okuma seemed to embody the qualities of the liberal statesman. He also had the advantage of close relations with Iwasaki Yataro, and a pool of devoted aides in the score or so of ambitious young bureaucrats who were expelled from the government in October because of their connections with him. Already by the end of 1881 some of these were, together with Omeisha leaders like Numa Morikazu, planning the setting up of a new party and on 16 March 1882 this came into existence under the name of Rikken Kaishinto (Constitutional Progressive Party) with Okuma as its president. Initially the Kaishinto drew its main support from urban intellectuals and from those men of substance who were disturbed by the radicalism of some Jiyuto supporters. In time, however, the parties converged as differences of principle or class support came to be eroded or superseded by essentially local rivalries, for where, as often happened, the prefectural branch of one national party was dominated by local notables from one or two *gun*, prominent figures from one or more of the other *gun*, concerned lest their own area might suffer from lack of political clout, would often affiliate with the other major party. The competition within the new prefectural assemblies over the routes which new roads should follow, and over other local construction projects which needed prefectural funding, naturally contributed to this kind of rivalry. It was partly because such rivalry was so strong that the People's Rights movement could never be fully united.

As the first national parties the Jiyuto and the Kaishinto have both attracted a great deal of attention from Japanese historians, but their importance should not be overstated. At first their membership was very small compared with that of all the local political societies combined. Even the larger Jiyuto had only 768 members (120 of them *shizoku*) on its roster in November 1882, and no more than 2,147 by May 1884. Nor were they active for very long in their initial phase. The Jiyuto dissolved itself on 29 October 1884, while the Kaishinto entered a period of stagnation after the resignation of Okuma and Kono Hironaka two months later. Even before 1884 both parties were declining in vigour, except in the Kanto (where the talented organiser, Hoshi Toru, was active) and in parts of central Japan.

Various reasons can be suggested for the failure of the national parties to make headway at this time. One would be that the promise of a national assembly cut much of the ground from under them by removing their main campaigning issue and thus condemning them to exist in a political limbo until 1890. Such an explanation, however, is not wholly compatible with the vitality which political activists displayed in 1882, when the number of public speech-meetings reached a peak of 1,817. A more important factor may have been the effectiveness of government restrictions, although this is not entirely supported by the statistics, for the increased interference with speech-meetings which occurred in 1882 (when fifty-three gatherings were banned and 282 ordered to discontinue) was reversed in 1883-4. A further factor of major significance was the severe deflationary financial policy which had been initiated in 1880 but which was more rigorously pursued by Matsukata Masayoshi (Satsuma) when he became Finance Minister in October 1881. The 'Matsukata deflation' was aimed at restoring the value of the yen by withdrawing the large amounts of paper money which had been printed in the late 1870s. By 1885 it had largely achieved this objective, but at the cost of reducing the price of rice and silk drastically and thus raising again the relative burden of national and local taxes. The resulting decline in peasant income increased internal divisions within the villages. Thousands of peasants were forced to sell their land between 1883 and 1890 because they were unable to pay their taxes, and others were pushed into debts which before long led to the same consequence. Frequently they ended up as tenants of the land they had formerly owned. One typical estimate suggests that the amount of land cultivated by tenants increased from 29 per cent in 1872 to over 40 per cent in 1888, and in some areas the rise was much sharper. Not all of the increase in tenancy was necessarily due to impoverishment, but the growth of inequality clearly weakened the sense of village community, and consequently the outbreak between 1884 and 1886 of several more serious, albeit localised, rural revolts in which Jiyuto members often played a prominent part must have alarmed some village leaders, especially when attacks on money-lenders and wealthy landlords were reported. Anxious to avoid accusations of encouraging subversion, and subjected to tighter governmental control, the party leaders decided to adopt a low posture and suspend their activities.

The People's Rights movement in the 1880s

The demise of the Jiyuto and the partial collapse of the Kaishinto have generally been seen as major setbacks to Japanese political party development. Such a view, however, tends to place too much emphasis on the national dimension and on the importance of centralised direction. Even between 1881 and 1884 much political activity remained local, and some of the fiercest conflicts between government authority and the People's Rights movement took place at the prefectural assembly level. Such confrontation between assembly members and prefectural governors became less intense after 1884, probably because of the increased efforts of governors to win over local notables. The framework of local party organisation, however, remained largely intact, ready to be built upon when national politics came into existence in 1890.

The existence of the Jiyuto and the Kaishinto was equally not a prerequisite for the other major form of political activity after 1881 – the debate about political principles. This had already begun in the 1870s and was carried on mainly in speech-meetings and in the press. A central theme of the debate, which was fuelled by translations of Western political philosophers such as Rousseau, Mill, Spencer and Bluntschli, was the question of natural rights, a concept attractive to theorists of the People's Rights movement, but open to challenge, as in Europe, from the standpoints of Social Darwinism and historical tradition. During 1881-2, however, the focus narrowed to the issue of the location of sovereignty, when Fukuchi Genichiro's assertion in the *Tokyo Nichi-Nichi* that it resided in the Emperor alone was vigorously rebutted in other newspapers. Supporters of Okuma and the Kaishinto, for instance, argued in favour of sovereignty being shared by the Emperor and the people's representatives in the British manner. Jiyuto supporters went even further, and it is indicative of the openness of debate and the weakness of official orthodoxy at this time that intellectuals could put forward the idea that popular sovereignty resided in the people without being regarded as extremists who were beyond the pale.

The most notable protagonists of the concept of popular sovereignty were the prolific young Tosa publicists, Ueki Emori, an adviser of Itagaki, and Nakae Chomin, the translator of Rousseau's *Social Contract*. Ueki's ideas were notable not only for their uncompromising assertion of democracy but also for his insistence that basic human rights should not be subject to the discretion of the state – even if popular sovereignty were accepted. This liberal view of the relative rights of state and citizen has often been claimed to be a crucial missing element in Japanese history, but it is worthy of note that it is also to be found in the Jiyuto leader, Itagaki Taisuke. In a speech in Kochi in 1882, for example, he argued that 'The interference of a government with the private affairs of the people is due to its ignorance of the distinction between politics and religion, public and personal matters. Government interference means the loss of independence'.[5] By this time, too, there was little if any, emphasis on distinctions between *shizoku* and other classes; moreover Ueki went so far as to advocate female emancipation, while Nakae criticised the discrimination which was suffered by the *burakumin* (or *eta*), the members of a pariah class who mostly lived in ghetto-like communities, particularly around Osaka.

In some People's Rights leaders, again including Itagaki, the concern for freedom extended to other Asian countries, notably Korea and China, and provided one of the idealistic strands of the pan-Asianism which emerged during the Meiji period. For many, however, attitudes to foreigners were dominated by resentment of Japan's unequal status in relation to the Western powers, and eventually other Asian countries came to be used, often under a pan-Asianist cloak, as instruments in the Japanese drive for greater national strength. In the 1880s, however, there was little popular pressure for expansionism, and party politicians generally were not in sympathy with the government's plans for a further military build-up. What primarily engaged public attention was the struggle to revise the unequal treaties with the Western powers; and here Western unwillingness to abandon their privileges seemed to play into the hands of the People's Rights politicians. To secure the promise of eventual restoration of tariff autonomy and a timetable for the ending of the extraterritorial rights enjoyed by foreigners since the opening of Japanese ports, Foreign Minister Inoue Kaoru in the mid-1880s had not only to agree to seek foreign approval for the Western-style legal codes which the Meiji government and its advisers were in the process of drawing up but also to the use of foreign judges in Japanese courts in cases involving foreigners. In addition the whole country was to be fully opened to Westerners. These concessions provoked considerable criticism not only in the press but even within the government, and in July 1887 the government withdrew its revision proposals.

[5] McLaren, *op. cit.*, p. 612.

Before it did so, however, a highly charged atmosphere was created which gave political parties renewed hope of public support.

The first significant attempt to revive nationally-organised opposition to the government had already occurred on 24 October 1886, when a conference organised by Hoshi Toru and Nakae Chomin met in Tokyo to discuss the formation of a *Daido Danketsu* (Union of Groups Emphasising the Same Priorities). Its instigators were mainly ex-Jiyuto members, however, and little headway was made until Inoue's treaty revision plan became publicly known in June 1887. The movement then developed swiftly into a campaign to bombard the government with petitions on the three major issues of treaty revision, tax reduction and freedom of opinion and assembly. Under the leadership of Goto Shojiro, the campaign achieved such momentum that Home Minister Yamagata Aritomo first banned the presentation of further petitions and then, on 26 December 1887, expelled over five hundred of the opposition leaders from Tokyo and its environs. These measures caused the latter some discomfiture but may indirectly have furthered the campaign by encouraging Goto and other national figures to stir up opinion in the provinces. As a result of their agitation the Daido Danketsu was finally established in October 1888. In the meantime, however, the government, concerned to prevent the formation of a genuinely all-embracing national opposition party, had persuaded Okuma to join the government as Foreign Minister in February 1888. Then, in March 1889, with the first parliamentary election scarcely a year away, Goto Shojiro was induced to take up the post of Minister of Communications. Although Itagaki refused a similar offer and continued to seek opposition unity, the Daido Danketsu split into two rival factions.

The Meiji government's response to the People's Rights movement

Depriving the opposition movement of its leaders was only one of the ways in which the government sought to counter its challenge. The Meiji leaders' most obvious weapon was the control they could impose on political associations and on the venting of critical opinions. As early as April 1880, regulations had been issued which subjected to police sanction the organisation of political societies; denied the right of membership to teachers and students; required official permission for the holding of public meetings; forbade the advertising of meetings by political associations; prescribed police intervention if the discussion seemed to threaten public order; and prohibited associations from combining and even communicating with each other. In June 1882 these regulations were re-issued and supplemented by a ban on the formation of branch organisations by political parties. The Public Order Preservation Ordinance of December 1887 represented a further attempt to control opposition. It is worth noting, however, that these controls and restrictions were generally applied in an uneven and spasmodic fashion, partly, no doubt, because of lack of personnel but also, possibly, because the more progressive members of the government (notably Ito Hirobumi) may have felt that a limited amount of popular political activity strengthened their hand against their reactionary or conservative opponents within officialdom.

Repressive measures were not the only way of limiting the growth of the People's Rights movement. More positively some attempt was made to draw unattached political groups into the Rikken Teiseito (Constitutional Imperial Party), which was formed by the *Tokyo Nichi-Nichi* editor, Fukuchi Genichiro, with the backing of Ito and Inoue Kaoru, in March 1882. Although this was rather an artificial creation, with its upper echelons dominated by bureaucrats and other functionaries, it did secure the affiliation of about forty local societies, not very many fewer than either the Jiyuto or Kaishinto. When, however, the latter both ceased to be active in 1884, the Teiseito was speedily disbanded. That the Meiji oligarchs would come to need organised popular support on a permanent basis was not yet appreciated by even the most far-sighted of them.

What does seem to have been appreciated was the desirability of driving a wedge between the political societies and the local elites. In some cases prefectural officials warned young men from respectable families not to become involved in political activity. More importantly, the scope of government patronage was increased by the expansion of the bureaucracy and by the restructuring of the local administrative system during Yamagata's tenure of the Home Ministry between 1883 and 1890. Much of this was carried out in the name of establishment of local self-government, but the existence of a political motivation is clearly indicated in the statement by Yamagata's German adviser, Albert Mosse, that it was vital 'to attract men of ability into local government work, because, if left out, they often become the instigators of anti-government activities'.[6] A substantial number of prefectural assembly members were indeed lured into local administration in the mid-1880s, while at a slightly lower level the reputation and status of many local notables became at least partly dependent on the government after May 1884, when the rules for town and village assemblies were amended so that the prestigious position of *kocho* (mayor) was no longer filled by public election alone but through appointment by the prefectural governor from among three to five elected candidates. Since the number of *kocho* was strikingly reduced at the same time from 25,831 to 10,603, so that each *kocho was* responsible for several communities, this position became even more highly prized than before.

Linked with the restructuring of local government was the weakening of local solidarity. That objective was evident in the 1884 redefinition of the boundaries of each *kocho's* office, and in 1888 the process was carried further by an administrative reorganisation which reduced the previously existing 71,314 towns and villages to 15,820 by forced amalgamation. Another way of undermining community solidarity was to accentuate distinctions of wealth by creating differential electoral rights, and this was incorporated in Yamagata's major local government legislation of 1888.[7] The complicated two and three-level voting systems then introduced were not all to prove long-lasting: in 1899 there was reversion to direct elections (by men who paid 3 yen in tax) for the *gun* and prefectural assemblies. But the idea behind them was to be reflected (and survive longer) in the provision for representation of the very highest taxpayers in the upper house of the national Diet which was introduced in 1890.

---

[6] Quoted by R.Hackett, *Yamagata Aritomo in the Rise of Modern Japan*, p.111.

[7] As a result of the 1888 changes those who paid less than 2 yen in tax per year were not allowed a vote in village and town assembly elections. Those who paid more were divided into two categories, with the wealthier minority electing the same number of representatives as the less affluent majority – the division being made at the point at which the tax payment of each group was equal. Elections to the *gun* assemblies were limited to the wealthier taxpayers and the members of town and village assemblies; and prefectural assembly members were in turn elected by the *gun* and city assembly members. City assembly members were elected by taxpayers divided into three categories on the same principle of preferential rights for the wealthy. See Arimoto Masao, 'Chiso Kaisei to Chiho Seiji' in *Iwanami Koza Nihon Rekishi*, vol. 14, pp. 202–4.

Some other forms of attracting élite support for the Meiji state were less direct. A change in conscription regulations in 1889, for instance, made it possible for graduates of middle schools (usually the wealthy) to serve just one year in the army as volunteer officer candidates instead of three years in the less pleasant conditions experienced by ordinary conscripts. Similarly, the gradual introduction of examinations as the main criterion for admission to the civil service meant that, as well as improving its quality, new opportunities for advancement became available to those who had attended one of the new academies or schools of law (which already by 1887 had 5,469 students compared with 256 in 1880). The Meiji state also strengthened itself by increasing the number of its servants. The bureaucracy almost doubled between 1880 and 1890, and during the same decade the army was also substantially expanded by the addition of seven new divisions. The growth of the police (from about 20,000 to 26,000) was less striking, but under the influence of a German adviser – Wilhelm Hoehn – they were spread more widely through the country by increasing the number of local police stations from 1,560 in 1880 to 12,832 in 1890.

It was no coincidence that the army expansion plans were formulated in 1882 during the high tide of the People's Rights movement. The alarm which this upsurge of opposition caused some government leaders is evident in a December 1882 memorandum by Iwakura Tomomi in which he likened contemporary developments to the French Revolution and recommended that 'considering this year and the outlook for next year we should take advantage of opportunity and at one stroke decisively suspend the metropolitan and prefectural assemblies. [...] Furthermore we should take in hand the power and authority of the navy, army and police, which comprise the weight of the state, face downwards imposingly, and make the people's hearts tremble'.[8] Although this was an extreme attitude, it helps to explain why the Home Ministry came to concentrate more on its role as guardian of law and order.

Even more significant in the long term, perhaps, than the enlargement of the Meiji state's power to defend itself or coerce its opponents by armed force was its more effective use of public indoctrination. Attempts to inculcate Establishment values took

[8] Quoted by Arimoto, *op. cit.*, p. 200.

several forms, beginning with the Admonition to Soldiers which the scholar-official, Nishi Amane, prepared for Army Minister Yamagata in 1878, and which not only exhorted soldiers to uphold the virtues of loyalty, bravery and obedience but warned that they must not petition concerning political matters and must never question state policies. This warning was not unrelated to a disturbing mutiny within the imperial guard in 1878 and to the suspicion that the disaffection had partly been caused by the influence of the People's Rights movement. With the great upsurge of that movement in 1880-1 a more far-reaching response was required, and an Imperial Rescript to Soldiers was issued on 4 January 1882. It went beyond the previous Admonition by stressing the concept of absolute loyalty to the Emperor in particular rather than the duty of obedience in general, and thus ran counter to the current Jiyuto assertions of popular sovereignty. Through the Rescript many thousands of conscripts were over the years exposed to what was in effect a simplified form of *bushido*, the samurai ethic.

There was one other means of inculcating loyalty to the state through the Emperor which could reach even larger numbers. It was hardly surprising that the Meiji government should perceive the relevance of education to the maintenance of the political system, for the Tokugawa Bakufu had consciously encouraged the establishment of Neo-Confucianism to give ideological support to their rule scarcely two centuries earlier. Initially one of the main functions of the Meiji education system had been to overcome conservative attitudes which posed an obstacle to 'civilisation and enlightenment', but by 1880 Confucian-based ethics had been reinstated to their traditional position of primacy. Although the amount of time devoted to ethics was slightly reduced after Mori Arinori became Education Minister in 1885, the government's control of textbooks was tightened and the principle that education should serve the needs of the state was clearly laid down. All this prepared the way for the issuing in October 1890 of the Imperial Rescript on Education, a document which owed much to Motoda Eifu and purported to be 'the teaching bequeathed by Our Imperial Ancestors, to be observed by Their Descendants and the subjects, infallible for all ages and true in all places'. It proclaimed loyalty and filial piety as the cardinal virtues, and by drawing upon what had been primarily the ideology of the samurai sought to counter the trend towards individualism and egalitarianism among the population at large. During the next two decades these ideas were to be elaborated and extended into what has been termed the '*kazoku kokka*' (family state) concept – a view of Japan as a unique polity wherein the people were seen as branches of one family and obedience was owed to the Emperor as head of the main line of that family. The Rescript was not immediately accepted with enthusiasm everywhere, but its regular reverential recitation in schools was calculated to make a deep impression on the minds of the young, who were obliged to memorise it, and the psychological appeal of a doctrine which proclaimed harmony and solidarity should not be underestimated.

The Emperor's position was also strengthened in a more material way during the 1880s, when the transfer of government-owned forest land to the imperial household was carried out on such a scale that the latter's estate increased in extent from 634 hectares in 1881 to over 3,500,000 in 1890. Hardly less striking was the parallel transfer of shares from government-controlled banks, companies and mines, the effect of which was to increase the value of the imperial family's private holdings from 1,700,000 yen in 1882 to 7,500,000 in 1887. With a further annual appropriation of 3,000,000 yen prescribed by the Imperial House Law of 1889, the imperial family was free from any future financial threat from the Diet; and its attachment to the established order was ensured by its being both the largest landowner and the largest shareholder in Japan.

The final buttress of the imperial family was the constitution which the Emperor promulgated on 11 February 1889. Its first article proclaimed that 'The Empire of Japan shall be reigned over and governed by a line of Emperors unbroken for ages eternal', and the fourth declared unequivocally that the rights of sovereignty were vested in him (although it added that he would exercise them in accordance with the constitution's provisions). That these principles would be enshrined in the constitution had been effectively decided by July 1881, when Iwakura had sent to Ito a set of guidelines which had been submitted to him by Inoue Kowashi. These had listed as essential the preservation of the Emperor's control over national administration, including the supreme command of the armed forces; the principle of ministerial responsibility to the Emperor, not to the Diet; and the restriction to the government alone of the right to initiate legislation. They also spelled out some of the more detailed arrangements which should be followed – a

House of Peers as well as an elected lower assembly, a property qualification for voting for members of the lower house, and the safeguard of reverting to the previous year's budget if the Diet should reject the government's finance bill. This list reflected the influence on Inoue of the German adviser, Hermann Roesler; and although Ito, in preparation for his great task, spent much of 1882-3 in Berlin and Vienna consulting, and being lectured by distinguished legal scholars, his studies abroad did not much affect the basic character of the Meiji constitution. What he did gain was a more sophisticated understanding of constitutional law (which stood him in good stead in the lengthy discussions of the draft document) and the satisfaction of discovering a moral justification for his approach in the concept of social monarchy, which assumed that with the growth of industrial capitalism there was a grave danger of bourgeois dominance of parliament and of endemic class conflict unless a hereditary monarchy, concerned with social harmony and the welfare of the whole nation, could protect the legitimate interests of the peasantry and improve the condition of the proletariat. But this would only be possible if the government were independent of parliament – hence the insistence by Ito and Prime Minister Kuroda, in public speeches immediately after the constitution's promulgation, of the necessity of 'transcendental' cabinets.

The ideal of social monarchy fitted in well with Confucian and Shintoist notions of the Emperor as the centre of the *kokutai* – Japan's unique national structure. But these had to be balanced against the need to prevent the possibility of despotic rule and the desirability of at least some measure of popular participation in the political process. The merit of the 1889 constitution was that Ito and his main advisers – Inoue Kowashi, Kaneko Kentaro, Ito Miyoji and Hermann Roesler – incorporated these different requirements sufficiently to make it more or less acceptable to all major political groups, and did so in an elaborate, carefully considered, form which won respect even from foreigners. The powers of the Emperor were buttressed by the creation of the House of Peers (*Kizoku-in*), which was to be composed of the two highest ranks (princes and marquises) and elected representatives of the three lower ranks (counts, viscounts and barons) of the nobility; and of imperial nominees, a category which covered not only appointed scholars and ex-bureaucrats but also representatives chosen by and from the fifteen highest taxpayers in each prefecture. At the same time, however, the Emperor's freedom of action was constitutionally limited by the requirement that his official actions be counter-signed by the appropriate minister, and the rule of law was further consolidated by constitutional guarantees for freedom of religious belief, publication, public meeting and association (within the limits of the law), as well as other basic rights such as freedom from unlawful arrest. Even more significantly, the House of Representatives (*Shugi-in*), the 300 members of which were to be elected (from 214 single-member constituencies and forty-three two-member districts) by the almost half a million men aged twenty-five years and over who paid 15 yen a year in tax, was, like the House of Peers, to have the right to make representations to the government, petition the Emperor, and also initiate bills – a rare deviation from the 1881 guidelines, albeit one which was to have no significant political effect in practice. Most important, it could also reject new legislation, including the budget – although in this case the government could fall back on the previous year's. The fact that the government could unilaterally effect changes (subject to subsequent ratification by the Diet) by means of ordinances, and that the Diet was normally to meet for only three months each year, admittedly detracted somewhat from its powers. Nonetheless, these offered more scope for the Diet to play an active role than might have been expected, and politicians looked forward to its opening in November 1890 as a real opportunity.

3

THE CONSTITUTIONAL
EXPERIMENT AND THE BEGINNING
OF COMPROMISE POLITICS, 1890-1905

The introduction of the Meiji constitution was regarded by contemporaries as an event of major significance in Japanese political history. What it would lead to, however, was by no means certain. Fundamentally different perspectives still divided the political parties and the established government leaders. Whereas the former saw themselves as the representatives of the people and condemned those in power as *han* cliques, the latter believed that their achievements entitled them to claim that they alone could be entrusted with the nation's destiny. Within a decade, however, the oligarchs were to retreat from their high-handed insistence that cabinets must transcend any connection with parties, while for their part the latter were to abandon their frontal attack on the government and pursue more limited ends.

The fact that the Meiji leaders had confined electoral rights to an affluent minority of men of property may partly explain this significant trend towards collaboration. So too may the gradual dilution of *hanbatsu* domination of government, as non-Sat-Cho bureaucrats recruited through examinations rose to important positions in various ministries. It was also produced by less predictable factors, one of which was the influence of foreign affairs. Between 1890 and 1905 Japan fought and won two wars – against China in 1894-5 and Russia in 1904-5 – and in 1902 entered into alliance with Britain. In the meantime Japan also at long last secured the replacement of the unequal treaties of 1858. This series of achievements inevitably increased the prestige of the Meiji oligarchs and intensified patriotic feeling; and whenever the nation was engaged in armed struggle, national solidarity became so imperative that politicians could hardly withhold support from the government. On the other hand, when oligarchic cabinets reverted to their customary caution in foreign policy, they rendered themselves open to the charge that they were betraying Japanese interests. Moreover, in order to gain Diet approval for the increased taxes which were required to build up the army and navy to the level at which Japan could assert itself against other countries, the Meiji oligarchs had no alternative but to make political concessions to the parties.

The growth of the economy also played a part in bringing the oligarchs and the parties closer together. In particular, the sharp rise in production following the 1895 Treaty of Shimonoseki (when Japan extorted a large indemnity from China and opened up new commercial opportunities on the Continent) increased the political weight of trade and industry, which, being both more lightly taxed than agriculture and more likely to benefit from military expenditure and imperialist expansion, were less inclined to oppose government policies. Equally, if not more, important, the growing involvement of local landlords in new banking and business ventures gradually aroused their interest in securing government subsidies for the development of roads, waterways, railways, harbours, schools, experimental stations and other vital elements of the local economic substructure.[1] These changes helped tilt the balance away from a politics of confrontation towards a more complex interaction in which cross-cutting alliances between oligarchs and party politicians were accepted by the former as necessary for the stability of government and by the parties as a means of sharing in power and advancing their interests.

The first Diet sessions

When the first Diet was convoked in November 1890, however, it was by no means clear how Japanese politics would develop. The general election held on 1 July 1890 had produced a majority of Diet representatives (171 out of 300) who were identified with political parties critical of the government, but at this stage allegiances were not always clear-cut, and members were often elected more for their local reputation than because they were party members. Very few of them could be described as professional politicians.

[1] After a change in government regulations the number of banks increased from 270 in 1892 to 1,867 in 1901. Most were local. Masumi, *Nihon Seito Shiron*, vol. 4, p. 6.

The typical representative was a fairly well-off landlord, although almost 100 members already had business connections of one kind or another, and approximately fifty were drawn from the liberal professions, such as the law, journalism, teaching and medicine. Over half had been members of prefectural assemblies, and thus were not entirely lacking in experience relevant to Diet procedure, including, in some cases, experience of disputes with prefectural governors. Almost two thirds of the total membership were under forty-three years of age, which meant that their political attitudes had been shaped within an environment of radical change and protest.

In this novel situation much depended on what stance the political parties would adopt towards the government and towards each other. In organisational terms they were still weak, being heavily dependent on personal ties between influential members of prefectural political associations, prominent regional leaders, and a handful of politicians of national stature. The disintegration of the *Daido Danketsu* movement in the spring of 1889 had left no fewer than five main groups, the most broadly based of which, regionally, was the Kaishinto. Of the other parties the Jiyuto was especially strong in the Kanto region, as was the Daido Club in north-east Japan, while Itagaki's Aikokukoto was concentrated on Shikoku and the Osaka area. The most specifically local organisation was the Kyushu Doshikai (Kyushu Association of Like Minds), which incorporated all the liberal elements in the south-western island. Efforts were made immediately before the election to unify the various organisations, and in May 1890 the Jiyuto, Aikokukoto and Daido Club actually decided to merge again, but the implementation of this agreement was postponed until August in order not to upset election arrangements. Following the election it was again shelved in favour of another attempt to establish an all-embracing popular party, but this too failed to materialise when the Kaishinto withdrew from the talks. Only in September did the previously planned amalgamation take place. Despite the incomplete nature of the merger, however, the new organisation, which adopted the name Rikken Jiyuto (Constitutional Liberal Party) was easily the major group in the Diet, its approximately 130 members considerably outnumbering the seventy-nine representatives who were loosely associated with the pro-government Taiseikai (Great Achievement Society) and the forty-one adherents of the Kaishinto.

The Diet tactics of the Jiyuto were affected by two main factors. One was the willingness or otherwise of the government to engage in genuine dialogue; the other was the pressure of those members of the party who were not Diet members. Of the sixty-nine members of the party organ entrusted with major decision-making, the *Jogi-in-kai* (standing committee), thirty-eight belonged to this category (known as *ingaidan*), and they were also in a majority in the five-man management committee (*kanji*). They tended to take a particularly hard line towards the government, and it was largely due to their pressure that the Jiyuto determined not to seek a prior agreement with the cabinet about the budget before it was presented to the Diet. This relatively intransigent approach was matched on the government side. The Prime Minister at this juncture was Yamagata Aritomo, who had built up a reputation for firmness as Home Minister during the 1880s and whose military background made him reluctant to yield ground. He showed little inclination to cultivate the sort of contacts with politicians which might have forestalled conflict, and as a result of this the first Diet session was a stormy one.

The central issue for both sides was finance. Battle was joined less than a month after the opening of the Diet when on 27 December 1890 the Lower House Budget Committee decided that the government's planned appropriations should be reduced by 11 per cent. Although the cuts were mainly in administrative costs rather than military expenditure, Yamagata and Finance Minister Matsukata resisted on the ground of constitutional principle. Their arguments did not persuade the Lower House, but in late February 1891 the deadlock was broken when twenty-six members of the so-called 'Tosa faction' of the Jiyuto were persuaded by Mutsu Munemitsu and Goto Shojiro to defect from the party and abandon their opposition. To treat the episode as a triumph for the oligarchs, as some historians have done, however, is to ignore the fact that, under pressure from Ito, who naturally wished the constitution he had worked on for so long to function effectively and was anxious to avoid an early dissolution, compromises were also made on the government side, with the result that the budget as passed incorporated almost three quarters of the cuts which had originally been demanded.

It is worth noting that many Diet members too did not wish the initial experiment with representative institutions to be seen as a failure, and that the 'Tosa faction' was before long accepted back into the Jiyuto. Their behaviour shows that they were already aware of the need to strike a balance between accommodation and confrontation. They were certainly not inclined to yield too easily to government demands; had they done so, they would have thrown away their most valuable weapon; and in any case, many of them were firmly opposed in principle to the tax increases the government favoured, especially if this meant a raising of the land tax. On the other hand, they were not unconscious that unremitting opposition might provoke the government into strong counter-measures – perhaps even suspension of the constitution. The feeling that they might have leaned too far in that direction may have been behind the changes which occurred within the Jiyuto in early 1891. In January the influence of the *ingaidan* elements was curbed when the standing committee's powers over Jiyuto Diet members were suspended and the special council set up in September 1890 to discuss and lay down specific guidelines for Diet tactics was abolished. Then in March 1891 the radical faction led by Oi Kentaro lost further ground when it was decided at the party's conference in Osaka to seek greater unity by installing a single leader, and Itagaki Taisuke defeated Oi by seventy-two votes to ten. In October the standing committee was abolished outright, and in June 1892 Oi and fourteen of his followers gave up their struggle and left the party.

The behind-the-scenes manoeuvres which led to these significant party changes are obscure, but by common consent a major part in them was played by Hoshi Toru. Born in 1850 the son of a small Edo shopkeeper, Hoshi had learned English and then been placed in charge of the Yokohama customs office at the age of twenty-four before being sent to London to study law. After returning to Japan he joined the Jiyuto and was twice imprisoned for being too outspoken in criticising the government. Absence abroad meant that he missed the first general election, but once back again he rapidly emerged as the principal architect of realistic compromise. His combination of political experience, organisational ability, and business connections gave him an exceptionally strong position in the party's dominant Kanto group.

These trends within the major political party offered some prospect of avoiding head-on conflict in the second session of the Diet, which was convoked in November 1891. That prospect was con-

ditional, however, on the government's willingness either to reduce the land-tax or to moderate its insistence that it stood above
and entirely separate from parties, and there was no sign of change
on either of these positions, even though Yamagata, who had experienced a difficult time as Prime Minister, had made way for
Matsukata. When the Diet called for substantial cuts in the new
budget, Matsukata, encouraged by Home Minister Shinagawa Yajiro
(who acted as Yamagata's main representative in the cabinet) attempted to overcome opposition by calling another election. It
was held on 15 February 1892 and ranks with those of 1890, 1924
and 1949 as among the most decisive in Japanese history. Although
the Home Minister engaged in intimidation and violence on a
massive scale, through both the police and strong-arm men (*soshi*),
and made lavish use of bribes and official recommendation of favoured
candidates, the electors still returned a majority of opposition members,
thus showing both their political spirit and the strong hold of local
leaders. The Matsukata cabinet made some attempt to remain in
office, but having lost the confidence of his fellow oligarchs, government officials and the Army and Navy Ministers, eventually had
no recourse but to resign.

The Ito cabinet and the Jiyuto

The relationship between the two dominant ex-*han* ensured that a
Satsuma Prime Minister would be succeeded by one from Choshu,
and since the hardline approach had failed it was natural that Ito
should now be given the responsibility. This ought to have been
the opportunity for the architect of the constitution to prove that it
could be made workable, but Ito's freedom to act was constrained
by the fact that his ideas had begun to diverge quite significantly
from those of his fellow oligarchs. Whereas most of the latter still
adhered to a strict policy of transcendental cabinets, Ito had reluctantly come to accept the necessity of establishing a government
party. Already in January 1892 he had gone so far as to recommend
this strategy in a memorial to the Emperor, but Yamagata and the
other elder statesmen had effectively vetoed any such idea of a permanent relationship with a party (of whatever kind), regarding it as
the first step on the slippery slope which would lead to party cabinets along British lines. Even though their alternative solution –
election interference – proved ineffective, they still did not waver

in their opposition to Ito's proposal The need for their cooperation meant that as Prime Minister Ito had to handle an awkward situation not of his own making without being able to apply the political remedy which he now considered appropriate. His tactical adroitness, and his willingness to establish contacts with Hoshi and other party leaders by using men such as Mutsu Munemitsu and Ito Miyoji, gave him some advantages over his predecessors, but there was little expectation that the pattern of Diet conflict would be changed.

As it turned out, Ito's ministry lasted until 1896, even though it too began with a budget crisis. This time the Lower House's demands for cuts were not confined to administrative costs but included the whole amount allocated to new warship construction. Moreover, on 7 February 1893, the Jiyuto combined with the Kaishinto to gain Diet approval of a petition to the Emperor condemning the cabinet. Instead of threatening dissolution, however, Ito defused the attack by having the Emperor issue a rescript in which he promised 1,800,000 yen over six years from imperial household funds for naval expansion and also required all government officials to contribute one-tenth of their salaries over the same period to the same end. Diet members were themselves affected by this provision, but at the same time the rescript went some way towards meeting their demand for economies.

The next session was again marked by acrimony, but this time the main focus of attack was the government's unwillingness to try to end the unequal treaties by applying strictly those provisions which could make life difficult for foreigners. Such pressure on the Western powers was in fact unnecessary – all of them were now resigned to the abandonment of their special rights, and a revised treaty with Britain was signed in July 1894 without recourse to threats – but the delicate negotiations which Mutsu was carrying on as Foreign Minister might well have been jeopardised if foreign suspicions of Japanese xenophobia, never far below the surface, had been re-awakened. Ito therefore needed to show that the government was firmly in control, and he did so by dissolving the Diet on 30 December 1893. That he felt able to act firmly, though, was due to his awareness of divisions between and among the popular parties. The Jiyuto was being accused by the Kaishinto of secret contacts with government members, and Kaishinto resentment was increased by the unwillingness of many Jiyuto members to join in the assault on the government's 'weak' foreign policy. The main force of Kaishinto displeasure was concentrated on Hoshi, who had not only been outspoken in his own counter-criticism but had laid himself open to attack by his involvement in a dubious trial and a shady business deal. Without full support from his own party, Hoshi was eventually expelled from the Lower House on 13 December 1893.

The removal of Hoshi was a less damaging blow to Ito than it might have been, for other Jiyuto politicians were now becoming conscious of the possible advantages of cultivating links with members of the government, even if this had to be done surreptitiously to avoid arousing the wrath of party activists. The Jiyuto certainly did not suffer electorally from the Kaishinto accusations of collusion, for in the March 1894 election the number of its Lower House members (which had been reduced to ninety-four in the 1892 election and further depleted by defections) rose to 120 (among them Hoshi) while the Kaishinto returned no more than fifty. Nevertheless, although it refrained from joining in the Kaishinto-led attack on the government's handling of the treaty revision issue, the Jiyuto did not yet abandon its opposition to the government altogether. In particular, it continued to proclaim the need for major administrative reforms, and in May supported another motion of no-confidence in the cabinet. Again Ito responded by dissolving the Diet, and in the September election both the Jiyuto and the Kaishinto lost some ground. By that time, however, the political situation had been transformed by a breakthrough in the struggle for treaty revision and even more by an almost simultaneous Japanese military challenge to Chinese control of Korea.

The 1894-5 conflict with China was probably the most popular war in modern Japanese history. National enthusiasm was fully reflected in the Diet, and neither of the two large budgets submitted to it during the war encountered any real difficulty. This late honeymoon came to an end, however, with the Triple Intervention of April 1895 when the Ito cabinet succumbed to German, Russian and French pressure for the return to China of the strategically important Liaotung peninsula in southern Manchuria, which Japan had just extorted, together with Taiwan, as part of the spoils of victory. The Jiyuto maintained its interest in cooperation, though, and in July 1895, after an approach by Ito Miyoji to Itagaki, it actually announced publicly that it would support the government. In return the government promised to consult it in advance on major government bills, not to increase the land tax, and to appoint Itagaki Home Minister. This last pledge was not redeemed by Ito until April 1896, but when it was, two party men were also admitted to key positions within the same ministry while Hoshi was made Japan's representative in the United States, a post not unconnected with his business interests. As a result of the agreement the cabinet was able to pass not only an unprecedented number of new laws but also a budget more than twice as large as the ones which had caused so much trouble in 1890 and 1891.

Despite the considerable benefits of cooperation this political compact was brought to an end in August 1896 in circumstances which suggest that Ito may have been anxious to avoid too close an identification with the Jiyuto. The immediate cause of the breach was Ito's proposal to fill two vacant cabinet positions with Matsukata and Okuma. Except for Kono Hironaka, all the Jiyuto leaders objected to the inclusion of Okuma, whose position had recently been strengthened by the amalgamation of the Kaishinto with several smaller groups to form the Shimpoto (Progressive Party), the Diet strength of which was almost equal to the Jiyuto's. When Ito persisted in his attempt to build a cabinet with a broader political base, the Jiyuto stood firm; and the Prime Minister, perhaps not entirely unwilling to relinquish for a time the cares of office, stepped down without waiting for the next Diet session.

Ito's obvious successor was Matsukata, who already had plans for an arrangement with Okuma which would give him the support of the Shimpoto. Significantly, he did not proceed with the formation of a cabinet until Okuma had agreed to enter it. Moreover, even though the government also depended heavily on strongly conservative Satsuma elements, the understanding with Okuma in practice gave the Shimpoto more than the Jiyuto had secured from Ito. Not only did Matsukata accept that the principles advocated by Okuma should become cabinet policy, but Shimpoto members were appointed to the two central posts of Cabinet Secretary and head of the Legislative Bureau, as well as to a number of government bureaus and prefectural governorships. Shimpoto prestige in the country was naturally increased by these developments, but the party's new influence was also used to the benefit of all political organisations when an attempt by pro-Yamagata bureaucrats in the Home Ministry to strengthen the regulations dealing with the suspension of publications was successfully resisted and the existing right of administrative action (without trial) against newspaper or magazine editors who offended the authorities was substantially restricted. Such successes, however, were resented by the Choshu members of the cabinet, and their hostility forced several of the Shimpoto bureaucratic appointees out of office. The resulting rupture of relations between Matsukata and the Shimpoto was soon followed by Okuma's resignation over the government's proposal to increase the land tax. An attempt was made by the leading Satsuma ministers to save the government by seeking the support of the Jiyuto through its leading Kyushu figure, Matsuda Masahisa, but this was successfully opposed within that party by Hayashi Yuzo and the 'Tosa faction', which had come to dominate the party in Hoshi's absence. Faced with a Diet motion of no-confidence, Matsukata resigned on 28 December 1897.

The 1898 impasse and the Kenseito cabinet

One of the reasons why Hayashi had opposed an alignment with Matsukata was that Jiyuto support was already being sought for another Ito cabinet by Ito Miyoji. However, the latter no longer had a full understanding of his patron and namesake, and whereas Ito Miyoji had developed close personal links through acting as go-between with Jiyuto leaders, the former Prime Minister had become increasingly dissatisfied with the idea of a temporary arrangement with one particular party. Experience had proved that this tended to make government partisan. When Ito formed his third ministry in January 1898, therefore, he aimed to secure Shimpoto as well as Jiyuto support.

In the event he gained neither. The Shimpoto was determined to make an advance on its previous partnership with Matsukata, and held out for four cabinet posts. The Jiyuto was less demanding, but continued to make control of the Home Ministry a prerequisite of cooperation. Ito Miyoji, who had become Minister of Agriculture and Commerce, pressed the Jiyuto case at a cabinet meeting on 13 April but opinion was divided and in the end the opposing view of Inoue Kaoru prevailed. The consequences for the government were serious. Ito Miyoji resigned, and the provisional support which the Jiyuto had given was now withdrawn. Although it refrained from joining the Shimpoto in condemning the government for inactivity while the Western powers were scrambling for concessions in China, it did not hesitate to vote against the budget, which included an increase in the land tax. In response, Ito dissolved the Diet once more.

The impasse over the 1898 budget marked a critical stage in the development of Japanese constitutional government. Three very different solutions presented themselves, and the one which was chosen was the least expected. It also signally failed to work, but its very failure opened the way to a resumption of the compromise between particular oligarchs and parties which, even though not wholly satisfactory to either side, was to provide Japan with a workable and fairly stable system.

The first solution put forward was Ito Hirobumi's. He had long felt the need for a national party which would not represent sectional interests or perpetuate People's Rights movement attitudes. As he envisaged it in 1898, it would be based on an amalgamation of the pro-government Kokumin Kyokai (National Association) with some other small conservative groups and independents. The new party would be more effectively organised, would involve the active participation and financial backing of businessmen, and would enjoy the advantages of government support and Ito's own prestigious leadership. His proposal did not come to fruition, however. Most of the businessmen approached were either unwilling to commit themselves to such an uncertain venture or were already connected with opposition politicians. More important, the other oligarchs, apart from Inoue, still regarded such a step as a betrayal of transcendentalism. Yamagata's hostility, in particular, was difficult to overcome since his influence, already strong in the army and the Home Ministry, had been growing in some departments, as the infiltration of party influence from 1896 aroused concern and resentment among career bureaucrats and impelled them to look for a staunch defender of their rights and position.

A second possible solution lay in the approach which Yamagata himself advocated. He too favoured the formation of a national or, as he termed it, a loyalist party (*kinnoto*), but in his scheme of things the government would stand clearly above and apart from such a party. Even if it was much less likely to secure a Diet majority than the one Ito envisaged, Yamagata believed that it could still give the oligarchs the extra leverage necessary to play off the main opposition parties against each other. Limited concession would certainly be necessary also, and possibly even bribery, although even more crucial in Yamagata's eyes was the maintenance of a firm, united stand by all the senior statesmen. Should all this prove insufficient, dissolution of the Diet, or the threat of it, might make its members more amenable; and if this failed to achieve its purpose, there was a last resort of an exemplary suspension of the constitution.

Whether Yamagata himself would actually have recommended this ultimate step is uncertain, but some of his henchmen did contemplate it as an alternative to the third solution: to acknowledge the importance of the Diet by giving the parties a significantly greater share in power. None of the oligarchs favoured this, but it became more difficult to resist after the unexpected merger of the Jiyuto and the Shimpoto into the Kenseito (Constitutional Government Party) on 22 June 1898. The fact that the Kenseito could muster an overwhelming majority within the Diet made prospects for the next session a daunting one, and on June 24 Ito resigned as Prime Minister. He suggested that Yamagata take office again, but the latter, aware that he would only have Ito's nominal support, declined. When Ito then proposed that the Emperor should invite Okuma and Itagaki, titular leaders of the new party, to form the next administration, the other oligarchs were left with no other options. Thus, on June 30, no more than four weeks after the first moves to form the Kenseito, Okuma became Prime Minister.

Ito's readiness to bring about what Yamagata described in a letter on June 26 as a 'great political revolution' should not be seen simply in terms of capitulation to superior force. The surprise of Okuma and Itagaki at being asked to form a government would suggest that they themselves were not conscious of possessing overwhelming strength. As in the 1881 political crisis, the explanation of Ito's action lies rather in his ability to adapt to new political circumstances and turn them to his own advantage. By installing Okuma and Itagaki he set a precedent which might make it easier for him to establish a party cabinet of his own in future, but he did so in the knowledge that the unity of Kenseito was far from tried and tested and that there was a good chance that it would not survive for long. Ito was also aware that both the constituent parties had already abandoned their outright opposition to increased government spending. Thus he could reasonably hope that, placed in a position of responsibility, the Kenseito would vote in the increased taxes which, if proposed by a non-party cabinet, would probably have been resisted for tactical reasons. That it would not attempt to go in the opposite direction and reduce military expenditure was guaranteed by the fact that both the Army and Navy Ministers (Katsura Taro – Yamagata's protégé from Choshu – and Saigo Tsugumichi) agreed to continue in office only if there was no military retrenchment policy. Furthermore, the House of Peers could prevent any undesirable laws from being passed. In short, the Okuma-Itagaki cabinet could be used to accelerate certain advantageous trends without any great risk of things getting out of control.

Given these limitations on the Kenseito's freedom of action, the new party could not reasonably have been expected to achieve a great deal in terms of the advance of popular power and rights. Even so, its performance was unimpressive. Apart from the abrogation of the repressive Public Order regulations of 1887, its only significant measure was the pruning of 4,500 bureaucrats, an economy measure intended at least partly to pay for the post-war programme of military and naval expansion which it had inherited. The most obvious reason for the Kenseito's lack of achievement was also the most conspicuous signal of its failure, namely the fact that after scarcely four months, and before it had even faced a Diet session, the party split and the cabinet was forced to resign.

The immediate cause of the Kenseito's split was the division of cabinet posts between ex-Jiyuto and ex-Shimpoto politicians. From the beginning the latter had enjoyed a slight advantage, but when Education Minister Ozaki Yukio was forced to step down after unwisely referring hypothetically to a Japanese republic in a speech, the way was opened to a more even balance. Instead of availing himself of this opportunity, however, Okuma had another of his own associates, Inukai Tsuyoshi (Ki), appointed. This move played into the hands of Hoshi Toru, who, having abandoned his diplomatic post in Washington when the Kenseito cabinet was formed, had his hope of becoming Foreign Minister rebuffed by Okuma and was now manoeuvring to undermine the new party. Other forces were working in the same direction. The hastily concocted merger had never had much grass-roots support, and although the party had won 260 out of a total of 300 seats in the general election which was held in August, the fact that more ex-Shimpoto than ex-Jiyuto men had been returned (and that some *gun* had been deprived of their expected right of running their own local man) inevitably added to the friction already produced by the selection of the new party officials. In addition both Ito Miyoji and members of the Yamagata faction had been orchestrating public criticism of the cabinet and encouraging their ex-Jiyuto contacts to withdraw from the party. Matters were brought to a head when Hoshi burst into a meeting of ex-Jiyuto leaders following Inukai's appointment in late October and browbeat them into agreeing to re-establish a separate party. Okuma's attempt to replace the 'Jiyuto' ministers with 'Shimpoto' men was then foiled by Katsura and Yamagata, who got Court officials to indicate to the Prime Minister that the Emperor's commission to form a government had been handed down to him and Itagaki jointly.

The Yamagata cabinet and the Kenseito

The demise of the Kenseito cabinet was followed quickly by the appointment of Yamagata as Prime Minister again. With Ito away in China, none of the other elder statesmen objected when Katsura canvassed their support for his patron. This was hardly surprising in view of Katsura's confidence, founded on his recent cooperation with Hoshi, that he could secure an alliance for Yamagata with the old Jiyuto – which now took advantage of Itagaki's influence in the Home Ministry to appropriate for itself the Kenseito name, while the Shimpoto elements retaliated by calling themselves the Kenseihonto (Original – or Main – Constitutional Government Party). The alliance was sealed in late November when the cabinet agreed to proclaim publicly its partnership with the Kenseito and to adopt its basic platform, including extension of the franchise. In return the party was to support the government in the Diet and agree to an increase in the land tax, albeit one limited to five years.

This agreement marked a significant change in the attitudes of both camps, for even though no party man received cabinet appointment, Yamagata effectively abandoned the original concept of transcendental cabinets while the Kenseito jettisoned, at least temporarily, what had hitherto been an almost sacrosanct party position. Moreover, it marked that party's willingness to pursue a more positive strategy with a broader appeal. Hoshi was already sensible of the advantages of attracting the backing of urban interests. As he somewhat cryptically put it to one of his followers: 'Although our Jiyuto historically has been strongly supported by the regions and peasants, it has lacked the trust of the Court and of businessmen. [...] In our national polity, however much popular trust there may be, without the trust of businessmen it is not possible to conduct state affairs satisfactorily. Therefore what the Jiyuto must strive for hereafter is to gain the trust of the Court and win over merchants and industrialists'.[2] Hoshi's close involvement with the Tokyo city assembly may have put him ahead of his party, but the acceptance of a higher land tax showed that the Kenseito had ceased to be a party of agrarian protest. It further indicated that many of the local notables who belonged to the party now recognised that greater national revenues could mean that central funds would be available (given sufficient political leverage) for projects which could not be financed by local means alone.

In seeking to attract businessmen the Kenseito was to some extent responding to signs of new political aspirations on the part of this rising class. A League for Land Tax Increase had already been formed by chambers of commerce to lobby both the government and the Diet, and in January 1899, at the instigation of wealthy entrepreneurs such as Shibusawa Eiichi, Okura Kihachiro and Yasuda Zenjiro, a League to Reform the Lower House Election Law was organised to press for more favourable treatment for cities. Their action was followed by similar campaigns by the chambers of commerce and by representatives of fifty-one cities. It was against this background that the Yamagata cabinet agreed to the introduction of a differential system in which the ratio of urban seats to population was made more generous than in the more rural areas. Each of the forty-two cities with populations of 30,000 or more became an electoral district, with larger cities having more than one member. At the same time the tax qualification for voting was reduced from 15 to 10 yen and secret balloting was introduced. Both these changes were in line with Hoshi's wishes, but a further change – the abandonment of the general principle of small single-member constituencies in favour of prefecture-wide, multi-member, districts (cities excluded) – was a devious attempt by the Yamagata faction to give independents and small parties a chance to return one or two members and thus limit Kenseito and Kenseihonto dominance.

Electoral reform was not the only area in which the burgeoning

<hr />

[2] Quoted by Mitani Taichiro, 'Seiyukai no Seiritsu' in *Iwanami Koza Nihon Rekishi*, vol. 16, p. 163.

strength of capitalism made itself felt. The interests of employers were also evident in the Peace Police Law (*Chian Keisatsu-ho*) of 1900, which, in its subsequently notorious Article 17, prohibited secret combinations among workers and denied the nascent trade unions any legal standing or protection. This article made it easier for strikes to be suppressed, and contrasted with the simultaneous relaxation of some of the surviving restrictions on conventional political activity, from which only women and minors were now barred. Significantly, the law was passed by the Diet virtually without discussion.

The Peace Police Law was not the only legacy of the second Yamagata cabinet which was to have a major influence on twentieth-century Japanese politics. Recognising the danger that parties in alliance with oligarchs would infiltrate the bureaucracy with their own nominees, Yamagata had three imperial ordinances issued in March 1899 (in a form which made it impossible to rescind them without imperial and Privy Council assent), which barred from almost all bureaucratic positions political appointees who had not passed the appropriate examinations. This was in due course to make it more difficult for party cabinets to assert full control over governmental departments. Similarly, at the cabinet level, further imperial ordinances in May 1900 restricted the positions of Army and Navy Minister to serving generals or lieutenant-generals and their naval counterparts.

These ordinances were clearly directed against the political parties and inevitably soured relations between the Yamagata cabinet and the Kenseito. Indeed, their alliance might not have survived more than one Diet session without extensive use of bribery (by way of Hoshi) and the raising of Diet members' annual salaries from 800 to 2000 yen in 1900. The further continuation of the cabinet would have been possible only if Yamagata had appointed Kenseito members to cabinet posts, but he preferred to resign rather than make such a concession. His intention was to propose Katsura to the other oligarchs as his successor, but the need to deal with the Boxer uprising in China obliged him to remain in office until October. By then another major political development had occurred, and instead of Katsura, Ito assumed office yet again.

The formation of the Seiyukai

The choice of Ito was made virtually inevitable by the fact that in September he had finally gone ahead with his long-cherished scheme to form a government party. In contrast to his earlier plan, however, the Rikken Seiyukai (Constitutional Association of Political Friends) was not an essentially new organisation, but was solidly based on the Kenseito. As far as possible, Ito tried to disguise this fact. Instead of agreeing to become president of the Kenseito when Hoshi approached him with the offer, he insisted that the Kenseito formally dissolve itself; and he attempted to draw businessmen and members of other parties into the new organisation. He also brought in some of his own supporters from the ranks of the bureaucracy, notably Saionji Kimmochi, a liberal-minded court noble, and Hara Takashi (Kei), an ex-newspaperman of high samurai birth and outstanding organisational ability. Hara became secretary-general of the Seiyukai, and the group associated with Ito filled seven out of the thirteen positions on its general affairs committee. Nevertheless, the bulk of the party's 150 Lower House members were ex-Kenseito men who, while conceding large powers to Ito as president, did so merely as a tactic for sharing in power, and continued to look to such party stalwarts as Hoshi and Matsuda for leadership. Political insiders were aware that this was so, as indeed was Yamagata, but his own recent alliance with the Kenseito – and its responsible behaviour during that time – deprived his objections of their former force. On the other hand, the Kenseito's transformation represented a further departure from the People's Rights movement tradition, a fact that was marked by Itagaki's withdrawal from active politics.

Despite his apparently impregnable position, Ito was not entirely happy to be returned to power so soon, and the short duration of his fourth ministry proved that his misgivings were justified. His difficulties came not so much, though, from the Lower as from the Upper House of the Diet, among the leading members of which were such ex-bureaucratic followers of Yamagata as Hirata Tosuke, Kiyoura Keigo and Yoshikawa Akimasa, all of whom strongly opposed Ito's close association with a political party. They were particularly hostile to the inclusion in the cabinet of Hoshi Toru, towards whom numerous allegations of corrupt practices had been levelled, and succeeded in forcing his resignation (soon to be followed by his assassination on 21 June 1901 by an indignant educationist). The

Peers were able to cause the government considerable embarrassment by blocking the tax increases which the Lower House had passed. Eventually Ito was able to force the budget through by having the Emperor insist to the Upper House chairman on the necessity of compliance, but only after his first suggestion of a reduction of the Upper House's powers by an imperial ordinance had been vetoed by the other elder statesmen. His evident loss of standing with his fellow oligarchs made it more difficult for Ito to exert control over the Seiyukai members, to whom his value depended in large part on his prestige and influence as an oligarch. Nor was his position helped when Finance Minister Watanabe Kunitake's insistence on retrenchment and the postponement of agreed public works provoked bitter protests from the five Seiyukai ministers. Faced with an internal conflict, Ito resigned in June 1901 intending to form a new, reorganised cabinet but failed to secure the approval of the elder statesmen.

Politics under the first Katsura cabinet

Ito was the last of the Meiji Ishin leaders (save for the atypical Okuma in 1914) to head a cabinet. His successor as Prime Minister was the Choshu general, Katsura Taro, born in 1847. Since all but one of the ministers in the new cabinet were, like Katsura, ex-protégés or ex-subordinates of Yamagata, the goodwill of the Peers was assured. To be effective, however, Seiyukai cooperation, or at least benevolent neutrality, was needed, and Katsura had to look to Ito to deliver this. Whatever Ito's personal feelings about the opposition he had encountered from Yamagata's bureaucratic supporters, his sense of responsibility did not permit him to reject such an approach. Other party leaders, however, were less inclined to give Katsura unconditional commitment, and after Ito had departed for Europe in September 1901 (in the hope of avoiding conflict with Russia by means of unofficial diplomacy) Matsuda and Hara, encouraged by approaches from the Kenseihonto, began to mobilise party opinion against the government. These particular efforts were short-lived, however, for Ito sent back a telegram indicating that the government should not be opposed at a time of international tension except for the most serious reasons.

Despite this invaluable support the Katsura cabinet still faced the same kind of financial difficulties which had beset its predecessors.

In some respects they were worse, since the land tax increase agreed in 1898 had been limited to five years, while on the other hand Japan was committed by the spirit of the alliance which had been concluded with Britain early in 1902 to increasing the size of its navy. Continuation of the higher rate of land tax was an obvious aim for Katsura and he was encouraged to pursue it in the winter of 1902 both by a vague oral indication of approval by Ito and by Yamagata's urging him to take resolute action by 'assaulting the centre'.

In the event Katsura's attempt to follow Yamagata's advice proved yet again that transcendental government would not work in Japan. Despite Ito's influence the Seiyukai, which had been successful in winning 191 of the 376 seats in the Lower House election of August 1902, had not become a tame government party. It was certainly not prepared to make concessions over the land tax without securing suitable compensation, and on this issue it was even willing to resume cooperation with the rival Kenseihonto. In the election which Katsura precipitately called in March 1903 this cooperation was reflected both in the similarity of their manifestoes and in their effort to foil one of Katsura's aims by returning sitting members to the Diet rather than engaging in expensive rivalry. Not very surprisingly, local rivalry prevented this intention from being fully executed. Nevertheless, the two main parties did succeed in restricting the number of their candidates to 332 compared with the 469 of the previous election, and the proportion who retained their seats was almost two-thirds, higher than in any election hitherto. Overall, the two main parties lost some ground to independent candidates, but their ability to block the cabinet's budget remained unimpaired. Although Katsura yet again attempted to outmanoeuvre them by appealing to Ito, the latter, constrained by his awareness of party attitudes, insisted on a compromise whereby the government agreed to find money for the navy through administrative cuts and new borrowing. The land tax increase was abandoned.

Even though Katsura had been forced to back down, the issue reawakened anti-government feeling within the Seiyukai and several of its Diet members gave vent to it by joining with the Kenseihonto in motions which criticised ministers for maladministration. For a government which was approaching the crucial final stage of its negotiations with Russia over Manchuria and Korea the situation

was highly uncomfortable, and Ito's ambivalent position was becoming increasingly questionable. On the one hand his power to
keep his party docile appeared to be diminishing; on the other his
presence made it more difficult for Seiyukai solidarity to be undermined by the sort of inducements or pressures which had sometimes
allowed governments to extricate themselves from similar predica-
ments in the past. Potentially, too, Ito was in a position to overthrow
a cabinet at almost any time if he ever allowed the Seiyukai off the
leash. In these circumstances it may have seemed to Katsura and
Yamagata that Ito's double role as party leader and elder statesman
was no longer tolerable; and when Ito at first rejected the suggestion that he should sever his links with the Seiyukai, Katsura did in
fact submit his own resignation (which was not accepted) on 1 July
1903. Not only Yamagata and Katsura but even Inoue Kaoru and
Ito Miyoji felt that Ito was being drawn too much into the orbit of
the party politicians. Their support for the proposal that he should
resign the Seiyukai presidency and become head of the Privy Council
apparently persuaded the Emperor to make a direct request to
Ito; and this time he complied.

In engineering Ito's elevation Yamagata and Katsura may well
have hoped that the Seiyukai would disintegrate as a result of
rivalries among its leaders and regional groups. Two groups had
already left the party because of differences over strategy or issues
of principle. If Katsura was looking for further defections on any
significant scale, however, he was to be disappointed, for the man
whom Ito named as his successor, Saionji Kimmochi, was in some
respects a more suitable leader. Not only was he less autocratic by
temperament, he had once, after returning from a lengthy period
of study in Europe, founded a newspaper which supported the
People's Rights movement; and as Minister of Education in the
third Ito cabinet he encouraged the introduction of progressive
textbooks. There was, however, no risk of his being regarded as a
dangerous radical since he belonged by birth to the ancient Court
nobility and had close connections with Sumitomo, one of the
growing *zaibatsu* (financial and industrial combines).

Another reason why the Seiyukai was able to maintain its unity
can be found in the international situation. With Russia refusing to
satisfy Japanese demands and war imminent, Katsura could not afford to confront internal opposition as well. Nor did the party,
despite its criticism of diplomatic secrecy during 1903, wish to cause

the government serious embarrassment at so critical a time. Not surprisingly, once Japan had taken the plunge and attacked Port Arthur in February 1904, the Diet voted in favour of the massive extra taxes which were necessary to support the war. Okuma and the Kenseihonto did, admittedly, continue to call for administrative reforms, but with muted voices. In view of the strength of public support for the war (save for a few socialists and Christians), not to have accepted a political truce would have been suicidal.

The Hibiya Park riots

As soon as the war ended, however, internal confrontation was renewed, for the terms of the peace treaty were widely regarded as a betrayal. Regular reports of victories by Japanese forces created expectations which were disappointed when the Japanese government failed to impose an indemnity upon Russia or force it to give up the northern half of Sakhalien. The Japanese success in driving Russian influence out of Korea and southern Manchuria (where Japan now took over the lease of the Kwantung peninsula and control of the South Manchurian Railway) was insufficient to prevent the swift development of a campaign of protest against the peace treaty. A major rally in Hibiya Park was planned by journalists, lawyers and (mainly minor) politicians associated with the Kowa Mondai Doshi Rengokai (Joint Council of Fellow Activists on the Peace Question), an *ad hoc* organisation incorporating the representatives of eight nationalistic groups. When, however, on the day it was due to be held (5 September 1905), the 30,000 demonstrators found that the police had closed the park, they broke down its gates. Further police attempts to restore control then led to armed clashes which spread, apparently spontaneously, to other parts of Tokyo. The riots lasted for three days and resulted in the destruction of several police stations and more than half the city's police boxes. At least seventeen people were killed, and 1000 wounded or otherwise injured, and 2000 were arrested. Whether the disturbances were inspired predominantly by overstimulated nationalism or whether they reflected more the development of a new kind of anti-authoritarian sentiment among the heavily burdened and more volatile lower and middle strata created by modern urban growth remains a source of controversy. What is beyond doubt is that passions were aroused throughout Japan – public meetings were held in almost every prefecture and the resolutions censuring the cabinet numbered at least 230 – and that the riots represented the greatest challenge to governmental authority for at least a quarter of a century. They signified in a dramatic fashion that the phase of modern Japanese history in which politics were confined almost wholly to the Diet and to the electoral process might not last much longer.

For all the strength of this outburst of popular feeling the Katsura cabinet managed to ride out the crisis. It was able to do so largely because the major political parties did not place themselves at the head of the campaign. The Kenseihonto was certainly critical of the government, but it was divided between those who wished to take an independent stand and those, such as Inukai Tsuyoshi, who sought cooperation with the Seiyukai in the hope of being able to form a joint party cabinet. Not until early September did the latter group discover that the Seiyukai, guided by Hara Takashi, was playing a double game. While keeping their options open by encouraging Kenseihonto approaches, Hara and Saionji had already reached an understanding with Katsura on 9 December 1904, when the latter, in return for Seiyukai support, promised to recommend Saionji as his successor when peace was re-established, provided that the latter did not establish a pure party cabinet. This promise having been confirmed on 14 August 1905, the Seiyukai leaders were little tempted to throw in their lot with either the Kenseihonto or a popular campaign, and despite some protests the party acquiesced in this decision. Its reward came when Katsura resigned on 21 December.

Although not even Yamagata had been initially consulted by Katsura about his nomination of Saionji, it would have been difficult given the circumstances for the *genro* (as the elder statesmen upon whose advice the Emperor still depended had come to be called) not to approve. After only a brief delay, therefore, Saionji formed his first cabinet on 7 January 1906. Although it included fewer party members in ministerial positions than had Ito's last administration, it was plain that, unlike Ito, Saionji mainly owed his position to the fact that he was a party leader. It would soon be apparent too that under his aegis Seiyukai policies were to be promoted to a greater extent than Ito would ever have allowed.

The declining role of the elder statesmen

Katsura's handover of prime ministerial power to Saionji thus marked a considerable step towards the recognition of political parties as legitimate participants not just in the constitutional process but in the exercise of governmental power and the determination of national policy. At the same time it also marked a significant, albeit surreptitious, shift of influence from the first to the second generation of Meiji leaders. Ironically, the removal of Ito from the Seiyukai presidency in 1903 had also partly undermined Yamagata's own position since it meant that he was no longer needed by Katsura to mediate with Ito, or to counteract the latter's influence and prestige. Yamagata, of course, still wielded enormous influence through his claims on the loyalty of those whose careers he had advanced, but even in Japan such loyalty was liable to be strained if protégés (*kobun*) felt that their own judgement and abilities were being slighted. Contemporary diaries provide various examples of private resentment by second-generation statesmen of interference by the 'old men'. In Katsura's case, his determination to go his own way was to cause a rift with Yamagata and lead to a major crisis within a few years.

If the power of the *genro* had passed its peak in 1905, however, their legacy remained potent. Despite their personal and tactical differences and despite their compromises and concessions, it was their policies which had shaped the development of the Meiji state. They had established Japan as a major East Asian power and secured international recognition of its continental interests while at the same time containing the more extreme xenophobic and expansionist pressures. They had succeeded in confining the political parties within the bounds of constitutionalism and had helped to make politics less violent and confrontational, if not less corrupt. Although they met with only limited success in their attempts to raise the land tax before the Russo-Japanese War, they did manage to keep government revenues generally in line with the growth of national income by introducing income tax and business tax (in 1887 and 1897 respectively), by expanding indirect taxes on consumption and by establishing government monopolies on the sale of salt and tobacco. Much of this increased revenue went to the armed forces, which in 1900, at the high point of naval expansion, were receiving 133 million yen compared with 20 million in 1890.

But there was also a steady growth in administrative expenditure, from 31 million yen in 1890 to 121 million in 1903. These latter figures were reflected in an increase in the total number of government employees during the same years from 79,000 to 144,000. While the Meiji oligarchs were giving way to some extent on the political front, therefore, they were at the same time unobtrusively consolidating the apparatus of state control. Whether the bureaucracy which they had thus built up would prove to be a major obstacle to the development of political party power was to be a key issue in the future.

4

POLITICAL PARTY CONSOLIDATION, OLIGARCHIC REACTION AND THE EMERGENCE OF NEW FORCES, 1905-18

The Russo-Japanese War was a landmark in Japanese political history not only because it led to the formation of a new cabinet by the president of the main political party – with the *genro* playing a passive role – but also because it transformed Japan's international position. Before 1904 Japan had been little more than a minor Far Eastern power; by the end of 1905 it had acquired a strong foothold on the Asian continent, with Korea coming under its protection (a prelude to annexation in 1910) and with the establishment of a Japanese sphere of influence in southern Manchuria. For some years the threat of a war of revenge by Russia exercised Japanese military men, but this possibility came to seem less likely when Japan and Russia signed a series of local agreements in 1907; and the process of Russo-Japanese rapprochement was further advanced in 1910 by an agreement to cooperate in protecting their railway interests in Manchuria against the threat of American capital.

Not every aspect of Japan's foreign relations improved during this period. In particular, the United States became more critical of Japanese policy and more sensitive to Japan's potential threat to the Philippines. But this did not significantly affect the new security which Japan enjoyed through being a partner of both the other major powers in East Asia. One result of the consequent diminution in international tension was a decline in Japanese nationalistic fervour, or at any rate a partial turning away from foreign affairs by a public now more conscious of the human cost of a major war. Certainly the Japanese people had become more aware of the continuing tax burden which the contest with Russia had imposed. Indeed the financial liabilities left by the massive (mainly foreign) war borrowing were to overshadow Japanese politics for the next decade, and the pressure for fiscal retrenchment produced by Japan's unfavourable balance of payments situation was to present problems for successive governments.

The political strategy of Hara Takashi

That fiscal difficulties would be so great was not immediately apparent when the first Saionji cabinet was formed in January 1906, and one of its earliest major decisions was to carry out the nationalisation of private railways at a cost, mostly in bonds, of 479 million yen. The immediate post-war boom also encouraged its dominant member, Home Minister Hara Takashi, to believe that the country could afford large-scale government expenditure on the economic development projects which he held dear, such as the extension of the railway system, the building or improvement of ports, harbours, roads and schools, and the expansion of the telephone network. As a native of Iwate, one of the six north-eastern prefectures collectively known as Tohoku, he was particularly sensitive to the relative poverty and climatic disadvantage which they suffered, and by directing aid towards the remoter areas he hoped to redress the imbalance between them and the wealthier central areas around and between Tokyo and Osaka.

Apart from his belief in economic growth and his concern about regional inequality Hara also had a very practical political motive for his 'positive policy'. He knew that at the prefectural assembly level there was now much support for government spending on the economic infrastructure. Given the shortage of local capital, this was often a prerequisite for the establishment of new enterprises or the expansion of existing ones. The popularity of the Seiyukai with local capitalists and men of influence could therefore be increased by Hara's policy, and if spending were directed towards those localities which returned Seiyukai representatives to the Diet or the prefectural assembly it would both reward them and induce politicians and electors in other areas to switch their allegiance to the Seiyukai.

Because the budget for 1906 had already been settled by the time the Saionji cabinet was formed, it was not until 1907 that Hara's positive policy could be fully deployed. In that year central government expenditures rose to 602 million yen, compared with

464 million in 1906 and 250 million before the war in 1903. A significant part of this increase was due to debt repayment (174 million yen in 1907 compared with 49 million in 1905 and 151 million in 1906). The military share was up too, from 130 million in 1906 to 198 million in 1907; while administrative expenses rose only slightly less sharply from 148 million yen to 197 million. Even if these had the lion's share, it was spending on economic development programmes which grew most rapidly. From 60 million yen in 1906 it virtually doubled to 120 million in 1907 and further increased in 1908 to 148 million. The types of expenditure which were of particular interest to local politicians and businessmen accelerated faster than the average. According to one calculation, railway expansion accounted for 33 million yen in 1908, as against 12 million in 1906; and expenditure on ports and harbours, waterways and other public works leapt from 4 million yen to 14 million. Though small in overall terms these injections of public money gave a significant boost to economic activity in many local areas.

To be politically effective the Seiyukai economic strategy depended on the cooperation of the prefectural governors, who as well as determining prefectural budgets had a major say in government decisions relating to their areas of jurisdiction. It was vital for these men to be sympathetic to the expansion of the local base of the party in power and to collaborate with its local representatives. Some governors had already shown themselves to be sympathetic to the Seiyukai and could be left in place, while others proved reasonably amenable to Hara's direction as Home Minister. Those, however, who were closely linked with hostile ex-bureaucrats such as Oura Kanetake (who now led the staunchly pro-oligarch Daido Club in the Diet), were liable to be suspended. Between 1906 and 1908 over a third of the forty-six governors were relieved of their functions, while a similar number were moved to different prefectures. At a higher level, new bureau chiefs were also appointed in the Home Ministry, while the Metropolitan Police Bureau was put in the charge of an official of whose cooperation Hara was assured. This was not the first time that bureaucratic appointments had been subjected to political manipulation, but the scale of intervention was now far greater and marked a significant step towards the politicisation of the bureaucracy.

Hara's success in implementing his positive economic policy and in extending his control over the Home Ministry was probably a major factor in the Seiyukai's success in the general election of May 1908, when it secured an absolute majority with 191 seats. That success, however, was deceptive, for the cabinet had been experiencing increasing difficulties since early 1907 and was not to last much longer. On the financial side it found itself under pressure from the Japanese banking world (represented by two *genro*, Inoue Kaoru and Matsukata Masayoshi) to reduce government expenditure and increase taxes because the ending of the post-war boom in 1907 threatened to lead to a serious revenue deficiency. So strong was the pressure that the cabinet felt obliged to admit Inoue and Matsukata to the meeting in December 1907 which approved the budget proposals for 1908. Its capitulation, however, had serious consequences. In January 1908 both the Finance Minister and the Communications Minister (whose railway construction plans had been cut back) resigned. Furthermore, the new taxes, and tax increases, which were imposed in 1908 aroused fierce opposition from the chambers of commerce (who were already protesting about the continuation of the special wartime additions) and provoked a national campaign by business organisations against the 'three evil taxes' on salt, textiles and the transit of goods.

At the political level, too, the cabinet suffered setbacks. Hara's bill to abolish the *gun* level of local administration encountered stronger opposition from Yamagata and his supporters than he had expected and was defeated in the House of Peers. Not only did Hara fail to achieve his main objective, but in making what turned out to be a futile attempt to establish Seiyukai influence in the upper chamber he damaged his relations with Katsura. The loss of the latter's benevolent neutrality made it more difficult for Saionji to resist the further pressure exerted by Yamagata in 1908, when that deeply conservative elder statesman decided that the cabinet (which had been prepared to tolerate the existence of a socialist party until the latter had adopted a more radical posture in February 1907) was insufficiently alert to the danger of subversive ideas. Yamagata first attempted to undermine Saionji's position by revealing to the Emperor that an open letter threatening his assassination had been posted by Japanese 'anarchist-terrorists' on the Japanese consulate in San Francisco in November 1907. In June 1908 a clash in central Tokyo between the police and anarchists who were waving red flags and proclaiming imminent revolution gave him a further chance to instil misgivings in the Emperor's mind. Shortly afterwards Saionji dismayed Hara and Matsuda, his chief lieutenants, by informing them of his intention to resign, which he put into effect on 4 July. Whether pressure from the Court (where one of Saionji's brothers was Grand Chamberlain) was the major factor remains uncertain. What is clear is that the Seiyukai was extremely unhappy but could only defer to the decision of a leader who by temperament was as much an oligarch as a party man.

The second Katsura cabinet and the Seiyukai

As his successor Saionji proposed Katsura, and when Ito's opinion was sought he concurred – almost the last political act by the elder statesman before his assassination by a Korean the following year. Thus the pattern of cabinets headed alternately by the two most prominent second-generation leaders was further established. As well as becoming Prime Minister, Katsura also assumed the post of Finance Minister, and he soon showed his intention of adopting a tighter fiscal policy by pledging the government to redeem existing public bonds and refrain from issuing new ones. Even railway construction and improvement, which were acknowledged to be essential and for which a special fund was set aside, were not to be financed by borrowing. The new tone of government policy, a mixture of financial orthodoxy and traditional frugality, was made especially clear to the public when the government banned a popular form of horse-race betting and postponed until 1917 an international exhibition which was to have been held in Tokyo in 1912.

If bankers and *genro* supported Katsura's policy, however, most ordinary businessmen were unhappy that it offered little hope of tax reduction. Their opposition, expressed through the chambers of commerce, was probably a significant factor in the failure of the pro-Katsura, anti-Seiyukai merger proposed by the so-called 're-form faction' within the Kenseihonto and by elements within the minor parties around this time. The issue of opposition to taxation provided a rallying point for those within the Kenseihonto, like Inukai Tsuyoshi, who retained both their old antipathy towards oligarchic government and their hope of a broad *minto* (people's party) coalition which would include the Seiyukai and force the *genro* and the bureaucrats to surrender a larger measure of their power. With the support of much of the press, the 'anti-reform' group within the Kenseihonto regained control at a special party

congress in March 1909 and secured the adoption of the slogan
'Strike down the evil of bureaucratic politics'. Shortly afterwards
the 'reform faction' was discredited by the exposure of some of its
leading members' complicity in a bribery scandal which involved
the proposed nationalisation, at an exorbitant price, of the Great
Japan Sugar Refining Company.

The 'reformists' within the Kenseihonto might have had more
success had their approaches to the government received a more
encouraging response. Katsura, however, true to the oligarchic tradition, from the start of his second cabinet proclaimed that he would
take an even-handed, impartial attitude towards the political parties. When, in January 1909, his budget proposals ran into opposition
in the Diet, his reaction was to seek an understanding with the
Seiyukai, which could deliver a majority in the Lower House. Hara
was abroad, but Katsura knew that Saionji would be inclined to
cooperate; and although the party reserved its right to reject measures which were not in line with Seiyukai policy, it provided the
government with invaluable support, most notably in ensuring the
rejection of a bill (which was backed by almost all the other members of the Lower House) to abolish the 'three evil taxes'.

The pattern of surreptitious cabinet dependence on Seiyukai
support was continued in the twenty-sixth Diet session in the
winter of 1909-10, but to maintain it Katsura was forced to reduce
some taxes, raise import duties on rice and withdraw some proposed legislation. His government's prospects in the next Diet were,
if anything, less favourable. Although some progress had been
made in redeeming bonds, Japan's economic position had not
much improved and there was little hope of additional revenue to
pay for the repair of flood damage in eastern Japan, the costs of
establishing a Japanese administration in Korea, the construction
of Dreadnaughts, and the widening of railroads (which the army
wanted). The cabinet was also open to criticism on a quite different
score. In May 1910 the discovery of a plot to assassinate the Emperor, the so-called Taigyaku Jiken (High Treason Incident), not
only shocked the public but also raised the question of responsibility for an action which would not, in the traditional view, have
occurred in a well-governed state. To some it seemed that the
heavy prison sentences meted out to socialists under the Katsura
cabinet, together with the latter's suppression of left-wing journals,
had driven radicalism underground and made it more likely to

take an unhealthy course. From this perspective even the twenty-four sentences of death which were handed down by Japan's highest court after a trial held in camera were criticised on the grounds of excessive harshness; Hara himself did so privately. Undoubtedly some of those condemned, including the best-known of the defendants, the anarchist Kotoku Shusui, were at most only peripherally involved in the conspiracy and appeared to have been punished for their ideas rather than their actions.

It was ironic that on 19 January 1911, only one day after the treason sentence, the *Yomiuri* newspaper questioned the government's own fidelity to the imperial tradition by pointing out that in dealing with the period in the fourteenth century when two different branches of the imperial family had been figureheads for competing military alliances, officially approved school textbooks treated them as though both had equal standing. Such an interpretation sat uneasily with the orthodox version of an unbroken dynasty whose right to rule had never been challenged throughout Japan's history. Katsura acted promptly to suspend the responsible textbook censor and have the Emperor pronounce that only the 'Southern Court' was legitimate, but to defeat an embarrassing motion of censure tabled by Inukai he had to rely yet again on Seiyukai support.

The textbook issue may have hastened the conclusion of a new deal between Katsura and the Seiyukai, for it was directly after its first being raised that a historic 'mutual understanding' was agreed between the Prime Minister and the party's leaders and sealed with a speech by the former at a luncheon given to all the Seiyukai Diet members on 29 January 1911. In this speech Katsura praised the party for seeking 'to contribute its services to the state on the basis of sound political views' – an unaccustomed tribute from an oligarch. His words reflected his appreciation of the fact that the Seiyukai leaders had pledged their support for most of the government's plans in the current Diet session, including the shelving of income tax reduction in order to complete a naval building project. But the agreement was not the one-sided bargain it superficially appeared to be. The well-informed Tokyo newspaper, *Asahi*, discerned this when it commented on 10 February 1911 that 'Cabinet decisions will not, hereafter, be the final government decisions. Where national affairs will be determined will be the conferences between the government and its party partner. They will become a

cabinet above the cabinet'.[1] Nor was this acceptance of consultation the only price for Seiyukai cooperation: Katsura also affirmed
his intention of standing down in Saionji's favour as soon as the
cabinet's pending business had been wound up.

These concessions were very considerable, but Katsura had little
alternative. In March 1910 the Kenseihonto had merged with two
smaller groups to form the even more anti-oligarchic Rikken
Kokuminto (Constitutional National Party). Had the Seiyukai responded to its overtures, Katsura would have been unable to get his
legislative programme through the Lower House. Nor could this
danger be safely ignored. By the end of 1910 much dissatisfaction
had built up among the Seiyukai rank and file over Katsura's unre-
lenting pursuit of financial retrenchment. Within party branches
and regional party congresses influential voices were calling for a
return to the positive policy which Hara had followed earlier, and
it was not impossible that the anti-mainstream movement which
was beginning to make its appearance might seek to respond to
Inukai's blandishments. The demand by some party men for the
open election of standing committee members instead of their
nomination by the leadership was only one token of a new mood
within the Seiyukai. It both forced Hara into negotiations with
Katsura and enabled him to put increased pressure on the Prime
Minister; and it may well have led Katsura to abandon the idea of
being succeeded by his Army Minister, Terauchi Masatake.

The actual conclusion of the 'mutual understanding' in January
had a striking effect on the government's legislative programme.
Several bills which the Seiyukai had successfully opposed in the
previous Diet session were now enacted, among them the first to
regulate working conditions in Japanese factories (although not
without some watering-down of its provisions by party representatives). Moreover, the Kokuminto's renewed attempt to abolish the
'three evil taxes' was easily repulsed. These successes allowed Katsura
to bow out in August 1911 with some sense of achievement.

The second Saionji cabinet and the death of the Emperor

The new Saionji cabinet was formed (after Katsura's recommendation to the Emperor and without any *genro* meeting) on 30 August

[1]   Quoted by Uno Shunichi, 'Dai-niji Katsura Naikaku' in Hayashi Shigeru and
Tsuji Kiyoaki (eds), *Nihon Naikaku Shiroku*, vol. 2, p.88.

1911. The very fact that Katsura had not attempted to delay the hand-over until after the prefectural elections in September (in which its ability to manipulate prefectural governors was to give the Seiyukai an advantage) indicated how the relations between the oligarchs and the major political party had changed. So too did the fact that Hara was able to insist that another minister was drawn from the Seiyukai and that the cabinet did not include any bureaucrats who belonged to the Yamagata camp. Hara himself chose to become Home Minister again rather than, as Saionji suggested, Finance Minister. Whether he would have been acceptable to the *genro* and financial circles as Finance Minister is uncertain – it was a responsibility usually confined to bankers and Finance Ministry bureaucrats, just as the Foreign Ministry had become the normal preserve of career diplomats, though neither were legally restricted to serving professionals as were the Army and Navy Ministries. Hara may, however, have later regretted not making a greater effort to install a party man or a more amenable banker, for the expert who was chosen, Yamamoto Tatsuo, soon proved much too orthodox for the Seiyukai's liking.

The main reasons for selecting Yamamoto were his standing in the financial world and the expectation that he would not defer to the views of his predecessor, Katsura. To Hara's distress, however, the new Finance Minister soon determined to take even tougher measures to restore financial soundness than the previous cabinet. Hara did not object to the main method proposed – the reduction of administrative expenses by each ministry – but he bitterly opposed the postponement of all new economic projects, including railway development. As he saw it, government borrowing for this purpose would soon generate enough profit to pay for itself, while at the same time it would increase national wealth and strength and help exports balance imports. 'Saionji and the other cabinet ministers cannot understand this', he lamented in his diary.[2] Only by threatening to resign did Hara salvage something of the Seiyukai's positive policy in the shape of 60 million yen for railway expansion.

Despite the limited allowance made for regional development, the 1912 budget did not alienate the Seiyukai's supporters, perhaps because cuts in the bureaucracy were always popular. Indeed, in

[2] Quoted by Banno Junji, 'Keion Naikaku to Taisho Seihen', *Iwanami Koza Nihon Rekishi*, vol. 17, p. 287.

the May 1912 general election the Seiyukai increased its Lower House majority by securing 209 of the 381 seats (compared with 191 out of 376 in 1908) and over half the popular vote. The cabinet's attempt to continue its policy of financial and administrative retrenchment in the budget for 1913, however, ran into much greater difficulty and was to provoke the biggest political crisis since the introduction of constitutional government.

The protest against the 1913 budget came not from the Seiyukai but from the army. Ever since 1907, when it drew up Japan's first national defence plan, the army had sought to expand its strength, but although the defence plan had accepted a peacetime target of twenty-five divisions, only two of the eight required to reach that figure had actually been created. Partly, no doubt, because Army Minister Terauchi Masatake did not wish, or dare, to challenge Katsura (like himself a general with a Choshu background but five years his senior), and partly because of the Japanese-Russian rapprochement, the army had yielded to the argument of financial necessity. The annexation of Korea, however, had brought additional defence responsibilities, and the eruption of revolution in China in October 1911 created concern (as well as hopes of new continental opportunities for Japan). The fact that the Saionji cabinet adopted a policy of non-interference in China only increased army irritation. Moreover, in contrast to its negative treatment of the two extra divisions which army leaders demanded, the cabinet seemed to accept that in an era of new battleship technology and increasing disharmony with the United States, provision had to be made for the navy's expensive building programme.

While tension was growing between the two services and between the army and the cabinet, two significant deaths occurred. One was of Army Minister Ishimoto Shinroku, who had been a staunch supporter of the Choshu clique. In the last stages of his illness, in April 1912, he was replaced by the Satsuma general, Uehara Yusaku, who was known to resent the domination which Choshu officers had established over the decision-making positions in the army. In the previous year, when non-Choshu officers had been manoeuvring to have him succeed Terauchi as Army Minister, Uehara had let the Seiyukai understand that he would be willing to accept further postponement of expansion if the financial situation required it. Once in office, however, his attitude changed, and his unexpected intransigence presented a difficult problem for

the rest of the cabinet. In previous years it might have been possible to resolve it through the mediation of Katsura, but he was
now less inclined to cooperate. Having become dissatisfied with
the way the 'politics of compromise' had developed, he had begun
to think (along lines rather similar to Ito's earlier) of establishing his
own pro-government party. It was partly with this in mind that he
embarked in the summer of 1912 on a European tour in the course
of which he intended to gain a better insight into the working of
Western politics. Before he had passed through Russia, however,
he was forced to return by the serious illness of the Emperor.

The Meiji Emperor's death on 30 July 1912 removed a significant stabilising element, especially since his successor suffered
from impaired mental faculties. The army now felt freer to press
its demands, while the public, stirred up by radical journalists and
increasingly politicised by campaigns against high prices and
monopolies in urban transport and utilities, sensed that now might
be the time for reform – for a Taisho Ishin which might emulate
the renovation which had marked the inception of the deceased
Emperor's reign. More particularly, the Emperor's death also provided Yamagata with the opportunity to have Katsura elevated to
the Court positions of Grand Chamberlain and Lord Keeper of the
Privy Seal, in which he would be responsible for advising the new
sovereign.

Yamagata may indeed have felt that Katsura's abilities were needed
to guide and protect the Emperor, but it is clear that this was not
his only motive. At the time there was suspicion that he was attempting to bring the new Emperor fully under the control of his own
bureaucratic faction: as well informed a politician as Hara thought
this to be the case. However, others who were closer to Yamagata
understood his action to be mainly due to the senior *genro's* distrust
of Katsura's political ambitions. The two men's personal relationship was no longer a warm one, especially since Katsura had been
raised to the highest rank of the nobility – equal to Yamagata and
above the other *genro* – in 1911, and Katsura's hints that Yamagata
might retire from public life altogether were not welcome to the
latter. But it was the younger man's political ambitions which were
crucial, and just as Ito's links with the Seiyukai had been severed by
his appointment as head of the Privy Council in 1903, so Katsura's
possible association with a new party would be – Yamagata could
assume – precluded by his new responsibilities as imperial adviser.

The Taisho political crisis

In this situation it was hardly surprising that the dispute between the army and the cabinet developed into a crisis. As early as 29 August Saionji approached Yamagata with a request for help, but the latter insisted on either the establishment of the two divisions or the completion of the army's re-equipment. The cabinet held firm, however, even rejecting a compromise proposal which Katsura was finally induced to make on 25 November. On 30 November it decided that Uehara should be pressed to step down and that if no replacement were forthcoming, all the ministers would resign. On 2 December, after being formally notified by Saionji that the army's expansion plan had been rejected, the Army Minister submitted his resignation directly to the Emperor. Three days later, having failed to secure a new Army Minister, the second Saionji cabinet came to an untimely end.

This sudden turn of events came as an unwelcome shock to Yamagata and the other *genro*. An open dispute between the army and the politicians, with the latter backed by public opinion, was highly undesirable in their eyes. The Seiyukai leaders were aware of this and hoped that Saionji would be asked to return to office (with pressure being put on the army to moderate its demands) in order to avert a crisis. This scenario was almost enacted, for the *genro* did seek an imperial rescript which would instruct Saionji to resume his position. The person responsible for advising the Emperor, however, was now Katsura, and his reluctance to open the way to conciliation meant that no rescript was issued.

Katsura's failure to cooperate can be explained in terms of his close links with the army and his resentment of the growth of Seiyukai power. It may also be, however, that he saw a chance of reviving his political career and putting into practice the ideas which he had been contemplating before he was elevated to his current position. Such an opportunity did, in fact, materialise. When the *genro* met to recommend the next Prime Minister it proved exceptionally difficult to find anyone who was willing or able to form a government. On 17 December, after eleven days of fruitless deliberations, Yamagata came to the reluctant conclusion that either he must shoulder the burden again or that Katsura must be brought back. His fellow *genro*, thinking, probably, that Katsura would seek a new basis for compromise, opted for the latter.

The re-emergence of Katsura incurred much public criticism, on the grounds both of constitutional impropriety (since he could be accused of having abused his position as imperial adviser to engineer his own return to power) and of favouritism towards the army. The latter accusation was not justified; Katsura did in fact accept that the two extra divisions must be postponed. But he soon provided more definite grounds for the former by having the Emperor instruct the navy to provide a Navy Minister, thus forcing it to abandon its attempt to prevent the similar postponement of the naval expansion plan. This blatant exploitation of the imperial prerogative by Katsura ran the risk of involving the monarch in political controversy and alienated Yamagata. The *genro's* misgivings were made even more acute when the Prime Minister embarked precipitately upon the formation of a party which he could lead personally.

Katsura's estrangement from Yamagata meant that many influential ex-bureaucrats declined to participate in the new party when its intended formation was announced on 20 January 1913. A number of younger bureaucrats, among them Wakatsuki Reijiro, Hamaguchi Yuko (Osachi) and Kato Komei (Takaaki), were prepared to take a chance, however, as were other sympathisers, such as Goto Shimpei. There were, too, several leading members of the Kokuminto who were willing to join a party which, with government backing, could hope to challenge Seiyukai dominance. To these forty-six ex-Kokuminto Diet members were added thirty-four from the conservative Chuo Club. But the more Katsura built up his support, the more he threatened the Seiyukai and the more remote became the prospect of a compromise deal with it. Although Katsura did not appreciate this, the party's attitude was changing radically as its rank-and-file members were caught up in the ferment of anti-oligarchic feeling produced by the Constitutional Protection movement.

This movement is usually said to have originated in a Tokyo club called the Kojunsha whose membership of journalists, progressive businessmen, politicians, and lawyers was dominated by graduates of Keio Academy. As early as 14 December, club members decided to launch a campaign with the slogan 'protect constitutional government, destroy cliquism', and five days later the Constitutional Protection Association which they had established held its first general assembly, with an impressive attendance of over 3,000.

The Kojunsha contribution was undoubtedly significant, for it not only brought together activists from both main parties, notably Inukai Tsuyoshi and Ozaki Yukio, but also sent out speakers to rallies in smaller cities, in a manner reminiscent of the People's Rights movement. Nevertheless, it is likely that there would have been nation-wide campaigning even without the Kojunsha. As early as November 1912, resolutions were beginning to pour in from local branches of the Seiyukai (and to a lesser extent the Kokuminto) calling for a firm stance against the military and the Choshu clique; and already on 9 December the Kanto Club (a Seiyukai organisation) had held a meeting which appealed for concerted action with other Seiyukai groups in order to 'sweep away the root of evil in the new Taisho era by restraining the domination of cliques'.

It is important not to attribute the Constitutional Protection movement too narrowly to a Tokyo club because its most significant feature was its nation-wide support and vitality. Rallies were held in the leading cities and towns of virtually every prefecture during December, January and February, and the fervour which they aroused among all classes, including manual workers, but especially among young men, attracted much comment. They culminated on 10 February, when a huge demonstration outside the Diet led to the destruction of property, arrests, injuries and losses of life on a scale which made the incident comparable with the Hibiya Park riots of September 1905. This clear indication of public dissatisfaction and the threat of further violence undoubtedly contributed substantially to Katsura's decision to resign later that day.

The fall of the third Katsura cabinet was due also to Seiyukai solidarity. In January it was still possible for Katsura to hope that he could ride out the storm of popular opposition if he could gain a majority in the Lower House. Only three Seiyukai members, however, succumbed to his blandishments. Thus when the new pro-government party, the Rikken Doshikai (Constitutional Association of Like Minds), was inaugurated on 7 February, it was clearly in a minority, and the ferocity of the attacks by Ozaki and others when the Diet was reconvened on 5 February made it plain that no quarter would be given. Katsura's last hope was Saionji. On 9 February he had the Seiyukai president summoned to the palace, where the Emperor expressed deep concern about the situation and indirectly but unmistakably requested Saionji to withdraw his party's backing

from the impending motion of no confidence. This was a dangerous tactic, since it again exposed the Emperor to the criticism that
he was being used on behalf of a particular group, but Katsura was
playing for high stakes. For a brief moment his ploy seemed to have
succeeded: the Seiyukai leadership saw no alternative but to accept
the imperial wish. Ordinary Seiyukai Diet members, however, were
not prepared to give way; and when on 10 February the party
leadership heard that Yamamoto Gonnohyoe, the senior Satsuma
admiral, had visited Katsura that morning to urge him to resign and
that Katsura had offered (in a moment of exasperation) to step down
in Yamamoto's favour, it decided to go ahead with the vote of no
confidence, disregarding Hara and Matsuda's advocacy of another
negotiated transfer of power. On the same day, a party congress
overwhelmingly confirmed the Seiyukai's refusal to back down.
Faced with this blow, with mass riots and with Yamagata's disapproval, Katsura, who was already suffering from the illness which
would send him to his grave later that year, had little option but to
resign. The Seiyukai triumph was confirmed when Yamamoto was
chosen as his successor (Saionji being out of the question because
of his inability to carry out the imperial message) and selected a
cabinet in which the party was more strongly represented than it
had ever been before.

The social and ideological background of the Taisho political crisis

The Taisho Political Change (Taisho Seihen), as this episode is
called, was clearly a landmark in modern Japanese political history
in that it represented a major rebuff for Katsura's attempt to re-
assert oligarchic control and confirmed the trend towards party
government. The most striking feature of the episode, though, was
the display of political consciousness among the population at large.
To appreciate the full significance of this, it is necessary to set it in
the context of the social trends and ideological developments of
the late Meiji period.

Ever since the Russo-Japanese War Japanese conservative leaders and bureaucrats had been concerned about the perceived
threat to the values of the Meiji state. The most striking example of
this threat was the appearance of socialists, some of whom not only
preached class conflict but also condemned Japanese imperialism.
The majority were relatively un-militant Christian socialists, but

even these in many cases had criticised Japan's involvement in war with Russia and could therefore be seen as subversive. It was tempting for the Japanese Establishment to regard them also as responsible for the wave of strikes which burst out in 1907, reaching the unprecedented figure of fifty-seven, many of which were in major dockyards or government arsenals. The suppression of a socialist party in 1901 and again in 1907 by no means removed the danger completely, for the socialists had considerable scope for expressing their views in the press. The most notable left-wing journal, the *Heimin Shimbun* (Commoners' Newspaper) was read widely – although it had fewer than 2,000 direct subscribers – and its influence extended well beyond the major cities. The newspaper was forced out of business by government pressure in January 1905, but its place was taken by *Chokugen* (Plain Speaking) and later by *Hikari* (Light), and although censorship was strict, this did not prevent the expression of carefully phrased critiques of Japanese society. Moreover, even when radical journals were suppressed, it was sometimes possible for socialists to vent their opinions in less committed publications.

The Japanese government (whichever cabinet was in office) was, indeed, regularly subject to journalistic criticism, for the press continued to display a healthy diversity of views and the stimulus given to circulations by war and the growth of urbanisation increased its vitality. Newspapers like the *Osaka Mainichi* and *Tokyo Nichi-Nichi* and magazines like *Taiyo* (The Sun), *Chuo Koron* (Central Review) and *Toyo Keizai Shimpo* (Oriental Economist) employed writers who were frequently in the forefront of popular campaigns against central or city government. In particular, they tended to support calls for tax reductions and oppose increases in the prices charged by public or semi-public utilities and services such as gas, electricity and trams; and they were usually eager to expose evidence of corruption in high places. Together with lawyers and academics they also played a prominent part in the campaign for general adult male suffrage which began in the 1890s and which resulted in a bill being passed by the Lower House of the Diet in 1911 – only to be rejected unanimously by the Peers.

Less obviously a threat to the Establishment – but still a cause of concern – were literary and academic trends. The growing popularity of naturalism encouraged novelists to concern themselves more with social reality, including its sordid and shameful aspects, but more significant (though less easily censored) was the growth of literary concern with the psychological problems of the individual. This latter trend was discernible not only in fiction but also in poetry. That even poems could be subversive was demonstrated during the Russo-Japanese War when the young poetess, Yosano Akiko, published one in which she urged her brother not to sacrifice his life for his country. Nor was the theatre free from 'undesirable' influences. The interest in new themes and rejection of traditional styles which were the hallmarks of the Shingeki ('new drama') movement after 1906 led to the staging of controversial modern Western plays – notably Ibsen's *A Doll's House* and Sudermann's *Magda* – which were even more disturbing in their challenge to established values in Japan than they were in Europe. Indeed, in the case of *Magda*, the Home Ministry went so far as to insist on the addition of an apology by the heroine for her unfilial conduct.

Perhaps the most radical development in the late Meiji literary and intellectual world was the appearance of the magazine *Seito* (Blue Stocking) in 1910 and the formation of a society (Seitosha) which was run by articulate upper-class feminists such as Hiratsuka Raicho. Their uncompromising ideas represented a fundamental break with the orthodox philosophy of female subordination as expressed in such time-worn phrases as *ryosai-kembo* (good wife, wise mother). Although the Seitosha did not engage directly in political activity, it was undoubtedly one of the sources of inspiration for the later movement for women's electoral rights.

To this catalogue of subversive trends should be added the writings of Tsuda Sokichi and Minobe Tatsukichi. Although these were not intentionally controversial, their anti-mystical interpretations of, respectively, the earliest Japanese chronicles and the Meiji constitution undermined both the historical and the legal bases of the orthodox version of imperial sovereignty, at least in the simplistic form in which it was commonly propagated. Tsuda's and Minobe's books were highly scholarly and therefore they were not widely read, but since their authors taught, respectively, at Waseda and Tokyo University, their audience included some of the future leaders of the country.

All the above developments, together with the unprecedented involvement of businessmen in anti-tax campaigns and a surge in the number of disputes between landlords and tenants in the years following the Russo-Japanese War, combined to create a sense of unease within the Japanese Establishment. This was reflected in the moralistic choice of the name of Taisho (Great Righteousness) for the reign of the new Emperor. It was also evident in the public debate over the ritual suicide of General Nogi soon after the Meiji Emperor's death, when a number of commentators argued that this act was a protest at the decline of moral standards and a warning about the way Japan was heading. A British diplomatic report of February 1912 had already noted that 'public opinion is slowly but surely emancipating itself from official control', and drawn attention to official concern:

... the socialist plot the year before last, the ever-growing complaints about taxation and the cost of living, the portentous apparition of the Chinese republic close at hand and the decay of the religious sentiment which the official class had ... identified with patriotism, are all contributing to cause anxiety to those in authority.[3]

In actual fact, those in authority had been taking steps to combat the new intellectual climate for some years before 1912. Some of these steps, such as the Great Treason trial, clearly had a repressive effect. The 1909 Press Law, too, which was passed unanimously by both Houses of the Diet, was similarly directed towards the suppression of socialism, its most significant feature being the restoration of the pre-1897 situation in which the Home Minister was able to ban by administrative action periodical articles which disturbed the public peace or were injurious to morals. This meant that even if it stayed within the limits of the law, a radical periodical would still be at risk.

Censorship and suppression were only part of the late Meiji government's attempt to maintain established values and authority. The Home Ministry, in particular, recognised the need for positive ideological reinforcement. It sought, however, to combine its pursuit of this objective with practical measures which would at the same time promote community solidarity and increase local capacity to bear the greater tax burden imposed by the Russo-Japanese War. The majority of these measures were launched during Katsura's period in office, but they were not opposed by the Seiyukai, although it did tend to stress the practical rather than the ideological dimension.

[3] Public Record Office, London. Foreign Office General Correspondence, Japan, F.O. 371, vol. 1387, no. 66, 29 February 1912.

The first Home Ministry attempt to combine the propagation of traditional values with practical encouragement was the promotion of *hotokusha* (repayment of virtue societies) in 1905-6. These were modelled on the local mutual-help associations established from the mid-nineteenth century by Ninomiya Sontoku, Ishikawa Rikinosuke and other agrarian reformers, and formed an important element in the *Nohonshugi* tradition, which emphasised respect for agriculture and village solidarity and remained a distinctive feature of Japanese rural society in the early twentieth century. The government not only encouraged the formation of such groups but also used them to emphasise the need for hard work (to repay the sacrifices made by parents and ancestors) and to reinforce the idea of obedience to superiors. At the same time Hirata Tosuke, a leading Agriculture and Commerce Ministry bureaucrat and protégé of Yamagata, made new efforts to promote and coordinate the *sangyo kumiai* (producer cooperative) movement, which he had begun in 1900 and which was designed to facilitate, through special tax privileges, saving and borrowing by middle and small cultivators, as well as cheap bulk purchasing. By 1914 the total number of such cooperatives was to rise to 11,160. In the meantime, both the *hotokusha* and the *sangyo kumiai* had been made part of a wider Rural Improvement (Chiho Kairyo) movement which Hirata, as Home Minister in Katsura's second cabinet, launched in 1909.

The Rural Improvement movement was not just concerned with the practicalities of economic growth. Ethical values held an equally central place, both because these were considered relevant to productivity and as means of strengthening or reasserting ideological and social control by the state. One of the initial purposes of the movement, in fact, was the organisation of societies to promote the reading of the Boshin Rescript, which Katsura and Hirata had the Emperor issue in 1908 and which called for hard work and thrift on the one hand, and social unity and rejection of class conflict on the other. Broader in scope, but basically similar in purpose, were the Young Men's groups (Seinendan) and Imperial Reservist Associations (Teikoku Zaigo Gunjinkai) which were established throughout the country. Both organisations were intended to strengthen the traditional sense of community solidarity (which the reformist early Meiji government had sought to undermine), but they were also used by officials to exhort the rural population not only to work hard and be frugal but also to revere ancestors and respect parents and other superiors. Devotion to the Emperor was also stressed, as it was in the newly-revised ethics textbooks used in elementary schools, where it was reinforced by being explicitly linked with ancestor worship and family ethics. Within the primary school system at this time examinations and competition were played down and greater emphasis was again being placed on a traditionally based moral education.

Partly to ensure the greater effectiveness of this indoctrination the period of compulsory education was extended from four to six years in 1907. The actual attendance rate rose, too, from 48 per cent in 1889 to 89 per cent in 1912, fees having been reduced in 1892 and removed in 1900, while extra provision was made for young men's night schools and business and agricultural-training schools. In February 1906 prefectural authorities were urged to continue the popular information activities which had been provided by the discussions, lectures and magic-lantern shows put on during the Russo-Japanese War. The Education Ministry continued to feel, however, that instruction based on the Imperial Rescript on Education needed to be followed up after children had left school, and in 1911 a Popular Education Research Committee was set up to recommend ways of achieving this. Its proposals for more extensive use of films, libraries and popular story-tellers received little financial support, though, and it was made fun of by the press. Equally ineffective was the Literary Committee established at the same time 'to encourage masterpieces beneficial to public morals and cause literary men to give thought to society and public morals and improve the social climate'. Its members, who included such prominent literary figures as Mori Ogai, Koda Rohan and Tokutomi Soho, soon became enmeshed in inconclusive argument and made no impact before the committee's abolition in 1913.

Even more Machiavellian, perhaps, than the attempted mobilisation of writers for state purposes were the Meiji government's plans to utilise religion. A report in January 1912 by the young diplomat, G.B. Sansom, later a distinguished historian of Japan, observed that 'From having displayed an ostensible impartiality in the matter of religion, it really looks as if the Japanese government are coming to conscious interference with religious freedom, which the constitution guarantees'.[4] Shortly afterwards the Home Ministry organised

---

[4] *Ibid.*, vol. 1387, no 5, 6 January 1912.

a conference of Shinto, Buddhist and Christian leaders for the purpose of cooperating 'to awaken the nation to a sense of the necessity
of religious faith in general, so that national morals may be built on
a sounder basis'. Even before this, however, official interest in making
religion serve the state had been seen in the campaign from 1906 to
1912 to consolidate Shinto shrines. If there were only one shrine in
each town or village, Home Ministry officials reasoned, it could be
more prestigiously maintained and could, with government subsidy, support a regular priest who would incorporate in his preaching
the State Shinto doctrines of the divine origins of the imperial dynasty
and the uniqueness of the Japanese *kokutai* (national structure). That
such a scheme could be devised is a testimony to the lack of understanding by rational Western-educated bureaucrats of the nature of
popular religion, and it is not surprising that in most areas the campaign succeeded only in reducing the number of shrines to one per
buraku rather than the desired one per village.

It is evident from the preceding account of government efforts
to stifle dissent and 'improve popular thinking' that there was considerable concern that the success of the early Meiji government in
imposing its values and pattern of control was in danger of being
eroded. The mass demonstrations of early 1913, however, suggest
that although the practical measures to assist the rural economy
may have enjoyed some success, the various efforts to inculcate
blind obedience to authority were less effective. Indeed, by emphasising ideal values, such as selfless service to state and Emperor,
they may even have worked against the oligarchs (especially Katsura)
in so far as the latter were now portrayed by the press as self-serving
men who had abused their positions to manipulate the Emperor
and come between him and his people. Moreover, in the larger
urban areas the government's propaganda tended to be too simplistic and old-fashioned to have the desired impact, certainly on the
more sophisticated opinion-makers. Nevertheless, the sheer weight
of indoctrination to which the Japanese public was exposed in the
closing years of the Meiji period makes it that much more remarkable that popular support of the Constitutional Protection movement
was so great; and the limited effectiveness of official propaganda,
especially compared with the conservative reaffirmation which was
to occur in the 1930s, lends support to those historians who claim
that 'Taisho Democracy' began after the Russo-Japanese War rather
than World War One.

The aftermath of the Taisho political crisis

If the significance of the political events of 1912-13 was great, their immediate results nevertheless left many of the more ardent suppo-rters of the Constitutional Protection movement disappointed. Once the danger of Katsura's new government party had been contained, the Seiyukai leadership moved back towards compromise with the oligarchs again and the popular campaign lost its impetus. This is not to say that the situation simply reverted to what it had been in 1912. On the contrary, the Seiyukai was now more in control of government than it had been when Saionji was Prime Minister. Not only was Prime Minister Yamamoto forced to accept, after some days' wrangling, the inclusion in the cabinet of three full party members (Hara, Matsuda and Motoda Hajime) as well as three men who were prepared to join the Seiyukai when they became ministers, but he also agreed to state publicly his support for the party's policy. Nor were these mere gestures. With Takahashi Korekiyo as Finance Minister the new cabinet at once responded to Seiyukai desires by embarking upon a positive policy of railway expansion and regional development and by borrowing from abroad again, ignoring the disapproval of the *genro* and the financial world. It also partly financed its economic programme by carrying out adminis-trative retrenchment, reducing the bureaucracy by more than 5,000 – an extremely popular action.

The unpopularity of the oligarchs and the army also made pos-sible two key reforms. One was the opening of the highest levels of the bureaucracy to free appointment by the cabinet, regardless of whether the nominee had passed the civil service examination. The other was the modification of the rule that the service ministers must be serving generals and admirals: now they could be drawn from retired officers of those grades as well. Neither of these changes had an obvious impact. No retired general or admiral ever did be-come an Army or Navy Minister, and there was no great influx of unqualified party appointees into the other departments of govern-ment. Nevertheless, the reforms gave cabinets greater leverage against both the civil and military bureaucracy, and they also represented a defeat for Yamagata personally, since it was he who had introduced the restrictions in 1899 and 1900. Not surprisingly, the cabinet's proposals were at first strongly opposed, but in July 1913 the Privy Council backed down over the issue of free appointment (after

Yamamoto and Hara had threatened to appeal to the public and either bypass the Council or ask the Emperor to purge it), while the army's objections to the new regulations about service minister eligibility were overruled by the Emperor in May.

As a result of these initial successes the prospects seemed good in 1913 for a further growth in Seiyukai influence. There remained, however, tensions between the government party and the navy, which Prime Minister Yamamoto represented and which now demanded a huge budgetary increase of 70 million yen. This would have left room only for expansion of the telephone network and port development – and would also have reduced the scope for tax reduction at a time when the chambers of commerce were pressing hard for the complete abolition of the business tax. As the call for tax cuts was taken up by the Kokuminto and other political groups, it became known that high-ranking naval officers had accepted bribes to order equipment for the cruiser *Kongo* from the German Siemens company. The scandal had an electrifying effect. Tokyo witnessed large-scale demonstrations, the biggest of which, on the anniversary of Katsura's overthrow, is believed to have involved some 50,000 protesters. Much of the obloquy inevitably attached itself to Yamamoto as the senior naval figure. With the cabinet seriously weakened, Navy Minister Saito agreed to a budgetary cut of 30 million yen, but this failed to satisfy public opinion. When in March the House of Peers rejected the naval supplementary budget outright, the cabinet, which also faced a vote of censure in the Lower House, resigned. Without popular backing it could not hope to overcome the combined strength of the Yamagata clique and its other bureaucratic and political enemies.

The Okuma cabinet and the rise of the Doshikai

One further reason why the cabinet collapsed so quickly may have been that Hara had become less interested in its continuation. The sudden death of Matsuda on 4 March had removed his only possible rival within the party and he expected to be recommended by Yamamoto as the next Prime Minister. However, the Seiyukai's reputation had suffered a major setback and it was easy for Yamagata to outmanoeuvre Hara by arranging a *genro* council to nominate Yamamoto's successor. Although the *genro's* first choice, the Upper House president, Tokugawa Iesato, declined the invitation to form an administration, and their more serious second choice, the ex-bureaucrat and Privy Council adviser, Kiyoura Keigo, gave up in the face of opposition from both the navy and the Doshikai, Yamagata and his fellow elder statesmen (Saionji excepted) were nonetheless determined to push back the Seiyukai's advance; and rather than choose Hara, they unexpectedly turned to the septuagenarian Okuma Shigenobu, who had been only peripherally involved in politics since being ousted from the presidency of the Kenseihonto in 1907. Okuma's advocacy of party cabinets was admittedly not to the *genro's* liking, but his popular reputation was an invaluable asset and he was prepared to make use of it, as requested by Inoue, 'to deliver a crushing blow against the Seiyukai'. He was aided in his task by the ready support of most non-Seiyukai Diet members (with the notable exception of Inukai) and his cabinet included not only the inevitable sprinkling of civil and military bureaucrats but also Ozaki Yukio and three members of the Doshikai (including its new leader, Kato Komei, as Foreign Minister). More fortuitously, his position was made easier by the outbreak of World War One, which engendered an atmosphere of greater national unity when the government quickly decided to join in on the side of its ally, Britain, and undertook a campaign against the German military base at Tsingtao. Despite some initial disruption of the money market, the war also gave a boost to Japanese industry by reducing imports and creating new export opportunities, with the result that the campaign for the abolition of business tax lost much of its force.

Despite these favourable circumstances the new cabinet's position was not wholly secure. It did not command a majority in the Diet, and although Hara avoided a confrontational approach, the Seiyukai's opposition meant that Okuma was unable to keep his promise to provide the army with its two extra divisions. This situation was to change dramatically as a result of the election held in March 1915. One of the most important in Japanese history, it ended the long period of Seiyukai electoral dominance and paved the way for an era of competition between two more evenly balanced parties. The Seiyukai won only 108 seats compared with the 202 it had held, whereas the Doshikai leaped from 93 to 153. Of the minor parties, Inukai's Kokuminto dropped to 27 and Ozaki's Chuseikai to 33 while the Okuma Support Association gained 12 seats and unattached members numbered 58. The election was notable not only for its results but also for its methods. Okuma's supporters in particular introduced ultra-modern campaigning techniques, including not only whistle-stop speech-making tours but also the playing of phonograph records made by prominent leaders. Less openly, Home Minister Oura Kanetake utilised to an unprecedented degree the various means available to win votes for government supporters, among them ensuring that the police kept close surveillance over opposition candidates and their agents while mainly turning a blind eye to the buying of votes by those who enjoyed official favour. In Hara's judgment it was the large sums of money disbursed in this way (some, supposedly, from imperial household funds) which had the biggest impact on the result.

The success of the Doshikai was not regarded by the *genro* with entirely unmixed feelings. Although they welcomed the setback suffered by the Seiyukai, they had no wish to see another party take its place, especially one led by Kato Komei. A man whose marriage into the Iwasaki family had made him financially independent – indeed it was largely his ability to provide funds which had been responsible for his becoming the Doshikai president – he was disinclined to follow the instructions of elder statesmen. His pronounced admiration for British institutions and procedures did not endear him to conservatives and traditionalists, and when in 1914 he discontinued the practice of consulting the *genro* on diplomatic matters, the latter protested strongly to Okuma. In early 1915 Kato went too far: his presentation of his soon-to-be-notorious '21 demands' for an extension of Japanese rights in China provoked antagonism both in that country and in the West, even though some of the demands were dropped from the ultimatum to which Kato eventually resorted. Subjected to strong pressure to resign by the *genro*, he did so in July 1915.

Despite this setback Kato did not give up hope of succeeding Okuma as Prime Minister in due course. From early 1916 the latter was intimating his intention to resign, and because he had established a closer personal relationship with the Taisho Emperor than Yamagata enjoyed, it seemed possible that his recommendation of Kato as his successor might be accepted. It may have been partly because he placed his trust in Okuma's influence that Kato showed little interest in the proposal for an all-party cabinet which the Choshu ex-general, Miura Goro, put forward at this time. However, not only Kato but Hara too lacked enthusiasm for exploring this possibility, and although a three-party agreement to sink their differences in the name of national unity was signed in May 1916, it had no effect on the political situation. The way was thus left open, when Okuma finally resigned on 4 October, for the *genro* to impose their choice, ex-Army Minister and Governor-General of Korea, General Terauchi Masatake.

The Terauchi cabinet and the resurgence of the Seiyukai

The need to thwart Kato seemed the more important to the *genro* in that the Doshikai was currently engaged in merger negotiations with two smaller parties which were to result in the still more formidable Kenseikai (Constitutional Party) on 10 October. Ironically the merger probably aided the new cabinet, for it meant that the Seiyukai was less likely to join in a united front with the Kenseikai now that it would be even more definitely the lesser partner. Some party members inevitably would still have preferred to engage in outright opposition to a cabinet which, despite its claims to be a cabinet of national unity, was composed mainly of members of the Yamagata faction and had not been well received by the press. For Hara, however, the way back to power lay in compromise rather than conflict. Already in 1914 he had begun to seek an understanding with Yamagata by regularly visiting his residence, discussing current affairs and seeking to persuade the old *genro* that party cabinets offered the best prospect of stability now that the Meiji leaders were retired or dead. It was a logical continuation of this policy to respond to Terauchi's request for cooperation with an assurance that his attitude would be one of firmness and impartiality: the Seiyukai would support the government so long as the latter's measures did not run counter to party interests. For the sake of its popular reputation, however, it chose to refrain from too close an association.

By contrast, Kato could not reconcile himself to the fact that he had been passed over. He apparently believed that Terauchi would not be willing to risk an election and would have to step down when he was confronted by an uncooperative Diet. His calculations did not work out as well as Hara's. After a no-confidence vote was passed by the combined forces of the Kokuminto and the Kenseikai in December 1916, Terauchi did in fact dissolve the Lower House, and in the ensuing election the government set out to achieve a Diet in which no party held a majority. To achieve this aim pro-government 'independent' or 'neutral candidates were specially favoured, but to reduce the Kenseikai's representation it was also necessary to give some electoral assistance to the Seiyukai. Although official interference was less blatant than in 1915, no fewer than twenty-seven prefectural governors were retired or moved to other areas immediately before the election. The effect of this favourable treatment was to boost Seiyukai representation to 165 seats (rather more than intended) while the Kenseikai slumped to 121. The unattached members upon whom the government could rely most surely, however, increased only marginally to sixty.

The restoration of the Seiyukai as the largest party gave Hara more leverage, but as during the first two Katsura cabinets he was prepared to bide his time. Meanwhile Kato's uncompromising stance ensured that the Seiyukai's support remained crucial to Terauchi, and over the next year Hara was able to re-establish his influence over government policy. Indeed, the small party into which most of the government's unattached supporters had been combined – the Shinseikai – split because the Finance Minister withdrew his budget proposals in order to incorporate Seiyukai amendments. Extra funds were provided for economic development as well as military and naval expansion, and Seiyukai pressure was also a factor in the cabinet's decision to accept a recommendation by a special advisory council on education that the Finance Ministry bear a substantial burden of primary school salaries – a long-time demand of local politicians.

By early 1918 Terauchi was ready to give up office. His relations with Yamagata had suffered because he, like Katsura, had been unwilling to act as a puppet of the *genro*, but Yamagata insisted on his soldiering on, since the government was engaged in extracting a new Sino-Japanese treaty from the warlord regime which it supported in Peking and, even more importantly, Japanese policy-makers were also in the throes of a debate over the question of sending an expedition to Siberia to protect allied (and advance Japanese) interests in the aftermath of the Bolshevik Revolution. That debate was settled in late July, when Hara, Saionji and Matsukata reluctantly agreed to a (supposedly limited) participation in an allied expedition. Before it became clear who was likely to succeed Terauchi, however, the government was confronted by the most violent wave of popular unrest since the revolts of the 1870s.

The rice riots and the Hara cabinet

The 1918 Rice Riots began on 3 August with a protest about the shortage of rice by a group of women in Toyama (on the Japan Sea coast) whose husbands were away in the north on poorly-paid fishing work. It quickly spread to other areas in central Japan; and by the time it began to subside around 12 September there had been disturbances in 38 cities, 153 towns and 177 villages. The number of protesters has been estimated as at least 700,000, of whom some 8,700 were tried and punished, often severely. The immediate and main cause of these unorganised uprisings was the price of rice, which by 1 August 1918 was more than three times higher than its 1917 average and, at its peak on 12 August, was almost five times higher. Partly underlying this rise was a steady increase in consumption resulting from the war-time boom in industry, but what should have been a manageable situation got out of control, firstly as a result of the government's decision to ban the import of foreign rice by small traders and reserve the right to only five companies, and secondly because of the speculative hoarding by dealers and large landlords who hoped that military purchases for the planned Siberian expedition would force prices still higher.

Serious though the spiralling cost of Japan's staple food was, the term 'Rice Riots' oversimplifies the nature of the disturbances. There had also been a sharp increase in the price of most other commodities, and even where these were less than the increase in the average wage level, they produced hardship and resentment among casual labourers and workers in traditional and home industries (which had profited less from the war boom than modern industry). Significantly, there were relatively few factory workers in the desperate attacks on rice warehouses or shops which seem often to have been instigated by members of the *burakumin* class, who generally had to take the worst-paid jobs. The effects of inflation, however, were felt at other levels of society too: tradesmen, journalists and teachers were also among those arrested. Indeed, anyone on a fixed salary was liable to experience a loss of purchasing power, and this included the lower levels of officialdom. One well-informed report by a foreign observer even suggested that the police had some sympathy for the protesters and could not

Two cartoons from the satirical magazine *Tokyo Puck*.

Right A depiction of the tribulations of Hara Takashi as Home Minister in the first Saionji cabinet in 1906. The weights causing the relatively liberal Hara to sweat are identified, from top to bottom, as the urban majority, the press, local assemblies, workers' organisations, and socialism.

Prime Minister Saionji Kimmochi shown in July 1912 as a hardworking peasant (indicating his government's concern with financial adjustment) about to see his work interrupted by the Navy Minister's demand for increased warship construction and by the Army Minister's insistence on the establishment of two extra divisions. The cabinet's refusal of these provoked the Taisho political crisis of 1912-13.

大正七年米騷動

Right Cartoon depiction of one of the many rice riots in August–September 1918. *Below* Photograph of a rice granary in Okayama burned down in one such riot.

always be relied upon to control them;[5] in at least one hundred places the army had to be called in.

There is no doubt that the Rice Riots were a major shock to the Japanese establishment. At least two cabinet ministers, Goto Shimpei and Den Kenjiro, regarded them as a harbinger of class war, and in some villages they took the form of attacks by tenant farmers on landlords. The concern of the ruling élites was revealed not only in the severe punishments inflicted on rioters but also in the gifts of money made for relief of the indigent by the imperial household (3,000,000 yen), by the Mitsui and Mitsubishi *zaibatsu* (1,000,000 yen each) and by the Suzuki company and Yamashita Denzaburo (500,000 yen each). Censorship of the press was also tightened. In mid-August Home Minister Mizuno Rentaro attempted to ban all comment on the riots or the price of rice and have only official bulletins published; and even when this injunction was relaxed in the face of strong representations, any newspaper which printed an article susceptible of being accused of disturbing public order ran a serious risk of prosecution, as the *Osaka Asahi* (a longstanding vigorous critic of the government) found to its cost on 26 August.

The Rice Riots ensured that the Terauchi cabinet would be replaced by a genuine party cabinet. This was not initially perceived by the Prime Minister, whose first reaction was that his duty required him to remain in office. Press and Kenseikai calls for the cabinet to accept its responsibility for Japan's troubles grew stronger, however, and criticism was forthcoming even from members of the House of Peers. Yamagata too, after first pressing in vain for the dismissal of three ministers whom he deemed unsatisfactory, came to favour a cabinet resignation. Moreover, although the Seiyukai and Kokuminto had tried to exercise a moderating influence during the crisis by calling for cooperation between government and people, there was growing pressure from the more radical members of the Seiyukai to withdraw support from Terauchi; and Hara seems to have been prepared, had his hope of a speedy transfer of power been frustrated, to join hands with the Kenseikai in an anti-oligarchic movement which could have rivalled that of 1912-13. Yamagata still hoped to avoid a pure party cabinet by persuading Saionji to head a cabinet of national unity, but the latter refused on

[5] Public Record Office, London. Foreign Office Confidential Prints, F.O.410, part xix. no.6, report by E.F.Crowe on 'Japan's After-War Problem' in Greene to Balfour, 19 September 1918.

the pretext of poor health and recommended that Hara be appointed. With Terauchi (once he had accepted that he could not continue) also favouring Hara as his successor, Yamagata eventually bowed to the inevitable. Unwilling, however, to recommend a party politician to the Emperor personally, he entrusted that duty to Saionji.

Hara formed his cabinet on 29 September, eight days after Terauchi's resignation. Except for the service ministers and the Foreign Minister its members were all party men, and it therefore qualifies to be termed Japan's first party cabinet (if the ephemeral 1898 Okuma cabinet is excluded, as it usually is). Its establishment was widely seen as a landmark in Japanese political history. As the British ambassador, Sir Conyngham Greene, expressed it:

the present situation is more or less the converse of what has hitherto obtained. That was a manipulation of parties by the bureaucrats. This should rather be the spectacle of a party in command manoeuvring with bureaucracy and the other complex influences of the Japanese political world.[6]

Ironically, Hara's reward for his major role in establishing a relatively stable political system may well have come too late. He was fond of impressing on the *genro* the futility of resisting the 'trend of the times' but his political philosophy was more attuned to the late Meiji era than to 1918. Even though Japan's military involvement in the First World War had been limited, the conflict had nevertheless transformed its economy. In the wake of increased industrialisation and urbanisation came new social problems and the rise of new social groups with different demands, and the subsequent collapse of the war boom in 1920 was soon to exacerbate the situation even further. It was the historical misfortune of the parties that they aspired to assume the mantle of the *genro* and establish the legitimacy of their rule at a time when government was becoming more difficult than it had been since the 1870s.

[6] Public Record Office, London. Foreign Office General Correspondence, vol. 3238, no 353, 27 September 1918.

5

PARTY CABINETS, RADICAL MOVEMENTS AND THE COLLAPSE OF TAISHO DEMOCRACY, 1918-32

The Hara cabinet came into existence at a time when the Rice Riots had aroused both foreboding and optimism in Japan. For many ultranationalilsts who later achieved fame or notoriety it was this episode which first alerted them to the need to prevent the disintegration of the sense of national solidarity which was so essential to their concept of a unique *kokutai*. For others the revelation of the potential power of mass action induced hope that this power might be channelled into radical causes. Even among those who were less alarmed or excited, the disturbances encouraged the feeling that the time was ripe for a fundamental re-examination and new initiatives.

The post-war ferment

Striking though the impact of the Rice Riots was, their main significance lay in the fact that they reflected an unprecedented social and intellectual ferment. That ferment, which especially characterised the years 1918-20, stemmed chiefly from the effects of the First World War. The economic boom which developed as the Japanese rushed into markets from which the European nations had been forced to withdraw created fortunes for some, but left others floundering in the wake of rapid inflation. Nor did the aftermath of the riots bring much relief: not until late 1920 did the price of rice drop significantly, and even then it did not return to the level of 1917. Meanwhile, the general cost of living continued to rise until the collapse of the boom in 1920. The Tokyo retail price index, which (based on 1934-6 =100) was at a level of 61.8 in 1914, 95.1 in 1917, and 124.6 in 1918, went up to 152.6 in 1919 and reached 167.8 in 1920 before falling back to 129.6 in 1921. Discontent caused by inflation was further fuelled by the ostentatious (and well-publicised) displays of wealth indulged in by some *nouveaux riches*. That such feeling could take a political direction was illustrated by the murder of the major *zaibatsu* leader, Yasuda Zenjiro, in 1921 by a young radical nationalist, Asahi Heigo, as a conscious protest against corruption and inequality.

The gap between prices and wages also had significant repercussions on labour relations. Strikes increased from 108 in 1916 to 398 in 1917 and 417 in 1918, reaching a peak of 497 (with 63,137 workers involved) in 1919, and the number of unions also rose dramatically (although this development followed rather than preceded the emergence of worker militancy). At least seventy-one new unions were formed during 1918 (making the total 187), compared with an estimated eleven in the previous year. This increase owed something to the activities of the anarchistic elements who established such unions as the Shinyukai (Faithful Friends' Society) and Seishinkai (True Progress Society), but far more to the moderate Yuaikai (Friendly Society), which had been founded in 1912 by the socially aware Christian, Suzuki Bunji. The numerous branches of the Yuaikai alone accounted for about 30,000 of the roughly 100,000 organised workers in 1919.

One of the most important developments in the Japanese labour movement was its acceptance in 1918 of the need for political as well as industrial action. Union leaders had frequently found it difficult to conduct industrial disputes as a result of the Peace Police Law which made any combination for strike action theoretically illegal and could only be repealed by the Diet. The most obvious way of changing this was to secure electoral representation through the movement for adult male suffrage, which, after two decades of unrewarded effort by a handful of liberal lawyers, journalists and socialists, now began to attract much greater support. Trade unionists comprised a substantial number of the many thousands of demonstrators who assembled in Tokyo on several occasions during the Diet sessions of 1919 and 1920, and they also participated in demonstrations in other major cities and in the numerous speech-meetings which were organised in almost every prefecture. The change in the character of the Yuaikai to a more militant and politically active organisation was marked in August 1919 by the alteration of its name to Dai Nihon Rodo Sodomei Yuaikai (Great Japan General Federation of Labour Friendly Societies) – it was usually shortened to Sodomei.

Unions were not the only organised element in the campaign for suffrage extension. No less important was the contribution of the urban political societies which flourished in the post-war years. They were particularly numerous in Tokyo, where forty-six were in existence in January 1921, but there were at least thirty-two more, spread fairly evenly outside the capital. Some of them were expressly concerned with electoral reform or constitutional government, although most also took a keen interest in city government and social problems. In several cases they were continuations or amalgamations of groups which had been active in the Taisho Political Crisis, but even more than at that period they were characterised by the involvement of young men's associations. For these young idealists the call for reconstruction and renovation was attractive.

One obvious reason for the appearance or increased vigour of political societies was the extra impetus towards urbanisation produced by the war. The number of people who lived in towns or cities with populations of between 20,000 and 50,000 rose from 2,934,000 in 1913 to 3,904,000 in 1918; in cities of 50,000 to 100,000 from 1,856,000 to 2,282,000; and in cities of more than 100,000 from 5,938,000 to 7,292,000. The number in Tokyo increased by almost 300,000 to 2,347,442, and in Osaka from 1,395,823 to 1,641,580. It was not just a matter of numbers, though. Despite the apparent fact that wages and salaries lagged behind prices for considerable periods, it seems likely that general purchasing power increased (partly because of the expansion of job opportunities, partly because some companies began to supplement the earnings of workers with extra payments based on family commitments and seniority). It is certainly clear that newspaper circulations and the production of books and magazines expanded. The sales of the *Osaka Mainichi*, Japan's largest newspaper, are believed to have risen from about 320,000 in 1914 to 600,000 in 1920 (reaching 1,110,000 in 1924) and there were approximately 6,000 retail bookshops in 1920, compared with 3,000 before the war. Many new magazines also appeared. Between 1916 and 1919 women's or children's magazines alone accounted for fifty-seven new titles. Others reflected such new interests as film, fashion, sight-seeing, and aviation, while at a more sober level there were numerous publications which specialised in such topics as how to pass examinations.

Of most direct political relevance was the wider dissemination through the press of liberal and radical ideas. Whereas previously they had been confined mainly to the *Heimin Shimbun* or to books or magazines which had a fairly select readership, they were now propagated or discussed in a number of more popular new magazines such as *Kaizo* (Radical Reorganisation), *Kaiho* (Emancipation), and *Warera* (We). The appearance of such magazines reflected the fact that the war had undermined conservatism both by showing that the old order was not immutable and by producing economic and social problems which could not be solved merely by preaching old values. A more rational approach based on new ideas became attractive to many and the widely-publicised plans of Japan's allies, particularly Woodrow Wilson's America, to reconstruct the post-war world on the basis of self-determination after the defeat of militarism and authoritarianism, provided additional encouragement for this approach. So too did the Russian Revolution, at least among that minority, often from ex-samurai families, who idealised direct action in the *shishi* tradition.

A notable role in popularising liberal ideas was played by university teachers, and among them the name of Yoshino Sakuzo stands out. Like the slightly older Minobe Tatsukichi (who, as the leading interpreter of the Japanese constitution, continued to counter the mystical view of the Emperor-state which officialdom had propagated and cultivated), Yoshino was a professor at Tokyo University, and it was not just his deployment of learning and reasoned argument but also his prestigious academic position that lent respectability to the concept of liberal democracy. He was careful, admittedly, to advocate *minponshugi* (government based on the people) rather than *minshushugi* (which implied democracy based on popular sovereignty), but at the same time he criticised traditionalists asserting that 'Those who argue that democracy is not compatible with the national spirit believe in the anachronistic and erroneous notion that the Emperor and people are mutually exclusive of each other'.[1] In practice, both *minponshugi* and *minshushugi* were alike in supporting the idea of government by parties responsive to public needs and concerned with people's livelihood. At the time, certainly, the men who were inspired to political action by Yoshino, including many idealistic students at Tokyo University, had few

[1] Quoted by T.Najita, 'Idealism in Yoshino Sukuzo's Political Thought,' in B. Silberman and H.Harootunian (eds), *Japan in Crisis*, p.40.

reservations about his commitment to democracy, especially after he engaged in a public debate on freedom of speech on 23 November 1918 with members of a patriotic right-wing society known for its use of intimidation. It was this incident which roused different sections of his admirers to form two groups – the Reimeikai (Dawn Society) and Shinjinkai (New Man Society) – which were to involve a number of other academics and part of the embryonic student movement in the various campaigns for social democracy.

One of the main reasons for Yoshino's importance was his willingness to express his ideas in popular journals such as *Chuo Koron*. He was not alone, however, in addressing himself to a wider readership. Kawakami Hajime, an economics professor at Kyoto University, wrote a series of articles in the *Osaka Asahi* newspaper in 1916 under the general title of 'Bimbo Monogatari' (Tales of Poverty), which brought home to an even greater number the harsh social reality of the slum areas. Together with the social worker, Kagawa Toyohiko (like Yoshino a Christian), who also publicised the desperate plight of the substantial fringe elements who had lost out under capitalism, Kawakami did a great deal to stir the social conscience of many Japanese, including some bureaucrats. It would be a mistake, however, to attribute to a handful of individuals alone the sudden expansion of social and political consciousness in Taisho Japan. The new emphasis on 'the people' came from several directions, including the pioneering studies of folklore and traditional customs carried out by Yanagida Kunio and the re-evaluation of popular art by members of the Shirakaba-ha (White Birch Group), an influential set of intellectuals and writers. Moreover, there were many other journalists and academics who regularly advanced progressive views even before 1918, among them Ukita Kazutami and Ishibashi Tanzan – the respective editors of the magazines *Taiyo* and *Toyo Keizai Shimpo* – and Oyama Ikuo and Hasegawa Nyozekan. They helped to create an atmosphere which encouraged not only the general campaign for male suffrage, but also movements on behalf of trade union legislation, female equality, non-discrimination against *burakumin*, and, from the early 1920s, tenant rights.

Just how far the new atmosphere permeated Taisho Japan is a matter of debate among historians. Acutely aware that liberalism was a casualty of the nationalist fervour which swept Japan only a decade later, many scholars have taken the view that the changes in attitude were superficial. Some have also emphasised the persistence of anti-modern elements in popular thinking (as exemplified by the parallel growth during this period of traditionally-based 'new religions' such as Omotokyo). However, even if the understanding and acceptance of progressive ideas was not universal, the marked trend in that direction was historically significant. It should be emphasised, too, that this trend was by no means confined to the cities or to the intellectuals. The historian, Kimbara Samon, has noted the appearance in various prefectures of new local magazines which, although presenting no overt challenge to the established order, focused on current issues and stimulated a more critical political and social consciousness.[2] Even more significant, perhaps, was the new mood among teachers. Young ones, in particular, reacted against authoritarian methods and subscribed to the ideals of the 'free education' movement which aimed to develop children more fully as human beings rather than treat them just as future servants of the state. During 1918-19 independent groups were formed in many areas with the object of examining educational techniques and subject matter, and despite obstruction from the authorities various experiments were tried, such as the use of colourful illustrations in primary schools. Equally significant was the shift in attention towards the children's own experience and talents. There can be little doubt that teachers played an important role in shaping popular attitudes and the influence of an appreciable number of them was now being exerted on behalf of idealistic liberalism.

The policies of the Hara cabinet

The response of the Hara cabinet to the new mood was generally rather conservative. On electoral reform it took a more cautious position than either the Kenseikai or the Kokuminto and when it extended the franchise in 1919 it did so only to those paying three yen in direct national taxes. The number of electors was doubled to 2,860,000, but they remained a minority, even of adult males. At the same time the replacement of large electoral districts mainly by single-member (but in some cases two- or three-member) constituencies may have been intended to prevent any socialist party from gaining seats (although it was also designed to give a particular

[2] See Kimbara Samon, 'Seito Seiji no Hatten' in *Iwanami Koza Nihon Rekishi*, vol. 18, pp. 274-5.

advantage to the Seiyukai, which, as the party in power, was likely
to win most single-member seats). The frustration of the universal
suffrage campaign was made more acute by the large victory won
by the Seiyukai in the subsequent election in May 1920, when it
secured 278 out of the 464 seats, far more than the Kenseikai's 110.

The government's reaction to industrial disputes was no less
conservative. Home Minister Tokonami encouraged all kinds of
strike-breaking, including the use of police and military police
units in some cases where public enterprises were being disrupted,
and the Peace Police Law was retained despite the fact that it was
even being criticised within the Home Ministry. The only non-
repressive step taken by the government was to support the
Kyochokai (Cooperation Society) which was established in 1919
by the business leader Shibusawa Eiichi, with Tokonami's assistance. This organisation had as its aim the promotion of 'humble
self-examination' by capitalists, the improvement of the workers'
position, and the settlement of disputes by conciliation. The decline in strikes after 1919, however, probably owed less to the
Kyochokai than to the 1920 recession, which caused considerable
unemployment and put labour on the defensive.

Large-scale unemployment was new to Japan, but it quickly rose
to more than 200,000 by 1921 and could not be entirely ignored
by the Hara government. A special bureau was introduced into the
Home Ministry to develop and coordinate the administration of
relief measures such as child welfare provision and public works,
and a central employment exchange was established under its aus-
pices. These were significant steps, for previously relief measures
had been mainly confined to elderly people without family and
incapable of working, wounded soldiers, or deceased soldiers'
dependants. However, because of the burden it imposed on local
government finances this more positive approach to social policy
soon faltered. It was, in any case, overshadowed by the 'Movement
to Cultivate the People's Strength' (Minryoku Kanyo Undo), which
the Home Ministry also ran and which once again attempted to
wage a 'thought improvement' campaign based on such slogans as
'the spirit of self-sacrifice and service', 'the glory of the *kokutai*',
'frugality and fortitude', and the 'promotion of economy and saving'. During the three years (1919-21) that this campaign was carried
out by local government officials, mainly using priests, young men's
associations, women's associations and producers' cooperatives, over

60,000 meetings were held, with a total attendance of over 17,000,000, and instructional films were seen by nearly 3,000,000.

The Hara cabinet's emphasis on moral exhortation lends support to the view, common among historians, that its fundamental attitude towards the Japanese people, namely that they could not be entrusted with complete freedom and required indoctrination, was very little different from that of its predecessors. Further evidence for this opinion is provided by the government's prosecution of both Morito Tatsuo (a young economics teacher at Tokyo University who published a partly critical but basically sympathetic exposition of Kropotkin's anarchism in his departmental journal in January 1920) and Aoki Tetsuji (a lawyer who received a four-month sentence for criticising the official emphasis on the supposedly unbroken dynastic line as the main pillar of imperial prestige and for arguing that *lèse-majesté* should not be a crime). Other writers were fined or had their articles or books banned. Nevertheless, prosecutions for violation of the Press Law diminished after 1918, and Hara himself, although hostile towards radicals, drew a distinction between his own approach and that of officialdom. 'The future rise of democracy', he informed Miura Goro in October 1917, 'is truly to be feared. It is something which disturbs me and the bureaucracy alike. There is a difference, however. The bureaucracy want to block this tide off; we want to prevent it from rising too high and causing great damage by drawing it off as appropriate'.[3]

It is doubtful whether, for Hara, radicalism and social unrest were the matters of greatest concern. He continued to be preoccupied with consolidating the Seiyukai's position within a stable political system and expanding national wealth and strength by means of a positive financial policy. With Inoue dead, Matsukata inactive, and Yamagata in semi-retirement, Saionji alone remained fully active among the *genro*, and Hara's objectives now seemed more attainable. On the financial front, of course, the cabinet was greatly strengthened by the First World War's transformation of an unfavourable balance of payments into a huge surplus. As a result there was no great outcry from banking circles when Finance Minister Takahashi Korekiyo presented a series of significantly larger budget proposals and greatly expanded government borrowing.

---

[3] Quoted by Oka Yoshitake, *Tenkanki no Taisho*, p. 89.

Much of the 46 per cent rise in government general account expenditure between 1918 and 1921 went to the armed forces, with the navy securing the lion's share. In 1921, indeed, the services' allocation amounted to almost half the total. However, substantial amounts were left for projects which would benefit local areas and win electoral support. Central government spending on construction leaped from 101 million yen in 1918 to 282 million in 1921, within which general figures are concealed still sharper increases in expenditure on harbours, ports, roads and bridges. Even the more detailed statistics do not tell the whole story, however, for the cabinet also committed its successors to major expansion projects which would have to be sustained for a number of years. The 1920 telephone network extension plan, for instance, which aimed to increase the number of subscribers to 430,000 (at a cost of 225 million yen), was not due to be completed until 1928; while the even more ambitious scheme of almost doubling railway line mileage (at a cost of 800 million yen) was to run for ten years from 1920. In another significant area, the cabinet's 1918 decision to expand higher education led to a six-year, 45 million yen programme for enlarging universities and establishing new high schools and specialised colleges. The location of these future railroads, exchanges and educational establishments was a matter of intense interest and provided the Seiyukai with tempting lures to dangle in front of local politicians, businessmen and community leaders.

While economic power played an even greater role than before in bringing local politicians within the orbit of the Seiyukai, the party also sought to extend its base (as, with less success, did the Kenseikai) by establishing connections with imperial reservist branches, young men's associations and agrarian societies. Some local politicians even tried to forge links with leaders of tenant unions. Such a strategy of building 'vertical parties transcending class', to use Kimbara's phrase, has been criticised as being an attempt to extend party power without seeking genuine mass support. Whatever the justification of that accusation, however, it should not be allowed to obscure the fact that the Hara cabinet did, in 1921, give the right to vote in city, town and village assembly elections to all taxpayers, and at the same time removed or (in cities) reduced the distinction between wealthier and poorer voters.

If the Seiyukai had sought to place its emphasis on democracy and put its trust principally in popular support, Hara would almost certainly have made little headway with his other strategy – winning over the Establishment. As it was, his evident determination to create a stable constitutional system, combined with his skillful use of government patronage, allowed him to make further significant inroads into the ranks of the conservative opponents of party cabinets. He wooed the leaders of the Kenkyukai (the largest of the factions in the House of Peers) with offers of directorships in government-controlled special banks and, in one case, with the post of Justice Minister; and he took care to consult them about cabinet policies. His reward was to experience much less difficulty than the Saionji cabinets in getting his legislation enacted. He was able to achieve his old aim of abolition of the *gun's* governmental functions in 1921 with little opposition; and he also succeeded in altering regulations so as to allow civilians to serve as Governor-Generals in Korea, Taiwan and the Kwantung leased territory. In addition more governmental posts (vice-minister, Home Ministry Police Bureau head, Tokyo Police Commissioner, chief secretaries of the two Diet chambers, Colonial Agency head, and the newly-established departmental councillors) were opened to non-bureaucrats. The placing of party men in the civilian ministries did not, as it happened, prove important. Much more effective was the gaining of bureaucrats' allegiance. The outstanding example of politicisation was the Home Ministry, where Tokonami persuaded all the top-level officials to become members of the Seiyukai; but party influence also began to infiltrate other ministries which had previously been immune to it. There was resentment, especially among junior bureaucrats; nevertheless, it was clear that the way to promotion now lay in identifying with political parties, not opposing them.

By the autumn of 1921, the Hara cabinet had lasted for a long time by Japanese standards, yet its continued survival did not seem threatened. Even Yamagata had come to appreciate that the government could not, in practice, be coordinated better than by the existing cabinet. The economic situation was admittedly less favourable, but it still seemed possible for Hara to maintain his positive policy, albeit on a slightly less ambitious scale. In foreign affairs, too, the failure of the Siberian expedition had discredited the military and justified Hara's original scepticism; and Japanese public opinion was now ready to accept a policy of cooperation towards the United States and greater restraint towards China which would be more in line with Hara's emphasis on internal development.

The strong position of the cabinet owed much to the Prime Minister himself. Hara may not have been a charismatic leader, and he was no orator, but more than any other Japanese politician he knew how to acquire influence and work the system. As well as ingratiating himself with Yamagata, infiltrating the bureaucracy, and neutralising the Upper House, Hara also earned the respect of the Lower House for the attention he gave to debate there. His handling of his party was no less important. He more than once declined a peerage because he felt that this would cut him off from its rank and file members. He lived simply, but as a director of the huge Furukawa company he was able and willing to bestow financial assistance upon less-favoured Seiyukai Diet representatives. Even so, his husbanding of the party's financial resources was marked by sufficient prudence that the 140,000 yen which he is said to have inherited when he became leader is believed to have grown to about 1,000,000 yen by the end of 1921. Unlike the aloof Kato Komei (whose colleagues did not presume to make jokes in his presence), Hara took a considerable personal interest in his party's members. He was loyal to old associates even when they were involved in scandals, but he could also be tough with troublesome colleagues. Above all, however, his overall grasp of political strategy and his pragmatism were more valuable assets to his party than Kato's dogmatic stand on the principle of pure party cabinets.

Seiyukai disunity and non-party cabinets

It was therefore an enormous blow to the Seiyukai when, on 4 November 1921, Hara was assassinated at Tokyo Station by a young railway worker. Nor was it just his followers who grieved for him. Yamagata, too, lamented Hara's demise, and even the newspapers which had been critical of his lack of idealism regretted his passing. Nevertheless, it still seemed that party cabinets might continue on the foundations which Hara had built. After once again declining to form an administration himself, Saionji persuaded Yamagata and Matsukata to accept Finance Minister Takahashi Korekiyo as Hara's successor, and when this intention was made known to the other Seiyukai leaders, they agreed, despite some reluctance by Home Minister Tokonami Takejiro, to nominate Takahashi as the new party president. The smoothness of the transition, however, disguised the fact that personal rivalry was about to exert a disruptive influence.

Rivalry among party barons was endemic in Japanese politics, and it was intensified by the growing importance of money in elections. Those leaders who could help out less well-funded Diet members were able to build up factions within the party, and this support strengthened their claims to influential party or cabinet positions. When Takahashi became Prime Minister, he was faced with persistent pressure from a so-called 'reorganisation' faction for the replacement of Railway Minister Motoda Hajime and Education Minister Nakahashi Tokugoro. After much dithering he requested their resignations in June 1922, but with the support of Tokonami and Agriculture Minister Yamamoto Tatsuo they refused, leaving Takahashi with no way of removing them but to resign himself and seek a commission from the Prince Regent to form a new administration. Takahashi did indeed take this step, but his manoeuvre failed, for the *genro* no longer believed that he could hold the Seiyukai together.

Takahashi's replacement posed a tricky problem for Matsukata and Saionji, now the only *genro* since Yamagata's death in February 1922. The Seiyukai remained the major party, but it was badly divided. One way out of the impasse would have been to nominate Kato Komei and hope that the Kenseikai would soon be able to win a working majority, but the distaste which Saionji felt for the ex-Foreign Minister was almost as great as Yamagata's had been, and there were serious question-marks over Kato's political ability. Saionji himself favoured Den Kenjiro, an able administrator and old associate of Yamagata, who had once been a Seiyukai Diet member and might be expected to be chosen as party leader if he were to become Prime Minister. However, being in ill health, Saionji left the decision entirely to Matsukata, who plumped for a fellow Satsuma man, the respected Admiral Kato Tomosaburo.

Kato Tomosaburo was surprised by the request to form a government and was inclined to decline until the Seiyukai leadership, having heard that Matsukata's alternative choice was Kato Komei, offered their party's full support. Regarding the situation as temporary, however, they chose not to nominate any Seiyukai

Right Hara Takashi, soon after becoming Japan's first commoner Prime Minister in 1918. *Below* Some of the leaders of his Seiyukai party at the time of his cabinet's emergence (from right to left: Takahashi Korekiyo, Motoda Hajime, Nakahashi Tokugoro and Noda Yutaro).

Above Demonstration calling for universal suffrage outside the Diet, 11 February 1920. *Below* Demonstration in 1925 protesting against the 'evil' Peace Preservation Law, introducing heavy penalties for anyone seeking to overthrow either the *kokutai* or the system of private property.

Above Three of the men (from right to left: Komaki Emi, Kaneko Yobun and Konno Kenzo) who founded Japan's first proletarian literary magazine, *Tanemakuhito* (Sowers of the Seed) in 1921. *Below* Three politicians (from right to left: Inukai Tsuyoshi, Kato Takaaki and Takahashi Korekiyo) who led their parties into the Second Constitutional Protection Movement, meeting in January 1924 at the home of ex-General Miura Goro.

Right The last *genro* (elder statesman), Saionji Kimmochi (left) with the last prewar Prime Minister to come from a political party, Inukai Tsuyoshi (right). *Below* The 'cabinet of national unity' under Admiral Saito Makoto, at the time of its formation soon after Inukai's assassination in May 1932 (Saito is in the centre at the front, to his right is future Prime Minister Hatoyama Ichiro, and on his far left is Saito's successor in 1934, Admiral Okada Keisuke).

men as ministers, and when Kato Tomosaburo did form a cabinet on 12 June, it was made up entirely of members of the House of Peers, career bureaucrats and military officers. There may have been some advantage for the party in not having to bear the responsibility for carrying out the destruction of surplus battleships according to the Washington Treaty quotas and, still more, for reducing the size of the army following the termination of the unsuccessful Siberian expedition. Nevertheless, the Seiyukai was jeopardising the fragile principle that party cabinets were the normal form of constitutional government, and it incurred much press criticism.

With Seiyukai support Kato Tomosaburo got through the 46th Diet session without undue difficulty. Indeed the government even secured the approval of both Houses for the introduction of the jury system in the trial of serious offences, an innovation which had been advocated by the Seiyukai since 1910. That it was by no means reactionary in spirit was shown also by its establishment of a committee in October 1922 to consider the question of universal suffrage. Its fiscal policy was less expansionist than the Hara cabinet's had been, but it nonetheless increased expenditure on ports and water control. Had he not been struck down by stomach cancer on 24 August 1923, Kato might well have remained in office for some time longer.

His replacement was another admiral from Satsuma – Yamamoto Gonnohyoe. Ten years earlier he had stood in for Saionji as head of a Seiyukai administration. Now the *genro* hoped that he would form a cabinet of national unity based on all parties and ensure a fair election in 1924. In again slighting the majority party Saionji was deliberately expressing his dissatisfaction with its continuing disunity and ineffective leadership. Both Takahashi and Kato Komei refused to join the government, but the acceptance of a ministerial post by Inukai (who had combined the Kokuminto with dissident members from other parties in 1922 to form the Kakushin (Reform) Club and who enjoyed a considerable reputation for his consistent stand for popular rights) helped it to receive a reasonable reception from the press. The inclusion, too, of such able bureaucrats as Den Kenjiro (as Minister of Agriculture and Commerce), Goto Shimpei (Home Minister), and Inoue Junnosuke (Finance Minister) betokened a government of real talent which would get to grips with Japan's economic and social problems.

This favourable mood, however, evaporated with bewildering rapidity, and by early November Saionji himself was expressing disenchantment.

The lack of ability which Saionji now discerned in Yamamoto could reflect the fact that the cabinet was confronted by several exceptionally difficult issues. Some of them resulted from the great earthquake which had struck the Tokyo-Yokohama region on 1 September 1923, just one day before the cabinet was installed, causing the loss of about 100,000 lives and damage to property estimated at over 4,500,000 yen. A more fundamental problem, however, was presented by the universal suffrage issue. The idea had strong support from Inukai and Goto, but some ministers from Satsuma whom Yamamoto had appointed urged that the cabinet should not alienate the Seiyukai by trying to introduce a bill which ran counter to the latter's declared policy, and on 6 December Yamamoto abandoned the proposal. To Inukai and Goto, for whom universal suffrage was an essential weapon in their plan to outmanoeuvre the major parties and set up a new one, this was a serious setback; and when on 27 December the Prince Regent nearly fell victim to an assassination attempt, Inukai strongly argued – along traditional lines – that the cabinet should take responsibility and resign. Sensing that the situation was likely to deteriorate, Yamamoto gave up office on 7 January.

Before Yamamoto's resignation moves had already been afoot within and between the two major parties to bring about a change of government, but despite some behind-the-scenes manoeuvring there had been no change in either party's leadership, and Saionji's continuing unwillingness to nominate either Kato or Takahashi led him to turn once again to someone who stood above party interests. On the advice of Hirata Tosuke, who as Lord Keeper of the Privy Seal acted on behalf of the throne in political matters, the *genro's* choice this time was the ex-bureaucrat and protégé of Yamagata, Kiyoura Keigo. However, he soon discovered that he had miscalculated yet again. Like Kato Tomosaburo, Kiyoura failed to persuade any representative of the main parties to join his government; unlike Kato, he did not secure Seiyukai support.

The appearance of yet another non-party administration increased the rank and file pressure for a Second Constitutional Protection movement which would repeat the success of 1913 and restore the parties' tarnished reputation. Within the Seiyukai,

Takahashi, Yokota Sennosuke and Okazaki Kunisuke responded positively to the idea but Tokonami, Nakahashi, Motoda and Yamamoto Tatsuo urged that the party should maintain its traditional attitude of prudent cooperation with the government. The issue exacerbated the divisions between the two wings of the party to such an extent that when Takahashi agreed to work with Kato Komei and Inukai to bring the cabinet down more than half the Seiyukai Lower House members defected to form a new party, the Seiyuhonto (Seiyu Main Party) under Tokonami's leadership. Takahashi himself decided to resign his peerage and stand in the coming Lower House election. His action reflected the main theme of the three parties' campaign – that a cabinet formed by members of the privileged orders would provoke class consciousness and conflict. In response, the cabinet's supporters claimed that it was the opposition movement which was stirring up class feeling. Ironically, popular involvement in the Second Constitutional Protection movement was much less marked than in its predecessor, even though the press generally supported it.

Even if passions ran less high than in 1913, the result of the election held in May 1924 showed that the national mood favoured party cabinets. Despite substantial government interference on the Seiyuhonto's behalf, its Diet strength dropped from 149 to 112. The Seiyukai also lost seats, though, and it was the Kenseikai which emerged as the largest party with 151 representatives. To disregard Kato Komei any longer would in these circumstances have invited serious political instability, and in June the Kenseikai leader was finally given the opportunity to form a government.

Reform and reaction under the Kato cabinet

Kato's period in office, which lasted until his death in January 1926, has often been regarded as the high point of 'Taisho Democracy'. Although it began with a coalition cabinet in which Takahashi and Yokota Sennosuke represented the Seiyukai and Inukai the Kakushin Club, the Kenseikai was clearly the dominant partner, and it brought into government some of the reforming ardour to be expected of a party which had long been in opposition. Its most notable achievement was the passing on 29 March 1925 of a law which gave to all males aged 25 (except an insignificant number who were in receipt of poor relief) the right to vote in general elections. The new act also replaced the small constituencies which Hara had created in 1919 with medium-sized election districts of three, four or five members. There was relatively little opposition from the Privy Council or the House of Peers. By contrast the upper chamber was far less willing to accept the limitations on its own powers and the changes in its own composition for which the Constitutional Protection movement had also campaigned; and Kato eventually disappointed radical hopes by accepting a compromise which in essence merely meant that the hereditary peers lost their prescribed numerical superiority over appointed members. That this was a token reform was confirmed when the Upper House subsequently did not hesitate to block bills passed by the Lower House.

The other main achievement of the Kato coalition government was the reduction of the army which was carried out by Army Minister Ugaki Kazushige (Issei). This was largely a result of the Kenseikai's determination to reduce public expenditure, but the abolition of four of the army's twenty-one divisions did involve the retiring of about 2,000 officers, and it both reflected and confirmed the relative decline in the army's power and status. Even though some of the money saved was diverted into military modernisation and some of the unwanted officers found employment in the military training programmes which were instituted in schools and universities, there was a keen awareness within the army that it had been forced to make concessions.

Apart from universal male suffrage and the assertion of greater influence over the army (though not to the extent of allowing civilians to become service ministers, as some liberals advocated) the reforming record of the three-party cabinet was not impressive. The Tenancy Conciliation Law of December 1924, which sought to direct disputes between landlords and tenant-farmers to the courts, was intended to protect the former at least as much as the latter and notably failed to to give legal recognition to tenant unions. On the industrial front the existence of labour unions was implicitly acknowledged by allowing them to elect a delegate to the International Labour Organisation, and in 1925 the article of the Peace Police Law of 1900 which made conspiracy to strike a criminal offence was repealed. Nevertheless, the cabinet failed to push through the Diet a bill drafted by the Home Ministry's Social Bureau which would have legally recognised unions and prohibited employers from penalising employees who joined them. In this respect politicians showed themselves to be more cautious, or more amenable to business pressure, than bureaucrats.

The reputation of the Kato cabinet has suffered less for the paucity of its reforms, however, than for its repressive measures against the more radical elements of the proletarian movement. In particular, the passage of the Peace Preservation Law in March 1925 has been seen as a major step away from liberal democracy. By introducing penalties of up to ten years' imprisonment for those found guilty of involvement in organisations which aimed at the overthrow of either the *kokutai* or the system of private property, the new law made it possible to punish communists, anarchists and other subversive radicals more harshly. Its adoption by the coalition cabinet after the Kenseikai had earlier expressed strong misgivings has lent weight to the charge that mainstream politicians either became reactionary as they felt threatened by left-wing forces or were prepared to make a cynical deal with more conservative forces in order to secure the passage of electoral reform.

There is justification for both allegations. Certainly the political climate had been altered since 1922, firstly by the revelation that a Japanese communist party had been formed in that year, then by the unearthing of an anarchist plot to kill General Fukuda Masataro (who had been responsible for the sometimes ruthless administration of martial law after the great Kanto earthquake), and finally by the attempted shooting of the Regent in December 1923, only months after the discovery of another plot against his life; and both the Diet and the press were much less critical of the law than they had been of a similar Justice Ministry proposal in 1922. It is also true that the Privy Council expressed a desire for a control law to counterbalance the suffrage extension. Nevertheless, it is doubtful whether in the aftermath of the Second Constitutional Protection movement either the Privy Council or the Peers would have dared to block electoral reform; and had not the Justice Ministry renewed its pressure, the cabinet might well not have given the Peace Preservation Law a high priority. Its introduction, therefore, may have owed more to bureaucratic initiative than to incipient reactionary tendencies within the parties or to dubious political deals. This is not to suggest that Kato and his colleagues were reluctant to sponsor such a law. It must be emphasised, however, that they envisaged that it would be implemented only against extremists. Perhaps the real charge which should be levelled at them is that they failed to realise that by bringing into the political arena the term *kokutai*, which had previously been confined largely to constitutional theory, they were giving currency to a concept which was (like the term 'un-American activities' in the United States during the McCarthy era) susceptible of being used not just against the intended victims but against progressive ideas in general .[4]

In 1924-5, however, what most occupied the cabinet's attention, and caused the greatest difficulty between the main coalition partners, was fiscal policy. Friction between the Kenseikai and Seiyukai on this issue was almost inevitable given the latter's traditional commitment to government spending for economic development and the former's more orthodox concern for balanced budgets, but the clash between the two approaches was particularly sharp in 1924. Partly because the post-war recession had seen a less sharp price drop in Japan than other major trading countries, Japanese exports had become relatively uncompetitive. On top of this basic problem the immense damage caused by the Kanto earthquake had forced an increase in the money supply and necessitated a further surge in imports. The Seiyukai would have been content to make minor adjustments and go on drawing on the huge balances accumulated during the First World War, but the Kenseikai took the view that the Japanese price-level must be brought down, and that the only way to achieve this was by major retrenchments in the government's own spending. Its ultimate objective was a return to the 'normalcy' of the old gold standard which Japan had been forced to abandon when the United States followed Britain off it in 1917. A third possibility – devaluation of the yen – which was to prove highly effective in the 1930s seems not to have been considered. The importance which Kato attached to the issue was shown when he insisted, against objections from Takahashi, on making Hamaguchi Osachi (Yuko) Finance Minister. Hamaguchi was even more dedicated to 'sound' finance than Kato. His initial plan was to cut government expenditure by about one-sixth but he encountered bitter opposition and his final 1925 budget proposal was only 6 per cent smaller than the previous year's. It was a retreat which Hamaguchi was reluctant to make,

[4] This is argued by Matsuo Takayoshi in 'Seiyukai to Minseito', *Iwanami Koza Nihon Rekishi*, vol.19. See especially pp. 85-92.

but he was overruled by Kato, who gave priority to the preservation of the ruling coalition.

Despite this compromise harmony could not long be maintained between the two main partners. In February 1925 Yokota Sennosuke, one of the chief Seiyukai supporters of coalition, died, and in April the resignation of Takahashi (both as a minister and as Seiyukai president) dealt it a further blow. Takahashi's central role as party leader was assumed by the leading Choshu general, Tanaka Giichi, who as Army Minister in the 1918-21 cabinet had cooperated closely with Hara and made a favourable impression on both the Seiyukai and Saionji. One month later Inukai Tsuyoshi dissolved the Kakushin Club and took his supporters into the Seiyukai. With this support Tanaka was less likely to continue to accept a junior coalition role for the Seiyukai, and in July two Seiyukai ministers, Ogawa Heikichi and Okazaki Kunisuke, provoked a cabinet crisis by refusing to accept Hamaguchi's budget proposals for 1926. It was evidently anticipated that Kato would be forced to resign and that a Seiyukai-Seiyuhonto rapprochement would then open up the possibility of a new coalition government from which the Kenseikai would be excluded.

The Seiyukai strategy succeeded in producing a cabinet resignation but it failed in its main objective. Casting aside his previous doubts about Kato, Saionji now decided that, having shown a proper sense of responsibility as Prime Minister, he should continue in office despite the Kenseikai's lack of a majority in the Diet. The new cabinet might have sought to remove this disadvantage by holding a new election, but the recent introduction of general male suffrage made it difficult to be sure that the electoral advantages of the party in power would prove as decisive as before. Instead Kato chose to seek cooperation with the Seiyuhonto, which had always been attracted to power but was divided between those, like Nakahashi Tokugoro, who were tempted to realign with the Seiyukai, and those, like Tokonami Takejiro and the Satsuma faction, who found the Seiyukai less attractive than the Kenseikai now that the former had a Choshu ex-general at its head. The timely provision of 300,000 yen to Tokonami from the pro-Kenseikai Mitsubishi company helped to tilt the balance in the government party's favour. Despite some Seiyuhonto defections to the Seiyukai, the Kato cabinet now had the effective support of the eighty-seven remaining Seiyuhonto members, and with a less controversial legislative programme it was able to get through the 1925-6 Diet session without a crisis.

The Wakatsuki cabinet and its difficulties

Whether Kato's reformist urge had been exhausted by this time cannot fairly be judged, for he died on 28 January 1926. As his successor, Saionji recommended Wakatsuki Reijiro, his choice being made straightforward by the Kenseikai's selection of Wakatsuki as its new leader within a day of Kato's demise. Like Kato, the new Prime Minister had a reputation for possessing a strong sense of public duty, but unlike his predecessor, he did not have direct access to abundant financial resources. More seriously still, he proved to lack both strength of character and political vision.

Some of Wakatsuki's limitations were soon revealed. In May-June he botched his negotiations with Tokonami about cabinet posts and lost Seiyuhonto support. He was also ineffective in countering the attacks which the Seiyukai increasingly mounted. A number of these, such as the regular criticism of the 'weak-kneed' approach of Foreign Minister Shidehara Kijuro, who had consistently abjured 'gunboat diplomacy' in China, involved genuine differences on policy, even if Seiyukai rhetoric was exaggerated. Others were more dubious, notably the hypocritical claim that the lenient treatment in prison of the young Korean, Pak Yul (known as Boku Retsu in Japanese), who had plotted to assassinate the Prince Regent in 1923, amounted to *lèse-majesté* on the part of the Kenseikai government. Wakatsuki's response to this attack was pusillanimous. Without consulting his cabinet colleagues, he chose to accept a compromise whereby, following the Taisho Emperor's death on 25 December, the three party leaders announced on 20 January 1927 that they would avoid undignified recrimination and unnecessary conflict in order that there should be an auspicious beginning to the reign of the new Emperor (for whom the reign-name 'Showa' – 'brightness and peace' – was chosen). What was not publicly announced was the price of this truce – Wakatsuki's agreement to resign in June or July.

Wakatsuki's action did not please his party. Many Kenseikai politicians felt that a better alternative would have been to call an election, and this criticism has been echoed by historians such as

Matsuo Takayoshi, who have condemned him for failing to seek popular support and for not countering the political slogan 'protect the *kokutai*' with an appeal for electoral support which would have emphasised policy as the basis of politics in the new era.[5] By not challenging the opposition campaign in this way, the Kenseikai leader is seen to have abandoned by default the only true foundation on which party government could have been established. Whether or not Wakatsuki's decision was as crucial as Matsuo suggests, it certainly provided the government with no more than a temporary respite. Admittedly the truce initially did seem to pay dividends, for it allowed time to negotiate, by March 1927, much closer Kenseikai-Seiyuhonto cooperation; and his position thus strengthened, Wakatsuki could hope that, even if he were to keep his promise and resign, he would be asked to form a new administration. Almost immediately, however, he was confronted with a challenge which his opponents might not have dared to mount had he gone to the country and secured a new mandate.

The challenge came from an unexpected quarter – the Privy Council – and over an unexpected issue. In the aftermath of the Kanto earthquake the Bank of Japan had provided massive financial support to banks and companies in the disaster area, but although most of the debts which had been discounted had since been repaid, a substantial number of 'earthquake relief bills' had been used to prop up enterprises which had sprung up during the easy conditions of the war but were now over- extended. In late 1926 the government decided to grasp the nettle and in effect write off the approximately 200 million yen's worth of remaining earthquake bills. Backed by the Seiyuhonto, it succeeded in getting its stabilising relief measures through the Diet, but in late March a full-scale financial panic developed when the Bank of Japan refused to extend further credit to the troubled Bank of Taiwan. In the ensuing crisis many banks had to close their doors. The government could not stand back and watch the semi-official Bank of Taiwan collapse, however, especially as the Kenseikai had connections with its main client, the Suzuki Company, so it decided to authorise the Bank of Japan to lend it up to 200 million yen against a government guarantee.

Had the Diet still been in session it would probably have approved this emergency measure quickly. Since it was not, the cabinet

[5] *Ibid*

had the choice of recalling it for a special session or issuing an imperial ordinance. Its decision to take the latter course proved disastrous. Imperial ordinances were customarily submitted to the scrutiny of the Privy Council, and that body included men, such as Ito Miyoji and Hiranuma Kiichiro, who were hostile to the Kenseikai. On 17 April the Council rejected the ordinance on the ground that it was unconstitutional because the urgency of the situation was not sufficient to prevent the recall of the Diet. This was an unexpected blow, but it need not necessarily have been fatal. The Privy Council was only an advisory body, and it was open to Wakatsuki to request the Emperor to issue the ordinance regardless. Some commentators argued that this would have been in keeping with the 'normal course of constitutional government' (*kensei jodo*), and even so conservative a cabinet member as Army Minister Ugaki favoured this course. Despite this advice, however, Wakatsuki submitted his cabinet's resignation straight away. Ironically, within three weeks a special Diet session had approved the contentious emergency relief measures.

The Wakatsuki cabinet's exit was an inglorious one, but it was not out of character. Although some party members would have been prepared to fight to stay in power, the Kenseikai leadership mostly consisted of ex-bureaucrats whose chief priorities tended to be the maintenance of political, economic and social stability. Significantly, its main achievement – the partial reform of the tax system so as to reduce the burden on poorer peasants – was partly designed to counter the attraction of extreme radicalism, and was matched by the introduction of youth training centres which gave a prominent place both to moral education and military drill.

Formation of the Minseito and the 1928 election

If the Wakatsuki cabinet's ambivalence about the onset of the era of mass politics harked back to the apprehensive attitude of the Hara cabinet, its successor adopted an approach more reminiscent of the Meiji oligarchs. This was not entirely surprising since the new Prime Minister, Tanaka Giichi, had been one of Yamagata's protégés. If his administration was to be more than an interim one, however, it had to increase its representation in the Lower House of the Diet, for in April 1927 it held no more than 166 seats and on 1 June its relative position was further weakened when all but a score of Seiyuhonto members joined with the Kenseikai to form the Rikken Minseito (Constitutional People's Government Party) under the leadership of Hamaguchi. The new party's programme indicated a greater awareness of the needs of the new era of mass political participation. In particular it emphasised the establishment of 'Diet-centred politics' and the relevance of the general will of the people, as well as recognising the importance of social justice and problems of economic livelihood.

By the time the next Diet session opened, on 27 December, the Seiyukai had increased its strength to 190 Lower House members, but this would not have been enough to prevent the passage of a no-confidence motion. A general election, the first to be held under the new electoral system, was thus held on 20 February 1928. For those who had hoped that the establishment of universal male suffrage would eradicate abuses it was a disappointment. Certainly the parties took the campaign for votes seriously: about 79,000 public meetings were held (an average of eighty-four per candidate), over 72,000 signboards were erected, roughly 35 million posters were put up, and as many as 150 million letters or leaflets (because house-visiting was prohibited) were reported to have been delivered to electors. The Seiyukai alone sent out approximately 1,000 campaign speakers, mostly armed with film of Prime Minister Tanaka. It is alleged that students, priests and even hucksters were specially recruited for this purpose. Despite all this activity, however, the proportion of electors who actually voted dropped from 88.9 per cent to 78.7 per cent. Moreover, according to a Justice Ministry report, vote-buying continued to be more effective than open campaigning. It was hardly surprising, therefore, that the new proletarian parties secured no more than eight seats in this unequal struggle. Nor was it unexpected that Home Minister Suzuki Kisaburo used his control of the prefectural governors to make the contest an uneven one. Any reference to Tanaka's alleged misuse of secret army funds, for instance, was banned; and the number of arrests of Minseito and proletarian campaigners (1701 and 3001 respectively) was hugely disproportionate to that of Seiyukai activists (164).

Despite all its advantages as the party in power, however, the Seiyukai failed to gain an overall majority, securing only 217 seats to the Minseito's 216. Indeed, the latter, with the same number of candidates, gained a slightly larger proportion of the total vote.

Significantly, it received support from many of the urban political societies and it scored a convincing victory over the government party in the major urban areas. With backing from some independents and small groups in the Diet the Minseito was able to pass a motion of censure on Suzuki on 3 May and force his removal from office.

The repressive policies and political difficulties of the Tanaka cabinet

Suzuki's ousting had little effect on the policy of repression which as Home Minister he had intensified with the arrest of almost 1,600 suspected communists (nearly 500 of whom were prosecuted in due course) on 15 March 1928. These arrests had then been used to justify the introduction in late April of a bill to strengthen the Peace Preservation Law by increasing the maximum sentence to death and rendered not just members of subversive organisations, but also sympathisers, liable to prosecution. The revision was exceptional in that it stemmed from a cabinet decision rather than originating in the bureaucracy, and even some Justice Ministry officials apparently argued that it went too far. It met with fierce criticism from the Minseito and other parties, and the sudden termination of the Diet session on 7 May was largely due to the prospect of a government defeat on this issue. Hypocritically disregarding its own criticism of Wakatsuki's recent attempt to settle the banking crisis by bypassing the Diet, however, the Seiyukai leadership now sought to revise the law by imperial ordinance. Such clearly unconstitutional and illiberal action provoked criticism from the press, from lawyers, from academics, and even from Seiyukai Diet members (who had not been consulted at any stage). All was in vain, however. Justice Minister Hara Yoshimichi, ex-Justice Minister Ogawa and the new Home Minister, Mochizuki Keisuke, all threatened to resign if the government drew back, and after a brief delay the bill was submitted on 12 June to the Privy Council. Even in this reactionary body objections were raised, and the proposal was only approved on 29 June.

To become a permanent law an ordinance had to be confirmed by the Diet at its next session. That seemed far from certain in June 1928. Not only did the Minseito appear resolute in its condemnation, but Seiyukai solidarity had been strained further by the

Prime Minister's controversial appointment of Kuhara Fusanosuke, a wealthy businessman but a political newcomer, as Communications Minister. Moreover the government was in difficulty on other fronts. In the Tokyo city assembly elections in June the Seiyukai lost its long-time dominance to the Minseito; while in foreign affairs a dangerous attack was launched by the Minseito on the government in July for signing the Kellogg-Briand treaty – not because of its renunciation of war as a means of solving international disputes but because, according to its preamble, this was done in the name of the respective peoples of the contracting powers. Disingenuous though the accusation that the government was contravening the principle of imperial sovereignty may have been, it caused severe embarrassment to Tanaka, and he had difficulty in securing the Privy Council's agreement to the treaty.

At this low ebb in its fortunes the government appeared to receive a reprieve when on 1 August Tokonami announced his departure from the Minseito. He was accompanied by twenty-eight of his old supporters and although they did not join the Seiyukai for another year, it was plain that their defection would have a decisive effect on the political arithmetic of the next Diet session. As far as the Peace Preservation Law revision was concerned, this proved to be so. Indeed, the Seiyukai eventually secured a majority of seventy-nine for it in the Lower House. Even so, Japanese politics had not developed to the stage where control of the elected chamber meant everything, and apart from the Peace Preservation Law revision only one legislative measure was to be enacted during the 56th Diet session.

The reason for this extraordinary outcome was not that the session was abruptly terminated – unlike many others it ran for the allotted ninety days – but that the Upper House turned against the cabinet. Why it did so to such an extent is not easy to explain. Ostensibly the reason was Tanaka's failure to answer the charge of using the Emperor's authority improperly in trying to prevent a minister from resigning after the previous Diet session. Behind this, it seems, lay resentment at Tanaka's lack of consideration shown to the Upper Chamber when he formed his cabinet. There may even have been a feeling that the Seiyukai had gone too far in its efforts to preserve its power: not only had its personnel changes in the Home Ministry been unprecedentedly far-reaching but in 1929 it had introduced a new electoral bill which smacked strongly of gerrymandering. Instead of the three-, four- or five-member constituencies which had been established by the coalition government in 1925, the Tanaka cabinet now put forward a scheme of one-, two- or three-member electoral districts which, as in Hara's 1919 revision, were designed to favour the Seiyukai. But whatever chance of acceptance this proposal may have had was made irrelevant when Tanaka became the victim of an unexpected turn of events as the result of which his continuation as Prime Minister was impossible.

Ironically, in view of Tanaka's military background, what caused his downfall was his inability to assert his authority over the army. In June 1928 the Manchurian warlord, Chang Tso-lin, was killed when his train was blown up, and it was suspected that the assassination had been carried out by officers of the Japanese Kwantung Army. Because of government censorship the Japanese press could for the most part only hint at this; and although the Minseito criticised the government at the 56th Diet session, it too was cautious. Nevertheless, Tanaka, conscious of Saionji's concern about the effect of the episode on Japan's international reputation and about the breakdown of army discipline, pledged to the Emperor in December that if Japanese officers were responsible, as seemed likely, they would be dealt with severely. This pledge proved impossible to keep. Although army leaders were well aware of the truth, they were adamantly opposed to admitting it in public and they refused to hold the court martial which Tanaka demanded. A decade earlier such intransigence might have been overcome, but the Choshu clique, of which Tanaka was the last major representative, no longer held unchallenged sway within the army. Faced with a solid front of opposition the Prime Minister finally abandoned the struggle and reported to the Emperor on 27 June 1929 that Japanese officers had not been guilty of the assassination after all.

The young Emperor's response was unexpected. Instead of acknowledging Tanaka's statement he tersely observed that it differed from what he had said in December and abruptly terminated the audience. Since he accepted without comment a similar report from Army Minister Shirakawa, the Emperor's unusual behaviour (which may have been influenced by Saionji) seems to have been prompted not just by the failure to maintain proper military discipline but also by a strong sense of personal dissatisfaction with a Prime Minister who had palpably misjudged the situation and was now attempting to conceal his failure to fulfil his commitment. Tanaka was deeply shocked and either decided to resign there and then, or, according to another version of these events, agreed to his cabinet's recommendation that he seek a second audience but then gave up when he was led to understand by the Grand Chamberlain, Admiral Suzuki Kantaro, that the Emperor had no wish to see him again.

Tanaka's discrediting, together with the Seiyukai's general unpopularity, made it inevitable that Saionji would now recommend Hamaguchi as the next Prime Minister. Like Wakatsuki, Hamaguchi hailed from Tosa and had been a Finance Minister bureaucrat, but unlike him he was strong-willed and decisive, as was shown by the fact that he assembled a cabinet within eight hours of his receiving the imperial command on 2 July 1929. The most surprising appointment was that of Inoue Junnosuke to the key position of Finance Minister, since Inoue had been associated with Takahashi Korekiyo and the Seiyukai and had recently expressed doubts about the wisdom of an early return to the gold standard, to which the Minseito was committed. Despite this background, however, he was to prove an extraordinarily loyal executor of the same fiscal policy for which Hamaguchi had struggled earlier as Finance Minister in the Kato cabinet: even when the catastrophic consequences of a rigid adherence to deflation and retrenchment had become all too apparent, he did not waver in his determination to see it through.

Financial retrenchment and the Naval Limitations controversy

A return to the gold standard was only one of the policies which the Minseito proclaimed at the outset of the Hamaguchi administration. Indeed, the cabinet took pride in its unprecedentedly comprehensive programme. But it was the economy which was its central concern, for the trade balance had continued to be unfavourable throughout the 1920s and some sectors of industry had not flourished. There was a general feeling that the Japanese economy could only be put in order by returning to the gold standard as all other major capitalist countries had done by 1928. The problem with such a policy was that almost all Japanese assumed that the yen should be restored to its pre-war value of roughly 49

American cents or 2 English shillings, which meant undertaking rigorous fiscal retrenchment to raise the yen from its mid-1929 value of about 44 cents. Not only were painful cuts projected in government expenditure on railways, ports, roads and the telephone network but in October 1929 Inoue also attempted the exceptional measure of clawing back 10 per cent of the salaries of all government employees who were paid more than 1,200 yen a year. The resulting trial of strength was brief. Faced by solid bureaucratic opposition the cabinet backed down after exactly one week.

Despite this setback the yen did rise to the desired level by the end of 1929, and on 11 January 1930 Japan was finally able to return to the gold standard. Encouraged by its achievement, the Minseito went to the country on 20 February and won an emphatic victory. The outcome of the election was admittedly not unaffected by the use of methods which the party had itself previously condemned, for Home Minister Adachi had replaced twenty-eight pro-Seiyukai prefectural governors and also made 118 other changes. Nevertheless, part of the Minseito's majority of ninety-nine seats over the Seiyukai was attributable to the widespread feeling that the Hamaguchi cabinet had the answer to Japan's economic problems; and the turn-out both at campaign meetings and the polling booths showed that this was an election which was concerned with real issues and which had raised political consciousness. It may well be, too, that the government's campaign to persuade people to buy Japanese rather than foreign goods had helped to identify the Minseito advocacy of economic self-discipline with patriotism.

The confidence which came from being in tune with national feeling was to last throughout 1930 and was to sustain Hamaguchi in his forthcoming struggle to ratify the London Naval Treaty, the most significant constitutional battle since 1913. In order to limit naval expenditure and maintain the relatively harmonious relations which had been established with the United States and Britain, the cabinet agreed to participate in a conference in London to consider the extension of the Washington Naval Limitations Treaty of 1922. If the two premier naval powers had accepted a less unequal 10:10:7 ratio for heavy cruisers than that set earlier for battleships and carriers, there would have been no difficulty in securing the Japanese navy's agreement to a treaty. But American naval thinking insisted that to have a good chance of defeating the

Japanese navy in a war in the western Pacific a 10:6 superiority was necessary. After the conference had reached a 'deadlock, a compromise was devised in March 1930 which in terms of its practical effect (but not its superficial appearance) came very close to the Japanese position; and with somewhat uncertain backing from the Navy Minister, and chief naval delegate, Admiral Takarabe, its acceptance was recommended by the leader of the Japanese delegation, Wakatsuki.

The fact that the proposed new treaty did not formally embody a 10:10:7 ratio was seized upon by those elements within the Japanese navy (usually known as the 'fleet faction') who had been unhappy even about the Washington treaty; and the Chief of Naval Staff, Admiral Kato Kanji, sought on 1 April to torpedo the agreement by taking advantage of his right of access to the throne to appeal directly to the Emperor before Hamaguchi could report the cabinet's decision to sign the treaty. Kato's attempt was frustrated, however, by Grand Chamberlain Suzuki Kantaro (who happened to be Kato's predecessor as Chief of Staff as well a a supporter of the opposing 'treaty faction'). Whether Suzuki brought direct pressure to bear or whether he merely used the pretext that the Emperor's schedule was too crowded to see Kato is unclear; the first version seems more likely, for when Kato did secure an audience on the following day, he apparently confined himself to the statement that the navy would make do with the treaty, difficult though this would be. By then, however, Hamaguchi had secured the Emperor's approval for it.

The outmanoeuvring of the fleet faction was far from the end of the matter. Indeed, the postponement of Kato's audience was itself to provide a focus for allegations that the supposedly non-political court officials had interfered improperly in political affairs on the cabinet's behalf. There were other grounds for criticism of the government, though, and the Seiyukai made the most of them during the brief special Diet session between 23 April and 14 May. Not only did it allege that the retreat from Japan's original naval demands jeopardised national defence, it also claimed that the size of the navy was the responsibility of the Chief of Naval Staff (who advised the Emperor on operational matters) rather than of the Navy Minister (whose province was naval administration). The fact that Hamaguchi had assumed the function of the Navy Minister during Takarabe's absence in London only gave added weight to the accusation that the right of supreme command had been violated. Although the Minseito's position in the Diet was strong enough to withstand the Seiyukai attack, the cabinet faced a more serious threat from the Privy Council. Hamaguchi was made of sterner stuff than Wakatsuki, however, and with the support of Saionji on the one hand and the leading newspapers on the other, he eventually won through in early October after more than three months' manoeuvring and persuasion.

Hamaguchi had won a major victory, but it was far from decisive. He had had to be careful not to claim that the cabinet had the sole right to decide the nation's military strength, and he also found it expedient to agree to a naval replenishment plan which absorbed 370 million yen out of the projected saving of 580 million. Moreover, some of his supporters within the navy were discredited in the eyes of their fellow officers. Both the Minister and the Vice Minister chose to resign in 1930 and other members of the treaty faction were to be purged in 1933. The most important casualty of the Minseito triumph, however, was Hamaguchi himself. On 14 November 1930 he was shot by a fanatical ultranationalist at Tokyo station, suffering wounds from which he was to die the following August.

Hamaguchi's removal was almost as much a turning-point for the Minseito as Hara's had been for the Seiyukai. He himself had enjoyed virtually unchallenged authority over the party, but there were divisions within it which came to the fore when the question of his replacement arose. An immediate decision was avoided by the cabinet's agreement that Foreign Minister Shidehara would act as Prime Minister for the time being; but the leadership, albeit temporary, of a party cabinet by a career bureaucrat who was not a party member was criticised, notably by such non-bureaucratic supporters of Home Minister Adachi as Nakano Seigo and Nagai Ryutaro. The resentment felt by the 'party faction' at the dominance of the 'bureaucratic faction' was accentuated by the timidity of the government in the 1930-1 Diet session, when it displayed little enthusiasm for reform. Feelings did not improve when the unmistakable deterioration in Hamaguchi's health compelled the Minseito, in April 1931, to select a proper successor. Instead of entrusting the choice to election by all its Diet members, as its constitution prescribed, those members of the cabinet who belonged to the party united to recommend Wakatsuki, a decision which then received the confirmation of the party executive committee and the approval of Hamaguchi. Adachi abandoned his own candidacy and his supporters' protest movement collapsed. A legacy of bitterness and disillusionment remained, however, which was to play its part in the collapse of the new Wakatsuki cabinet before the year was out.

The Depression and failures of the Minseito cabinet

Even if Hamaguchi had recovered from his wounds the prospects for the Minseito would not have been bright. Although it was not yet fully apparent by the end of 1930, it is clear in retrospect that the government's financial and economic policies were doomed to failure. No more unpropitious a time could have been chosen to return to the old orthodoxy. As the American Depression spread to other countries, trade declined and world prices plummeted. The result was a massive slump in Japanese exports and a dramatic surge in unemployment. Distress was widespread, notably among school-leavers and graduates. Unemployment among the latter, whose numbers had increased sharply since the war, rose to well over 50 per cent, leading to much agonised comment in the press and the entry into popular usage of the term '*interi-lumpen*' (intelligentsia-lumpen proletariat). No less grave was the plight of the farming villages, which were severely affected by the decline in the price of rice and raw silk. The situation was particularly bad in the Tohoku region in 1931, when local weather conditions led to a 20 per cent fall in crop. While no other areas suffered to quite the same extent, the fact that, according to one survey, 211,990 of the 569,432 factory workers who lost their jobs in 1930 (283,951 out of 657,114 in 1931) returned to their home village, meant that the agricultural sector everywhere shouldered a disproportionate amount of the burden of depression.

The economic crisis was bound to undermine confidence in the Minseito, but it has been argued that the damage to its political standing would have been less if it had been as steadfast in its commitment to social and political reform as it was obstinate in its adherence to an unrealistic gold standard. The cabinet's position on workers' organisation, in particular, has been seen as crucial. Having in December 1929 accepted the need to legalise trade unions, it met with concerted opposition behind the scenes from the *zaibatsu*-dominated Japan Industrial Club and other business organisations, and by the time a bill was eventually submitted to the Diet in February 1931 its provisions were so watered down that the Tokyo *Asahi* newspaper called it a 'veritable labour union control law'. Even then it was talked out in the House of Peers. The sharp contrast between the cabinet's lukewarm attitude on this issue and its tough line on strikes and the propagation of radical leftist ideas was only too obvious.

The fate of the labour union bill was matched by the outcome of the government's attempts to expand political rights. In January 1930 it set up, at Adachi's instigation, a Lower House election reform study commission, with members drawn from both sides and both chambers, but although it adopted the commission's proposal to extend the franchise to all males aged 20 or over, the resulting bill did not even get beyond a Lower House committee. A parallel proposal, stimulated by the vigorous campaign for female suffrage, to allow women aged at least twenty-five the vote in city, town and village assembly elections and remove the ban on female membership of political parties or societies, did get through the Lower House but failed to overcome the conservatism of the Peers.

Whether a strong commitment to social reform would have saved the Minseito cabinet from its disastrous collapse in late 1931 must be questionable. Even if this had won broader popular support without alienating some of the other interests which the Minseito represented, it would still probably have been insufficient to counteract the effects of its other policies. In particular it is doubtful whether it could have sustained the cabinet against challenge from the army, which was bitterly critical of the apparent encouragement given to rampant Chinese nationalism by Foreign Minister Shidehara's conciliatory approach towards China and strongly resentful of the cabinet's insistence on further military cuts. The resignation in April 1931 of the relatively flexible Army Minister, Ugaki Kazushige, made a serious clash even more likely.

Military subversion and the Mukden Incident

Other factors also contributed to the growing military-civil tension. There was a tendency for low-paid officers steeped in patriotism and *bushido*-style ethics to condemn the corruption of politicians and the affluence of businessmen who financed them;

one group of officers even thanked the proletarian writer Hosoda Tamiki, when they encountered him in Tokyo, for 'revealing the truth about the evils of capitalism to the Japanese masses and peasants' in a novel which the Tokyo *Asahi* serialised during the first half of 1930.[6] Such social consciousness was only one aspect of the increasing politicisation of the army. Even more ominous was the formation of societies such as the Futabakai, the Mumeikai and the Issekikai. These were composed mainly of colonels and majors who had graduated from the Military Academy between 1907 and 1916. They were originally concerned with internal army reform (primarily the ending of Choshu dominance) but their discussions soon encompassed foreign policy too. Partly as a result of contacts with civilian ultranationalists such as Kita Ikki, Okawa Shumei and Yasuoka Masaatsu, some of them came to contemplate the possibility of engineering a political crisis which would end the era of party cabinets.

Despite their shared desire for both a strong line in Manchuria and a different political system in Japan, army officers were by no means agreed on which aim should have priority. Some, such as Colonel Itagaki Seishiro and Lieutenant-Colonel Ishiwara Kanji, who from 1928 served together on the Kwantung Army staff, advocated the staging of a dramatic incident in Manchuria which would unleash national feeling and make it easy to sweep away constitutional liberalism. Others argued that the overthrow of party cabinets in Tokyo must come first. One protagonist of the latter view was Lieutenant-Colonel Hashimoto Kingoro, a specialist on Russia in the General Staff Intelligence Division who in September 1930 formed the Sakurakai (Cherry Society). This had about 100 members, mainly middle-level officers in the Army Ministry and the General Staff. With backing from this group, Hashimoto proceeded to plan a *coup d'état* in early 1931. His scheme involved the staging (with the assistance of Okawa Shumei and the national socialists, Akamatsu Katsumaro and Kamei Kanichiro) of a mass demonstration outside the Diet, accompanied by bomb explosions at the Prime Minister's residence and both the Minseito and the Seiyukai headquarters. The army would then force the cabinet to resign on the grounds that it did not have the trust of the nation, following which Saionji would be induced to have Ugaki chosen as head of a cabinet dedicated to the renovation of Japan.

The 'March Plot' failed to reach fruition. Although Hashimoto had the support of Vice-Chief of Staff Ninomiya, Intelligence Division Chief Tatekawa and Military Affairs Bureau Chief Koiso, his ideas were regarded as ill-conceived by key members of the Futabakai, notably Lieutenant-Colonel Suzuki Teiichi and Colonels Okamura and Nagata. Whatever chance the plot had was ended when General Ugaki ordered its termination. However, the abandonment of this clandestine conspiracy did not mean that friction between the army and the cabinet diminished. On the contrary, a series of incidents in Manchuria increasingly aroused military feeling during 1931, and army officers did not hesitate to stimulate public indignation by supplying newspaper reporters (whom Foreign Ministry officials held at arm's length) with slanted information and accusations. Shidehara was soon forced to adopt a tougher line towards the Chinese, but his change of tack was too little and too late for Ishiwara, Itagaki and other ranking staff officers of the Kwantung Army, and in the summer of 1931 they decided to establish full Japanese control over Manchuria.

The Kwantung Army officers' scheme was far more audacious than army headquarters in Tokyo were yet prepared to contemplate, but they nevertheless succeeded in securing private assurances of support or sympathy from many of the key division, bureau or section chiefs. It was impossible, however, to prevent rumours of the impending action from being picked up by reporters and in early September they reached the Emperor's ears. His warning to the Army and Navy Ministers that discipline must be maintained resulted in the despatch of a high-ranking officer to Manchuria to prevent any untoward incident. The mission was sabotaged, however, firstly by a series of telegrams which Hashimoto sent urging the conspirators to act before it was too late, and secondly by the choice as emissary of one of the men whom Ishiwara and Itagaki had won over, Major-General Tatekawa. Instead of preventing an unauthorised military initiative, therefore, his mission precipitated the small, but momentous, explosion on the South Manchurian Railway just outside Mukden which was blamed on the Chinese and which served as the pretext for the Kwantung Army to implement its emergency plan of operations.

The overpowering wave of nationalist feeling which was unleashed as the Mukden Incident grew into the Manchuria Incident was to render hopeless the League of Nations's attempts to insist on compliance with the rules of international behaviour laid down in its Covenant. Some historians have argued, however, that if the Minseito cabinet had stood firm, the escalation of the incident could have been prevented. In particular, it is claimed that the government should have brought the military to heel by persisting in its original refusal to approve retrospectively the sending of re-inforcements by the Japanese military commander in Korea, which had taken place without the Emperor's permission. Significantly, even though there was a danger that Army Minister Minami might bring down the cabinet by resigning, some cabinet ministers, including Shidehara, were indeed prepared to stand firm; and their position was strengthened on 20 September when an attempt by Chief of Staff Kanaya to bypass the cabinet and secure direct im-perial approval for the troop reinforcements was blocked by the prevarication of the Minister of the Imperial Household, Ichiki Kitokuro. Prime Minister Wakatsuki, however, was anxious to avoid a confrontation, and two days later the cabinet reluctantly approved the Korean Army's action by agreeing to make financial provision for it.

Whether this surrender was crucial is not easy to judge. It is important to note, however, that it was not completely one-sided. In return Minami and Kanaya had to pledge that they would en-force the official policy of avoiding any expansion of the fighting while Shidehara sought a diplomatic settlement through bilateral negotiations with China. That this compromise was not seen with favour by the army is indicated by the fact that a new plot to over-throw the government was hatched by Lieutenant-Colonel Hashimoto. This 'October Plot' (which like the March one was aborted when superior officers learned of it) was supposedly aimed at the assassination of the whole cabinet and the installation of a renovation government, this time under the strongly nationalistic General Araki Sadao. It has been suggested that the plan was not genuine but an elaborate pretence masterminded by the General Staff, the true purpose of which was not the establishment of an Araki cabinet but the intimidation of the Wakatsuki cabinet.[7] The evidence for this argument is mainly circumstantial, however, and it seems unlikely to supplant the established view that Hashimoto's

[7] Fujimura Michio, 'Coup d'état to shite Manshu Jihen' in Miyake Masaki *et al.* (eds), *Showa Shi no Gunbu to Seiji*, vol. 1 pp. 81-118.

scheme foundered primarily because of the existence of basic differences of political approach (intertwined with personal and factional rivalries) within army headquarters.

The collapse of the second Wakatsuki cabinet

Although the 'October Plot' was an ominous warning to Minseito ministers, the collapse of the Wakatsuki cabinet less than two months later can be more clearly attributed to two other factors. One was the decision of Great Britain, soon followed by various other countries, to go off the gold standard on 21 September. What had previously been a slow drain of specie out of Japan now became a flood as banks decided to sell yen for dollars in antici-pation of the devaluation which their own actions made even more certain. Sooner or later the government would have had to admit that the policy on which its whole strategy had been based had lost its credibility. As if this were not enough, the Wakatsuki cabinet was being undermined from within by the Adachi faction, which had never supported its financial and foreign policies wholeheartedly. In late October Adachi met Wakatsuki to discuss the government's difficulties, and the idea of a coalition with the Seiyukai was suggested as a way of overcoming them. Whose suggestion it initially was is unclear, but it is not disputed that Wakatsuki asked Adachi to sound out the Seiyukai. When Shide-hara and Inoue heard of this, however, they objected forcefully that partnership with the Seiyukai would mean the abandonment of the policies to which they had dedicated themselves; and with Saionji sceptical too, Wakatsuki instructed Adachi not to pursue the idea.

This Adachi was not willing to do. He had received a favourable response from Kuhara Fusanosuke, Tokonami Takejiro and a number of other Seiyukai leaders (though not Inukai or Suzuki) and his supporters were aware that a coalition might provide him with the opportunity to re-assert his claim to leadership of the Minseito. It could be argued, moreover, that at a time of national crisis the political parties' interests would be best served by the formation of a cabinet of national unity (following the example of the national government in Britain), and this position was put forward in a document drawn up in December by Kuhara and Adachi's Minseito ally, Tomita Kojiro. When it was presented to

Wakatsuki on 10 December, however, the Prime Minister did not deign to read it, and other cabinet ministers pressed Adachi either to abandon the idea or resign. Instead the frustrated Home Minister chose a third course: he refused to attend the cabinet meeting on the following day. Faced with an unprecedented 'strike' by a key member, the rest of the cabinet decided to resign *en bloc*.

The Inukai cabinet and the May 15th Incident

Its replacement was speedily decided. Saionji did briefly consider the reconstitution of a Minseito administration without Adachi, and the idea of a broad-based cabinet of national cooperation – with Ugaki as Prime Minister, though, rather than a politician – was mooted by the Lord Keeper of the Privy Seal, Makino; but it was important to avoid complications and stabilise the situation, and Saionji scarcely hesitated before following the 'normal course of constitutional government' and nominating Inukai Tsuyoshi, the Seiyukai president. Unusually for a party leader of this era, Inukai was a genuine, even idealistic, politician of non-bureaucratic background; and his selection as Tanaka Giichi's successor by the Seiyukai in 1929 had only occurred because of a deadlock (and extreme mutual antipathy) between the more powerful contenders for the leadership, Suzuki Kisaburo and Tokonami Takejiro .

As a compromise third choice Inukai clearly lacked political clout. Nevertheless, his standing received a boost from the Seiyukai's sweeping victory in the general election of February 1932, when it won 303 seats against the Minseito's 146. Moreover, his choice of Takahashi Korekiyo as Finance Minister meant that Japan was very quickly set on the road to economic recovery. Takahashi's first action was to reimpose the embargo on the export of gold, and he then proceeded to reverse his predecessor's other policies, casting economic orthodoxy to the winds. By encouraging demand and allowing the exchange rate to depreciate by almost 50 per cent, he paved the way for a rapid revival of exports, a mushrooming of new companies, and a very sharp rise in gross national product. The full success of Takahashi's policies was, admittedly, far from apparent in early 1932, but had the Inukai government survived it would have received the credit for steering Japan out of depression.

Inukai might also have hoped to avoid a major conflict with the army. In recent years the Seiyukai had adopted a more nationalistic, pro-military stance and of the two generals (usually there was only one) who were nominated as suitable candidates for Army Minister by the 'big three' (the outgoing Minister, the Chief of Staff and the Inspector-General of Military Education) Inukai opted for the hawkish Araki Sadao rather than Ugaki's associate, Abe Nobuyuki. This meant that he went some way towards satisfying some of the renovationist officers. Moreover, at Araki's insistence the restraints on the Kwantung Army were removed. Within a few months of the changeover from a Minseito to a Seiyukai government the whole of Manchuria was under Japanese control and the new, purportedly autonomous, state of Manchukuo had been set up.

Despite these concessions to military and nationalist feeling, Inukai still tried to maintain a balance between moderation and extremism. Although he was prepared to accept Manchukuo as a *fait accompli*, he did not intend to challenge the tenets of the post-war international order by giving the new state formal recognition, and he hoped to utilise his old contacts with Chinese nationalists to negotiate an agreement with the Nanking government. He is also said to have considered requesting the aid of the Emperor in order to assert control over the army. Whether Inukai could have held the line against the more extreme nationalists is doubtful, but before his leadership could be fully put to the test he had fallen victim on 15 May to yet another assassination plot.

Inukai's murder was the third successful attempt on the life of a public figure in the first half of 1932. On 9 February Inoue Junnosuke had been shot and on 5 March Dan Takuma, the chief executive of Mitsui, was similarly killed. Both assassinations were carried out by members of Inoue Nissho's Ketsumeidan (Blood Brotherhood), a group composed mainly of idealistic students who had been inspired by the fervent conviction of their leader that he could be the agent of Japan's renewal. Inoue was a highly orthodox Buddhist priest who during the 1920s had come to realise, as he later put it, that 'Japan, unlike other countries, was a state which had developed basing its national structure (*kokutai*) on cosmic law' and that to return it to the true course from which it had deviated he should lead 'a movement for destruction and reconstruction'. He saw his ultimate aim as being 'to reconstruct the world by the implementation of the principle of absolute equality.'[8] Inspired by his sense of mission he had drawn up a list of various Establishment figures whose elimination he considered imperative, but before anyone else could be attacked he and his civilian followers were arrested. His influence was not wholly extinguished, however. The motley assortment of radical young navy officers, army cadets and young peasants belonging to Tachibana Kosaburo's Aikyojuku (Land Loving Academy) who carried out the May 15th Incident had all been connected with Inoue.

The May 15th Incident marked the end of an era. No cabinet after Inukai's was to be headed by a party politician again until 1946. This was not, however, clearly foreseen in 1932 and it would be a mistake to assume that Saionji was as yet prepared to write off political parties. It is sometimes suggested that he no longer had any real choice because of the army's objection to party cabinets but it is doubtful whether it was really this which led the *genro* to bypass party politicians when deciding upon the next Prime Minister. The existence of factional divisions within the army meant that a new party cabinet could probably have secured an Army Minister from among generals associated with Ugaki, if Araki had refused to continue in office. More important, arguably, was the absence of any politician whom Saionji could consider a suitable candidate. No Minseito leader could be considered because of the party's recent crushing defeat, while the Seiyukai was riven by factionalism. Even though, in the aftermath of Inukai's murder, the latter temporarily achieved unanimity in the choice of Suzuki Kisaburo as its next leader, it seemed unlikely that he would remain unchallenged; and in any case his advocacy of direct imperial rule and his other reactionary attitudes had aroused Saionji's deep distrust. The *genro* chose, therefore, to act as he had after the collapse of the Takahashi cabinet ten years earlier, and once again it was a moderate and widely respected admiral – this time Saito Makoto – who was drafted as an interim leader. It is significant that the Emperor had, exceptionally, made known to Saionji his opposition to anyone who was 'close to fascism' (by which he has been assumed to have been vetoing Suzuki and Hiranuma Kiichiro), and it is noteworthy, too, that

[8] Inoue Nissho, *Ume no Mi*, cited by Hashikawa Bunzo, 'Showa Ishin no Ronri to Shinri', in Hashikawa Bunzo and Matsumoto Sannosuke (eds), *Kindai Nihon Seiji Shiso Shi*, vol. 2, p.224.

the *genro* consulted ex-Prime Ministers Wakatsuki, Kiyoura and Yamamoto, as well as Field Marshal Uehara, Admiral of the Fleet Togo and Lord Keeper of the Privy Seal Makino, before reaching his decision. Saionji found a consensus for Saito and a national unity cabinet, but not for a 'transcendental' one which sought to disregard political parties. Rather it was hoped that Saito would be able to secure bi-partisan support. This hope was not disappointed: the new cabinet included four men who were associated with the Seiyukai and two from the Minseito. Only three of the thirteen cabinet ministers, however, were members of the Lower House.

The weaknesses of political parties

While the eclipse of the parties was by no means total, it remains the case that except for a brief period in 1936-7 their fortunes steadily declined after 1932. Their fate was closely connected with the waning of Western influence as Japan's international position became isolated and military priorities became dominant, although it was not irrelevant that in the 1930s, unlike the preceding decade, international trends shifted towards totalitarianism and away from democracy and constitutionalism. To attribute the major setback experienced by Japanese political parties solely to international factors would be far too simple, however. As contemporary critics were quick to point out, the parties were open to attack on many counts. Bribery and corruption scandals had become more numerous as politicians acquired more power and influence, and although little was known for certain about the parties' relationships with business interests, it was widely believed that the Seiyukai was dependent on Mitsui and the Minseito on Mitsubishi. It would be unduly simple, however, to identify either party as the instrument of one particular *zaibatsu*, for both received money from a variety of sources; moreover, the Seiyukai had a considerable number of Diet members who were employed by or connected with Mitsubishi, and there were Mitsui men in the Minseito as well as the Seiyukai. One writer, while recognising the importance of financial contributions from the major *zaibatsu*, has argued that these were not made in return for specific favours (unlike some gifts from individual businessmen) but were based on historic ties; and he compares them with the backing by fans of baseball teams.[9] A closer analogy might be with the patronage of *kabuki* actors, for funding rarely, if ever, went to the party as such, and often not to the party leader, but rather to particular politicians with whom business leaders had personal ties. Such politicians, like the wealthy businessmen who entered politics directly, were in a position to earn the party president's gratitude or to build up their own influence by bestowing 'pocket-money' on less well-endowed Diet members. The support of thirty of these 'adopted sons' (*kanji*) was said to be enough to become a minister. Even if this was an exaggeration, there can be no doubt that the provision of financial largesse opened the way to membership of the party directorate (*kambu*), and this gave the *zaibatsu* some indirect control over the parties.

In some, although not all, cases, financial considerations played a vital part in deciding who should be party president. Kato Komei's long tenure as leader of the Kenseikai, for instance, owed a great deal to his links with Mitsubishi; while Tanaka Giichi's swift transformation from retired general to Seiyukai president was mainly due to the party directorate's anticipation that he would bring with him a 'dowry' of five million yen as a result of his connections with the Mitsui and Yasuda *zaibatsu*. These expectations apparently proved unduly optimistic, but Tanaka appears to have made up for the initial disappointment at the time of the 1928 general election, for it was claimed by an informed commentator that he had drummed up as much as 8,000,000 yen, and allegations of corruption and misappropriation of secret army funds were rife.

It was, in fact, elections which made the parties so dependent on outside funding. Regular expenses amounted to no more than 200,000 yen a year normally (much more, even so, than the income received from party dues), but from 1915, especially, election expenses increasingly dwarfed routine organisational costs. Few, if any, candidates for the Diet from the major parties remained within the legal spending limits, and by the early Showa period outlays from 20,000 to 80,000 yen were said to be normal. The many hundreds of arrests, usually for vote-buying, made by the specially assigned detachments of the local police attest to this widespread lubrication of the election machinery. Diet candidates themselves were rarely caught red-handed, however, for the money

[9] Masumi Junnosuke, *Nihon Seito Shiron*, vol. 5, p. 232. Most of the following details about party finances, structure and organisation are taken from this source.

quickly passed down from their election officers, via friendly prefectural or city assembly members, to town, village and ward assembly members or to other local men of influence (*yuryokusha*) who acted as election 'brokers'. This vote-securing network, in which a Diet politician's *jiban* (political base) was built on the *jiban* of lower-level politicians and local notables, was not solely dependent on money – the primary concern of most politicians' supporters after all was to secure adequate representation of their local interests, and it would be rare for them to turn to an outsider or newcomer, however wealthy he might be – but without the ability to offer financial inducements the prospects of electoral success would normally be slight. Although a few members could run their campaigns from their own independent means or with the help of local backers (together with the subsidy of about 10,000 yen which party headquarters provided for officially recognised candidates), an increasing number became dependent on a particular leader for aid. In this way party factions grew up which were based less on regional associations, as in the past, and more on financial manipulation; and since the largest providers of money were assumed to be the *zaibatsu*, the parties could easily be accused of pandering to the interests of their paymasters.

This accusation could not easily be dismissed. The postponement of the implementation of factory legislation and the dropping, by more than one party cabinet, of plans to legalise trade unions was clearly due to pressure from large employers, while the relatively unrestricted rice imports of the 1920s (long after the danger of renewed rice riots had ended) favoured business and industry at the expense of agricultural producers by helping to keep the cost of living, and thus wages, low. On the other hand, there did exist differences between the main parties, notably over fiscal policy, which cannot be convincingly explained in terms of the parties' links with business interests. Moreover, while the growth of indirect dependence on *zaibatsu* funding by many Diet members contributed to the tilting of the balance within the parties towards the centre and away from the regions, it can hardly be said that either party turned a deaf ear to the continual demands for expenditure on local development projects, at least until the Minseito cabinet attempted its drastic retrenchment policy in 1929-31. If the Kenseikai was more inclined than the Seiyukai to put financial orthodoxy first and less willing to accommodate requests for regional development, this can better be explained by its greater electoral dependence on urban areas and by the larger number of ex-Finance Ministry bureaucrats among its leaders than by any *zaibatsu* influence. Nevertheless, public opinion did associate the parties with the *zaibatsu*, and when the latter were condemned, whether from the left or the radical right, for their ruthless pursuit of economic rationalisation or for their apparent lack of concern for the national interest in selling yen in 1931, some of the opprobrium was inevitably transferred to the established parties. It is significant that 1930 saw the formation in Tokyo, Osaka, Nagoya and Yokohama of a number of new, albeit short-lived, parties, the names of which suggest that their membership was centred on small businessmen who were dissatisfied with the existing political set-up.

Other parallel developments similarly tended to distance the parties from their grass roots. At the level of Diet membership the proportion of party representatives who had previously served as metropolitan or prefectural assembly members had declined to less than one-half by the late 1920s, as against almost three-quarters in the 1890s. The reduction was related to the fall in the number of landlords, who accounted for only 15 per cent of Lower House members in 1930 compared with almost 50 per cent in 1890. By contrast lawyers, newspapermen, doctors and teachers had together risen to 29 per cent in 1930. Bureaucrats and military officers were beginning to make an impression too, although they were still very much in a minority in 1930. The proportion of members whose principal occupation was in business or industry was about one-quarter in 1930 (less than in 1917), although over half had business connections.

These changes in the composition of the parliamentary parties during the 1920s were not dramatic but they did reflect a continuing trend towards centralisation. That trend was also evident at the higher levels of the parties. Under the presidencies of Inukai and Wakatsuki only 15 per cent of the members of the party directorates had prefectural assembly backgrounds, and on average no more than one ex-prefectural assembly man found a place in the last five party cabinets. By contrast, two-thirds of the ministers during that period were ex-bureaucrats. Nor did the established parties go much beyond slogans in seeking to gain support from the urban and rural proletariats. According to one scholar, 'the party branches, being clubs of local Diet representatives and pre-fectural or metropolitan assembly men, possessed no interest at all in the reform of branch organisation or the expansion of branch activity. Even after the universal suffrage law came into effect, the branches remained just as they had been. Their efforts were mainly directed towards colluding with the prefectural governor to carry out metropolitan or prefectural government for party benefit'.[10]

This emphasis on gaining electoral support by manipulating the distribution of central and local government expenditures, rather than by attempting to build up a large membership which identified with party policies and attitudes, meant that both the Seiyukai and, to a lesser extent, the Minseito lacked really solid foundations. If events at the centre were to lead to the discontin-uation of party cabinets, their strategy would be disrupted, for prefectural governors would not be under the same pressure to comply with party demands. When this actually happened in 1932, it was, ironically, accompanied by sharp increases in relief expen-diture as the Saito cabinet sought to respond to the unprecedented depression. Such a display of positive administration helped to produce rural recovery and inevitably overshadowed the benefits which parties had offered. Moreover, the latter's local position was also being undermined by social changes. By the end of the 1920s the increasing attraction of the urban areas and the growth of tenant unrest had led both to the departure from the villages of many of the wealthier landlord families and to the gradual emer-gence of a new leadership in the shape of the so-called *yakushoku meiboka* – men drawn largely from the owner-cultivator middle stratum who became village heads, local assembly men or directors of producers' cooperatives by virtue of their ability, not their family's traditional reputation. This new village leadership, it has been asserted, was happy with any system, even bureaucratic or military control, which provided it with government aid. Mean-while, in the urban areas the old élites of shop-owners, small businessmen, labour contractors and other quasi-paternalistic 'bosses' (*oyakata*) were losing their dominance as the growing influx of peasants led to the establishment of new *jiban*. If the esta-blished parties had adapted in the 1920s by actively cultivating

[10] *Ibid.*, p. 309.

the up-and-coming men of influence, they might have been better placed to respond to adversity in the 1930s. When the Minseito did eventually launch a recruiting drive in 1936, it was too late to make any difference.

A similar pattern of conservative élitism was visible at the highest level of party leadership. Although by the 1920s ordinary Diet members could express their views in various party committees, only the Policy Affairs Research Council had much influence on party policy, and its chairman, like that of all committees, was normally appointed by the party president. Essentially both parties continued to be run in an oligarchic manner, with the executive council (Somu-in), and even the larger consultative council (Hyogi-in), being generally nominated by the party president or selected in advance by the party directorate. The annual party conference usually lasted only two days a year and rubber-stamped whatever the leadership put to it. In such circumstances it would have been surprising if the non-bureaucratic career politicians and ex-journalists in the Diet had not felt some frustration, and this certainly played some part in the damaging alienation from the Minseito of the Adachi faction.

It is sometimes suggested that the failure of the parties to develop into more democratic organisations with mass support was due to their being pushed into a defensive reaction by the rise of the Left. This view tends to obscure the fact that there was actually a great deal of political debate in the 1920s and early '30s about how to improve the people's livelihood and raise the level of education and political consciousness. Moreover, although party cabinets repressed extreme radicalism harshly, the moderate left was treated far less severely. Most politicians, in any case, had little reason to be alarmed by the electoral performance of the proletarian parties; with only a handful of left-wing candidates winning seats in the 1928, 1930 and 1932 elections, Diet members' *jiban* were in general far more threatened by their traditional rivals than by this new opposition.

A more plausible explanation of why the parties were seen less and less as the spearhead of a broad popular movement is that they gained access to real political power. Indeed, since at least the turn of the century, long before left-wing ideas had made any real impact, the parties had been moving away from a stance of pure opposition as more and greater concessions were made to them by the oligarchs. By incorporating bureaucrats and business-men into their ranks they increased their respectability and made themselves more eligible for the role – which the Meiji oligarchs had formerly played – of coordinating the various sectional inter-ests within government. Some have seen this as the process whereby a manipulative Establishment adjusted to changed circumstances and transformed the parties into defenders of the existing social and economic order. Such an interpretation, however, is open to the criticism that other élites were actually reluctant to concede power to the parties, and in the early 1930s there was still much resentment among them of the parties' advance. The latter's new position therefore remained precarious. If party government had worked well in practice, the 'normal course of constitutional government' might indeed have been consolidated despite the constitutional weakness of the parties and their lack of committed grass-roots support. If their policies failed, however, then their new role could be challenged, for none of their institutional rivals, and certainly not the military or the bureaucracy, had been deci-sively subordinated to their control.

'Taisho Democracy' and the new social movements

The collapse of the Inukai cabinet is often taken to mark the end of the period of 'Taisho Democracy'. Not all historians find this term meaningful, however, and even those who do accept it differ considerably in their emphases. Some stress the generally progre-ssive character of the age, as well as the strength of American and European influence, and regard the major parties, for all their faults, as part of the movement towards a more democratic system, even in the late 1920s. Many other historians, however, identify Taisho Democracy almost exclusively with the new popular movements and emancipatory forces which developed after the Russo-Japanese War and flourished immediately after the First World War. This period, rather than the later 1920s, is seen by them as the high point of Taisho Democracy, for although some of the new organisations went on expanding, the possibility of a political and social transformation faded as extreme radicalism was effectively suppressed and even the moderate elements were driven onto the defensive.

However one relates it to the question of Taisho Democracy,

there can be no doubt that the containment of the new social movements was an extremely significant feature of Japanese political development in the 1920s. At the beginning of the post-war period the growth of a new political consciousness had been remarkable and, for the conservative Establishment, ominous. Most notable had been the sudden explosion of strikes and the rapid growth of labour union membership, but on a smaller scale this was parallelled by the emergence in 1922 of the Suiheisha (Levelling Society), which sought equality for the hundreds of thousands of *burakumin* (virtual outcastes) who mostly lived in ghettos around Osaka, Kyoto and Tokyo and continued to suffer from social discrimination despite having been granted legal equality in 1871. Women too were beginning to express dissatisfaction with their inferior status, and in 1920 the New Women's Association (Shin Fujin Kyokai) was formed with the object of securing female suffrage as a means of improving their position. Although this organisation collapsed in 1922, it was followed in 1924 by the League for the Achievement of Female Suffrage (Fujin Sansei-ken Kakutoku Kisei Domeikai), and numerous smaller groups with similar aims proliferated throughout Japan during the later 1920s, including several with a proletarian character. Nor was the new mood confined to the cities and towns. Whereas before the First World War the number of disputes between tenants and landlords rarely exceeded thirty, by 1918 it had rocketed to 256, and, after another sharp jump from 408 in 1920 to 1608 in 1921, it continued to rise steadily until 1926 when a peak (for the 1920s) of 2713 was reached. Most of the early disputes occurred around Osaka, Hyogo and Kyoto, where absentee landlordism was more prevalent and the change from war boom to post-war recession was more acutely felt. The increased militancy of tenants was both reflected in and stimulated by the appearance of tenant unions. By 1921 there were 681, and by 1922, when the first nation-wide federation, the Japan Peasants Union (Nihon Nomin Kumiai), was founded, their number had leaped to 1114. Their growth was maintained until 1927, when they reached their peak of 4,582 (with a membership of 365,331).

Despite these impressive advances the Left always suffered from a lack of solidarity. Quite apart from the inevitable difficulties of cooperation between the urban and rural proletariats, the union movement was bedevilled by rivalries among individual labour bosses, as well as by suspicion of outsiders and by the persistence of localism (which particularly impeded collaboration between unions in the Tokyo-Yokohama area and those based on the Osaka-Kobe-Kyoto region). As a result no labour union except the Japan Seamen's Union included all the workers in a single industry, and there was no general federation which included all, or even most, labour unions. Unions were also extremely heterogeneous in character. Many were confined to a single enterprise (*kigyobetsu kumiai*), and a considerable number were '*goyo-kumiai*', company unions which had been set up by management itself to prevent the intrusion of external labour organisers and were scarcely more independent than works councils.

Company unions were only one means by which management defused the threat of labour militancy. In large concerns, particularly, there was a widespread adoption of techniques which have since become a noted characteristic of the Japanese industrial relations system. Some of these, such as special allowances for workers' dependants, had originally been introduced to cope with the problem of rapid wartime inflation, while others, including additional payments based on length of service, were devised to give skilled workers an incentive to stay with the company which had trained them. In the 1920s such practices began to be combined with other benefits, such as the provision of housing and welfare facilities, relatively high wages, regular bonuses, and a virtual guarantee of employment if conduct was satisfactory, to produce a workforce which had much to lose from engaging in strikes, especially as most large modern companies also employed non-established or seasonal workers of lower status who could easily take the place of regular workers. Moreover, large companies also adopted more selective recruitment policies, hiring mainly youths with good educational records from middle-level farm households. The emergence of such a new industrial relations system meant that workers in large factories played little part in any of the union federations, and their lack of involvement deprived the labour movement of what theoretically ought to have been its spearhead.

Even if the modern sector of Japanese capitalism had adapted less successfully to post-war conditions, the proletarian movement would still have faced daunting obstacles. Police pressure and right-wing strike-breaking made life difficult for unions even after the partial repeal of the Peace Police Law in 1925. The traditional ethos of Japanese society, too, with its emphasis on harmony and hierarchy, hardly provided an encouraging environment for organisations which by their very nature were bound to stress the idea of different class interests. In the countryside, emphasis on conflict was particularly inhibited by the custom, still strong in the less developed areas, of depending upon landlords for assistance in hard times; and although the sense of village community had been somewhat eroded by absentee landlordism, there was during the depression caused by the steady decline of agricultural prices in the 1920s evidence of a recrudescence of the *Nohonshugi* (agrarianism) ideal of mutual cooperation and self-help both in the advocacy by some writers and local leaders of *'isson ikka'* (one village acting as one family) and in the doubling of the membership of village cooperatives. Moreover, whereas after 1927 tenant unions became numerically weaker, conciliation unions, which included both landlords and tenants, continued to grow. By 1929 they had more than 200,000 members, and by 1936 they had surpassed tenant unions in total membership. For all the unfairness of the tenancy system, the continuing need for village solidarity was not conducive to radicalism. It was also significant that, although almost half of the arable land was under tenancy, the number of peasants who were tenants pure and simple was smaller than the number of those who owned at least some of the land they cultivated (1,486,133 as against 2,370,544 in 1930).

In such circumstances it is not surprising that the proletarian movement was plagued by ideological disunity and organisational problems. Apart from the differences of interest between labour and tenant unions, there was a fundamental cleavage between, on the one hand, those who acknowledged the limitations imposed by Japanese socio-political conditions and were ready to be satisfied with gradual improvements in their position and, on the other, those who thought there was, or might soon be, a real possibility of revolutionary change. The former camp was dominated by labour bosses such as Matsuoka Komakichi and Nishio Suehiro, together with the founder of the Yuaikai, Suzuki Bunji. The latter camp contained a number of socialists such as Sakai Toshihiko, Yamakawa Hitoshi, Arahata Kanson and Katayama Sen, and anarchists like Osugi Sakae, who had been influenced by Kotoku Shusui in the late Meiji period, but also many younger intellectuals and students, including most of the politically active members of the Shinjinkai. Some of them had their consciousness stimulated and their enthusiasm kindled by the Russian Revolution, but others were more attracted by anarcho-syndicalist ideas of direct action by the workers and played down the need for a political movement. It was not until 1922, when the post-war depression had forced labour unions onto the defensive, seeking to maintain jobs rather than improve wages and hours, that the anarcho-syndicalists lost out to the 'Bolshevik' elements on the radical fringe of the labour movement.

The reverse suffered by the anarcho-syndicalists marked the end of a chapter but it by no means concluded the basic struggle for domination of the main federation, Sodomei. Although pragmatic labour bosses had gained control in most areas, their influence was frequently challenged by more radical elements, especially in the Kanto region. In May 1925 this struggle was resolved when the prospect of universal male suffrage and the possibility of establishing a proletarian political party persuaded the 'realistic socialists' to expel those communist-led unions whose presence might expose the mainstream of the proletarian movement to the danger of official suppression. The price of respectability proved to be a high one, however. The expelled unions immediately combined to form a leftist federation, the Nihon Rodo Kumiai Hyogikai (Council of Japanese Labour Unions). With an initial membership of 10,7778 workers in thirty-two unions, Hyogikai was not much weaker than Sodomei, and for three years it was to constitute a significant additional barrier to labour unity.

Notwithstanding this internecine conflict unionisation gradually increased throughout the 1920s. By 1931 7.9 per cent of the total industrial work-force had joined the 818 unions then in existence. The onset of the Depression saw a sharp rise in the level of industrial action, with strikes increasing from 329 in 1928 to 490 in 1929 and jumping to 761 in 1930 (when the number of workers involved was highest at 64,374) before reaching a peak of 853 in 1931. Sabotage and slow-down action also became more common, as did lockouts. It should be noted, however, that the number of strikers never surpassed the figure for 1918; that most strikers did not belong to unions; and that labour had returned to the defensive, fighting to maintain wages and preserve employment rather than extend the concessions that had previously been secured.

The moderate union leaders were also on the defensive politically. Although Hyogikai was suppressed by the Tanaka government in April 1928, Sodomei was soon threatened on its other flank. Some of the unions which had been sponsored by management or used in strike-breaking increased their membership and began to form nationalistic labour federations such as the Buso Rodo Renmei (Chivalrous Labour League) in 1929, and the Nihon Sangyo Rodo Kurabu (Japan Industrial Labour Club) in 1933. By 1936 the main right-wing labour front could claim 134,000 members. Faced with this substantial new challenge, the moderate right and centre of the labour movement finally managed to overcome the differences which had impeded their cooperation hitherto. In June 1931 they established the Nihon Rodo Kurabu (Japan Labour Club), a loose confederation of fourteen labour organisations, of which Sodomei was the most prominent. By September 1932, when it was renamed Nihon Rodo Kumiai Kaigi (Congress of Japanese Labour Unions), the confederation had increased its membership from 224,000 to 280,000.

Left-wing political parties

The early history of Japanese proletarian parties parallelled that of labour unions and generally reflected the latter's organisational disunity. After a premature initial attempt in 1921, the extreme left was quick to establish the Nihon Kyosanto (Japanese Communist Party) in July 1922, and much of the ensuing political debate and controversy within the proletarian camp revolved around the questions of whether and how to accommodate, control, isolate or eliminate this significant minority. The problem was complicated by fluctuations in communist policy, inevitable in a new and illicit organisation with highly committed and individualistic members, but exacerbated by differences of interest between the Kyosanto and the Comintern and differing interpretations of Japan's actual stage of historical development. In the 1920s many Japanese communists were tempted to assume that a bourgeois revolution had already occurred in Japan and that the way was therefore clear for the pursuit of a socialist revolution. As expounded by Yamakawa Hitoshi and Inomata Tsunao in the magazine *Rono* (Workers and Peasants), such an analysis had the considerable attraction that the focus of attack could be on monopoly capitalism and the established political parties, both of which could be criticised with less risk than the Emperor, the military and the other 'feudalistic' élites. From the Comintern viewpoint, however, this Ronoha position was less attractive than the opposing Kozaha (Lectures Faction) approach, since it diverted the leftist attack away from the army (the institution which most threatened the Soviet Union's Far Eastern position) towards the more pacific and internationalist elements. These fundamental differences of approach were never fully reconciled. Even when the Comintern accepted in 1927 that there existed in Japan 'the objective prerequisites for the rapid transformation of the bourgeois revolution into a socialist revolution', it added the important qualification that 'the ideological backwardness of Japan ... is a great impediment and stumbling block'.[11]

There were also disagreements among the communists over the correct revolutionary tactics. The Comintern generally emphasised the need to infiltrate workers' and peasants' organisations, undermine the social democratic elements and establish control over a legal party of the Left, but it also insisted on the maintenance of a communist party. In February 1924, however, after the first Kyosanto had been weakened by the arrest of many of its leaders in June 1923, the party decided to dissolve itself in line with the argument of Yamakawa Hitoshi that a communist party was premature and communists should concentrate on developing mass organisations and on forming a united front of workers and peasants. When in December 1926 the Kyosanto was re-formed after pressure from Moscow (but without Yamakawa, Arahata and other Ronoha members) the Comintern found that it had to contend with another deviation, since under the slogan 'unity through separation' the party's new intellectual leader, Fukumoto Kazuo, not without opposition, switched the emphasis to the creation of an ideologically pure revolutionary vanguard, thus jeopardising the supposed chance of securing leadership of the mass organisations of the centre and extreme left. Fukumoto-ism smacked too much of Trotskyism for Stalin and Bukharin, however, and in mid-1927 Fukumoto and his supporters were replaced in the top Kyosanto positions by more acceptable leaders.

The greater ideological unity which the Kyosanto enjoyed after mid-1927 proved of little practical value, for its activities were severely attenuated as a result of the mass round-ups of extreme

[11] See G.M.Beckmann and G.Okubo, *The Japanese Communist Party, 1922-1945*, p. 121.

leftists by the Tanaka government on 15 March 1928 and 16 April 1929. Although a fragmentary party organisation was kept in being, the Kyosanto ceased to be much more than a bogey to the authorities, and in 1933 the well-publicised renunciation both of international communism and of opposition to the Emperor-system by two imprisoned communist leaders, Sano Manabu and Nabeyama Sadachika, marked the retreat of the radical Left in the face of rampant nationalism. By this time communist literary figures had also been silenced, and only a few theorists who had developed the art of veiled criticism remained cautiously active.

The other sections of the Left were slower to form political parties even though they, unlike the communists, could hope to secure legal acceptance. In December 1923 a Seiji Mondai Kenkyukai (Society for the Study of Political Problems) was set up with broad leftist support to prepare the way for a proletarian party, but in 1925, after it had become dominated by communist or pro-communist elements, it was abandoned by the moderates. Following the introduction of full adult male suffrage, Kagawa Toyohiko and Sugiyama Motojiro, the leaders of the main pea-sants' federation, the Nihon Nomin Kumiai, attempted to bring into existence an all-embracing socialist party, but their effort was frustrated by Sodomei's objection to the participation of pro-communist organisations. When the party – the Nomin Rodoto (Peasant-Labour Party) – was formed on 1 December 1925 it in-evitably had a more radical complexion than had originally been envisaged and was instantly banned by the government.

The Nihon Nomin Kumiai leaders now tried a different tactic. They first reached agreement with Sodomei to form the Rodo Nominto (Labour Peasant Party) with Sugiyama as chairman and social democratic policies, but soon after its establishment on 5 March 1926 they sought to broaden it by accepting extreme Left involvement on an individual basis. Again, however, Sodomei leaders chose to opt out rather than cooperate with pro-commu-nists. As a result the Rodo Nominto soon passed into the control of Hyogikai and Seiji Mondai Kenkyukai. In response Sodomei leaders on 5 December set up their own party, the Shakai Minshuto (Social Masses Party), with the backing of Yoshino Sakuzo, Abe Iso (who became its first chairman) and other noted intellectuals. The Shakai Minshuto was to some extent modelled on the British Labour Party, and aimed at securing support from small shopkeepers and white-collar groups as well as manual workers, but its potential strength was limited by the fact that it did not embrace all the non-communist elements of the proletarian movement. Already in October 1926 the agrarian leaders, Hirano Rikizo, had set up the Nihon Nominto (Japanese Peasants Party), and on 9 December a Sodomei faction leader, Aso Hisashi (an ex-student of Yoshino Sakuzo), deserted the Shakai Minshuto to form the Nihon Ronoto (Japan Labour-Peasant Party). Feeling that Sodomei had become obsessed with the communist threat and too ready to cooperate with capitalism, he hoped that the Nihon Ronoto would help the other parties to come together in a united socialist front. In practice, however, the formation of a new labour federation, the Nihon Rodo Kumiai Domei (League of Japanese Labour Unions), from among Aso's unionist supporters helped to ensure that factional fragmentation was further institutionalised within the proletarian camp.

It was unlikely that the proletarian movement could make a sudden electoral breakthrough after 1925 for it had to contend with the *jiban* and the local loyalties built up by established politicians, but its prospects were further hampered by the fact that in some areas candidates from different proletarian parties competed against each other. In the 1927 prefectural elections, only twenty-eight out of 216 proletarian candidates were successful; while in the 1928 general election a mere eight were elected, all from major conurbations or industrial areas (Osaka, Kyoto, Fukuoka, Tokyo and Hyogo), and the eighty-eight proletarian candidates secured just 5 per cent of the total vote. The 1930 results were no more impressive. Even with ten more candidates the left-wing parties did not increase their proportion of the total vote and their number of seats actually dropped to five. Part of the explanation may lie in the popularity of the Minseito government, but the centre and extreme Left may also have suffered from the confusing realignments which occurred after the banning in 1928 of the Rodo Nominto. The latter was eventually replaced in November 1929 by the Ronoto – the normal abbreviation of the Shin Rodo Nominto (New Labour-Peasant Party) – but support was lost particularly from the peasant movement, and in the meantime, in December 1928, some of its ex-members had merged with the Nihon Ronoto to form the Nihon Taishuto (Japan Masses Party).

Following the 1930 election the proletarian party movement

continued to change in a kaleidoscopic manner, with the Nihon Taishuto combining with the small centrist Zenkoku Taishuto (Nationwide Masses Party) in July 1930 and then merging with both the Ronoto (which had lost or jettisoned some of its pro-communist members) and a splinter group from the Shakai Minshuto to form the Zenkoku Rono Taishuto (Nationwide Labour Masses Party) in July 1931. While this amalgamation brought together most of the extreme and centre Left and some moderates, however, the party was soon weakened by the expulsion of Kato Kanju and some other militant centrists who had come to share, to some extent, the communist perception of the social democrats and moderate unions as 'social fascists' and had consequently opposed the Nihon Rodo Kurabu which had been established in June 1931. Their concern was not ungrounded, for elements within the proletarian movement were significantly shifting their political stance in 1931. Both Akamatsu Katsumaro and Kamei Kanichiro were accomplices in the military coup planned by Hashimoto Kingoro in March, and after the outbreak of the Manchurian Incident Akamatsu, who had already moved from communism to advocacy of 'realistic socialism' in the spirit of 'scientific Japanism', came out openly in favour of Japanese expansion. In collusion with Shimonaka Yasaburo, Okawa Shumei and other ultranationalists, he embarked in 1932 upon a campaign to convert the Shakai Minshuto to national socialism. His efforts were aided by the dismal experience of the 1932 general election, when only thirty-five candidates were put forward, only 287,853 votes gained, and three (out of five) seats were won by nationalistic socialists. In April Akamatsu's proposal for a new party founded on reverence for the *kokutai* and the rejection of internationalism only just failed to secure acceptance by the Central Executive Committee of the Shakai Minshuto. He then broke with the party and proceeded to form the Nihon Kokka Shakaito (Japan State Socialist Party).

Akamatsu's challenge, the shock of the election results, and the movement towards cooperation by the main labour federations all contributed to overcome the obstacles which since 1926 had stood in the way of a broadly-based proletarian party. In contrast with an abortive attempt in 1930, the proposed merger between the Shakai Minshuto and the Zenkoku Rono Taishuto now resulted in the formation on 24 July 1932 of a new party – the Shakai

Taishuto (Social Masses Party) – with Abe Iso as Chairman and Aso Hisashi as Secretary-General. To consider this achievement of a broad measure of unity as a real advance, however, would be misleading, for by 1932 the proletarian movement was almost wholly on the defensive. Labour union hopes of achieving improvements in their position through political means were fading, and the tendency for them to confine themselves to 'sound unionism' was growing. Increasingly they were withdrawing from the pursuit of socialism, moving away from internationalism, and abandoning their criticism of Japanese imperialism. The peasant movement had suffered an even greater setback. Although the number of disputes with landlords rose steadily in the early 1930s, their scale was much smaller than before, for they no longer originated predominantly in concerted campaigns by tenants to reduce rents but in desperate resistance to attempts by hard-pressed small landlords to reclaim the right of cultivation. When the pressure for national unity intensified following the outbreak of the Manchurian Incident, there was a real danger that proletarian organisations might lose even the limited acceptance they had secured. Having been in the vanguard of 'Taisho Democracy', they were by 1932 effectively in retreat.

6

THE PURSUIT OF GREATER NATIONAL
UNITY AND THE WAR STATE, 1932-45

By 1932 both liberal ideas and socialist hopes had received setbacks from which they were not to recover until after 1945, and nationalism had reasserted itself as the dominant force. Much of its revived strength was due to the peculiar combination of increased insecurity and inflated pride, as Japan simultaneously defied the League of Nations over Manchuria and displayed its military prowess. Even so, the real threat to Japan from outside was not that much more considerable than before, and its international isolation was far from total. To appreciate why nationalism became so pervasive and virulent in Japan – to such an extent that historians customarily refer to it as ultranationalism – it is necessary to take other factors into account.

The upsurge of fundamentalist nationalism

One of those factors was undoubtedly the widespread feeling that modernisation along Western lines had been a mistake, or at least had been carried out indiscriminately. As the bureaucratic and academic compilers of the *Kokutai no Hongi* (Basic Principles of the National Structure), the bible of official nationalism, put it in 1937:

The various ideological and social evils of present-day Japan are the result of ignoring the fundamental and running after the trivial, of lack of judgement, and a failure to digest things thoroughly; and this is due to the fact that since the days of Meiji so many aspects of European and American culture, systems and learning have been imported, and that, too rapidly.[1]

At a more popular level there was criticism of those manifestations of Western influence, such as new styles of dress, cafés and dance halls, which could be regarded as causes of the moral decline implied by the common characterisation of the era as one of 'ero,

[1] *Kokutai no Hongi*, p. 52.

guro, nansensu' (eroticism, grotesquerie and nonsense). Not all the moralisers of the early 1930s were fundamentally anti-Western or anti-modern, but the unprecedented depth of the economic crisis and the apparent bankruptcy of the approaches advocated in the previous decade meant that many Japanese turned to older national traditions for ways out of the *hijoji* (time of abnormality). Influenced, perhaps, by the Minseito's repeated claim that the causes of the crisis were international, but unwilling to accept that nothing could be done, they called for a Showa Ishin (Showa Renovation) which, like the Meiji Ishin, would renew Japan and rescue the country from its difficulties. For some the desire to recreate the past took on an even more atavistic form: Gondo Seikyo, the leading Nohonshugi ideologue, attracted support with his appeal for a return to an ancient, supposedly uncorrupted, age of self-governing rural communities. Only a few were as extreme as this, but even thoughtful intellectuals began to use the phrase '*kindai no kokufu*' (overcoming modernity).

The upsurge of anti-Westernism and anti-modernism goes a long way towards explaining why eighty-seven nationalist societies were formed in 1931 and 196 in 1932 (compared with one in 1920, sixteen in 1925, and forty in 1930), and why the number in existence rose from 330 in 1932 to 988 in 1940, with membership increasing from 306,857 to 587,128 during the same period. One further contributory factor, however, also needs to be mentioned. During the previous decade Japan had undergone considerable social and intellectual change and was now much closer to becoming a modern mass society (albeit one which was still traditional in important respects). Among the causes of change was undoubtedly the propagation of democratic, liberal and socialist ideas by politicians – the more frequent use of words such as *kaizo* (reconstruction), in particular, made people less fatalistic than they would have been in the past – but developments in the media and everyday life were also important. Far more Japanese were proceeding beyond the minimum level of compulsory education and becoming acquainted with contemporary problems through books, magazines and newspapers. Aided by fierce competition and price reductions, for instance, the *Osaka Mainichi* newspaper increased its circulation to well over one million copies a day by 1924, while in 1927 the publishers of the radical journal *Kaizo* initiated a policy of producing cheap books in popular editions. The opportunities for tapping the potential new mass readership were best seized, however, by the founder of the Kodansha publishing company, Noma Seiji, whose outstanding success – a magazine entitled *King* – was so well attuned to popular taste that by 1927, within two years of its launch, its sales had reached the million mark. Significantly, it included regular historical serials of a kind likely to foster national pride.

The growth of mass culture helped to raise political consciousness and encourage the feeling that not just elites but the *kokumin* (the people at large) had the right to share in political decision-making. Up to 1930 it could have been expected that this would favour democratic trends, but the sensational manner in which much information was presented was not conducive to the attainment of a high general level of political understanding or discrimination; and when internationalism and constitutional government seemed to have failed Japan in the early 1930s, the tendency to seek refuge in simple alternatives without perceiving their dangers became evident. In particular, the naive belief that all would be well if there was total national unity gained almost complete sway. For some the conviction was grounded in a semimystic sense of Japan as a great extended *kyodotai* (community) which might almost be described as tribalistic nationalism. For others it was connected with the concept of the unique relationship between Emperor and people, as expressed in catchphrases such as '*kunmin itchi*' (ruler and people as one) or '*tenno no kokumin, kokumin no tenno*' (the Emperor's people, the people's Emperor). Both approaches drew on the late Tokugawa view of Japan as *shinkoku* (the sacred country) and on the *kazoku kokka* (family state) myth which had been officially propagated in the Meiji period, neither of which had been allowed to disappear entirely from popular education, even in the 'liberal twenties'.

The result of the combination of anti-Westernism, anti-modernism, mass culture and popular indoctrination was a phenomenon which has since been seen in other Asian societies: a fundamentalist reaction against those elements which were perceived as obstructing national unity and undermining traditional values. In practice, however, total national unity was to prove elusive. Indeed, the nationalist movement itself displayed a remarkable degree of disunity. For various reasons, including ideological differences, personal rivalries, the strength of localism, and the Japanese preference for groups in which there is personal contact between leaders and followers, attempts at amalgamation met with extremely limited success. Some societies, admittedly, established themselves on a national scale: the Rikken Yoseikai (Society of the Cultivation of Constitutional Justice), which according to Home Ministry records was the largest at the end of 1935, had at that time 214,373 members in thirty-two prefectures, while the next biggest, the Showa Shinseikai (Showa Sacred Society), had 84,916 spread over all forty-seven prefectures. Nevertheless, most societies were small and local, and rather than consolidating into a mass organisation they continued to proliferate throughout the 1930s.

The divisions within Japanese ultranationalism

The great number and variety of different groups (most of which have never been studied) makes analysis of Japanese nationalism extremely difficult. Historians have tended to favour a dualistic division into *kokkashugi* (pro-Establishment statist nationalism) and *kokuminshugi* (anti-Establishment people-oriented nationalism), or alternatively, totalitarian (or renovationist) Right and idealist (or Japanist) Right. Both of these approaches have their merits, as has the division between nationalists who were mainly concerned with Japan's power and international position and those who were primarily anxious to preserve Japan's distinctive culture. From the viewpoint of political (as opposed to intellectual) history, however, a dualistic division is too simple, and it is necessary to acknowledge the existence of at least three broad camps.

Probably the most clear-cut position within the nationalist movement was held by those organisations which sought above all to return to Meiji values and restore the political system to what the Meiji oligarchs had intended it to be. Ranging from strongly conservative to outright reactionary in their attitudes, their membership included bureaucrats, senior military figures, capitalists and members of the House of Peers, the best-known of such organisations being the highly respectable Kokuhonsha (National Foundation Society), which Hiranuma Kiichiro founded in 1924. Hostility to democracy was always one of their distinguishing characteristics, although their opposition to party cabinets was effectively limited by their fear of creating political instability if they provoked a crisis. No such constraint restricted their attack on left-wing movements, which they saw as a threat not only to property but also to the myth that class conflict was alien to the Japanese *kokutai*. Similarly, their lack of sympathy for internationalism in foreign policy was overshadowed by their invincible hatred of the Soviet Union. The ideological edifice which they erected was buttressed by, if not founded upon, ideas drawn from Confucianism and Shinto, and it placed great weight on the unbroken imperial line, on the sovereign Emperor's embodiment of the traditional virtues, and on the necessity of absolute loyalty to the throne; ironically, the advocacy of direct imperial rule by some of their leading figures paid little heed to the current Emperor's own support for constitutionalism.

In sharp contrast to the reactionary or conservative brand of nationalism (except for a shared hostility towards communism and the existing political parties) stood the radical Right. Unlike their more traditionalist counterparts, the radical nationalist groups sought basic reconstruction (*kaizo*) of the existing political and economic system, and in some cases their aims would have merited their description as revolutionary. Indeed, their membership included a considerable number of ex-socialists, and like leftist organisations they came under the surveillance of the Home Ministry's special political police. They superficially resembled their reactionary counterparts in that many of them looked to the Japanese past for inspiration, but differed significantly in that they usually sought it in the Meiji Ishin. Moreover, instead of blaming Japan's contemporary predicament on the fact that the work of the Meiji oligarchs had been challenged from below, they believed that the wrong course had been taken earlier – in or soon after 1868 – when the introduction of Western methods and institutions had been used to establish and consolidate the power of a privileged minority. To them the sense of special community which was unique to Japan had been damaged by individualism, liberalism, materialism, competition, and gross economic inequality.

The radical wing of the nationalist movement embraced a very large number of organisations, not all of which had identical recipes for national salvation or even identical views of the Emperor and the state. There was a huge gulf between the peasant supporters of radical *Nohonshugi* (which itself encompassed a variety of positions but generally opposed industrialisation) and national socialists who derived support from right-wing labour unions. The vast majority of radical nationalists, including the young officer groups, fell somewhere in between these extremes, and can perhaps be most aptly, if imprecisely, described as advocates of a Showa Ishin in view of of the prominence of this concept in their thinking. Outside the established élites in most cases, and frequently influenced or inspired by unorthodox (or at least non-mainstream) religious or intellectual traditions such as Nichiren Buddhism (particularly in northern Japan) or the Oyomei school of Confucianism (which remained strong in Kyushu), their views were generally held intensely and expressed vituperatively. Their excoriation of the corruption of the privileged classes and the current holders of power was usually matched by a xenophobic approach to international relations; and as economic conditions within Japan improved, their attention tended to switch from internal reform to the eradication of Western influence in East Asia. All emphasised the aim of oneness between Emperor and people, although in some cases the invocation of the Emperor's name probably served an essentially amuletic purpose – that is, of warding off the danger of being treated as subversive Leftists. That may well have been true of the best-known ultranationalist – Kita Ikki – whose early socialist background carried over into his advocacy, in his book, *An Outline Plan for the Reorganization of Japan*, of radical change, including land reform, the elimination of the *zaibatsu*, and suspension of the constitution, together with the imposition of martial law. He frequently invoked the idea of a unique bond between the Japanese Emperor and people, but when in 1937 he was executed for his alleged complicity in an attempted military coup, he declined, at this final moment, to express reverence for the Emperor by shouting '*Tenno Heika Banzai*', instead calling this hallowed incantation a 'banal slogan'.[2]

Most active nationalists belonged to either the radical or the reactionary wings of the movement, but perhaps the most crucial role was played by a less ideological grouping of modernising, technocratic and fascistic nationalists. Like the radical reconstructionists they sought far-reaching reform, but not primarily out of a sense of injustice or indignation and usually not by assassination or *coups d'état*; like the reactionary nationalists they already had some degree of power and influence (or connections with those who did), but they were decidedly not supporters of the status quo, let

[2] See B.A.Shillony, *Revolt in Japan*, p.206.

alone of turning the clock back. They tended to be highly educated – having often studied abroad at some stage – and to be acutely
aware of contemporary world trends and developments. The desire
to catch up with and surpass the West was particularly strong in
some of them, and especially for the most dynamic and forceful
element – the mainly middle-ranking military officers associated
with the Tosei (Control) group – it seemed vital that military
technology be modernised, economic planning implemented, and
popular support mobilised in preparation for the new kind of
total warfare which Europe had already experienced between 1914
and 1918. In their pursuit of a new political and economic structure which would concentrate power and provide more effective
coordination of governmental functions they found allies among
'progressive' politicians who had broken with their parties and
younger 'revisionist' bureaucrats. In the late 1930s, moreover, the
attraction of what has sometimes been called 'military fascism'
drew some support away from the other wings of the nationalist
movement and even from the socialist Shakai Taishuto.

Not all of these groups, clearly, had exactly the same interests or
motives as the Tosei officers. Many bureaucrats, especially, were
probably more technocratic than nationalistic, and their pressure
for greater governmental centralisation and intervention was a
natural response to the turmoil and instability produced in the 1920s
and early '30s by an economic system which was largely beyond
their direct control. Nevertheless, those who sought reorganisation
from within the system were in general more modern in outlook
than other nationalists; and while they may have paid lip-service to
Japan's 'imperial way' or to the *kokutai*, they sought to achieve
national unity and efficiency not so much through dependence on
Japan's unique traditions and spiritual values as through the
strengthening of governmental machinery, the extension of
bureaucratic control and the elimination of constitutional and political restraints. In practice, they constituted the most totalitarian
element within the nationalist movement, and although very few
of them applied the label 'fascist' to themselves, it was from these
groups that the main impetus for alliance with Germany and Italy
was to come in the later 1930s.

The Saito cabinet

Lack of unity within the nationalist movement meant that, even if its general impact on the political atmosphere was great, it was unlikely to bring about a political revolution. A number of further plots to assassinate cabinet members were hatched during 1932 and 1933, but in each case the arrest of the plotters prevented their implementation. Meanwhile, with the blessing of Saionji and with differing degrees of support from the Seiyukai and the Minseito, the compromise Saito cabinet went some way towards fulfilling its mission of restoring stability. Urban unrest was reduced by a major expansion of public works schemes, and similar help was given to the villages by local governments. In 1933 a Rice Control Law extended the 1931 provision for government intervention in the market to prevent the price from falling below a fixed level. Even more important was the general revival of the economy which resulted from the devaluation of the yen, Takahashi's reflationary policy, declining interest rates, and the fuller utilisation of the production capacity which had been lying idle. Between 1931 and 1934 the number of companies in Japan leaped from 57,226 to 78,198 and the tide of unemployment receded at a faster rate than in other major countries. The Japanese spoke less often of *hijoji*, and the sense of crisis and foreboding which had been prevalent in 1930-1 gradually dissipated.

In the area of foreign policy, too, the Saito cabinet attuned itself to the popular mood by recognising Manchukuo as an 'independent' state in September 1932 and by terminating Japanese membership of the League of Nations in March 1933. Despite these gestures of defiance towards the international community, however, the cabinet was more interested in stabilising the international situation than embarking on new adventures. It withdrew Japanese troops from one part of north-east China after concluding the Tangku truce in May 1933, and it refused to allow itself to be pushed into a military confrontation with the Soviet Union, as some key military officers, including Army Minister Araki, wished. In a series of Five Minister (Prime, Foreign, Finance, Army and Navy) Conferences in October 1933, Foreign Minister Hirota Koki and Finance Minister Takahashi resisted Araki's demand for preparation for war with the Soviet Union by 1936, and with Saito's backing they confirmed that Japan's policy should emphasise the settlement of current problems by diplomatic means.

This rebuff for Araki was soon followed by another. In November and December a committee of eight ministers set up to coordinate internal policy was faced with a strong demand by Agriculture Minister Goto Fumio for increased expenditure on farming village relief measures. Goto was supported by Araki but firmly opposed by Takahashi and Railway Minister Mitsuchi, and the impasse was resolved only by re-allocating funds which had been committed to the army. While this concession did little to check the trend of steadily rising army expenditure, it further diminished Araki's standing with those headquarters staff officers who already felt that he was running too great a risk of provoking the Soviet Union into counter-measures by constantly dwelling on the idea of an imminent international crisis. Araki had already disappointed the younger officers who had idolised him before 1932 and had expected him to bring about a Showa Ishin when he became Army Minister. When in January 1934 he became ill with influenza, he used this as a pretext to resign, thus opening the way to an important shift of power within the army.

One other significant factor played a part in Araki's resignation – the renewal of criticism of the military by the political parties. Both Seiyukai and Minseito members objected to the size of budgetary allocations to the armed services proposed in late 1933, and they argued that it was hypocritical of the army to wax indignant about the plight of the peasantry while swallowing more national resources itself. Their attack prompted the issuing in December 1933 of a joint army-navy pronouncement which admonished the parties for trying to divide the military from the people. Instead of quelling political criticism, however, this warning stimulated it further. Meetings were held to promote cooperation between the two parties, and it seemed possible that the budget might be rejected by the Diet. With the resignation of Araki on 23 January, however, and the public acknowledgement both by his successor, the more cautious General Hayashi Senjuro, and by Navy Minister Osumi Mineo, that the military should not involve themselves in politics, the likelihood of a major confrontation diminished.

Whether the parties would have gone to the extreme of rejecting the budget is doubtful. Some government proposals had previously been frustrated by Seiyukai opposition, but such an outright challenge was a different matter. If Saito then chose to call a new election, the Seiyukai, no longer the party in office, might well lose its commanding majority. Even if it did not, the establishment of a Seiyukai cabinet could still be blocked by army or *genro* opposition. On the other hand, the Seiyukai's position and prospects would be considerably improved if the Seiyukai and Minseito could show themselves capable of combining to form a party-based 'cabinet of national unity'; and, harking back to the 1880s and the People's Rights movement, there was much talk of a new *Daido Danketsu*. In April 1934, however, this flurry of activity subsided, when Suzuki Kisaburo ordered that inter-party agreement must be limited to policy alone. His decision was not unconnected with his belated realisation that under the cloak of organisational cooperation the Kuhara and Tokonami factions intended to undermine his leadership of the Seiyukai by making an agreement with the Minseito to support another Prime Ministerial candidate. In effect Suzuki repudiated the efforts of the previous six months and compelled his party to pin its hopes on a resumption of the normal course of constitutional government when Saito decided that his task had been accomplished.

As it happened, the Saito administration was to last only one more month. The main reason for its demise was not difficulty with the army or the Diet but a series of scandals or embarrassments, the most important resulting from the accusation that several ministers had improperly profited from the irregular acquisition of shares in the Imperial Rayon Company. The cabinet's resignation, however, gave only brief satisfaction to its enemies, for it was replaced by one of a basically similar complexion, the most striking resemblance being that it too was headed by a moderate retired admiral – in this case Okada Keisuke. The method of his selection was not quite the same as that of his predecessor, though, for it resulted formally from a meeting of the *genro*, the Lord Keeper of the Privy Seal (Makino), the head of the Privy Council, and the surviving ex-Prime Ministers – a body to be known collectively as the *jushin* (senior retainers) which was intended by the eighty-five-year-old Saionji to take over his responsibility of recommending a suitable Prime Minister. In actuality, the *jushin* merely ratified the consensus which had already been established through the behind-the-scenes consultations conducted by Saionji's agent, Harada Kumao, and Makino's aide, Kido Koichi.

The Okada cabinet and the Minobe affair

The choice of Okada was partly determined by the concern of the Court moderates to have a statesmanlike admiral at the helm when the naval limitation treaties reached their term in 1936, but a still more crucial factor was that as a political neutral he could hope to preserve the balance which had been maintained for the past two years. There was, however, one significant difference between Okada's cabinet and Saito's which made the former's task harder: the Seiyukai (though not the Minseito) refused to allow any of its members to become ministers, and when Tokonami Takejiro and two of his faction members ignored this injunction, their names were removed from the party list. Moreover, the fact that yet another Prime Minister had not been drawn from the ranks of the Seiyukai, despite the latter's majority in the Diet Lower House, revived interest within the party in cooperation against the government, and in late 1934 there was some response from the Minseito when it was casually slighted by Okada over the summoning of a special Diet session. However, the new mood was again dispelled before long by the Suzuki faction – this time through a flagrant lack of consultation in the Diet – and when on 20 January 1935 Machida Chuji, a member of the Okada cabinet, succeeded Wakatsuki as Minseito president, the chance that the parties might combine again in a common cause was further weakened. It was finally extinguished when the Minseito agreed to participate in the Cabinet Deliberative Council (Naikaku Shingikai), a high-level body created in May 1935 to assist in the establishment and coordination of long-term government policy. In sharp contrast the Seiyukai expelled the two senior party members who had joined.

Continuing political frustration soon led the Seiyukai into a more insidious form of opposition. During the early 1930s the assault by extreme nationalists on the radical left had been extended to include well-known scholars whose words they considered subversive of the *kokutai*. At the forefront of the witch-hunting campaign was a lecturer named Minoda Muneki who had established a nationalistic society in 1925. His attack on Takikawa Yukitoki, a Kyoto University law professor, had led to the latter's dismissal in 1933, and to a much-publicised incident in which Education Minister Hatoyama Ichiro contemptuously rejected the law faculty's demand for his re-instatement. Minoda had also set his sights on Minobe Tatsukichi, the distinguished Tokyo University law professor, whose great offence was to have interpreted the Japanese constitution in line with modern German legal theory by locating sovereignty in the state rather than the Emperor (whom he regarded as its highest organ). Minobe's prestige was such that even when, in February 1935, the retired Major-Generals Eto Genkuro and Kikuchi Takeo took up the attack on him in the Lower House and House of Peers respectively, it seemed unlikely that their efforts would have much effect. By the summer the issue of 'clarification of the kokutai' had escalated into a major political controversy as other forces joined in the campaign, some with ulterior motives. Prominent among them was the Seiyukai.

The Seiyukai's involvement in the Minobe affair has customarily been condemned as a short-sighted decision which aided the forces of obscurantism and Emperor-centred extremism. At the time, however, the issue did not seem so clear-cut. In the first place Minobe himself had, since 1932, ceased to be an advocate of party cabinets. Instead he supported the idea of a cabinet of national unity and also proposed the establishment of a council (drawn from not only political parties but also the military, business and labour) which would advise on basic national policy and help to insulate it from the potentially disruptive effects of party rivalry and political fluctuation. Since he had also explicitly criticised the Seiyukai as well as publicly contesting its constitutional arguments on such issues as the Hamaguchi cabinet's right to sign the London Naval Treaty, it is not difficult to understand that party's willingness to attack Minobe. The campaign also had a further objective, however. By calling for official condemnation of a man who was not only one of the cabinet's principal intellectual supporters but could be regarded as a spokesman for the liberal-conservative wing of the Establishment, its promoters could hope to place Prime Minister Okada in a position where, unable to satisfy an inflamed public opinion, he would feel compelled to resign. This would be to the Seiyukai's advantage, for it would still be the majority party and could hope that its leader would be called on to form the next administration. If it tried to bring the cabinet down by rejecting the budget on the other hand, this might well result in an election, in which the government would be likely to favour the Minseito.

In seeking to profit from the surge of fundamentalist feeling which the issue of clarification of the *kokutai* stimulated, the Seiyukai was by no means alone. The reactionary supporters of Hiranuma, who had always asserted that sovereignty resided in the Emperor, were no less keen to do so, especially since Ichiki Kitokuro, who had been chosen as President of the Privy Council instead of Hiranuma in 1934, was himself closely associated with the 'Emperor-organ' theory. Within the army, too, Inspector-General of Military Education Mazaki Jinzaburo hoped that the cabinet would be brought down by public indignation and that General Araki would then be chosen as next Prime Minister (with Mazaki himself as Army Minister). While he rejected any open collusion with the Seiyukai, he did, in May, meet Kuhara Fusanosuke, one of the promoters of the party's campaign, and reach an understanding on the desirability of coordinating tactics. Mazaki had already issued a public declaration that Minobe's theory contravened the *kokutai*, and he may well have exerted more influence behind the scenes, in particular on the Imperial Reservist Association. The unprecedented involvement of that 3 million-strong organisation in petitions and rallies was one of the most striking – and for the Establishment one of the most alarming – features of the anti-Minobe movement.

This extraordinary popular ferment eventually achieved its aims, or at least those which its instigators declared. Many of Minobe's scholarly works were banned and a number of other professors who shared his views were suspended; while in October the cabinet was obliged to issue a denunciation of theories which held 'that the subject of sovereignty is not the Emperor but the State'. It is doubtful, however, whether either the Seiyukai or Mazaki gained any direct political advantage from the outcome. Although Okada had to give ground, the Emperor and his closest advisers had little sympathy with the cause of the cabinet's enemies. Indeed, one of the ironies of the affair was that the Emperor himself privately stated his own preference for Minobe's interpretation, adding that 'if there arise in the universities two contending theories ... is that not to be admired as a restraint on the despotic tendencies of the monarchical sovereignty theory?', and he expressed his irritation to his chief military aide by commenting: 'Is it not a great contradiction that the military should proceed to attack the organ theory in opposition to my views?'[3] In these

---

[3] Quoted by F.O.Miller, *Minobe Tatsukichi*, p. 236.

circumstances Okada did not feel obliged to resign and the cabinet even felt emboldened to mount a partial counter-attack; Mazaki was removed from his position as Inspector-General of Military Education, while the Seiyukai found that its activities came under particularly close official scrutiny in the prefectural elections which were held in late 1935.

Factional struggle in the army

Mazaki's ousting was not just the result of Establishment displeasure over his part in the Minobe affair. It was also the culmination of a long struggle for control over the army. During the 1920s there had been considerable bitterness as the old Satsuma resentment of Choshu dominance had come to be more widely shared, especially by officers from Saga (Hizen), Fukuoka and Kochi (Tosa); while at the same time regional rivalries were reinforced by the impatience of a new generation of professional soldiers who saw the existing leadership as an obstacle to rapid military modernisation. When Ugaki Kazushige became Army Minister again in 1929, the situation was further complicated, for although he had been the protégé of the last important Choshu general, Tanaka Giichi, he himself came from Okayama and he actually removed a number of Choshu officers from active service or key planning positions. In place of the Choshu faction, in fact, a loosely-knit Ugaki group emerged as the new mainstream element in the army. As well as various personal friends and associates, among them some younger generals from Oita (in Kyushu), it included a number of military specialists who had graduated from the cavalry course or the accountancy school; while on its fringes was a group of slightly younger ex-graduates of the Staff College, mostly colonels whose talents Ugaki had recognised by appointing them to central planning positions as section chiefs in the Army Ministry or General Staff. Although this latter group tended not to feel the same loyalty to Ugaki as did his older supporters, they appreciated his concern with army modernisation, even if they had some doubts about his links with politicians.

Other younger officers associated with the Issekikai and other army societies were less satisfied with Ugaki, especially after he showed himself unwilling to back the *coup d'etat* plot of March 1931. For the achievement of their more radical aims they looked to Araki (who came from Tokyo), Mazaki (from Saga), and Hayashi Senjuro (from Ishikawa), three lieutenant-generals who had recently served as heads of either the Military Academy or the Staff College. When Araki became Army Minister in the Inukai cabinet in December 1931 and Mazaki was made Vice-Chief of Staff under Prince Kanin (an uncle of the Emperor who was expected to be a figurehead) they satisfied the expectations of their more ardent supporters by purging the Army Ministry and General Staff of many of Ugaki's adherents. Although its leaders never acknowledged its existence (which would have been contrary to army regulations), the Kodoha, as the faction soon became known because of Araki's tendency to use terms such as *kodo* (imperial way) in his public pronouncements, appeared to have gained full control.

Kodoha dominance was not to remain unchallenged for long, however. When Araki resigned as Army Minister in January 1934, the Kodoha plan to have Mazaki succeed to his position was blocked by Prince Kanin. In the end the Chief of Staff agreed to the Kodoha's second proposal – the promotion of Inspector-General Hayashi Senjuro and Hayashi's replacement by Mazaki – but ironically the appointment of Hayashi as minister did not work out well for the Kodoha. By overriding Araki's opposition to Nagata Tetsuzan's becoming Chief of the Military Affairs Bureau in the Army Ministry, Hayashi showed that he would not be a Kodoha puppet, and thereafter he leaned more and more towards the Tosei movement (sometimes called the Toseiha [Control Faction], but this is inappropriate since one of its main objectives was the elimination of factionalism). This loose group of Staff College graduates around Nagata had originally had high expectations of the Kodoha. They had been disillusioned, however, by its lack of interest in long-term planning and its emphasis on ideology rather than technology, and they were further alienated by the continuing Kodoha vendetta against the Ugaki group. Apart from these concerns they were also worried by the apparent Kodoha willingness to embark on a preemptive war against the Soviet Union, which ran counter to Nagata's emphasis on the need for much fuller war preparations. With encouragement from these middle-and lower-level military bureaucrats, and in alliance with the top leaders in the General Staff, Hayashi presided over a series of transfers and retirements which soon whittled down the number of Kodoha officers in influential positions at central headquarters.

The inability of the Kodoha to sustain its position was partly due to the paucity of Kodoha officers sufficiently senior to be eligible for the highest positions. As a result Araki and Mazaki in most cases accepted Hayashi's personnel changes without much resistance for fear that he might resign and be replaced by an Ugaki supporter. Nor were the Kodoha's enemies to be found only within the army. Within the Establishment it was suspected of encouraging subversive tendencies. To some extent the suspicion was unfounded, for the faction's leaders themselves did not insist that national policy should be dictated by the army. Indeed, they regarded Tosei plans for a tightly controlled economy as a form of state socialism, and therefore improper. Ironically too, Araki had earlier repudiated the 1931 October Plot, while Mazaki had serious reservations about the radical ideals of the much more junior young officers who were known to favour a radical Showa Ishin, and took care to avoid direct contact with them. Nevertheless, the fact that the young officers saw the Kodoha generals as the most likely leaders of their envisioned new Japan inevitably aroused concern, especially in Court circles. When, in July 1935, Mazaki's dismissal was finally decided upon by Hayashi and Prince Kanin (in disregard of the convention that, as Inspector-General, and therefore one of the army 'big three', his own agreement was also required), the Emperor's confirmation was immediately forthcoming. Mazaki was not even allowed an imperial audience to appeal against his removal.

His dismissal had speedy repercussions. On 12 August a pro-Kodoha officer, Lieutenant-Colonel Aizawa Saburo, marched into the office of Major-General Nagata, whom he saw with some justice as the mastermind behind the purge of the Kodoha and, in a sensational act of retaliation, cut him down. Hayashi felt obliged to take responsibility for the incident by resigning in September, but its consequences did not end there; when Aizawa's murder trial began on 28 January 1936, it was used to make accusations against Nagata, Hayashi, Prime Minister Okada and Lord Keeper of the Privy Seal Saito: Mazaki's dismissal, it was alleged, constituted an encroachment upon the right of supreme command. Mazaki himself appeared as a defence witness on 25 February, when he gave the court to understand that he was in a position to reveal secret information concerning the background of his transfer and the Aizawa incident if he were given imperial permission to do so. Before this tactic could achieve its full effect, however, the trial was interrupted by an even more dramatic development – the February 26th Incident (Ni-ni-roku jiken).

The February 26th Incident

The February 26th Incident was the culmination of a decade of discontent among young officers. Their movement involved about a hundred lieutenants and a few captains, who, unlike the majors and colonels in headquarters positions, mostly had close contacts with ordinary soldiers and were primarily concerned with social justice rather than economic and technological preparation for war. Their distrust of what they considered the fascistic tendencies of the military planners may have found a resonance in the resentment felt by many regimental officers towards the elitism of the central staff officers, who had all been picked out for study at the prestigious Staff College as top graduates of the Military Academy. The removal of Mazaki and the court-martial of Aizawa caused them to fear that the Establishment was strengthening its grip on power, and stimulated them to contemplate direct action to overthrow the government. When in late January 1936 it was learned that the First Division, in which many radical young officers were serving, was to be transferred from Tokyo to Manchukuo, the decision was made to carry out a *coup d'état* while they still had the chance.

If the score of young officers involved in the plot had been entirely on their own they could have had no hope of success. They believed, however, that they would enjoy at least the tacit support of many fellow officers, including Mazaki (whom they intended to have appointed as Prime Minister), while the new Army Minister, General Kawashima, was considered to be malleable. Some sympathy and financial support was forthcoming from Kuhara Fusanosuke, the ambitious Seiyukai faction leader and founder of Nissan. Even within the inner Establishment itself the young officers had some friends, the most important being the Emperor's brother, Prince Chichibu, who was himself a regimental officer.

The initial execution of the coup was impressive. The area of Tokyo south of the imperial palace which contained most of the government offices was seized, and although some of the Establishment figures who were slated for assassination either escaped or hid or were merely wounded, the Lord Keeper of the Privy Seal (and ex-Prime Minister) Saito, Finance Minister Takahashi, and Inspector-General of Military Education Watanabe were ruthlessly murdered. For a brief period it seemed as if the young officers might achieve their objective. Army Minister Kawashima met their leaders and appeared to be sympathetic to their demand that some Tosei officers be dismissed. He certainly ordered that the manifesto in which they justified their action should be circulated throughout the army, and he himself read it to the Emperor. Then, on the afternoon of 26 February, the Supreme War Council agreed to issue a declaration which acknowledged the sincerity of the young officers' motives and pledged support for the implementation of their ideals. Most significantly of all, a proclamation of martial law – which Kita Ikki, whose radical nationalist ideas had influenced the young officers, had regarded as a crucial step towards the success of a military coup – was signed by the Emperor on 27 February after the cabinet had yielded to the Army Minister's pressure.

It was not long, however, before the conspirators' hopes of success foundered. Opposition was soon forthcoming from the navy, which swiftly brought warships close to the capital and landed marines; while within the army itself the General Staff adopted a markedly different stance from the Army Ministry. Vice-Chief of Staff Sugiyama Hajime was determined to treat the young officers as rebels, and he was strongly backed up by the head of his Operations Section, Ishiwara Kanji, on whom the young officers had counted for vital support. Ishiwara may actually have intended to play a double game initially; certainly his actions on 26 February suggest that he believed that political advantage might be derived from such an incident. He first burst into an emergency cabinet session and demanded (without success) to present the army's views and then proposed to both the rebels and Sugiyama (again without success) the appointment of a new cabinet acceptable to both wings of the army. Nevertheless from the start he insisted that the incident was a mutiny, and he also told the young officers personally that they must lay down their arms. Later, on 28 February, he brusquely rejected an attempt by General Araki and other War Councillors to avoid the forceful suppression of the rebels.

The most important obstacle to the success of the coup, however, was the Emperor himself. From the beginning he took a strong stand, refusing to allow the cabinet to resign (even though Prime Minister Okada was for twenty-four hours believed to have been killed) until the mutiny had been crushed. With the army rent by internal division, and in the absence of any clear consensus among his ministers, the Emperor was in the unusual position of being able to make decisions himself; and encouraged by such close advisers as Imperial Household Minister Yuasa Kurahei and Kido Koichi, the secretary to the Lord Keeper of the Privy Seal (and son of Kido Koin), who shared his indignation at the murder of Saito and the wounding of Grand Chamberlain Suzuki, he refused to make any concessions to the rebel officers. Had the latter given the same priority to control of the Emperor as had Okubo, Saigo and Iwakura in 1868, the outcome might perhaps have been a Showa Ishin. But they only had 1,400 troops at their disposal, and their somewhat half-hearted attempt to seize the imperial palace with eighty of them was easily rebuffed. By the evening of 28 February several of the high-ranking officers who had shown sympathy towards the rebels had come to accept that their cause was lost, and this awareness was soon communicated to the young officers themselves. When tanks were brought in on the 29th, the rebellion collapsed. Most of the officers involved chose not to commit suicide, hoping either for lenient treatment or a public trial, but in this too their hopes were to be disappointed: after a series of secret court martials seventeen officers or ex-young officers, among them Aizawa, and three civilians, including Kita Ikki (who had been only marginally involved), were sentenced to death.

The increase in military influence on government

The political consequences of the February 26th Incident may sometimes have been exaggerated, but they were certainly considerable. In a classic analysis Maruyama Masao maintained that the incident resulted in the defeat of 'fascism from below'. Whereas he regarded this as paving the way for fascism from above', though, others have seen it as ushering in a 'conservative reaffirmation'.[4] Both these views now seem oversimplified. Even if it is accepted that Japan experienced fascism – a view which most Western scholars

[4] See, in particular, his essay 'The Ideology and Dynamics of Japanese Fascism' in M. Maruyama, *Thought and Behaviour in Modern Japanese Politics*, edited by I.Morris.

and a growing number of Japanese would not endorse – it must be noted that the young officers saw themselves as radical Japanists, not as fascists. Furthermore, the principal beneficiaries of the incident were the middle-ranking officers in army headquarters, not their seniors or other conservatives. Indeed, one Japanese historian has recently concluded that there was a virtual coup within the army in 1936 which effectively placed control in the hands of the forty-seven-year-old Colonel Ishiwara Kanji, the forty-four-year-old Lieutenant-Colonel Muto Akira, the latter's ex-classmate at the Military Academy, Lieutenant-Colonel Tanaka Shinichi, and the even more junior officers who served in the key Operations Division of the General Staff and the politically crucial Military Affairs Bureau of the Army Ministry.[5]

This may slightly overstate the case: while the new Army Minister, General Terauchi Hisaichi, was effectively chosen by Ishiwara and Muto and was as much a 'robot' (a contemporary attribution) as Chief of Staff Prince Kanin, the new Vice-Minister, Lieutenant-General Umezu Yoshijiro, was unusually strong-minded. Moreover, personal relations between Ishiwara and his adherents (sometimes called the Manchurian faction) and the equally forceful, but less unorthodox, Muto and Tanaka were not close. Nevertheless, it was these middle-level (*sakan*) officers who seized the initiative in the early days of March. At Muto's behest, the forty-year-old Major Arisue Seizo bluntly informed General Kawashima on 2 March that, in the view of his fellow officers, the Army Minister should accept responsibility for what had happened by resigning; and he then visited Generals Abe, Hayashi and Araki with the same uncompromising message. Only Araki, and later Mazaki, attempted to challenge what was effectively an ultimatum, and their resistance soon collapsed. This remarkable instance of *gekokujo* (subordinates usurping the functions of, or manipulating, their superiors) was followed by similar purges of other officers – whether pro-Kodoha, pro-Ugaki, or schemers like Hashimoto Kingoro – who were regarded as responsible for factional dispute or internal dissension within the army. Moreover, to ensure that none of the ousted leaders would be able to make a comeback in the event of

---

See also G.M. Wilson, 'A New Look at the Problem of "Japanese Fascism" ', in H.A. Turner (ed.), *Reappraisals of Fascism*, New Viewpoints, 1975.

[5] Tsutsui Kiyotada, *Showa-ki Nihon no Kozo*, pp. 261-73.

a change in the political climate, army regulations were changed in May so as to allow only generals on the active list to become Army Minister – a reversion to the situation which had obtained before 1913.

The change in army regulations would also make it easier for the army to bring down a cabinet or prevent the formation of one to which it objected. Already by this time, however, the Okada cabinet had accepted responsibility for the February 26th Incident by resigning, even though the general election which had been held as recently as 20 February had strengthened its position by elevating the Minseito (which enjoyed some covert government support) to majority party (with 205 seats) and reducing the Seiyukai from 301 to 174 Diet members. As Okada's successor Saionji nominated Prince Konoe Fumimaro, a prominent figure in the House of Peers and a high-ranking hereditary noble, whose Rightist tendencies he regretted but whose public standing could be utilised to restore stability and confidence. However, Konoe, who was something of a dilettante and disinclined to make difficult decisions, declined the invitation on rather dubious health grounds. As an alternative the name of Foreign Minister Hirota Koki was tentatively put forward by Court advisers Ichiki, Yuasa and Kido, and when Saionji concurred Hirota was prevailed upon to accept. In neither case was there a *jushin* conference.

It was at the stage of deciding the composition of the cabinet that the army was able to impose its wishes. With the Establishment desperate to restore stability and fearful of another outbreak of violence, it was possible for Terauchi (prompted by Muto) to insist on the exclusion of four ministers-designate and to press successfully for the inclusion as Finance Minister of Baba Eiichi, who was willing to risk inflation and impose higher taxes to satisfy the military's desire for more funds. A further demand that the number of politicians in the cabinet be halved from the intended two from each party was firmly resisted by Hirota, but he did concede that the Home Ministry should not be held by a party man.

This pattern of strong army pressure was maintained throughout the ten months' duration of the Hirota cabinet. In foreign policy the Anti-Comintern Pact, which was signed in November with Germany and had a secret clause promising cooperation against the Soviet Union, was largely the result of the army's own diplomacy; and the drawing up of a new National Defence Plan in the summer of 1936 was partly intended to justify a larger budget for the army over the following years (although Ishiwara was unable to prevent the navy from staking its claim too). These developments by no means fully satisfied Ishiwara, however. He also organised the establishment of a War Leadership Unit in the General Staff, himself becoming its first head; and he enlisted outside expertise – in the form of Miyazaki Masayoshi, a South Manchurian Railway economist – to draft a five-year plan for coordinated industrial development in Japan and Manchuria on a sufficiently massive scale to match the expansion in the Soviet Union's strength. Although the plan did not become official government policy (partly because the Military Affairs Bureau raised objections to it) Ishiwara's initiative was an indication that the new generation of army leaders was no longer content to leave control of the economy solely in the hands of the captains of industry.

Army dissatisfaction with the status quo also extended to the organisation of government. Ever since the Meiji Ishin there had been differences over the relationship between policy-making and administration, but not even in the 1870s were they as acute as they became in the 1930s. On the one hand, the demise of party cabinets had left a vacuum at the centre, with no single force or group, not even the army or the bureaucracy, capable of coordinating the various branches of government. On the other hand, governmental organisation had itself become more complex as the tendency after 1914 for the state to assume new social and economic functions began to affect Japan as well. One result was the increasing specialisation of government departments: for instance, separate ministries were set up for Railways in 1920 and Colonial Affairs in 1928, while the Agriculture and Commerce Ministry was divided in two in 1922. Another was the establishment of special bureaux, such as the Social Bureau (within the Home Ministry) in 1920-2 and the Resources Bureau (attached to the Ministry of Commerce and Industry) in 1930. An even more striking proliferation of government agencies occurred with the creation of special committees and investigative organs; by the mid-1930s these numbered more than one hundred, and attempts to abolish or reorganise them were conspicuously unsuccessful.

A number of attempts were made during the Saito and Okada cabinets to counteract the tendency towards departmental sectionalism. In 1933 Five Ministers' Conferences (Gosho Kaigi) were instituted to determine foreign policy in the light of defence and fiscal considerations, and Internal Policy Conferences (Naisei Kaigi), which were attended by eight of the thirteen cabinet ministers, helped the Saito cabinet to resolve some differences over domestic priorities. Under Okada the Cabinet Deliberative Council was established with members drawn from senior politicians, leading businessmen, and ex-bureaucrats, but this was intended primarily to justify the claim that the cabinet was one of national unity and to secure party support in the Diet. It was abolished by the Hirota cabinet in May 1936. More important was the Cabinet Research Bureau (Naikaku Chosakyoku) which was set up at the same time. Unlike other government bureaux it was not limited in the scope of its investigations and proposals, and its members (among whom 'revisionist bureaucrats' and army officers were prominent) were encouraged to regard it as a governmental general staff.

The strengthening of the Cabinet Research Bureau was one of the army's aims in 1936, but the plan for administrative reform which it put to Hirota in September went much further than this. Drafted originally by Major Sato Kenryo, of the newly-established Policy Unit within the Military Affairs Bureau, it also included proposals for centralising control of the bureaucracy through a new Personnel Office, for amalgamating several ministries, and for curtailing the powers of the Diet. Many of the suggestions were left rather vague, but even so it was clear that the basic idea behind them was to concentrate more power in the hands of the Prime Minister so that through him the army and its allies among the revisionist and renovationist bureaucrats could impose upon the various ministries a more coherent programme in line with their own objectives. Needless to say, the proposals encountered considerable opposition from both party politicians and the majority of bureaucrats. Although those which related to the Diet had to be partially disavowed by Army Minister Terauchi, the others could not be so easily dismissed. By January 1937, after extensive discussion in ministerial committees, it seemed as though army demands would be met, albeit incompletely, by the strengthening of the Cabinet Research Bureau and the introduction of a Personnel Bureau. At this point, however, the cabinet collapsed.

The partial party revival and the Hayashi cabinet

The circumstances of Hirota's resignation indicated that the army's unprecedented intervention in political affairs had finally provoked an effective reaction. Just as conventional bureaucrats were disturbed by the proposed administrative charges, so big business was alarmed by the huge budget increases which Finance Minister Baba had proposed for 1937. With rumblings of dissatisfaction from these quarters in the background, politicians were tempted to assert themselves once more. Their own public image had improved somewhat, partly as a result, ironically, of the efforts to purify elections which the Home Ministry had made since 1932. The major parties, moreover, had easily overcome the challenge of the two new nationalistic pro-army parties in the general election of 20 February 1936. The Showakai (Showa Association) had secured only twenty seats and the Kokumin Domei (National Alliance) no more than fifteen, and both were outstripped by the major proletarian party, the Shakai Taishuto, which leaped from five to twenty-two. The particular success of the Minseito (whose support of the Okada cabinet was rewarded by the Sumitomo *zaibatsu's* provision, arranged through Saionji, of a million yen for its election expenses) had even encouraged hopes, until the February 26th Incident cut these short, of a return to party cabinets. During the Diet sessions of 1936 a number of speeches critical of the military received considerable acclaim, and it was when one of these, made by the Seiyukai's Hamada Kunimatsu, led to a sharp exchange with Army Minister Terauchi that the latter insisted that the Lower House be dissolved and new elections held.

Behind Terauchi's tough stance lay the intention of taking advantage of the Hamada incident to make the major breakthrough which politically minded officers like Ishiwara desired. By December Ishiwara had instigated discussion of a new party (to be recruited from the more amenable members of the existing ones and led by Prince Konoe), which would provide solid backing for a cabinet fully committed to the establishment of the national defence state of which the army planners dreamed. His plan proved premature, however, for Konoe felt that the opposition to such radical changes was too strong to be overcome. Despite this setback Terauchi continued to demand a dissolution, apparently thinking that an election would teach the parties a lesson. Most of the party members in the cabinet, however, not unnaturally saw things rather differently, and it was the resulting impasse which bought about Hirota's resignation on 23 January.

The events which followed showed the army's political inter-ference reaching a new peak. When General Ugaki was invited, at Saionji's suggestion, to form a government, Terauchi flatly refused to recommend anyone to serve as Army Minister. A consensus had been reached by various section chiefs in the Army Ministry, ap-parently under pressure from Ishiwara, that certain generals and admirals, among them Ugaki, were unacceptable as Prime Minis-ter. Undeterred, Ugaki put forward three ways of overcoming army opposition: either he should take charge personally, without a minister being appointed; or a suitable retired general should be appointed after being put back on the active list; or the Emperor should personally order a qualified general to cooperate. The Emperor's advisers, however, lacked Ugaki's resolution: Yuasa Kurahei, who had succeeded Ichiki as Lord Keeper of the Privy Seal, rejected Ugaki's request on the grounds that it was 'unthink-able to set the Emperor on a boat which was sailing against a strong current'.[6] Thus one of the last chances to reassert political control over the army was thrown away.

The view that it might have been possible to call the army's bluff is borne out by the rapid reappearance of cracks in that service's unity. When Ugaki abandoned his attempt to form a government on 29 January, Saionji agreed to nominate Hiranuma Kiichiro (who declined), and then Hayashi Senjuro, who was considered to have acted responsibly as Army Minister in 1934-5. At first Ishiwara was delighted with this development, for Hayashi had expressed even more sympathy than Konoe for the planned national defence state plans and initially he was willing to allow his cabinet to be chosen for him by Ishiwara's associates, Sogo Shinji and Asahara Kenzo. His hopes were quickly dashed, however. When Hayashi agreed to appoint Ishiwara's old Kwantung Army co-conspirator, Itagaki Seishiro, as Army Minister, Vice-Minister Umezu and the army 'big three' let it be known that Itagaki was unacceptable because he was supported by radical reformists and also lacked seniority. When the navy also objected to the proposed Navy Minister and some other prospective cabinet members refused to serve, Hayashi

[6] Quoted by Eguchi Keiichi, 'Hayashi Naikaku' in Hayashi Shigeru and Tsuji Kiyoaki (eds), *Nihon Naikaku Shiroku*, vol. 3, p. 426.

realised that his association with the Ishiwara group was likely to prove unproductive. Speedily changing tack, he dismissed Asahara and Sogo from his headquarters.

The Hayashi cabinet was formally installed on 2 February. Its composition gave some reassurance to business and financial circles, but no real concessions were made to the political parties: although cabinet positions were offered to the Seiyukai's Nakajima Chikuhei and the Minseito's Nagai Ryutaro, both offers were conditional on their giving up party membership and both were declined. Despite the cabinet's lack of a political base, however, the Diet was not particularly obstructive, since the most contentious proposals put forward by the previous cabinet were either withdrawn or considerably attenuated. Nevertheless, perhaps because he sensed that the parties would not be satisfied with their total exclusion from power for much longer, and apparently anticipating that an election would encourage the advocates of a new party, Hayashi unexpectedly had the Lower House dissolved as soon as the budget had been passed in March.

If Hayashi really believed, as has been suggested, that a new party could be formed in time to participate in the election which was due to be held on 30 April, he was politically naive. Not only did it fail to materialise, but the only two existing parties which supported the cabinet – the Showakai and the Kokumin Domei – won fewer seats than the Shakai Taishuto, which increased its representation from twenty-two to thirty-seven. The Minseito (though reduced to 179 members) and the Seiyukai (with 175) easily maintained their joint dominance of the Lower House. Significantly, there was some attempt (facilitated by Suzuki's recent resignation and replacement by the four-man team of Maeda Yonezo, Nakajima Chikuhei, Hatoyama Ichiro and Shimada Toshio) at cooperation by the Minseito and Seiyukai headquarters. With the intention of showing solidarity in the face of the threat of a new party and of protesting against the 'anti-constitutional' dissolution, they encouraged the idea that sitting members should be returned without contest, a tactic reminiscent of 1924 or, even more closely, of 1903, when an election had similarly been called prematurely by a Prime Minister who was also a general; and although local rivalries in most cases impeded its implementation, in four constituencies the existing members were returned without contest, while the number of candidates from the two main parties went down from 638 in 1936 to 534. Even though the voting rate dropped from 77 to 70 per cent (in big cities from 72 to 57 per cent) there was a general feeling (however obliquely it was expressed) that the election was a battle between parliamentarism and military dominance. Hayashi was reluctant to acknowledge defeat, and initially thought of dissolving the Diet yet again, but this seemed pointlessly provocative, even to army leaders. When they made it clear that he had lost their confidence, the Prime Minister quickly resigned.

The first Konoe cabinet and the China Incident

Whether the next cabinet would be better able than Hayashi's to accommodate the various interest groups and restore some stability seemed doubtful. Even the choice of the next Prime Minister proved contentious. The aging Saionji was partly responsible for this because, having instituted a new procedure whereby the duty of nominating the next head of government was assumed by the Lord Keeper of the Privy Seal, he then objected when Yuasa, after consultation with Konoe, Kido, and Harada, accepted Hayashi's suggestion that his successor should be the outgoing Army Minister, Sugiyama Hajime. To the *genro* the appointment of another general seemed unwise, and he again urged that Konoe was the most appropriate man for the job. His view prevailed, and on this occasion Konoe acceded to the appeal to his sense of duty.

Initial responses to Konoe's assumption of office in June 1937 were overwhelmingly favourable. The forty-five-year-old nobleman enjoyed an unique political position in Japan. His range of contacts and sympathies were unusually wide, and various elements, notably the current army leadership but also the discredited Kodoha officers, the Court advisers, the *zaibatsu*, the pan-Asianists, and even the political parties, looked to him to further their aims or interests. Paradoxically, because he was not clearly identified with any one group, there was also a widespread impression that a Konoe cabinet could provide Japan with the unity which had proved so elusive. Such an attitude was naive, for in practice it would not have been possible for Konoe to satisfy all expectations, as he himself soon discovered when he was rebuffed in his attempt to secure imperial approval of an amnesty for all those who had been involved in the assassinations and attempted coups of 1932 and 1936. Before he had really begun to face the challenge of how to reconcile conflicting interests and demands, however, the balance of forces within Japan was again distorted by Japanese military action in China, this time after a clash near the Marco Polo Bridge close to an important railway junction south of Beijing.

The outbreak of the so-called 'China Incident' in July 1937 seems to have been unplanned, but it followed several years of Japanese pressure and a recent series of anti-Japanese incidents. Despite his pan-Asian tendencies, Konoe did little to prevent this new incident's escalation. Although he occasionally wavered in favour of a negotiated settlement, he basically shared the widespread view that the Chinese, and particularly the ruling Kuomintang led by Chiang Kai-shek, needed to be taught a firm lesson. This view was held no less strongly by the other cabinet members; and the party members who had become ministers, Nakajima Chikuhei and Nagai Ryutaro, were particularly eager for punitive measures. Even the Shakai Taishuto, which, despite displaying distinct nationalistic tendencies since the early 1930s, had opposed withdrawal from the League of Nations and advocated genuine independence for Manchukuo, succumbed almost completely to nationalistic fervour. By early 1938 it was calling for an all-party front to support the (undeclared) war, thus matching the declaration of the largest union federation that it would renounce the right to strike and launch a 'home front' campaign. The smaller left-wing party, the Nihon Musanto, under the leadership of Kato Kanju resisted almost alone the bellicose mood, but its attempt to form a popular front against the war resulted only in the party's forced dissolution in December 1937. The one possibility of halting the escalation of the conflict lay, ironically, in the concern of Ishiwara (now head of the General Staff Operations Division) and his fellow long-term planners to avoid a costly involvement which was likely to impair their preparations for war with the Soviet Union. They were outnumbered, however, by more hawkish officers, including those in the field armies on the continent; and in a striking reversal of past roles Ishiwara's assertion of the need for caution was undermined by some of his own subordinates, notably Muto Akira. Even though the Vice-Chief of Staff, General Tada, shared Ishiwara's concern, he was outmanoeuvred in his effort in January 1938 to offer reasonable terms to Chiang; and on 16 January 1938 Konoe himself made a settlement more difficult by publicly stating that Japan would no longer negotiate with the Kuomintang. Already before this, though, what remained of Ishiwara's political influence had been effectively ended by his posting to the Kwantung Army.

Contrary to Konoe's assumption in early 1938, and despite the Japanese capture (or 'rape') in December 1937, at horrific cost to the Chinese population, of the capital of Nanking, there was to be no speedy collapse of Chinese resistance. As a result about 700,000 Japanese troops were caught in the Chinese quagmire, fighting innumerable engagements, not only in north China but also in the centre and south. Within Japan the most immediate effect of the conflict was the further intensification of nationalism. Little was left to chance by the government. In September the Cabinet Information Committee was upgraded into an expanded Cabinet Information Division and immediately set to work, together with the Home and Education Ministries, on a national spiritual mobilisation campaign. It did not have to start from scratch, for the Hayashi cabinet had previously approved a Cabinet Information Committee plan to promote the 'enlightenment of the nation', and in the recently published *Kokutai no Hongi* it inherited an imposing, if somewhat recondite, elaboration (prompted by the Minobe controversy) of Japan's special social and political values. This reformulation of official ideology was buttressed by the suppression of surviving Marxist academic factions and by a yet further extension of censorship.

The China Incident also had a major impact on the Japanese economy. There was a severe tightening of import restrictions, while the expansion of heavy and chemical industry, which had already grown from one-third of industrial production in 1930 to a half in 1936, was given a further boost. Inevitably, too, government expenditure rose sharply, necessitating heavier taxation, increased borrowing, and price controls. In the prevailing atmosphere of heightened patriotism, opposition to such extra burdens and restrictions was bound to be muted, and the parties did not dare to block, in March 1938, the passage of the National General Mobilisation Law, which conceded to the government sweeping emergency powers over labour, industry and banking, potentially depriving them of much of their remaining political leverage.

The heavier weight given to military priorities also tilted the scales with regard to administrative reform. As one of its last acts the Hayashi cabinet had, in May 1937, converted the Cabinet Research Bureau into the Planning Office (Kikakucho). In October this became the Planning Board (Kikakuin), and was assigned the significantly expanded role of coordinating the work of each ministry to ensure that it was in line with national strategy. The drafting of the National General Mobilisation Bill was largely its work. Its impact on government, however, though considerable, was to be less profound than some army officers and revisionist bureaucrats had hoped. It was never able to overcome completely the opposition which it encountered from the various ministries, particularly the Finance Ministry, and departmental divisions were even reflected to some extent within the Planning Board itself.

Konoe's other efforts to unify decision-making were also less effective than anticipated. His support for the establishment of an imperial general headquarters in November 1937 proved fruitless since, unlike in earlier wars, the military did not accept any civilian presence; indeed the two services' own mutual rivalry was so intense that even between them coordination was mostly minimal. An attempt to overcome this obstacle through the institution of an imperial headquarters-government liaison conference proved to be premature: the army did not welcome interference, and no meeting was held after January 1938 for over two years. In the hope of improving decision-making, and in particular of finding a solution to the China Incident, Konoe re-established the Five Ministers Conference, and he also brought into the government General Itagaki as Army Minister (with the Emperor's help), General Ugaki as Foreign Minister, and the Mitsui director, Ikeda Seihin, who was strongly internationalist and carried great weight in the business community, as both Finance Minister and Minister of Commerce and Industry. He further sought to overcome military independence and intransigence by agreeing strategy with Ikeda and Ugaki in advance of the weekly or twice-weekly meetings of the Five Ministers. Again, however, the effects were negligible. Itagaki was easily manipulated by his subordinates, while Ugaki abandoned his post within four months when the Foreign Ministry lost its responsibility for Chinese affairs to the newly-established Koain (Asia Development Board) under General Yanagawa.

Had Konoe himself been more decisive and dynamic, the obstacles of sectionalism or polycentrism might have been overcome. But although he had the benefit of much advice, notably from the Showa Kenkyukai, an unofficial brains-trust of revisionist bureaucrats, ex-bureaucrats and academics, he was temperamentally unsuited to leadership. Perhaps because of his aristocratic background, perhaps because of lack of self-confidence, he was extremely reluctant to take a firm stand or risk a confrontation and tended to be reserved in meetings. As Ikeda complained in December 1938, 'It is very difficult when the Prime Minister silently looks on while the right wing and part of the army interfere with what I am trying to do'.[7] Easily diverted from his purpose, Konoe often became defeatist and frequently expressed a desire to abandon his Prime Ministerial responsibility.

Konoe finally did resign on 4 January 1939, probably because he wished to avoid difficult choices on two issues which had become particularly pressing. One was the question of strengthening the Anti-Comintern Pact, which Germany and Italy were now seeking to extend to cases of conflict with not just the Soviet Union but other countries too. The second issue arose out of dissatisfaction with the national spiritual mobilisation movement, which had been criticised as being too bureaucratic and insufficiently coordinated. There was general acknowledgement of the need for greater popular involvement but considerable divergence over the form this should take. Whereas the Agricultural Minister, Arima Yoriyasu, wished to emphasise the producers' cooperatives (*sangyo kumiai*) and other agrarian groups over which his ministry had influence, the Home Ministry sought to control the campaign by having its officials supervise either such existing organisations as those of the reservists, young men, patriotic and religious groups or, as its Local Administration Bureau proposed, new associations, modelled in part on the neighbourhood groups of the Tokugawa period and comprising all the inhabitants of each hamlet and urban ward. A number of prominent political figures, such as Home Minister Admiral Suetsugu, Justice Minister Shiono Suehiko, Akita Kiyoshi (ex-Seiyukai), and Aso Hisashi (Shakai Taishuto), adopted a significantly different position by urging, more often in rivalry than in unison, that only a new mass political party could

---

[7] Quoted by A.E. Tiedemann, 'Big Business and Politics' in J.W.Morley (ed.), *Dilemmas of Growth in Pre-War Japan*, p. 313.

both mobilise popular energies fully and provide the effective leadership necessary to achieve real national unity. The leader of such a party would naturally have a great advantage in his relations with the various élite groups and might even be able to bring the army to heel. Inevitably, however, the creation of such a party would provoke great opposition. Only under Konoe's leadership would it have any chance of acceptance, and there was thus considerable competition among its various protagonists to secure his agreement to their particular scheme. Konoe, however, was evidently wary of being used in this way, and his resignation was probably intended in part to remove the pressure to which he was being subjected.

Before he resigned, Konoe sounded out Hiranuma Kiichiro to discover whether he would be willing to replace him, and he also gained the understanding of Ikeda and Kido for this transfer of responsibility. When Yuasa consulted Saionji, his agreement was forthcoming too. The need to split the reactionary Right from the radical Right had led the *genro* finally to agree to Hiranuma's promotion to head the Privy Council after the February 26th Incident, and in that role Hiranuma had shown that his primary concern was to maintain political order. His disbandment of the Kokuhon-sha helped to prove his soundness. Now that the political parties had lost their pre-eminence, his attitude towards them had moderated. He included two party members in his cabinet and in a statement to the Diet acknowledged that political parties could not be ignored. Significantly he disclaimed any thought of a restructuring of national organisations or a new political party movement, and he dropped Home Minister Suetsugu, one of the most committed opponents of the existing parties.

The Hiranuma and Abe cabinets

The obvious lack of enthusiasm by Hiranuma for radical reorganisation, together with Konoe's reluctance to lead a new party, led to a sharp drop in the political temperature. Neither the Seiyukai nor the Minseito was now inclined to challenge the government in the Diet. Although the National General Mobilisation Law had (contrary to Konoe's earlier promise) already been invoked, its implementation had been restrained, largely as a result of Ikeda's stiff defence of business interests within the cabinet, and the major parties were not disposed to jeopardise the patriotic image they had been cultivating by contesting the government's action. In any case, both were preoccupied with problems of internal disunity, and the Seiyukai was facing a bitter leadership struggle between the relatively inexperienced Nakajima Chikuhei, who was interested in making the Seiyukai the nucleus of a new, pro-government party, and the less renovationist Kuhara Fusanosuke, Hatoyama Ichiro, and Suzuki Kisaburo. The result was a party schism, with one group electing Nakajima as their leader, while the rest chose to follow Kuhara. Meanwhile, on the other side of the Diet, an attempt to create a progressive party with a mass base by the amalgamation of the Shakai Taishuto and the Tohokai (a party founded in 1937 by the ex-Minseito progressive, Nakano Seigo, which enjoyed some support from Communications Ministry workers and had links with the producers' cooperatives movement) also engendered a dispute over leadership and finally came to nothing.

If domestic politics presented relatively few problems for the Hiranuma cabinet, the same could not be said about foreign policy. The hope of achieving a settlement of the China Incident through the defection of Wang Ching-wei, one of the most prominent Kuomintang leaders, soon faded when neither warlords, generals, politicians nor public opinion rallied to his call for a compromise peace. More thorny still was the question of the strengthening of the Anti-Comintern Pact, which the army demanded even more insistently after hostilities broke out between the Kwantung Army and the Soviet Far Eastern forces in May at Nomonhan on the Mongolian-Manchukuo border. Significant support also came from within the navy, although the terms proposed by Germany made conflict with Britain possible; but Navy Minister Yonai Mitsumasa and Vice-Minister Yamamoto Isoroku stood firm against it, despite attempts at intimidation by right-wing nationalists. The army was also opposed by Foreign Minister Arita Hachiro, who received strong backing from the Emperor and from Ikeda. Even after some seventy top-level meetings the army did not give up, and the dispute only ended in August 1939 after Germany, in preparation for its attack on Poland, signed a non-aggression treaty with the Soviet Union. This betrayal of the existing Anti-Comintern Pact dumbfounded the Japanese government and Hiranuma resigned.

It was not only Hiranuma whose reputation was damaged by the Anti-Comintern Pact fiasco. The army was even more open to the accusation that it had tried to set Japan on a misguided course with an untrustworthy partner, and its position was further weakened by the refusal of the Kwantung Army (until it had suffered humiliating setbacks) to abandon its continuing border conflict with Soviet forces. The extent of the Japanese military's loss of standing was not immediately evident, and Army Minister Itagaki did not hesitate to veto Hirota as Hiranuma's successor, notwithstanding the fact that Konoe, Hiranuma and Yuasa had reached preliminary agreement on the former Prime Minister. Itagaki also made it clear that Ugaki, whose candidacy was supported by Ikeda, Machida Chuji, and Okada, remained unacceptable. Yuasa would have proposed Ikeda, but was dissuaded by Konoe's objection that this would be seen as a complete turn about and should be delayed until the army was less powerful. For the Emperor's advisers the avoidance of internal conflict remained the highest priority, even though the possibility of resisting military intervention in politics was stronger than it had been for at least two years. Instead of making a bold choice they accepted one of the army's two suggestions – the relatively unknown General Abe Nobuyuki.

If Yuasa and Konoe were unduly cautious, the Emperor was not. Angry at the way in which Itagaki had served as mere mouthpiece for his subordinates, he informed Abe, in an unprecedented exercise of his authority, that the two generals who were being considered by the army 'big three' as next Army Minister were not acceptable and that the choice must be confined to either Umezu or Hata Shunroku (both of whom had the reputation of being strong upholders of discipline). Moreover, in addition to the now customary injunctions to respect the constitution, avoid unnecessary international friction, and cause no drastic upheavals in the financial world, the Emperor also sternly informed Abe that he must be conciliatory towards Britain and the United States and must exercise particular care in selecting the Home and Justice Ministers – the latter demand probably reflecting the Emperor's dissatisfaction that his complaints to Hiranuma about the organisation of anti-British rallies by right-wing groups had been in vain.

This show of imperial will had a considerable psychological impact. Nevertheless, although the army accepted Hata as its new minister, it was still able to exercise political influence, even if it had to act more discreetly. Indeed, in the choice of civilian cabinet members it had a major say, for Abe, being politically inexperienced, relied heavily on the advice of Colonel Arisue Seizo, a member of the Military Affairs Bureau. One of the results was that the army's desire for a smaller cabinet was realised, with several of the new government's members assuming responsibility for two related ministries (although the experiment was abandoned before the end of the year). The personal composition of the cabinet was also rather unbalanced, for Abe and six other ministers, as well as the Chief of the Legislative Bureau and the Cabinet Secretary, were also members of a mainly bureaucratic group called the Jiji Kondankai (Current Affairs Discussion Association). Only Railway Minister Nagai Ryutaro was a party man, and his presence was by no means an indication of party support, since army pressure had had to be exerted on Machida Chuji not to have Nagai expelled from the Minseito if he accepted Abe's invitation.

The Abe cabinet was very soon in need of extra support, for its record was one of almost total failure. An attempt to strengthen the power of the Prime Minister was abandoned in the face of Privy Council objections, and a similarly army-inspired proposal to set up a Trade Ministry aroused such opposition from Foreign Ministry officials, over a hundred of whom offered their resignations in protest, that the government had to make an embarrassing retreat on this issue too. Nor was it any more successful in its attempts to carry out the Emperor's instruction to improve relations with Britain and America. In particular it was unable to negotiate a new trade agreement with the United States after the latter had unilaterally abrogated the 1911 treaty in July in response to Japanese activities in China. The absence of a treaty did not prevent trade from continuing, but it foreshadowed the imposition of economic sanctions. To cap the cabinet's misfortunes, the fixed rice price had to be raised in November as a result of a severe drought, and with consumer goods in short supply because of wartime trade restrictions popular resentment began to manifest itself.

Despite its growing unpopularity, none of the major party leaders were eager to attack the cabinet, for there still seemed little likelihood that any of them would be invited to form a new government. An increasing number of Diet members, however, were becoming impatient with their lack of influence, and some were tempted to believe that they might be able to regain some of it by combining in a new reformist party with the Tohokai and other minor parties and forcing Abe out of office. As soon as the Diet session began on 26 December, a no-confidence resolution was drawn up by 240 members representing all parties, and on 7 January no fewer than 276 members joined in a petition calling for the cabinet's resignation. Abe was not disposed to give in, and planned to dissolve the Diet and form an alliance with Kuhara, but like Hayashi three years earlier he had come to be regarded as a liability by the army. On 14 January 1940, after a week of constant pressure by Muto Akira (now head of the Military Affairs Bureau) and other officers, Abe bowed to their demand and resigned.

The Yonai cabinet and the new party movement

Ironically, within a few months of helping to block Abe's scheme, Muto was himself planning to make use of Kuhara (among others) to build a new pro-government party. His change of tack can be partly explained by army dissatisfaction with the new cabinet. In recommending a new Prime Minister, Lord Keeper of the Privy Seal Yuasa acted with a determination which contrasted sharply with his caution four months earlier and quickly secured the acquiescence of Saionji and some ex-Prime Ministers in the appointment of another moderate admiral in the tradition of Saito and Okada – Yonai Mitsumasa. His unusual decisiveness may, it has been suggested, have been prompted by his awareness of his sovereign's wishes.[8] The Emperor certainly liked Yonai personally and appreciated his stubborn resistance to the army's pressure over the proposed new Anti-Comintern Pact; and he may well have regretted the failure to appoint someone in September who would really strive to maintain the status quo. If the Emperor did indeed indicate to the Lord Keeper of the Privy Seal the person whom the latter was to recommend for the imperial nomination, it would represent an intriguing reversal of the constitutional convention that the monarch held nominal power but left decision-making to his advisers.

The new cabinet was certainly different from its predecessor in one significant respect. Acknowledging the importance of the

[8] See Takeyama Morio, 'Yonai Naikaku' in Hayashi Shigeru and Tsuji Kiyoaki (eds), *Nihon Naikaku Shiroku*, vol. 4, p. 214.

Lower House of the Diet, Yonai sought and obtained the entry into his cabinet of four politicians as explicit representatives of the major parties – two from the Minseito, one each from the main Seiyukai camps – and for the first time since Takahashi a party man held the sensitive position of Finance Minister. This more conciliatory policy seems to have paid off, for there was negligible Diet opposition to the government's legislative programme, even though a major revision of the tax system substantially increased almost everything from income tax to the tax on geishas' tips. The most controversial incident during the early 1940 Diet session was actually one which had only an indirect connection with the Yonai cabinet. In early February Saito Takao, a Minseito member noted for his independence and anti-authoritarianism, made an impassioned Diet speech in which he criticised past government policies and asserted that to call the conflict in China a holy war was hollow hypocrisy. His brave, but possibly ill-judged, diatribe not only outraged the army but also paved the way towards a fundamental realignment of party politics, for those who wished to establish a new party, or were moving towards this idea, found an opportunity to join together in calling for Saito's expulsion from the Diet. The ensuing struggle between, on the one hand, the mainstream Minseito leadership under Machida Chuji, the Hatoyama group in the Seiyukai, and the less nationalistic members of the Shakai Taishuto, all of whom opposed expulsion, and, on the other hand, the Nagai Ryutaro faction in the Minseito, both the Nakajima and Kuhara branches of the Seiyukai, the Aso faction in the Shakai Taishuto, and the various smaller parties ended on 7 March when Saito's expulsion was decided by a large majority. The handful of Seiyukai members who voted against the motion were forced out of their party for doing so, as were ten Shakai Taishuto representatives who absented themselves from the chamber in protest, and when the latter group tried to establish a new proletarian party, it was prohibited by the Home Ministry on the grounds that it would instigate class struggle and obstruct national solidarity.

In the wake of Saito's expulsion a new organisation – the League of Diet Members for Carrying to Fulfilment the Holy War – which openly called for the establishment of a 'great new party' was formed on 25 March with the participation not only of the smaller parties but also some Seiyukai and Minseito members.

It was this development which aroused Major-General Muto's interest, and the Military Affairs Bureau supported the new venture by urging the Seiyukai leaders to associate themselves with it. Whether these efforts by themselves would have been fruitful, given the degree of personal rivalry which existed, is uncertain. In mid-May, however, the situation began to change dramatically as the German war-machine started to overrun Western Europe. Not only did the Western colonial empires in South East Asia seem likely to fall into Japan's lap if the cautious Yonai cabinet were replaced and Germany induced to acknowledge Japanese hegemony in that region, but the German victories offered persuasive evidence of the advantages of a one-party state. There was a widespread feeling in Japan, just as elsewhere, that world history was at a major turning-point, with both the old imperial order and the new internationalism about to give way to regional blocs, while liberalism and pluralism would be swept aside by totalitarian nationalism. Konoe too seems to have been affected by the prevailing mood, for in early June he made a public statement in which he said that he believed that a strong new political party was necessary. When he resigned from the presidency of the Privy Council on 24 June with the avowed purpose of contributing to the establishment of a new structure, the expectation that this would finally come about became overwhelming; and to fulfil Konoe's condition for their participation in the new scheme of things, the Diet politicians successively dissolved the parties or groups to which they belonged – the Shakai Taishuto on 6 July, the Kuhara faction on 16 July, the Nakajima faction on 30 July, and finally, after the Nagai group had broken ranks on 26 July, the Minseito on 15 August.

Swiftly though the parties acted, the political situation was developing even more rapidly. Konoe's change of heart had also revived Muto's hope of another cabinet under his leadership, and in order to grasp the opportunities which French, Dutch and British disarray appeared to present, it seemed vital not to 'miss the bus'. To achieve the speedy removal of the existing cabinet, Army Minister Hata was pressurised into threatening resignation, and when Yonai's refusal to step down forced Hata to carry out his threat on 16 July, the army made it clear that no replacement would be forthcoming. Yonai then gave up, and Konoe was nominated the same evening by the new Lord Keeper of the Privy Seal, Kido Koichi.

Konoe and the new political structure

Konoe's return to office opened up the prospect of the immediate establishment of a new political structure, but great differences remained over what should be the nature of the new order and which groups and individuals should play the leading roles in it. More than fifty proposals were put forward by study groups, academics, politicians and political commentators, and the competition for Konoe's attention was intense. As in 1938, there was a fundamental division between those who emphasised the need for a mass political organisation and those who believed that national energies could best be mobilised by the development of a more effective, but non-political, network for organising home front activities and disseminating propaganda. The former were a particularly motley camp. At one extreme were the politicians belonging to the Kuhara, Nakajima and Nagai factions who had established by 8 August an Association for the Promotion of a New Structure and who hoped that, having rid themselves of their more liberal fellow-members, they would be regarded as the obvious nucleus of a new party. At the other end were elements which sought a much more radical shift in power (and were generally also more eager for alliance with Germany). The label 'fascist' has been applied rather sweepingly by Japanese historians writing on the pre-war period, but in this particular case it is impossible to ignore the similarities between some of the advocates of a new political order and the followers of Hitler and Mussolini. Such proletarian leaders as Akamatsu Katsumaro, of course, had since the early 1930s been self-proclaimed 'national socialists' and had more or less abandoned the pursuit of social justice at home in favour of the cause of Japan as a 'have-not' nation internationally; and the same term could also be used to describe Aso Hisashi and Kamei Kanichiro. As early as 1934 they had concluded that the best chance of achieving proletarian aims was through collaboration with the army in the establishment of state controls over the economy, and the lead taken by the Shakai Taishuto in the dissolution of the political parties represented a triumph for their ideas. From a more mainstream political background Nakano Seigo publicly professed his admiration for Hitler and Mussolini as national leaders and had the youth section of his Tohokai wear black shirts, black combat hats and red ties.

In mid-1940 he joined the National League for the Construction of East Asia, together with such like-minded men as Hashimoto Kingoro (who after his dismissal from military service had organised a Great Japan Youth Party along Nazi lines) and ex-Admiral Suetsugu Nobumasa.

Although most members of the renovationist right had little interest in borrowing foreign labels when 'Japanism' (Nihonshugi) bore so high a premium, the influence of the European dictatorships was strong. On 11 June, for instance, a Tokyo *Asahi* report based on a talk with Konoe's long-time associate, Arima Yoriyasu, suggested that ' a national political organisation like the German Nazis' was being considered. What particularly attracted Arima and the other renovationist bureaucrats, journalists and academics who belonged to the Showa Kenkyukai, however, was not so much the leadership principle as the idea of an almost totally planned society within a corporate state. Like Nakano and Nagai Ryutaro, many of them had been regarded as progressives in the 1920s, and in their own eyes still were. They had considerable influence on the Cabinet Planning Board, and in Justice Minister Kazami Akira, Home Minister Yasui Eiji, Cabinet Secretary Tomita Kenji and Legislative Bureau Chief Murase Naokai they had close allies within the new cabinet. Kazami, Yasui, Tomita, Murase, Arima and Goto Ryunosuke (another Showa Kenkyukai member and mentor of Konoe) were all made members of the twenty-six-strong New Structure Preparatory Commission or its eight-man standing committee.

The six sessions of the Preparatory Commission which were held between 28 August and 17 September were, not surprisingly, marked by disagreement and acrimony. Whereas the politicians wanted a new political party built out of their own (nominally deactivated) organisations, some of the Showa Kenkyukai members advocated a fundamentally different political system based on occupational associations, notably the *sangyo kumiai*. Between these two extremes fell the Military Affairs Bureau's proposal for a party in which representatives of various institutions or groups, including politicians but also the military, would play a role. As it turned out, however, the crucial issue in the discussions was not the nature of the proposed party but whether there should be a party at all. Although Konoe's previous statements had encouraged the feeling that there would be, his introductory remarks to the first meeting, when he drew a distinction between a political movement and a political party, left his intentions unclear. One reason for his waning enthusiasm, it has been suggested, was that on becoming Prime Minister he realised that his aim of controlling the army by constructing a powerful national party was unrealistic in the prevailing circumstances. Perhaps more convincing, however, is the argument that he was disturbed by the accusation that a new Bakufu was being established which would encroach upon the Emperor's supreme authority and subvert the *kokutai*. Equally worrying may have been the assertion that the government was seeking to introduce a Japanese version of the Communist Party of the Soviet Union or Germany's Nazi party. These criticisms were made most forcefully by the 'idealist right', which among others included the Hiranuma camp, ex-Kodoha generals and pro-Kodoha military societies, members of the House of Peers, and various notorious ultranationalist activists such as Toyama Mitsuru (a revered extremist 'godfather'), Inoue Nissho (the founder of the Blood Brotherhood) and Mikami Taku (another of the conspirators of 1932). The propensity of the latter three for taking direct action could not easily be disregarded.

Nor was the Japanist Right alone. Although less vocal at this stage, some politicians in the Machida and Hatoyama camps were expressing misgivings about the threat to the Diet, as were business leaders about the plans for direct State control of industry which were being concocted by the Planning Board with the help of the Showa Kenkyukai's Ryu Shintaro. The elder statesmen and Court advisers, including Saionji, who was still mentally alert in his ninety-first year (though he was to die in November), were also concerned about the renovationist character of the proposed new order; and the Emperor is reported to have asked Konoe whether it did not infringe the spirit of the Constitution. Perhaps the most important of all the Japanist right's allies, however, was the powerful Home Ministry, whose bureaucrats were highly suspicious of any movement which might encroach upon their local control and were already implementing their own plans for improving the effectiveness of the spiritual mobilisation campaign by incorporating the whole nation in a network of neighbourhood associations.

At the Preparatory Commission's second meeting on 3 September two Japanist members indicated their doubts about the proposed

new structure, and Konoe appears to have been sufficiently concerned by these and more public warnings to drop the word 'party'.
This retreat, however, provoked an angry response at the following meeting from Muto, who asserted that if there was no need for
a party then there was no need for Konoe as Prime Minister. Nevertheless, the army was in no mood at this stage, with a German
alliance in the offing, to bring down the government, and on 10
September it accepted the compromise term 'association' for the
new organisation, which on 17 September was prospectively named
the Imperial Rule Assistance Association (Taisei Yokusankai). The
radical character of the new structure was also undermined at the
10 September meeting by the abandonment of the idea of basing
the organisation on vocational or cultural associations. Renovationist
hopes were further blunted by the speech which Konoe made at
the inauguration of the Imperial Rule Assistance Association on 12
October. Having discarded the positive drafts which Arima had
given him the previous evening, he dumbfounded his audience
by stating that there was no proclamation or platform other than
'carrying out the way of the subject in assisting the imperial rule'.

The emasculation of the new structure

Such bland language indicated that Konoe had lost interest in
making major changes, and this impression was confirmed by his
failure during the next six months to defend the Imperial Rule
Assistance Association against its critics. Significantly, the Showa
Kenkyukai disbanded itself in November, although four of its
members were nevertheless to be arrested on 8 April 1941 on the
ground that, under cover of the new economic structure plans
which they had persuaded the Cabinet Planning Board to adopt
the previous year, they had been trying to import socialism. Thirteen others were taken into custody in this 'Cabinet Planning
Board Incident', but already before this the strong business
reaction to the 'red' aspects of the plans had led to the removal
from office of two of the planners' high-level supporters – Kishi
Nobusuke, the Vice-Minister of Commerce and Industry, and
Hoshino Naoki, the head of the Planning Board. The plans
themselves were substantially diluted before they received cabinet
approval on 7 December 1940. Both profit limitation and close
bureaucratic direction (under the formula of 'separation of

management and capital') were jettisoned in return for the agreement of business leaders to give proper weight to national interests and to accept control associations for every industry. When the latter were, somewhat belatedly, introduced in late 1941 and early 1942, they were in all cases headed by a leading industrialist, not a bureaucratic planner.

The emasculation of the new economic structure was parallelled by the crippling of the political reorganisation. Not much of the initial bold conception of a new order had survived the formation of the Imperial Rule Assistance Association, but the new body did have a considerable proportion of renovationists on its directorate and in its five bureaux. In December 1940, however, the Association lost much of its support within the cabinet as a result of Konoe's decision to remove the two principal renovationist ministers, Kazami and Yasui, and replace them by General Yanagawa and Baron Hiranuma. Moreover, pressure for further changes was soon forthcoming from the Diet, where in order to regain some political leverage the majority of politicians had by 20 December combined to form a Diet Members Club. Their position was that much stronger because big business had been so antagonised by the proposed economic controls that the Imperial Rule Assistance Association was no longer able to rely on private funding and the government was therefore compelled to seek money for its continued operation from the Diet. The price proved high, however. Not only did the Lower House politicians insist on a reduction of the amount requested from thirty-seven to eight million yen, but Arima, Nakano, Hashimoto and other renovationists were forced to resign from their positions in the Association, while Yanagawa was brought in as Konoe's deputy director. Meanwhile the Lower House had also secured, through negotiations between Konoe and Machida, a postponement of both the widely proclaimed electoral reform plans and the election which was due in May 1941.

In the nine months from July 1940 to April 1941 Japan had swung wildly from a mood which favoured sweeping political and economic change to a more sober acceptance that institutions could only be modified gradually and by agreement. This lowering of the political temperature clearly owed much to the reassertion of conservative and moderate forces. To understand why this opposition was able to express itself so much more effectively in late 1940 than in the summer, and how it was possible to overcome army wishes, it is necessary to examine the change in Japanese perceptions of the international situation.

It is universally accepted that the upsurge of the new structure movement in June-July 1940 was closely connected with the excitement caused by the prospect of the collapse of the Western colonial position in South East Asia, but it has generally escaped attention that, at least among policy-makers, the mood of euphoria gradually dissipated during the autumn and winter. Although Japanese military pressure was able to secure the stationing of troops in northern Indochina in September, and although the dynamic diplomacy of new Foreign Minister Matsuoka Yosuke resulted in the signature on 27 September of a military alliance with Germany, Japanese expectations were otherwise disappointed. Britain did not submit to Germany, and although Matsuoka eventually (though not until April 1941) secured a neutrality pact from Stalin, the improvement of relations with the Soviet Union was not sufficient to free Japan from concern about a possible northern threat. Even more important, the spectre of active American opposition to Japan's establishment of a Great East Asia Co-Prosperity Sphere loomed much larger. In July 1940 the United States had for the first time imposed official sanctions – on high-quality aviation oil and scrap iron – and further embargoes followed from late September. Although the Tripartite Pact provided for German support for Japan if the country should be attacked by the United States, the American decision in June 1940 to build a two-ocean navy meant that, even with its new super-battleships, Japan would soon be left so far behind in tonnage volumes that it would be impossible to risk war. During the winter of 1940-1, the desire of the top navy leaders for caution became apparent to their army counterparts. By March 1941 even Major-General Tanaka Shinichi, the hawkish new head of the General Staff Operations Division, had come to the conclusion that the policy adopted in the previous July, which had envisaged the possibility of using force if necessary to establish Japanese hegemony over South-East Asia, was no better than waste-paper – a judgement with which the other division heads concurred.[9] Within the Army Ministry, Muto had himself become extremely concerned about the American danger. It was against this background of doubts and uncertainties on the military side that the opponents of a

[9] See Boeicho Boeikenshujo Senshishitsu, *Daihonei Rikugunbu*, vol. 2, p. 214.

Japanese-style one-party state were able to halt and turn back the tide which had seemed irresistible only a few months earlier.

Politics and foreign policy in 1941

The truce which was concluded in early 1941 between the government and the Diet was not to be challenged for the rest of the year. Nevertheless, by October there had been two further changes of cabinet, both caused by differences over foreign policy. The first stemmed from Foreign Minister Matsuoka's conviction that only if Germany was successful in destroying the established international world order would Japan be able to overcome Anglo-American opposition to the Great East Asia Co-Prosperity Sphere. This led him to try to sabotage the talks in Washington between Secretary of State Hull and the Japanese Ambassador Nomura, which aimed at a Japanese-American rapprochement (and which threatened to undermine the deterrent value of the Tripartite Pact). It also led him to urge in June that Japan join in Germany's assault on the Soviet Union, disregarding the Neutrality Pact which he himself had negotiated with Stalin in April. Matsuoka's colleagues, however, saw things rather differently. Although an attack on the traditional number-one enemy was favoured by some elements in the Army General Staff and by fanatical anti-communists, most military men preferred to avoid another test of strength and to wait until the Soviet Union collapsed. For its part, the navy was so anxious to prevent such an outcome that, with too little consideration of the possible consequences, Navy Minister Oikawa threw his weight behind an alternative proposal for the acquisition of bases in southern French Indochina. Almost by chance, the resulting resumption of its southward military movement finally set Japan on a collision course with the United States, for President Roosevelt now agreed to freeze Japanese assets in the United States and impose new restrictions on trade. By September these had turned into a de facto total embargo, and Japan was faced with the very real prospect of running out of oil and becoming militarily impotent within two years.

Yet another ironical aspect of the events of mid-1941 was that Matsuoka almost alone opposed the move into southern Indochina (as likely to provoke a hostile Anglo-American reaction), yet by the time it took place in late July, he had been removed from office because he had come to be seen as a major impediment to the improvement of relations with America. Since he had considerable support from some renovationist elements, his outright dismissal could have been politically risky, so Konoe instead engineered his removal through the devious procedure of a resignation of the whole cabinet on 18 July and its immediate reconstitution without him. The change of Foreign Minister opened the way for a more determined and realistic pursuit of an accommodation with the United States, but the plan on which Konoe placed his chief hope – a summit meeting between himself and Roosevelt – came up against the implacable opposition of Secretary of State Hull. Meanwhile, in early September, after intense pressure by Major-General Tanaka and other General Staff members had overcome the misgivings of their naval counterparts, an imperial headquarters–government liaison conference (in practice the supreme policy-making body since mid-1940) took the decision to embark upon war if there were no prospect of diplomatic success by mid-October. No opposition was forthcoming from Konoe, and although the Emperor showed some inclination to voice his own doubts at the Imperial Conference held to ratify the decision on 6 September, he was dissuaded by Privy Seal Kido from doing so directly.

Konoe's willingness to go along with the military in September was clearly connected with his hope that the summit meeting proposal would produce sufficient improvement in the situation to defuse the international tension and allow the decision for war to be cancelled. He failed, however, to take fully into account how much more difficult it would be to oppose the advocates of war once a deadline had been set. When, in early October, with the Americans still unaccommodating, Konoe sought more time to pursue a compromise through diplomacy, he ran into Army Minister Tojo Hideki's objection that he was seeking to overturn an Imperial Conference decision. Tojo suspected, with some justice, that the navy too was secretly trying to wriggle out of its commitment to war, and his indignation boiled over in a cabinet meeting on 14 October. If the cabinet was not prepared to accept responsibility for what had been decided in September, the Army Minister asserted, then there was no alternative to resignation. Faced with this uncompromising stand by a military leader who was very conscious of the General Staff's demanding mobilisation requirements, Konoe had no choice but to resign.

In the circumstances the choice of a new Prime Minister was both unusually urgent and peculiarly difficult. From the point of view of the Court it was essential that the person selected should have sufficient standing to maintain control of the army should the decision for war be suspended or rejected, and to Konoe it seemed that Prince Higashikuni, an uncle of the Emperor and a serving general, best fitted the bill. The same conclusion had been reached by Tojo. The key figure in the nomination process, however, was Kido, and the Lord Keeper of the Privy Seal was determined not to allow the imperial family to be involved in politics. Instead, he gambled by putting forward Tojo, the very person who had brought the previous cabinet down. Conscious that Japan's fate was in the balance, he felt that the problem of army pressure could best be dealt with by giving the Army Minister overall responsibility. If war still was not avoided and things turned out badly, it would be the army which would have to shoulder the blame.

Initially it seemed as if the gamble might pay off. When, after the *jushin* had accepted Kido's arguments, Tojo was summoned to the Palace on 17 October to be informed of his unexpected appointment, he accepted without question the imperial instruction that the new cabinet should review national policy without being bound by the Imperial Conference decision of 6 September. Moreover, Tojo rejected Military Affairs Bureau interference in the formation of his cabinet. He himself became Home Minister while retaining the position of Army Minister, but the most significant new appointment, as Foreign Minister, was a professional diplomat known for his opposition to alliance with Germany – Togo Shigenori. Furthermore, when Togo demanded an extension of the diplomatic deadline and insisted on presenting to the United States an alternative proposal for a short-term agreement, he was supported by the Prime Minister. But there were limits to how far Tojo was prepared to go. In particular, he could not agree to the American demand that Japan withdraw all its troops from China within a clearly specified period of limited duration. His objections were shared not only by the military but by almost all his cabinet colleagues, and consequently on 1 December another Imperial Conference gave the final go-ahead for war. A week later much of the American Pacific fleet had been put out of action by Admiral Yamamoto's surprise attack upon Pearl Harbor, and within a few months the whole of South-East Asia had passed into Japanese control.

Tojo, the 1942 election and war-time politics

Japan's overwhelming initial success confounded the pessimists and inevitably strengthened Tojo's political position. With an election due in April 1942 he sought to capitalise on the early victories and bolster his prestige by reinforcing the government's support in the Diet. To ensure this, a semi-official political association, the Yokusan Seiji Kyogikai (Imperial Rule Political Assistance Conference), was formed on 17 March with the purpose of selecting suitable candidates, preferably uncontaminated by old party connections, for endorsement in the coming election. Because the branch members were to be appointed by prefectural governors, and because the Home Ministry recommended that reservists should be specially favoured in this process, it was anticipated that the influence of those local *yuryokusha* who had maintained the political bases of the old party politicians would be largely eliminated. Such expectations proved unduly optimistic. In practice many existing and previous Diet members became leaders of the new organisation, and only fourteen branches followed central guidelines fully in recommending candidates for endorsement. The eventual list included 235 current Diet members (including all the mainstream faction leaders other than Hatoyama) and eighteen with previous Diet experience, as against 213 newcomers (some of whom had party connections); and of the 381 endorsed candidates who were elected, 212 had sat in the Diet before. Of the eighty-five non-recommended candidates who were returned, fifty-five were either sitting or previous members.

It would therefore be an over-simplification to regard this war-time election as an overwhelming triumph for the government. Official endorsement did not prove an infallible guarantee of success: even the 82 per cent success rate for endorsed candidates can be considered deceptive in that many of these men were returned primarily because of their local standing. Moreover, the virtual elimination of the need to secure party backing and (since vote-buying and other inducements were even more strictly prohibited than in 1937) the much lesser importance of political funding meant that many more *gun* felt free to seek representation by their own men, and localism flourished as never before. As a result there was a record number of 1079 candidates, a statistic which may well explain why an election which engendered little general enthusiasm produced a turn-out of nearly 83 per cent, 10 per cent higher than in 1937. In practice the continuing strength of grass-root loyalties and local alignments limited the scope for government interference. Admittedly, favoured candidates appear to have received some assistance, and sixty-one established Diet politicians were apparently persuaded to withdraw, but, except in a few areas such as Kagoshima and Nagano, the government avoided any blatant totalitarian action which would have damaged its image. In any case, many prefectural governors had connections with local politicians and would have been extremely wary of some of the new men who were trying to bury the old politics.

This was especially likely where the radical Right and the Dai Nihon Yokusan Sonendan (Great Japan Young Men's Assistance Corps) were involved. The latter organisation (usually abbreviated to Yokuso) was formed on 16 January 1942 at the instigation of the Military Affairs Bureau, and was intended by the military renovationists and other enemies of the old order to play the leading role in 'enlightening' the electorate in the coming campaign. Its membership of about 1,300,000 men, mainly in their twenties and thirties (in 10,059 town and village branches), included a significant number of activists belonging to the Marxist-influenced (according to the police) Noson Kyodotai Kensetsu Domei (League for the Establishment of Farming Village Communities); and, particularly in the north, renovationist agrarian leaders frequently succeeded in becoming Yokuso branch chiefs. The Home Ministry, however, was apparently concerned not to allow it to become a Nazi-style auxiliary support base for the army, and only forty of Yokuso's members were elected to the Diet in 1942.

Despite the survival of most of the older political leaders, however, the election did pave the way for the establishment, on 20 May, of the Dai Nihon Yokusan Seijikai (Great Japan Imperial Rule Assistance Political Association). The new body (usually known as the Yokusei) incorporated the Imperial Assistance Diet Members League (formed after the Diet Members Club split), but other groups, such as the Dokokai (which Hatoyama had set up in late 1941) also decided to join it. Their action may well have helped them to fend off criticism from the radical Right, for the Young

Men's Corps, in particular, continued to pose a threat even though its influence was diminished by Muto's transfer from the Military Affairs Bureau in April 1942. In the town and village assembly elections held in May, Yokuso was able to claim that some 30,000 of the victorious candidates belonged to its branches, and it successfully opposed Yokusei's demand for permission to set up its own local branches. However, if the government was not prepared to allow Yokusei to undermine Yokuso's local organisation, neither was it willing to jeopardise Yokusei cooperation in the Diet in order to satisfy the aspirations of radical agrarian leaders. Whereas Diet politicians were rewarded in June 1942 by the establishment of consultative committees for each ministry, with their memberships drawn mainly from the Lower House, the Young Men's Corps was shocked in early 1943 when the government announced that the practice of endorsing election candidates, which had been criticised in the Diet, was to be discontinued. Yokuso hopes of using the system to score a major success in the next prefectural and metropolitan elections thus received a significant setback. When the organisation was further neutralised by the government's imposition of changes in its upper echelons in December 1943, Yokuso local leaders became increasingly frustrated. The Corps was finally dissolved in 1945.[10] Its fate was a testimony to the deeply ingrained authoritarianism which ensured that in the last resort Japan's government preferred to rely on centralised control, even at the risk of causing alienation and loss of morale, rather than unleash popular forces, however patriotic.

Yokuso's decline was also connected with the weakening of Tojo's political position. Superficially there was no sign of this before 1944. In November 1942, indeed, Tojo had been able to force through a reduction in the number of bureaucrats and also, at the cost of Foreign Minister Togo's resignation, to place responsibility for relations with South East Asia in a Great East Asia Ministry. In November 1943 he further assumed control of the new Ministry of War Procurement, which incorporated the Planning Board, part of the Ministry of Commerce and Industry and some of the economic

[10] A valuable examination of wartime political organisations and their problematic relationships, a hitherto neglected topic, is to be found in E.J.Drea, *The 1942 Japanese General Election*. See also his briefer treatment, 'Yokusan Seiji no Jisso', in Miwa Kimitada (ed.), *Nihon no 1930 – Nendai*, pp. 250-68.

sections of the armed services; while as late as February 1944 he went so far as to combine the two major military functions by making himself additionally Chief of the Army General Staff and Navy Minister Shimada Chief of the Navy General Staff. But these latter steps represented desperate attempts to cope with a deteriorating war situation rather than genuine increases in political power, and sometimes had to be accompanied by concessions.

Essentially Tojo's standing depended on military success, and the turn of the tide after Japan's initial victories was bound to undermine his cabinet. The naval reverse suffered at Midway in June 1942 might be concealed, but the first actual loss of territory in the Solomon Islands after the long drawn-out battle of Guadalcanal in the winter of 1942-3 was a different matter, and the attempt to cover up such defeats under the euphemistic phrase 'advance by changing position' became an increasingly transparent disguise with every repetition. Not that there was any danger of open criticism of the government, for although the censorship system was occasionally breached or circumvented, in general it effectively constrained those newspapers which had been allowed to remain in existence after the government had forced many to discontinue production or amalgamate on economic grounds in 1941. Nor was popular dissent likely. Not only did war propaganda pervade the various media, but the whole of the nation had, between 1940 and 1943, been compelled to enrol in neighbourhood associations which the Home Ministry used both to carry out various local functions (including the distribution of rations) and to maintain patriotic feeling and collectivist conformity; while industrial workers, whose living conditions generally deteriorated more than those of the rural population during the war, had been deprived of any scope for autonomous action by the dissolution of labour unions to make way for the nation-wide organisation – on an individual workplace basis and with management involvement – of the officially sponsored patriotic labour association, Sangyo Hokoku-kai (Sampo).

The growth of opposition to Tojo

At a higher and less public level, however, Tojo and his cabinet did not remain above criticism. Within the army itself there were those who resented Tojo's dominance, as well as others (notably Tanaka

Shinichi until he was transferred from the General Staff in 1943) who felt that he had made too many concessions to the navy. Many naval officers, on the other hand, believed that Admiral Shimada had allowed himself to be used by Tojo, and wanted to see both of them replaced. Such views generally had to be expressed with great discretion, however, for those who dared to put them forward were liable to find themselves, or their family members, posted to dangerous or remote assignments. They might also be subjected to the menacing attentions of the dreaded Kempeitai, the military police force which came under Tojo's control as Army Minister and which operated with ruthless zeal.

The same danger also faced Diet politicians, but their status and privileges as members of the legislature did give them slightly greater freedom than ordinary citizens, and some bolder spirits began to make use of this from late 1942. First among the critics of the Prime Minister was Nakano Seigo, who had re-established his party, the Tohokai, before the 1942 election and had put up forty-seven candidates, seven of whom had been returned. Nakano was joined by other politicians, mostly of non-bureaucratic background, such as Hatoyama Ichiro and Miki Bukichi, in remonstrating against the government for riding rough-shod over the Diet's sensitivities, and in particular for severely curtailing the duration of its sessions and forcing it to rubber-stamp legislation. In March 1943 some thirty Lower House members went so far as to vote against an amendment to the criminal law, and in June Nakano and Hatoyama were among six who withdrew from membership of the Imperial Rule Assistance Political Association. The intensity of Nakano's detestation of the Prime Minister's bureaucratic approach led him to be both more active and less discreet than Hatoyama, and in October 1943 he paid the penalty by being arrested, along with about 100 members of radical Rightist societies. Because a new Diet session was about to begin, Nakano was detained only for a few days, but shortly after his release he committed suicide.

The reasons for Nakano's drastic action have been much debated. He may have intended it as a defiant protest, in the tradition of Oshio Heihachiro, Saigo Takamori and other tragic heroes of the Oyomei school of Confucianism, against Tojo's semi-dictatorial conduct; alternatively he may have been driven to it by threats against his family, as the chief of the Tokyo Kempeitai, Colonel

Shikata, was not ashamed to hint later.[11] Whatever his motive or motives, Nakano had undoubtedly been attempting to undermine the cabinet and had been seeking to involve a number of eminent and influential persons, among them Prince Higashikuni, Prince Konoe, ex-diplomat Yoshida Shigeru, and probably General Ugaki. These men shared Nakano's desire to secure Tojo's removal, though mainly because they were concerned about the danger of a military-led social revolution if Japan went on fighting to the bitter end. Konoe, in particular, was already anxious by early 1943 to bring to power the retired Kodoha general, Mazaki Jinzaburo, or some comparable military figure, such as General Ugaki or Admiral Kobayashi Seizo, who could be trusted to suppress the crypto-communist tendencies which he believed some of the military planners to harbour. To prevent such a threat to the established order it was also desirable to negotiate an early peace, although even Konoe, privileged as he was, could not speak of this outside his circle of intimate friends. The replacement of Tojo would be a step towards the achievement of both objectives, and from about December 1942 Konoe sought this. Typically, he occasionally wavered in his attitude, but he represented a much greater danger than Nakano to Tojo.

Between late 1942 and mid-1944 the clandestine anti-Tojo movement grew as Konoe's group, which already had links with the Kodoha, found sympathisers among the *jushin* (especially the naval ex-Prime Ministers) and the imperial princes. In August 1943 the *jushin* entertained the hope that by intimating to Tojo that there was dissatisfaction with his conduct of government, they might induce him to resign, but although a meeting was held with this purpose, it proved fruitless. The most obvious alternative method was to involve the Court, but neither the Lord Keeper of the Privy Seal nor the Emperor seem to have shared fully Konoe's apprehensions about a disguised communist threat and both were reluctant to act in a way which might be deemed constitutionally improper. As a result Tojo was able to remain in office even when the desire for a change had become so widespread in informed circles that the Speaker of the Lower House, at a Prime Ministerial reception for Diet members on 25 March 1944, felt able to call for his resignation.

---

[11] See L.R. Oates, *Populist Nationalism in Pre-War Japan*, p. 112.

Not until the loss of Saipan (in the Mariana Islands) on 7 July 1944 brought American air-power within striking distance of the Japanese home islands did the pressure for a major change at the highest level of government become overwhelming. On 13 July, after he had apparently become concerned about both the cabinet's failure to make any moves to end the war and Tojo's and Shimada's dismissal of a Navy Ministry plan for an operation to regain control of Saipan, the Emperor indicated, first through Kido, then directly, that the Prime Minister should separate the service ministries from the general staffs again, replace Navy Minister Shimada, and bring some *jushin* into the government. Although Tojo was prepared to meet the first of the Emperor's requirements, the third proved to be beyond his reach, for although General Abe might have been willing to join the cabinet, Admiral Yonai resolutely declined to do so. To make the situation more difficult for Tojo, one of the current Ministers of State, Kishi Nobusuke, whom the Prime Minister had requested to resign to make room for a *jushin*, refused to do so unless the whole cabinet stepped down. Two other ministers also advocated this latter course, as, on 17 July, did the *jushin* and two imperial princes. In addition, rumours were rife that the Imperial Rule Assistance Political Association might be about to withdraw its support. Faced with these unmistakable signs of elite dissatisfaction, Tojo bowed out of office on 18 July.

The Koiso and Suzuki cabinets and the peace party

The fall of the Tojo cabinet left the Japanese political situation in a state of some confusion. Opposition to Tojo had come from various quarters, not from one coherent movement, and no-one had emerged as an obvious successor. Consequently, when the *jushin* were convened by Kido to nominate the next Prime Minister, various opinions were expressed. Eventually consensus was reached in favour of the least provocative option – the appointment of another general. Rather surprisingly Konoe did not press the claims of Mazaki, and after Tojo had vetoed Field Marshal Terauchi, the mandate passed to General Koiso Kuniaki, a one-time Colonial Minister and conspirator in the abortive March coup in 1931. At Konoe's suggestion, however, Kido recommended to the Emperor that, in order to guarantee full navy cooperation and the presence of a strong voice for moderation, Admiral Yonai should share the responsibility for the cabinet's formation. Yonai's involvement helped to give it a more balanced complexion, for his personal friend, the liberal newspaperman, Ogata Taketora, became a Minister of State, and three politicians, the most since Yonai's own 1940 cabinet, were also included.

The Koiso cabinet was inevitably a weak one. It had to take responsibility for the ever-deteriorating war situation and for the lack of adequate defences against the heavy bombing raids which began to wreak devastation on Japan's cities and industry from November 1944, yet little could be done to reverse the tide of defeat. Some efforts were made, notably the replacement of the imperial headquarters-government liaison conference by a supreme war leadership council in August 1944, but this proved scarcely more than a change of name; for it to have functioned as a true war cabinet, closer coordination between the two services would have been necessary, but that goal became ever more elusive as the army came increasingly to emphasise a strategy based on the land-based defence of the home islands. Needless to say, the navy was fiercely opposed both to this and another idea mooted by the army leaders – a merger of the two services.

At the level of mass mobilisation the Prime Minister's efforts were similarly unproductive. His plan to revitalise the Imperial Rule Assistance Association, the Imperial Rule Assistance Political Association and the Young Men's Corps by merging them into a supposedly more autonomous body was successfully resisted by the Political Association; and there was further friction with both the other organisations when Koiso foisted upon them new leaders with whom he had close connections. In addition, the replacement of General Abe as head of the Political Association by the relatively moderate Admiral Kobayashi and the re-institution of the system of parliamentary vice-ministers encouraged a revival of factional activity among politicians; and when in March 1945 the Political Association was abolished to make way for another new body, the Dai Nihon Seijikai (Great Japan Political Association), which would, it was claimed, act as an effective national political party, ninety members of the Lower House declined to join it. The final demonstration of Koiso's weakness, and of his cabinet's lack of solidarity, came when his plan to negotiate a Chinese peace settlement with Miao Pin, a secret agent of Chiang

Kai-shek who had come to Japan in March, was blocked by Foreign Minister Shigemitsu Mamoru, Army Minister Sugiyama, Yonai and Kido. Further discouraged by Kido from pursuing the idea of a major governmental change, Koiso resigned on 5 April.

The fact that Koiso's departure was partly prompted by the failure of his Chinese peace plan was ironic, since he saw it as a first move towards an ending of the wider war, which was also the aim of several of the men who sabotaged the plan. However, past experience of unofficial negotiations with China gave no grounds for optimism, and in any case the fact that Koiso was also known to be contemplating resignation opened up the prospect of bringing in someone less committed to the military point of view. The person whom Konoe now favoured, and for whom he canvassed support in late March among his fellow *jushin*, was the seventy-eight-year-old ex-admiral, Suzuki Kantaro. Having once been Grand Chamberlain, Suzuki was known to be absolutely loyal to the Emperor, and in the last resort could be trusted to place the preservation of the imperial house and the *kokutai* above all other considerations, including unwillingness to accept the fact of defeat. Suzuki himself was taken by surprise by his nomination on 5 April but in the face of an established consensus and an appeal by Kido to his sense of duty he reluctantly acquiesced.

Initially Suzuki's appointment appeared to make little difference. Indeed, his first steps as Prime Minister were to introduce new measures for the more effective prosecution of the war. One such was the establishment in April of yet another organisation for mobilising the people, the Kokumin Giyutai (National Patriotic Corps), in which all males between the ages of fifteen and sixty and all females between seventeen and forty were supposed to enrol. In June it replaced or absorbed all the other surviving patriotic bodies, including the Imperial Rule Assistance Association. By then Japan's war leaders were becoming desperate. Production had been drastically cut as a result of the sinking of most of the merchant fleet and the bombing of industrial areas. At the beginning of April the tide of American advance had reached Okinawa, and on the day Koiso resigned, the Soviet Union ominously gave notice that it was terminating the 1941 Neutrality Pact (although it was technically bound by its terms for a further year).

Despite the worsening situation the basic army position remained one of reliance on all-out resistance, in the hope that the

Right A *Tokyo Puck* cartoon satirising the mid-1930s campaign for clean elections led by Home Minister Goto Fumio (pictured speaking) by suggesting that behind the fine words the working classes were being exploited by finance capital. *Below* Three leaders of the Shakai Taishuto (from left to right, Aso Hisashi, Asanuma Inejiro and Kawabe Shigeo) celebrating their party's success in doubling its representation in the 1937 general election.

Right Konoe Fumimaro, three times Prime Minister between July 1937 and October 1941. *Below* Some of the key members of his second cabinet (from right to left: Tojo Hideki, Yoshida Zengo, and Matsuoka Yosuke) discussing the future direction of Japan with him at his Tekigaiso residence on 19 July 1940, just before the cabinet's formal inauguration.

Saito Takao making his controversial Diet speech criticising Japan's China policy in February 1940: it was to lead, after bitter debate within the various political parties, to his expulsion, and contributed to the mood favouring the dissolution of political parties in 1940 that culminated in the establishment of the Imperial Rule Assistance Association.

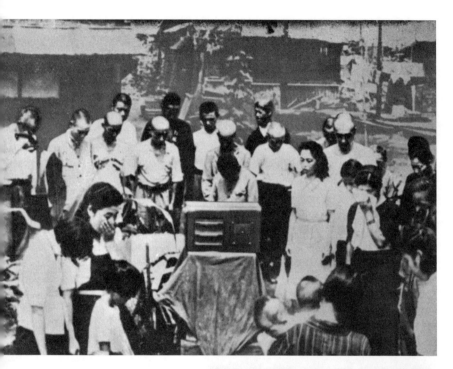

Above Japanese listening to the Emperor's surrender broadcast on 15 August 1945.
Right SCAP GHQ, General MacArthur's headquarters in the Daiichi Sogo building opposite the Imperial Palace, where lights glowed late at night as American occupation officials worked on the postwar reform of Japan.

Americans would be deterred from invasion by their prospective losses and would offer acceptable peace terms. Within the Establishment generally this policy increasingly seemed suicidal, but anyone who advocated that Japan sue for peace risked assassination or imprisonment. Even Konoe was threatened by ultranationalists in April, and some of his close associates, among them Yoshida Shigeru, were actually arrested and held in custody for about six weeks by the Kempeitai. Probably an even greater obstacle to peace, however, was the American insistence that Japan's surrender, like Germany's, must be unconditional. Although arguably justifiable in that it ensured that the United States would have a free hand in eradicating Japanese militarism after the war, this demand virtually precluded any direct approach by the Japanese government. Some unofficial soundings were made in early 1945, via Switzerland and Sweden, in the hope of eliciting an indication of American flexibility, but being indirect and noncommittal these were disregarded. When the Suzuki cabinet was formed, Togo Shigenori, who had again reluctantly agreed to become Foreign Minister, succeeded in having all military personnel other than the Army and Navy Ministers and Chiefs of Staff excluded from the supreme war leadership council, but that body then overrode Togo's arguments and decided to bolster Japan's bargaining position by seeking improved relations with the Soviet Union. Not until 7 July, after the Emperor and Kido had added their weight to the pressure for a settlement, did the council seek peace. Even then the approach was not a direct one. Instead, the leadership continued to clutch at straws by offering Stalin major territorial concessions and hegemony in North-East Asia in return for Russian mediation.

Japan's attempt to play power-politics was a disastrous failure. Not only did Stalin fail to rise to the bait, but its gambit allowed the Japanese government to continue to indulge in vain hopes and thus contributed to Suzuki's decision not to make a serious response to the Potsdam Declaration of 26 July, in which the Allied powers warned that if Japan did not 'proclaim now the unconditional surrender of all Japanese armed forces', the alternative would be 'prompt and utter destruction'. Precisely what that last phrase signified was not spelled out, but on 6 August the population of Hiroshima learned its meaning when most of their city was reduced to ashes by an atomic bomb, an experience which the inhabitants of Nagasaki were also to undergo three days later. In the meantime, on 8 August, the Soviet Union declared war and began to overrun Manchukuo.

The decision to surrender

The sequence of disasters which befell Japan between the 6th and 9th of August had a decisive effect on the Japanese leadership, although their close juxtaposition in time makes it impossible to determine which of the blows had the greatest impact. Nevertheless, the issue of war or peace was still not resolved completely. At the supreme war leadership council meeting on 9 August the two army members and the Chief of the Naval General Staff insisted that the Potsdam Declaration should be accepted only, among other conditions, if Japan were allowed to disarm her own forces and if any military occupation were strictly limited. Against this Togo maintained, with support from Yonai and Suzuki, that Japan should only hold out for the maintenance of the Emperor's position. This deadlock was not broken even after a prolonged cabinet meeting, but following several further hours of agonising debate at an Imperial Conference during the night, Suzuki took the unprecedented step of requesting the Emperor to decide, and the latter's judgement in favour of Togo was accepted without dispute both by the Conference and by the subsequent cabinet meeting. Thus, on 10 August, Japan offered to accept the terms of the Potsdam Declaration on the understanding that the Emperor's 'prerogatives as a Sovereign Ruler' were not prejudiced.

The American Secretary of State's reply was equivocal. 'The ultimate form of government of Japan', he stated, 'shall ... be subject to the Supreme Commander of the Allied powers'. Into such language could easily be read the intention of destroying the *kokutai*, and not only did Army Minister Anami, Army Chief of Staff Umezu and Navy Chief of Staff Toyoda urge rejection, but even Suzuki for a time hesitated to acquiesce in surrender on such terms. Although the majority of the cabinet supported Togo's reiterated demand for acceptance on 13 August, it was once again left to the Emperor to overcome military opposition in another Imperial Conference the following day. He followed this up with another unprecedented action – a broadcast (which some army headquarters staff vainly attempted to prevent by seizing the imperial palace) in which he called upon the Japanese people to 'endure the unendurable' and devote their strength to 'construction for the future'. Some army leaders, notably Anami and Sugiyama, chose instead to commit *harakiri*, and at least 524 other Japanese preferred suicide to living with the shame of defeat. A number of army officers and fanatical nationalists defied the imperial pronouncement to the extent of attempting to stage *coups d'état*, but despite these incidents there was a remarkable lack of opposition when American forces under General MacArthur arrived on 28 August to begin the occupation and reform of Japan. The Emperor's actions thus marked the apogee of the political role of the throne at the same time as they prepared the way for the dismantling of the Emperor-system.

7

THE POST-WAR RESHAPING OF JAPANESE POLITICS, 1945-52

It is one of the ironies of history that the Japanese attempt to establish an autonomous empire ended in Japan's being even more at the mercy of a Western power than it had been in the 1860s. Not that the full extent of the nation's humiliation was spelt out in the broadcast in which the Emperor announced Japan's surrender on 15 August 1945. Indeed, while referring to America's use of a devastating new weapon as the principal reason for the termination of the war, he avoided any explicit admission that Japan had been defeated, going only so far as to concede that the conflict had developed 'not necessarily to Japan's advantage'. He then proceeded to exhort his subjects to 'beware most strictly of any outburst of emotion ... or any fraternal contention and strife which may create confusion, lead ye astray and cause ye to lose the confidence of the world', and urged them to devote themselves to building the future while continuing 'as one family from generation to generation, ever firm in its faith in the imperishableness of its sacred land'.[1]

Conservative expectations and initial Occupation policy

This choice of language was clearly designed to make surrender less unpalatable to the armed forces and to ultranationalist diehards, but it also reflected the intense concern of the Establishment to maintain continuity and minimise disruption. On the face of it there should have been little ground for confidence with regard to this second desire. The Japanese were, after all, psychologically unprepared either for defeat or occupation, while on the other hand the objectives outlined by the United States and Britain in the Potsdam Declaration were potentially extremely far-reaching.

[1] Quoted by W. Macmahon Ball, *Japan: Enemy or Ally*, p. 47.

Nevertheless, Prince Konoe and other civilian leaders, while anticipating that America and its allies would take drastic measures against the Japanese military, did not foresee unrestricted punitive or destructive action by the conquering powers. On the contrary, far from sharing the fears inculcated by wartime propaganda, they seem to have considered that American involvement in Japan would be a stabilising factor. In particular, it would provide a safeguard against the danger that the masses, possibly led by radical army officers and incited by Soviet agents, would blame the ruling élites for what had gone wrong and support revolution. The fact that the Supreme Commander for the Allied Powers (SCAP), General MacArthur, upon his arrival did not establish direct military government but instead set up sections within his General Headquarters which exercised indirect surveillance over the Japanese government encouraged the feeling that the process of reform would be largely left to the Japanese themselves and that moderate conservative elements might be able to regain the strong position which they had held before 1931.

Such conservative hopes were soon to seem like wishful thinking, when on 4 October SCAP (an acronym which became commonly applied not only to MacArthur but also his general headquarters) issued its first major directive. In accordance with the Initial Post-Surrender Policy for Japan – the gist of which had been sent to MacArthur from Washington on 29 August – it required the Japanese government (which had been headed since 17 August by Prince Higashikuni, the Emperor's uncle) to release all political prisoners, including communists, remove the existing Home Minister, and repeal the laws (notably the Peace Preservation Law) on which official suppression of radicalism had been based. The cabinet, which had actually been planning to tighten its control by enlisting ex-army officers into an expanded police force, was so rocked by this demand that it decided to resign forthwith.

The shock of the 4 October directive was soon followed by further indications that SCAP was not concerned simply to eliminate the Japanese military. On 11 October, MacArthur communicated to the new Prime Minister, the respected ex-diplomat Shidehara Kijuro, his conviction that to fulfil the requirements of the Potsdam Declaration women should be enfranchised, labour unions encouraged, education liberalised, and the economy democratised. These demands, which were implemented, at least in part, by the end of the year by no means represented the limits of Occupation intentions. SCAP's targets also included the punishment of all those who bore responsibility for Japanese aggression. Konoe himself was among the twenty-eight military and governmental leaders designated on 6 December for trial as major war criminals, but rather than undergo such an ordeal he committed suicide. Whether he would have received the sentence of death which three years later was passed on seven of the accused, among them Tojo and Hirota, cannot therefore be known. The Emperor was not indicted, although he was required to disclaim his supposed divinity in a rescript on 1 January 1946.

Of greater political significance than the Tokyo war crimes tribunal was the attempted eradication of undesirable influences. Some leaders were removed from office in late 1945, but the sweeping nature of the purge only became apparent in January 1946, when all Diet representatives who had been members of the Dai Nihon Seijikai during the war were disbarred from standing for election again and all identifiable ultranationalists and militarists were banned from public office or important positions in industry. Since all ex-officers of the now-disbanded armed forces, as well as the close relatives of politicians, were affected by this broader disqualification (with important business leaders being added to the list in 1947), the number of those purged ultimately amounted to over 200,000. For a few the ban proved to be temporary, but in most cases it was terminated only towards, or after, the end of the Occupation in 1952, and many, though by no means all, found it difficult to resume their previous careers.

By the beginning of 1946 it was plain that those 'old Japan hands' in the United States, such as ex-Ambassador Grew, who shared the belief of Japanese moderate conservatives that the period between 1931 and 1945 had been a militaristic aberration in modern Japanese history, had been forced to give ground to those who maintained that there was something fundamentally unhealthy and undemocratic about Japan's whole process of modernisation since 1868. Like the Japanese Marxists who were beginning to establish their intellectual sway over Japanese historical writing, many Americans, especially among those who had been trained during the war for service in Japan, saw it as their mission to eradicate from Japanese life what they saw as the 'feudal legacy'. As the radical American journalist, Mark Gayn, described it in his 7

December diary entry: 'This is an exciting place at an exciting time in history. [...] Headquarters is full of 'reformers'. Lights burn late in the buildings where these young men work on a blueprint for a new Japanese democracy. [...] There is wrecking aplenty, but this is a feudal land, and no democracy can rise here until the old structure is demolished'.[2]

The divergence between the expectations of the Japanese conservatives and the radical character of American actions in the first year of the Occupation was subsequently attributed by the former to an initial American misunderstanding of Japanese society and politics. Although such a view considerably oversimplifies matters, it is nevertheless relevant that the initial American plans for Japan were originally drawn up by an interdepartmental committee representing the Army, Navy and State Department during 1944-5, when attitudes were bound to be strongly influenced by wartime feeling and propaganda as well as by the expectation that only a bitterly contested invasion and occupation would secure Japan's surrender. In such circumstances the desire for retribution was probably a factor in the general enthusiasm, even among military men who might in other circumstances have been suspicious of so radical an approach, for the uprooting of the injustices and traditional attitudes which, it was plausibly argued, had nurtured Japanese ultranationalism. This would help to explain the ready acceptance of the necessity not just of demilitarisation but also of democratisation – and in social organisation, the economy and education, as well as politics. Such an approach found solid support from those (sometimes called the 'China crowd') who sympathised or identified with nationalist China and hoped to see that country emerge as the major East Asian power and America's ally. It should further be noted that among the roughly 2,000 members of SCAP headquarters were some who had been involved in Roosevelt's New Deal measures and regarded Japan as highly suitable for a more extensive experiment in social engineering. Such men were particularly prominent in the Government Section, which was most directly concerned with Japan's political democratisation.

The influence of the radical reformers who served under MacArthur in Tokyo was eventually to decline, but in the crucial early months of the Occupation they played a major role. They were in most cases given full rein by MacArthur, who found

[2] M. Gayn, *Japan Diary*, p. 5.

congenial the mission of bringing American values to Japan and whose presidential ambitions stood to be furthered if he could claim the credit for the successful transformation of America's erstwhile enemy. What the Supreme Commander most emphatically did not want, however, was interference by the Far Eastern Commission. This body, formally the supreme authority with regard to Occupation policy, was pressed upon the US government by Britain and the Soviet Union in December 1945. It was to have members from eleven nations and was to be based in Washington (with a smaller Allied Council for Japan made up of representatives of the United States, the Soviet Union, the British Commonwealth and China, advising MacArthur in Tokyo). In practice it was not to play a very active role, the US government having limited its concession by insisting on a clause which required unanimity for Far Eastern Commission decisions, thus leaving effective control in American hands. Nevertheless, MacArthur was not disposed to trust Washington to maintain his de facto power, and was therefore eager to press ahead before the Far Eastern Commission came into formal existence in March 1946.

Constitutional reform

The most notable examples of SCAP's haste were the imposition of a new constitution and the holding of a general election. In July 1945 the Potsdam Declaration had laid down, as one of the conditions for the withdrawal of the occupying forces, the establishment 'in accordance with the freely-expressed will of the Japanese people' of 'a peacefully inclined and responsible government'. MacArthur's pressure on the Shidehara cabinet in October 1945 to set up a constitutional revision committee, though betraying some impatience, was not necessarily incompatible with this basic approach. But in early February 1946, only a month after Washington had sent him a set of guidelines for the reform of the Japanese government which included the explicit instruction that 'only as a last resort should the Supreme Commander order the Japanese Government to effect the above listed reforms', MacArthur effectively cast aside this official policy. After the very limited constitutional revision proposals being considered by the Japanese government committee under Matsumoto Joji became known through publication of a leaked version of them in the *Mainichi* newspaper on 1 February, he handed down to General Whitney, the head of his Government Section, a list of guiding principles which should be incorporated in the new constitution. First among his essential requirements was that the Emperor should be 'at the head of state', but this was qualified by the insistence that he would exercise his powers 'in accordance with the Constitution and responsive to the basic will of the people as provided therein'. Also laid down was the cessation of the feudal system (meaning the special political position of the peerage) and, most radically, the abolition of war as a sovereign right of the nation. The latter provision was made even more specific by the addition of the sentence: 'No Japanese Army, Navy or Air Force will ever be authorised and no rights of belligerency will ever be conferred upon any Japanese force'. Scarcely a week later, on 13 February, Whitney presented to the cabinet a draft based on MacArthur's guidelines which had been drawn up at hectic speed by members of Government Section – principally Colonel Kades, Commander Hussey and Lieutenant-Colonel Rowell – and which was far more explicitly democratic and liberal than anything which the Japanese establishment would have willingly contemplated. Initially the Shidehara cabinet was clearly unwilling to adopt it, and only did so after Whitney was reported to have said that this was 'the only way of protecting the person of the Emperor from those who are opposed to him'.

In reality this veiled threat that the Emperor might be deposed or even tried as a war criminal was almost certainly a bluff. Not only had MacArthur been favourably impressed by the Emperor's conduct ever since the latter had, in September, paid a personal visit to SCAP headquarters and apparently offered to take responsibility for everything that had been done in his name, but both MacArthur and the US government were keenly aware that Japanese public opinion could turn sharply against America if the Emperor were put on trial. Even so, Japanese conservative leaders could scarcely ignore such a danger (or the possibility of their own replacement, if uncooperative, by left-wing leaders more in tune with Government Section's thinking), and thus the unenviable task of securing the passage through the Diet during 1946 of a new constitution was reluctantly undertaken, first by Shidehara and subsequently by his successor, Yoshida Shigeru. Despite the toning down of some of its provisions in the process of translation and in the course of discussion with SCAP, it did not go uncriticised in either House. In particular, its assertion that sovereignty resided in the people (which the Far Eastern Commission, in one of its rare interventions, managed to make completely unambiguous) and its diminution of the Emperor's position to a symbol of the State with a purely formal and ceremonial role, were condemned by some as destructive of the Japanese *kokutai*. But the majority of Diet members were aware of SCAP's determination and, like the government, bowed to the inevitable; in the Lower House only the five Communist members voted against it, while in the Peers no formal vote was taken. It was duly promulgated on 3 November 1946 and put into effect in the following May.

There can be no doubt that the 1946 constitution (which, to avoid political complications, such as the need to convoke a special constituent assembly, was passed under the technical guise of a revision of the Meiji constitution) was effectively, if not explicitly, imposed upon the Japanese government. Nevertheless, to regard it as a wholly American production, as is commonly done, is not altogether correct. Even though the version first revealed to the Japanese public betrayed some traces of translation from English, Kades and his colleagues had many drafts by Japanese at their fingertips, and one in particular – the work of the Kempo Kenkyukai (Constitutional Study Association), a group of liberal or socialist academics, journalists and lawyers, including Suzuki Yasuzo, Morito Tatsuo, Ouchi Hyoe and Takano Iwasaburo – provided a foundation for their efforts. In view of this major Japanese input it is less surprising that, for more than half a century after the end of the Occupation, the constitution remained intact and unaltered despite several campaigns by conservatives to reject it as a foreign implant. Admittedly revision was made extremely difficult by the requirement of not only a two-thirds vote in both Houses of the Diet but also a majority in a popular referendum. Equally important, though, was that the constitution was not out of keeping with the popular mood in Japan in 1946 and continued to meet with wide acceptance thereafter. It contained far-reaching guarantees of human rights, including freedom of thought, religion, assembly, association, speech, press, emigration and marriage; it provided for judicial independence, subject to popular review, and for the election of local officials, including prefectural governors; and it placed the choice of the Prime Minister directly in the hands of the Diet.

The Diet itself was changed by the abolition of the House of Peers and its replacement by a House of Councillors (*Sangi-in*), with members elected from either nation-wide or prefecture-wide constituencies for fixed six-year terms (in contrast with the maximum of four years for the members of the House of Representatives). Unlike the Peers, the Councillors, in the last resort, had to yield to the Representatives in cases of conflict.

Although most conservative Japanese felt the change in the Emperor's status to be unnecessary, only one article of the constitution was to be seriously controversial – Article 9, which renounced war and, uniquely, stated that land, sea and air forces, as well as other war potential, would never be maintained. The origins of this abrogation of a basic sovereign right are still obscure: MacArthur insisted on its inclusion but claimed that the idea had first been suggested by Shidehara. Although Shidehara corroborated this, however, he may himself have been prompted by Kades. Alternatively, the Supreme Commander may have read too much into a favourable reference by the Japanese Prime Minister to the Kellogg-Briand 'no-war' pact of 1928. Most plausibly, perhaps, MacArthur may have been influenced by his knowledge that the 1935 Philippine constitution renounced war but realised that the provision would be more acceptable if its authorship was believed to be Japanese. Whatever its provenance, Article 9 has certainly provoked resentment from some Japanese conservatives and nationalists. Nevertheless, in practice it was not interpreted so strictly as to prevent the establishment of substantial Self-Defence Forces. Ironically, the initial move in this direction – the creation of a 75,000-strong Police Reserve in 1950 – was carried out at the insistence of the US government, as part of the unacknowledged 'reverse-course' which was to reshape American policy before the end of the Occupation.

Closely connected with the hasty moves to introduce a new constitution was the decision in January 1946 to hold the first post-war general election two months later. Most of the members of the existing House of Representatives having just been prohibited from standing again, it could plausibly be argued that it was now time to replace the tainted wartime body with a more democratic one which would have the moral authority to approve the proposed constitutional change. Some members of the Far Eastern Commission complained that the election was premature, since the conservatives' electoral bases still survived and could not yet be effectively challenged by new political forces, but even the 'New Dealers' within Government Section, who were sympathetic towards the Japanese socialists and had successfully opposed Shidehara's move to dissolve the Diet in December, saw no reason for delay. The main reason for speed, in fact, was probably MacArthur's desire to avoid the possibility of outside interference, and it is unlikely that it was motivated by any intention to favour a particular party or camp. Indeed, it would hardly have been possible for anyone to predict the outcome of the election with confidence. The reduction of the voting age to twenty, and the extension of the suffrage to women, were only two causes of uncertainty. Another was the revision of the election law. By the introduction of prefectural-size, multi-member constituencies, with electors being given two votes, independent candidatures and smaller parties were encouraged; and largely as a result 1946 saw a record number of candidates – 2,770. Even more important, the major parties were still in disarray.

The revival of political parties

The post-war revival of political parties was fraught with difficulties. Both the Seiyukai and the Minseito had already been deeply divided by 1940, and the involvement of most Diet members in the Imperial Rule Assistance Political Association had further blurred party identities and loyalties. If this were not enough, their legacy of past failures and dubious compromises also indicated the need for some degree of political reorganisation. Among major politicians the first to see this situation as an opportunity was the ex-Seiyukai anti-mainstream leader, Hatoyama Ichiro. As early as 15 August 1945 he began discussions with his associates about the formation of a new party based partly on those who had formed an unofficial opposition during the war and partly on liberal journalists and academics such as Ishibashi Tanzan and Minobe Tatsukichi. He even contemplated an alliance with right-wing socialists such as Nishio Suehiro, but their talks on 23 August quickly made it clear that their different backgrounds precluded any formal merger. When Hatoyama's new party was officially founded on 9 November, it significantly harked back to the People's Rights Movement by adopting the name Nihon Jiyuto (Japan Liberty

Party) and included only forty-three existing Diet members (some of whom had belonged to the Minseito before the war). In Kono Ichiro and Miki Bukichi it had two of the ablest up-and-coming politicians. No less important, however, was the financial support of Kodama Yoshio, an ultranationalist who had come into possession of a substantial fortune immediately after the war when the government engaged in a massive illicit operation to forestall the expected demand for reparations by disbursing stockpiles of materials to trade associations and to companies and individuals with whom the armed services, especially, had political or business connections. Kodama was only one of a number of shadowy figures who were thus able to exercise behind-the-scenes influence on politics in the post-war decade.

Most of the existing Diet members chose to continue their wartime association by joining the Nihon Shimpoto (Japan Progressive Party), which also sought, when it was formally established on 16 November, to claim a respectable pedigree by resurrecting a name from a less tarnished era of Japanese political history For a time it seemed that General Ugaki Kazushige might finally enter politics as its leader, but this might have appeared provocative, given the new atmosphere of anti-militarism, and Ugaki proved in any case to lack fund-raising ability. Instead the aged Machida Chuji was made interim Party President on 18 December. His term of office was even shorter than expected, however, for he was one of of 260 (out of 274) Shimpoto Diet members who in January were officially banned from standing again. As a result the party entered the election campaign with no more established politicians than the Jiyuto (which had thirty of its forty-three members purged). Neither party could expect to inherit the commanding position which the Seiyukai and Minseito had enjoyed before the war. Many of their new candidates were relatively young and inexperienced; and a large number of prominent local politicians whose backing might have been enlisted by the major parties in normal times were tempted to stand as independents or as members of minor parties. Among the latter the Kyodoto (Cooperative Party), which drew support from producer cooperatives in many villages, was the most important.

The disruption caused by the purge was a considerable setback to the conservatives, but the major problem confronting them was the challenge of the Left. At the political level this meant primarily the Nihon Shakaito (Japan Socialist Party) which Nishio Suehiro took the lead in establishing on 6 November 1945. The Shakaito combined the various elements which had been able to operate legally before the war in the Shakai Taishuto and Nihon Musanto. However, the divisions which had split the pre-war movement still persisted within the new party. In particular, the unwillingness of Nishio's faction to call for the ending of the notorious Peace Preservation Law or the release of political prisoners in September, aroused suspicions on the left; and whereas Nishio and the Christian Social Democrat Katayama Tetsu inclined towards the idea of Shakaito participation in a broad-based cabinet of national salvation, the left-wing Socialists, encouraged by their contacts with sympathetic Occupationnaires, hoped that SCAP's need to find willing collaborators and allay rising popular discontent (largely caused by food shortages) would help to lead to a socialist government.

The fact that the left-wing held only four of the seventeen seats on the Shakaito executive committee made the adoption of an uncompromising approach unlikely. Nevertheless, the political situation at this period was unpredictable. One of the factors creating uncertainty was the position of the newly-legalised Nihon Kyosanto (Japan Communist Party), which was gaining considerable influence at the popular level through the creation of intellectuals', students', women's and *burakumin* groups. Until the beginning of 1946 the Kyosanto was controlled by men such as Tokuda Kyuichi, who had refused to recant their political beliefs during their many years in prison and who, after their release following Occupation intervention in October 1945, were understandably militant. On 13 January, however, Nozaka Sanzo returned from exile with the Chinese communists in Yenan to urge a broad united front which would include even the right-wing social democrats. He also argued that even though the Emperor-system had to be ended, the Emperor need not be removed as a figurehead. To the Shakaito leaders (who at the party's inaugural ceremony had led the assembled members in the traditional incantation of loyalty to the Emperor) the prospect of a moderation of the Kyosanto's uncompromising stance made the idea of cooperation in a popular front less objectionable. Although the left wing of the party's proposals for an immediate broad left alliance and a constitution based on popular sovereignty were defeated on 16 January, some modification of

Shakaito policy was evident in its acceptance that a popular front should be formed after the forthcoming election.

In the event cooperation between socialists and communists at the political level failed to materialise. The strongly anti-Shakaito Tokuda, who, like some left-wing socialists, had delusions of Occupation and Far Eastern Commission support, remained influential on the communist side; and the publication of the 'government' constitution on 6 March further separated the two parties. Whereas the Shakaito broadly accepted the proposed document – once it had recovered from its initial dismay at losing one of its best electoral cards by the unexpected conservative decision to embrace full democracy – the Kyosanto continued to insist on the complete eradication of the Emperor-system and the establishment of a people's republic. Not surprisingly, no electoral pacts were arranged between socialist and communist candidates when the nation went to the polls in April.

The 1946 election and the purge of Hatoyama

The outcome of the 1946 election gave no party an overall majority but revealed that the bases of conservative support still remained substantially intact. Hatoyama's Jiyuto had the greatest success, returning 140 candidates, while the Shimpoto secured second place with ninety-four, followed closely by the Shakaito with ninety-three and more distantly by the Kyodoto with fourteen and the Kyosanto with five. Of the 118 independents who were victorious, over 100 in due course attached themselves to one or other of the conservative parties. No fewer than thirty-nine out of the seventy-eight women candidates were elected – a figure which was not to be matched in subsequent elections.

Although it only came third, the results marked a striking advance for the Shakaito over the pre-war peak, and conservative disunity put the socialists in a position to exert a decisive influence on the post-election situation. There was also a feeling that a coalition between the Shakaito and the Shimpoto (which had dutifully ensured the passage of all the government's Occupation-inspired measures during the recent Diet session and had invited Shidehara to become its president on 17 April) might not be unwelcome to SCAP, both because it would assist stability during the period of constitutional revision and because it would keep out

Hatoyama, who had publicly criticised the use of atomic bombs in September (before press censorship was reimposed) and whom SCAP was pressing the cabinet (albeit without success) to purge. Any hope that such a scheme might succeed, however, ended when the Shakaito, instead of succumbing to the temptation to share power with the Shimpoto, called for a constitutional protection movement and took the lead in the establishment on 19 April of an *ad hoc* alliance between the Shakaito, Jiyuto, Kyodoto and Kyosanto. In the face of such unexpected opposition Shidehara stepped down on 22 April.

At the time of the previous cabinet change Shidehara had been appointed on the recommendation of Lord Keeper of the Privy Seal Kido after consultation with one of the senior statesmen, Hiranuma Kiichiro (although SCAP approval was also sought before the decision was formalised). In the meantime, however, both Kido and Hiranuma had been indicted as suspected war criminals, and in these circumstances Kido's role was taken over by Shidehara who, despite his involvement with the Shimpoto, was not expected to put party interest above considerations of political stability. He seems to have encouraged Hatoyama to reach an agreement with Shakaito Secretary-General Katayama, and Hatoyama certainly sought Socialist participation in a coalition cabinet; but despite the wishes of its right wing, the party rejected Hatoyama's overtures and agreed only to promise to support the government in securing passage of the constitution and in dealing with the food shortage. This limited understanding having been reached, Shidehara recommended Hatoyama's appointment to SCAP on 3 May.

Hatoyama was not, however, to become Prime Minister in 1946. Behind the scenes members of both Government Section and the Communist Party had been seeking to undermine his position by raking up the less savoury aspects of his pre-war record, including his praise of Mussolini; and they prompted the reporter, Mark Gayn, to criticise him at a press conference. This led the recently established Allied Council for Japan to take up the question on 17 April, and Government Section was then able to kill two birds with one stone by moving against Hatoyama while simultaneously appeasing the Council (which had been given cause for complaint by SCAP's blatant initial attempts to negate its functions). Despite Hatoyama's recent success in Japan's first democratic election, a purge order was issued against him by SCAP itself on the eve of his assumption of office. Occupation archives show that Government Section justified its purge recommendation to SCAP by claiming that Hatoyama's removal would have 'a salutary [*sic*] effect upon Japanese politics in forcing a more realistic alignment of political parties, for the breakup of the Jiyuto would almost inevitably follow, with alignment of liberal elements of that party with the Shakaito and the most conservative elements with the Shimpoto'.[3] This was either disingenuous or a remarkable example of wishful thinking.

The first Yoshida cabinet and the challenge of the Left

Deprived of his party position and the chance to form a government, Hatoyama sought an acceptable substitute. After considering two other possibilities he decided on Foreign Minister Yoshida Shigeru, whose imprisonment in early 1945 and exclusion from the Hirota cabinet at army insistence in 1936 were excellent credentials. His professed desire to have nothing to do with party organisation was a further advantage as far as Hatoyama was concerned. Yoshida seems only to have insisted that he should not remain party leader longer than he wished, that he should not be responsible for fund-raising, and that Hatoyama should not interfere with the selection of his cabinet members. He became Jiyuto president on Hatoyama's recommendation on 15 May and formed his cabinet one week later. It included four Shimpoto and four non-party members and only five from the Jiyuto itself. At this stage no-one could have foreseen that Yoshida would head four more cabinets and dominate Japanese politics for the next decade.

The installation of the Yoshida cabinet came as yet another blow to the Shakaito, for Hatoyama's purge had encouraged the party to assume that SCAP did not favour the Jiyuto and that there was a chance of a coalition cabinet under Shakaito leadership. Despite this setback, however, it could still be hoped that the series of massive demonstrations organised mainly by the fast-growing labour unions to protest about the desperate food shortage would induce the conservatives to yield the reins of power. Such hopes were shown to be illusory when on 20 May 1946, the day after more than 200,000 demonstrators turned out for a 'food May Day' protest, General MacArthur issued a public warning that because

[3] Quoted by S. Nolte, *Liberalism in Modern Japan*, p. 321.

the 'growing tendency towards mass violence and physical pro-
cesses of intimidation under organised leadership' constituted 'a
menace not only to orderly government but to the basic purposes
and security of the Occupation itself', the 'physical violence which
undisciplined elements are now beginning to practice will not
be permitted to continue'.[4] Not only did he thereby imply a
willingness to support the emerging Yoshida cabinet with force if
necessary, but he also followed up his statement by making foreign
rice available. With an improved harvest soon to come, the food
problem rapidly ceased to be a major political factor.

Despite SCAP's intervention, however, the Yoshida cabinet was
still confronted by a formidable radical upsurge. As a means both of
'democratising management' and attempting to keep wages in
line with the rampant inflation, labour unions were increasingly
resorting to 'production control', a tactic which meant that, instead of striking, workers took over company operations (often
increasing output). The threat which 'production control' posed to
the industrial base of conservative support was matched by that
which the landlord interests faced from the spectacular growth –
from 300,000 at the end of March 1946 to 1,500,000 by the end of
December – in the membership of peasant associations, most of
which were affiliated to the radical Nihon Nomin Kumiai (Japan
Peasants Union). This phenomenal development was partly stimulated by hostility towards government grain delivery requirements
but, as the widespread use of the slogan 'land to the peasant' indicated, it was also due to dissatisfaction with the very limited land
reform introduced by the Shidehara cabinet in late 1945 and to
resentment of attempts by landlords to strengthen their position
by repossessing tenanted land. Not surprisingly the campaign
for land reform was often extended to include demands for democratisation of village government and agricultural organisations.

Left to itself the Yoshida cabinet would probably have been unable either to suppress or come to terms with this huge wave of
popular militancy. Its fate, however, was effectively taken out of its
hands. SCAP secured endorsement for a much more far-reaching
measure of land reform from the Allied Council for Japan in June,
and then imposed it on Yoshida. Passed by the Diet in October
1946, it satisfied most tenant expectations by requiring the sale of
all agricultural land owned by absentee landlords (as of November

[4] Quoted by Gayn, *op. cit.*, p. 231.

1945) and of all but a limited amount held by cultivating landlords. The process of expropriation was supervised by local, prefectural and national committees on which tenants were strongly represented, and the the result was that over a third of all Japan's agricultural land passed into the hands of the families which had previously cultivated it as tenants. As an additional bonus, repayment could extend over twenty-four years; and as a further blow to the landlords, the level of compensation bore little relation to the real value of the land and was further diminished by the subsequent acceleration of inflation. Painful though it may have been to landlords, however, land reform was to prove an enormous boon to conservative politicians, for it removed the main cause of peasant radicalism and opened the way for the rural constituencies to become a natural bastion of electoral support when the reformist fervour had receded. Moreover, the Nihon Nomin Kumiai split shortly after it had achieved its main objective, thus adding to the factional disunity within the Shakaito, with which it had significant links.

The threat from the militant labour unions was dealt with in a rather different manner. Instead of compelling the government to give way to radical pressure, SCAP's Civil Intelligence Section and Public Security Division, overriding the Labour Division (which had sought to nurture trade unionism), urged the adoption of a firm stand against production control. At SCAP's prompting the proprietors of the *Yomiuri* newspaper dismissed the journalists who had taken over editorial control of the paper, and on the same day (13 June 1946) the cabinet issued a statement warning that production control would be treated as an illegal breach of management rights. With the aid of armed police and strike breakers such disputes were soon brought to an end.

As yet, however, the unions were by no means ready to accept defeat. Their growth had been even more phenomenal than the peasant unions' – from 378,481 at the end of 1945 to 3,748,952 (out of an estimated total of 9,305,070 workers) by July 1946. Significantly, the labour federation which benefited most from this expansion was the Zen Nihon Sangyobetsu Rodo Kumiai Kaigi (All Japan Industrial Labour Unions Conference, usually known as Sanbetsu) which was established in August 1946 and was strongly influenced by communists and left-wing socialists. In place of production control, Sanbetsu reverted to strike tactics, especially simultaneous coordinated strikes; and its vitality and mass appeal forced the more cautious Sodomei (which was broadly aligned with the Shakaito mainstream) to join in the strike campaign. In an effort to contain it, the Yoshida cabinet in October hastily brought into effect the newly passed Labour Relations Adjustment Law which, in addition to encouraging the use of conciliation, mediation and arbitration committees to settle disputes, prohibited policemen, firemen, prison officers and employees of national, prefectural or municipal governments from engaging in acts of dispute, and imposed a thirty-day cooling-off period for intending strikers in public utilities. Nevertheless, the new law did not prevent a series of strike victories by unions in the private sector in October, and aided by these successes Sanbetsu was able to draw Sodomei and other union federations into a new campaign aimed nominally at securing wage rises in the even less well-paid government service but in reality at the overthrow of the government and its replacement by a people's republic. The means by which this political revolution was to be accomplished was a general strike, and the date set for this was 1 February 1947.

What would have been the result of a general strike, had it been carried out, is hard to estimate. In view of the fact that Yoshida had exacerbated feeling by condemning the militant union members as subversive elements in a New Year's broadcast, that the Joint Struggle Committee which was set up represented almost all unionists, and that two rallies held in Tokyo to galvanise popular feeling each attracted over half a million people, it would seem that at the very least the continuation of the cabinet would have become almost impossible. As it was, however, the strike was called off at the last moment when, after previous SCAP warnings had been ignored, MacArthur personally issued a direct prohibition on 31 January. Those communists who had persisted in regarding the Occupation forces as an army of liberation and argued that they would not block the pursuit of radical change through mass action were again proved to be guilty of wishful thinking.

Whether MacArthur's direct intervention was basically motivated by concern to protect the capitalist system or by a fundamental conviction that order and authority must be maintained, it proved that there were limits which Japanese radicalism would not be permitted to overstep. To deduce from this that SCAP's reforming ardour was spent, however, would be a mistake. Under Occupation pressure a number of important measures were sponsored by the Yoshida cabinet, among them a highly progressive and idealistic Fundamental Law of Education in March 1947, and, at the same time, a School Education Law which increased the period of compulsory education to nine years and abolished élitist differences at middle-school level (although it did not prohibit private schools). Another notable change was the establishment of a Fair Trade Commission in April 1947 with the function of administering the newly-passed Anti-Monopoly Law. Meanwhile plans for splitting up companies which were considered to hold too dominant a position in their particular industries were drafted. That SCAP did not, at this stage, lean towards capital rather than labour was shown not only by the extension of the purge in January to business executives who had held influential positions in major companies during the war, but also by the enactment of a Labour Standards Law which provided, in theory at least, for an eight-hour day, equal pay for men and women, and other conditions which were more generous to workers than those to which they were accustomed.

Even at the political level the support which had effectively been given to the cabinet by the banning of the general strike soon proved to be double-edged. Having failed to defuse popular discontent by his unsuccessful attempts to bring the Shakaito into the government, Yoshida and his Jiyuto colleagues were held to be partly responsible by SCAP for the fact that MacArthur had been forced to invoke his ultimate authority. In these circumstances the distaste which a significant element within Government Section felt for the Jiyuto was quick to manifest itself. Under the pretext that the inauguration of the new constitution required a new Diet, but probably in the hope of securing a more satisfactory political balance, Yoshida was ordered on 7 February to hold a new election in April.

Socialist-led coalition government

The possibility that an election might produce a weakening of the Jiyuto became more likely in late February when Ashida Hitoshi, a liberal ex-diplomat, defected from it as a prelude to becoming the head of a projected new party, which was expected to be more progressive that the Jiyuto. When this party – the Minshuto (Democratic Party) – was established on 31 March 1947, it incorporated most of the Shimpoto, some other defectors from the Jiyuto and a score or so of Diet members recruited from the minor parties and was, with 143 seats, the largest party in the Diet. Its hopes of becoming the major partner in a new post-election cabinet, however, received a setback when in the April election, held after a new election law restoring the pre-war system of three-, four-, and five-member constituencies had been pushed through by the cabinet in disregard of SCAP disapproval, it secured the return of only 121 of its candidates, slightly fewer than the Jiyuto's 131. It was in large part because of this almost equal division of conservative support that the Shakaito, which had itself received no more than 26.3 per cent of the total vote (only a fraction more than the Minshuto's 25.89 per cent and less than the Jiyuto's 26.71 per cent), won 143 seats and became for the first and only time in its history the largest single party. This surprising success made it likely that the Shakaito would be able to play a leading role in the formation of the next government.

That opportunity soon arrived, for Yoshida immediately decided to resign, and Ashida, who had been made aware of SCAP's desire for a government which would be more in tune with the popular mood, accepted that the next Prime Minister should be the respected Shakaito chairman, Katayama Tetsu. There were some doubts on the socialist Left as to whether it was wise to enter a coalition, but the possible advantages to be derived from establishing the party at the centre of power induced the Shakaito leadership to pay the price which its prospective partners demanded. Not only did it agree to set aside such major planks of its election platform as the nationalisation of key industries, a minimum wage system and a further measure of land reform, it also accepted that measures likely to cause social unrest would be avoided, that state secrets would not be leaked, and that its left wing should be excluded from cabinet membership. Despite these concessions, however, the Jiyuto eventually declined to participate in the new government, and when its composition was finally decided on 1 June 1947, a week after Katayama had become Prime Minister by receiving 420 out of the 426 votes in the House of Representatives and 205 out of 207 in the House of Councillors, it consisted of seven members from the Shakaito, seven from the Minshuto, two from the Kokumin Kyodoto (People's Cooperative Party), and one from the Ryokufukai (Green Wind Society), an independent faction in the House of Councillors.

In succumbing to the lure of office, the Shakaito did not, as things turned out, improve its long-term prospects. It may possibly have increased its respectability and perhaps gained some initial credit for not shirking its responsibility, but if so it was at the cost of alienating many of its supporters and deepening internal party differences. The new cabinet certainly pressed ahead with the remaining democratising measures which SCAP favoured, such as the abolition of the Home Ministry, the replacement of pre-war legal codes, and the extreme decentralisation of the police. But to achieve the economic revival which was essential if living standards were eventually to be raised to a tolerable level, it was deemed necessary to stimulate increased production by sharply raising prices (in the case of rice and coal by almost 200 per cent) while at the same time appealing for wage restraint. With key industries further favoured by receiving priority treatment from the Reconstruction Finance Bank, industrial recovery did get under way; but the accompanying acceleration of inflation inevitably strained relations with the labour unions, which had at first cooperated with the Katayama cabinet by resorting to strike action less frequently. Shakaito support was further undermined when a government bill to establish a limited measure of state control over the coal industry was emasculated because of objections from the Minshuto and outright opposition from the Jiyuto. In November 1947 the dismissal and subsequent defection (together with fifteen supporters) of Agriculture Minister Hirano Rikizo tilted the balance within the Shakaito towards the Left. It began to adopt a less compromising attitude towards its coalition partners, and a cabinet split seemed on the cards. Before this could happen, however, the left-wing chairman of the House of Representatives' budget committee, Suzuki Mosaburo, engineered the defeat of a controversial government proposal to pay for an increase in public workers' supplementary allowances by raising train fares and postal charges, and on 10 February 1948 Katayama resigned.

The fall of the Katayama cabinet did not mark the end of the experiment with coalition government, for despite left-wing disenchantment with this first experiment in power-sharing, the Shakaito had no wish to see another Jiyuto-led cabinet. To prevent Yoshida from being elected Prime Minister, therefore, the Socialists threw their weight behind Ashida. As a result, although Yoshida received the votes of twenty-five ex-members of the Minshuto

who, led by Shidehara, had defected because of the government's
interference with the coal industry and were soon to merge with
the Jiyuto to form the Minshu-Jiyuto (Democratic-Liberal Party),
Ashida was able to defeat Yoshida in the decisive House of Representatives ballot (the Councillors' small majority in Yoshida's favour
thus proving in vain). In return the Shakaito was not only rewarded
with eight cabinet posts (one more than under Katayama) but was
even able to nominate two left-wing members, including Kato Kanju
as Labour Minister.

The change in American policy and the return to conservative control

The reconstruction of the coalition gave the Shakaito a temporary
reprieve rather than a new lease of life. Shakaito popularity showed
a marked decline in opinion polls and in July the endemic internal
division cost the party the defection of a further fifteen members.
What really spelled doom for the Shakaito's hopes of strengthening
its position, though, was the campaign which had been developing
in Washington since early 1947 to switch the emphasis of American policy towards Japan from radical change to economic recovery.
It was led on the one side by businessmen, journalists and lawyers
with Japanese interests or connections (and possibly some Japanese
funding), and on the other by State and War Department officials
who saw Japan as a potential ally or as a vital link between the
American and South East Asian economies. The subsequent
successes of the Communists in the Chinese civil war and the intensification of the Cold War, not to mention growing Congressional
irritation at the continuing need to provide Japan with economic
aid, further strengthened the pressure for reassessment of American
objectives. The advocates of such a course, however, faced a major
obstacle in General MacArthur, who resented the implication that
the policies for which he had claimed credit might not have been
in the United States' best interests. Instead of a sharp U-turn, therefore,
a gradual modification of SCAP's original approach took place from
late 1947 onwards, as MacArthur tacitly readjusted his approach
under increasing pressure from Washington.

As a result of the change in American priorities SCAP's desire
for a willing partner to promote democratisation diminished, while
at the same time its increasing concern to clamp down on what

were seen as disorderly or subversive forces intensified the divisions within the socialist movement. As in early 1947 it was the activities of labour unions which provoked SCAP to action. Even though their aims were less politically motivated than at the time of the planned general strike, government workers, whose wages had lagged well behind those of workers in the private sector, led a new wave of dispute actions in early 1948. On 27 March SCAP banned a proposed nation-wide strike by communications workers, and on 22 July, in an open letter to Ashida, MacArthur shocked the Japanese labour movement by calling for the revision of the National Public Service Law so as to prohibit not only strikes by government employees but also their right of collective bargaining. The cabinet treated the letter as an instruction which had to be obeyed and did so by issuing an ordinance on 31 July. Such alacrity suggested that some ministers were only too happy to comply with SCAP's wishes, and it made the Shakaito's continued participation in government extremely questionable. Before the issue could be resolved, however, the cabinet suffered further injury, this time self-inflicted, in the form of the Showa Denko (Showa Electric Company) affair. Even though only one person was ultimately convicted, those arrested in the autumn of 1948 on suspicion of receiving bribes from Showa Denko included the prominent right-wing socialist, Nishio Suehiro (who had recently been forced to resign as a minister for not reporting a major political donation from a construction company). Subsequently Ashida himself was arrested, but by then he was no longer Prime Minister, the cabinet having decided to resign directly after Nishio's arrest on 6 October.

While the Showa Denko scandal would appear to be a wholly Japanese affair, some of those involved later argued that, like so many other instances of corruption in the shadows of Japanese politics, it would have escaped exposure had there not been a lessening of SCAP support for a centrist coalition. It was even alleged that the Counter Intelligence (G-2) Section under General Willoughby (who had opposed the purge even in 1946 and was an admirer of Mussolini and Franco) encouraged the Minshu-Jiyuto to publicise the rumours of a scandal and prevented Government Section, which still favoured the Ashida cabinet, from limiting the damage by supporting a cover-up. Government Section's position was weakened, it was further alleged, by the rumour that through

Viscountess Torio (who was reputed to be Colonel Kades' mistress) some of its own members may have been recipients of Showa Denko largesse. How much truth there is in this version of the fall of the Ashida cabinet may never be known, but in so far as it suggests that the supporters of a middle-of-the-road political course were becoming less influential, or even isolated, it is consistent with subsequent developments.

The formation of the next cabinet revealed the weakening of Government Section's position still more clearly. In the hope that another relatively progressive government might be constructed, Colonel Kades tried to persuade the Secretary-General of the Minshu-Jiyuto, Yamazaki Takeshi, to stand against Yoshida in the Diet ballot for the Prime Ministership on the understanding that he would receive the support of all three of the parties involved in the previous coalition. It was hoped that the Minshu-Jiyuto would then break up, leaving Yoshida on the political fringe. Implausible though this scheme might seem to be, it could conceivably have succeeded if enough members of the Minshu-Jiyuto had become convinced that SCAP was determined to block Yoshida's return to office. It came to nothing, however, because Yamazaki, after first appearing responsive, suddenly backed away, going so far as to resign from the Diet to ensure that he could not be pressured into standing. Whether or not G-2 Section had anything to do with his change of attitude, it was evidently a disappointment to Kades, who soon afterwards returned to the United States.

Yamazaki's withdrawal left the way open for Yoshida. In forming his second cabinet he chose not to seek an alliance with any of the other main parties, intending to call a new election in the near future in order to take advantage of the unpopularity of an opposition which was still tainted by scandal. Nor surprisingly, the other parties sought to avoid a dissolution of the Diet. Once again, however, the shift in Occupation attitude worked to Yoshida's advantage. Initially Government Section maintained that the only specific provision in the new constitution which allowed for premature dissolution was Article 69 (which stated that a government must either resign or hold a new election if a no-confidence motion were passed by the House of Representatives) and argued that Yoshida's plan of requesting the Emperor to dissolve the House, using his power as head of state under Article 7, was an undemocratic abuse of authority. By November, however, it had been decided to give Yoshida what he wanted by 'persuading' the opposition parties to submit the necessary no-confidence motion within a limited period. As a result Japan's third post-war general election was held on 23 January.

The 1949 election proved to be one of the most decisive in Japanese history. By increasing its number of seats from 152 to 264 the Minshu-Jiyuto won an absolute majority, a triumph which exceeded all expectations. Its main opponents, by contrast, slumped catastrophically, the Minshuto dropping from ninety to sixty-nine, the Kokumin Kyodoto from twenty-nine to fourteen and the Shakaito from 111 to a mere forty-eight. Many of the Socialists' supporters, disillusioned by the party's ineffectiveness and lack of principle, switched to the Kyosanto, which leaped to within range of its left-wing rival by winning thirty-five seats, an increase of thirty-one. Yoshida attributed his success not only to the unpopularity of the coalition partners but also to the general desire for strong, sound and stable government; and if this was the case, the Minshu-Jiyuto probably benefited from the unusually large number of high-level bureaucrats who figured among its candidates. The possibility cannot be ignored, however, that the party also had the advantage of being the recipient of exceptionally large financial contributions from business leaders who wanted both a tougher line to be taken against the unions and a relaxation of some of the early Occupation reforms.

If big business did support Yoshida for these reasons it was to be rewarded, for in 1949 the shift to a 'reverse course' became even more pronounced. However, it was not the cabinet's own policies which had the greatest impact, but the economic guidelines which were dictated to it by Washington. Believing that the key to Japan's recovery lay in the classic remedies of reducing government expenditure, balancing the budget, and encouraging exports by restoring price competitiveness, the US government sent a nine-point programme to Japan on 18 December 1948. To ensure that it was properly implemented this was followed, on 1 February 1949, by the despatch of Joseph Dodge, an ultra-orthodox banker.

Dodge's insistence on discontinuing the Reconstruction Finance Bank (the main source of loans to industry) and producing a budgetary surplus in order to repay government debt was reminiscent of the Minseito deflationary policy of 1929-31, and, as then, it proved costly in terms of bankruptcies among small and middle-sized companies. It seemed harsh even to the cabinet, but pleas for a less drastic adjustment foundered in the face of Dodge's conviction that the economy had for too long been cushioned against reality. Inflation was brought to a halt (although it had actually been levelling off since the previous September), and overall production continued to grow, but because of stagnating sales, stockpiles accumulated and the danger of a recession was only averted by the American 'special procurements' which followed the outbreak of the Korean war in mid-1950. The effects on labour and labour unions were even more serious. Quite apart from the undetermined number of workers in private companies who lost their jobs, administrative retrenchment by the government itself resulted in the redundancy of some 200,000 public employees by September 1949. With unions almost impotent against this onslaught, their membership, which had risen to 6,896,208 by March 1949, dropped back to 5,773,908 by June 1950, while the numbers involved in disputes declined by half during 1949.

One reason for the decline in union militancy was that both the government and many companies took advantage of the situation to dismiss left-wing activists. This tough line had American support, for SCAP had itself since 1947 been following a policy of encouraging the growth of moderate unionism through the promotion of 'democratisation leagues' (*mindo*) within unions. Partly because many unions were based on a single enterprise, often having a special relationship with its management, SCAP efforts had met with some success; and by February 1948 a Sanbetsu Democratisation League had been established under the leadership of Hosoya Matsuta, who had been expelled from the Kyosanto. During late 1948 and 1949 Sanbetsu was increasingly split between pro-communist and democratisation league factions, but with the latter gaining ground because of the vulnerability of the former to dismissal. Meanwhile, within Sodomei the left wing had become the dominant force in October 1948, and this opened the way for merger discussions with the Sanbetsu Democratisation League. Although neither was as moderate as SCAP would ideally have liked, the desirability of eliminating Sanbetsu as a major force led SCAP's Economic and Scientific Section to support the scheme. Things did not go quite to plan, for Hosoya objected to the extent of American involvement, and his movement did not initially join the two-and-three-quarter million-strong federation known as Sohyo when it was established by Sodomei and several independent unions in July 1950. Nevertheless the chief aim of separating the communists from the mainstream of the labour movement was largely achieved.

That objective had become even more important to SCAP in 1950. In January the Kyosanto had come under strong criticism from both the USSR-dominated Cominform and the Chinese Communist Party for being too receptive to Nozaka Sanzo's advocacy of seeking to achieve revolution through parliamentarism. During the spring of 1950 the Kyosanto leadership began to move towards a new position of opposing US imperialism by violent means, and on 30 May some American troops were assaulted by demonstrators in Tokyo. SCAP's response was to purge the twenty-four members of the Kyosanto Central Committee on 6 June; and when the Korean War broke out on 25 June communists in other areas of public life were dismissed. Altogether over 10,000 people were affected by this 'red purge', which ironically occurred at the same time as many of the men who had originally been regarded as a threat to Japan's future were depurged. Like the creation of the National Police Reserve, which took place at American insistence in July, it showed how far the reverse course had proceeded.

The end of the Occupation

How much American policy had changed was also shown by the manner in which the Occupation itself was brought to an end. When plans for a peace treaty were first drawn up (both by MacArthur and the State Department) in 1947, it was still envisaged that there would be a comprehensive settlement between Japan and all its wartime enemies, and that this would leave the country demilitarised not only in the sense of having no armed forces of its own but also in having no foreign troops stationed on its soil. When, however, a peace treaty was eventually signed in San Francisco on 8 September 1951, it was accompanied by a security treaty between the United States and Japan which allowed for the continued American use of military bases (even, if deemed necessary, for the suppression of internal subversion); and not only the Soviet Union and the Chinese People's Republic but also India refused to become party to the peace settlement. The United States sought substantial Japanese rearmament as well, but with much less success. Although Yoshida was prepared to pay the price of America's continued military presence in order to restore Japanese sovereignty and safeguard Japanese security, he remained, like the Foreign Ministry but unlike some Japanese conservatives, reluctant to risk the revival of Japanese militarism.

Yoshida's successful resistance to American pressure owed something to the support which he received from MacArthur (until the latter's dismissal in April 1951 as a result of his open disagreement with his own government over the conduct of the Korean War). He was also helped by fierce controversy in Japan over the peace and security treaties, for this meant that the United States could not be too demanding lest it provoke an even stronger popular reaction. In consequence the San Francisco settlement was basically satisfactory for Yoshida, even though he was forced to commit Japan to recognition of Chiang Kai-shek's regime in Taiwan as the legitimate government of China. By contrast, it was a disaster for the Shakaito. Whereas its right wing and centre were prepared to accept the peace treaty, its left wing, which maintained that Japan should adopt a neutral stance in world affairs, insisted that a treaty signed with only one of the opposing camps was unacceptable. The dispute inescapably brought to the fore the fundamental division over whether the Shakaito should be a class-based, possibly revolutionary, socialist party which regarded imperialism as the chief threat to peace or a social democratic one which emphasised the need for broad national support and parliamentarism and saw communism as the main danger. This disagreement had previously been papered over by verbal compromises, but no such fudging was possible when the Diet voted on the treaties. The result was that the party split into two essentially separate organisations (both of which claimed for themselves the name of Shakaito). Although they were to come together again in 1955, their reunification was to last only for four years until a further, more permanent, separation.

The Occupation finally came to an end in April 1952. Because its effects extended to all Japanese institutions its impact on politics was complex. There can be no doubt that its early radicalism ensured that reforms were introduced which would otherwise have taken much longer or not been enacted at all, nor that this democratisation 'from above' contributed greatly to the rapid extension of political rights and freedom. Whether these initial effects were negated by the subsequent changes in SCAP attitude, particularly towards labour unions, is a matter for debate. On the one hand it must be admitted that most of the institutional reforms were not abandoned, and there is some substance in the claim, made by certain ex-SCAP officers who deny the existence of a reverse course, that the phase of radical reform needed to be followed by a period of assimilation and could not have been expected to continue unabated. From a different angle, however, it can be argued that even the initial democratic stage of SCAP intervention distorted Japan's political development to the ultimate detriment of the Left. On the assumption that democracy cannot be conferred from outside but has to be fought for from within, it is possible to maintain that a policy of non-interference in Japan's internal affairs might have been more appropriate to the achievement of the objectives which the United States had originally proclaimed. By enforcing constitutional change, legalising labour unions and imposing land reform, SCAP may have accelerated the process of development, but it may also have inhibited the growth of a more genuine political consciousness rooted in the experience of sustained struggle for popular rights. Had SCAP deliberately tilted the political scales more positively in the left's favour, this effect conceivably might have been partially counterbalanced. But instead it was further accentuated by MacArthur's hostility towards disruptive action from below. His warning in 1946 against violent demonstrations, and his later ban on general strikes, together ensured that left-wing movements were prevented from engaging in major tests of strength which might have had catalytic political effects. Against this, of course, it can reasonably be held that a policy of standing back and allowing the Japanese to reconstruct their own society by their own efforts and in their own way might have led, at least in the short term, either to anarchy or to a revival of authoritarianism and repression. Nevertheless it would be hard to deny that by forcing conservative politicians, landlords and capitalists to give up what otherwise they would have clung to – and thus removing the major political and social grievances – the Occupation paradoxically laid the foundations of the stability and conservative predominance which characterised the post-1952 era.

8

THE '1955 SYSTEM' AND THE ERA OF L.D.P. DOMINANCE, 1952-93

When Japan emerged from Occupation in April 1952, the prospect of political stability seemed distant. Although the government had since 1949 been controlled by a single party, there were indications that the ruling Jiyuto (as the Minshu-Jiyuto had been renamed in 1950) would fall victim to the same tendency to splinter to which all previous Japanese political parties had been prey. Even if it held together, the odds that it would win another overall majority in the next election were not high; and the existence of a rival party, the Minshuto, which had shown itself capable of cooperating with the Socialists, suggested that there might, as before, be frequent transfers of power and that cabinets might have great difficulty in pushing legislation through the Diet. Yet from 1955 until 1993 one party would enjoy a dominance which was not only greater and more sustained than any of its predecessors had achieved, but was unmatched by almost any political party in a non-totalitarian state.

The fact that Japan was to experience relative stability for nearly four decades is the more remarkable because in other areas of Japanese life these same years witnessed exceptionally rapid change. Most strikingly, the Japanese economy underwent a transformation, as the proportion of the labour force employed in primary industry (agriculture, forestry, and fisheries) dropped from 48.3 per cent in 1950 to only 8.8 per cent in 1985, while those in secondary industry rose from 21.9 to 33.1 per cent, and those in tertiary industry climbed from 29.8 to 56.5 per cent. No less striking, though, was the increase in the manufacturing production index: from 146.9 in 1950 (based on 1945 = 100) to 3555.4 in 1985. Not surprisingly, Japanese exports also soared from 820 million dollars in value in 1950 to 130 billion in 1980 (when they accounted for 6.9 per cent of world exports, as against 1.4 per cent in 1950). Overseas direct investment, although it was slow to develop, displayed a similarly remarkable growth, rising from 1.9 billion dollars in 1971 to 29 billion in 1982 and 259.8 billion in 1993.

Such an economic transformation could not be unaccompanied by changes in Japanese attitudes and in Japan's international position. From being in the 1950s an impoverished nation conscious of its economic weakness and of the stigma attached to it as a result of its recent military humiliation, the Japanese could by the beginning of the 1990s take pride in the fact that they had proved their economic prowess and regained a significant degree of international esteem. They might still be the object of foreign opprobrium, but even when they were criticised – notably for their excessive exports and their barriers to imports, but also for such perceived failings as their passivity during the Persian Gulf War in 1991 – those attacks tended to reflect a feeling of frustration or resentment that Japan was clinging to old ways which might have been acceptable when it was weak and vulnerable but which did not befit its enhanced strength and status. That their country had come by the 1960s to be regarded by influential journals like *The Economist* as a model not only for late-developing nations but also for the major Western powers themselves could not but be gratifying to most Japanese; and when Americans and Europeans appeared to beg for Japanese investment, plead for export restraint, and depend on Japanese purchases of foreign government bonds, the Japanese could hardly fail to welcome the reversal of roles which seemed to have taken place. Inevitably national pride – visible most clearly in the proliferation of writing on what made the Japanese different and special (*Nihonjin-ron*) – began to reawaken, and the Japanese self-image became much less marked by the assumptions of inferiority which had been widely prevalent after the Pacific War.

Changes in Japanese self-consciousness reflected the fact that by the 1970s and '80s the Japanese possessed far more direct knowledge and experience of foreigners, and foreign realities, than they had previously. In that respect the aim of internationalisation, which was officially proclaimed in the 1980s, was becoming a reality. More foreigners (4.2 million by 1996) visited or worked in Japan – including in schools – and there was a vast increase in the number of Japanese travelling and living abroad – 10.6 million visited foreign countries in 1991 (and no fewer than 16.7 million in 1996). Meanwhile, the expansion of the media led one Japanese academic in 1972 to claim that the amount of information was increasing by over 10 per cent each year and to attempt to coin the term 'information pollution'. These phenomena were testimonies to Japan's growing commercialism and affluence. So too was the expansion of education, where by 1983 the number of students continuing beyond the compulsory age of sixteen had risen to 93 per cent, while from the early 1970s roughly one-third of eighteen year-olds (1,828,256 in 1973) were proceeding to higher education. Such changes, like the massive growth of urbanisation – 70 per cent lived in cities by 1970, compared with 38 per cent twenty years earlier – and the partial desertion of the villages, might have been expected to lead to a greater political consciousness. In some respects this does seem to have occurred: the mass demonstrations over the revision of the Security Treaty with America in 1960 and the widespread student protests in the late 1960s were the most newsworthy examples, but no less significant was the proliferation of campaigns by citizens' movements against pollution or other threats to their local environment resulting from ill-considered development by large companies – often in collusion with local government. The most dramatic case – although not the most typical, since the object of attack was the national government and the protesters were mainly cultivators of agricultural land – was the long and violent resistance in the 1970s to the building of the new international airport for Tokyo at Narita. However, over time the governing party became more wary of courting controversy, and greater political consciousness at the local level did not prevent increasing apathy as far as the political parties and the Diet were concerned.

The persistence of American influence

The termination of the Occupation in April 1952 did not end American influence over Japanese politics. The United States retained an obvious interest in Japan's adherence to the recently signed Security Treaty, and the conclusion of the Korean War in June 1953 did not lessen American determination to maintain their military bases in Japan, especially Okinawa. In addition, US interest in Japan as a trading partner, which had partly prompted the change of emphasis in Occupation policy from reform to economic recovery from 1947 onwards, remained no less important a factor in American thinking. Inevitably the American government was concerned that Japan should not become politically unstable – hence its inclusion in the Security Treaty of a highly unusual clause providing for American military intervention in Japanese affairs if requested by the Japanese government. Such intervention, however, might have been counter-productive and was never resorted to. The temptation to pursue American ends through surreptitious political funding, on the other hand, seems to have been irresistible. Money was to become an even more important weapon in post-Occupation politics than it had been in earlier decades, and it was capable of having a significant bearing upon not only the balance of strength between and within parties but also the extent to which rival parties opposed or cooperated with each other. For the American government (and to a lesser extent also for the Soviet Union) to employ such means would make good political sense, provided that its action remained secret. Consequently, historians have given credence to the revelations (by American ex-officials who claimed to have been involved in the transactions) in the *New York Times* on 9 October 1994, that the LDP received funding from the CIA and that financial assistance was not confined to the ruling party but was also directed to the JSP and labour organisations.[1] The amounts involved are alleged to have varied from 2 million to 10 million dollars per year from 1955 through the 1960s, but in view of the sensitivity of the issue it may not be known for a very long time, if ever, exactly how far post-1952 politics in Japan was subject to such outside interference.

Even if there had been no direct US involvement, whether through the CIA or other channels, after April 1952, there still would have been indirect American influence, for the shadow of the Occupation continued to hang over Japanese politics. Most obviously, the division of the Japanese Socialists into separate parties was at least nominally due to the different attitudes of the left and right wings of the previously unified party towards the peace treaty which the United States had negotiated with the Japanese government. The conservatives too, however, were at odds in large part because of the Occupation legacy. Even before SCAP ceased

[1] Cited by W. LaFeber, *The Clash: A History of US-Japanese Relations*, (NewYork W.W. Norton, 1997), pp.318, 326 and 336. In the introduction to his collection of writings by E.H. Norman, *Origins of the Modern Japanese State*, J. Dower claims that the American government also launched an ideological campaign against the Japanese Left from the early 1950s.

to exist, a struggle for leadership of the ruling Jiyuto had commenced when politicians who had been barred from holding public positions in the early period of the Occupation were depurged in 1950-51. The most notable of those frequently embittered men was Hatoyama Ichiro, who had, in his view, entrusted the Jiyuto to Prime Minister Yoshida only temporarily (and who apparently believed that the fact that he was among the last to be depurged – in August 1951 – was due to Yoshida's desire to cling to power). Not surprisingly, those who had suffered from the purge were rather less attached to the changes introduced during the Occupation than were those who had worked with SCAP and had assumed responsibility for the post-war reforms. Above all the former group resented the American imposition of a constitution in 1946, and particularly the treatment of Japan as an international pariah by depriving it of the right of belligerency and by banning it from maintaining armed forces. The fact that the American government had repented of its original inclusion of Article Nine, and that it had even insisted on its partial negation by the establishment of a potential military force under the guise of a National Police Reserve in 1950, made Yoshida's hostility towards constitutional revision and large-scale rearmament particularly frustrating to the revisionists.

Conservative division and Yoshida's ousting

The desire by depurged politicians to revise the constitution and pursue a systematic 'reverse-course' policy was not the only cause of animosity within the conservative camp. Another was the carry-over from the pre-war period of Seiyukai-Minseito rivalry. On top of this many politicians resented the entry into politics, especially in 1949, of ex-bureaucrats and the immediate promotion of a significant number of them to governmental positions, some at a very high level. It had not been forgotten that in the pre-war period bureaucrats had generally regarded themselves as superior to politicians and had been a major obstacle to political party cabinets. The fact that the Prime Minister, himself an ex-bureaucrat, had surrounded himself with such men (the so-called Yoshida school) only intensified the dissatisfaction which had already led to him being criticised as 'one-man Yoshida' for his high-handed manner.

From 1952 Japanese politics entered a period of turbulence as Yoshida struggled to keep his adversaries at bay. That it took over two years to achieve his overthrow was not mainly due to the extent or solidarity of Yoshida's support: in the House of Representatives election of October 1952 (in which 139 depurgees were returned), only seventy-three of the 240 successful Jiyuto candidates belonged to his faction, and some of his most powerful backers, notably Ogata Taketora and Hirokawa Kozen, came to feel that it was time for him to go. Nor could it be put down to his political skill: his expulsion in September 1952 from the party of two heavyweight allies of Hatoyama – Ishibashi Tanzan and the forceful politician, Kono Ichiro – achieved nothing, and soon had to be rescinded, while in the following year a careless insult to a Socialist in a Diet session resulted in the passing of a no-confidence motion and forced him into another, basically unnecessary, election. What principally kept Yoshida in office was the fact that his three main enemies could not easily cooperate because they all had competing ambitions to become the next prime minister. One was Shigemitsu Mamoru, the war-time Foreign Minister, who had become leader of the Kaishinto (Progressive Party) when this was formed in February 1952 from the Minshuto and several small conservative groups. Another was Hatoyama, Yoshida's rival within the Jiyuto, who enjoyed the support of such senior party figures as Ishibashi Tanzan, Kono Ichiro, and Miki Bukichi, and could therefore hope to become party president and Prime Minister himself if Yoshida could be induced to resign by pressure from within the party. Meanwhile, the third potential leader, Kishi Nobusuke, (like Shigemitsu an ex-bureaucrat and war criminal) was biding his time, possibly inhibited in campaigning against Yoshida by the fact that his brother, Sato Eisaku, was one of the Prime Minister's leading protégés. The situation was further complicated in that, given the probability of a roughly equal balance of strength between conservative rivals, any challenge to Yoshida was likely to need Socialist support. The latter had shown clear signs of recovery from their 1949 debacle in the 1952 House of Representatives election, when the Right Socialists won fifty-seven seats and the Left Socialists fifty-four, and in the 1953 election they further increased their representation to sixty-six and seventy-two members respectively. As long as the conservatives sought to contain labour militancy by such methods as the 1953 Strike Control Law, however, any alliance between them and the radical camp was unlikely to materialise.

In the aftermath of the Occupation, Yoshida's popularity steadily declined, and his position was further weakened when the pro-Hatoyama group, after supporting the Socialists' successful no-confidence motion, defected from the Jiyuto in March 1953. In the ensuing election, in April, the Jiyuto representation in the House of Representatives dropped to 199 seats. Had the non-Jiyuto Diet members combined to support Shigemitsu as Prime Minister, as the leader of the Sohyo labour federation, Takano Minoru, advocated, Yoshida might have been ousted at this point, but in the end Takano's 'united-front' approach did not find favour with the Sohyo-backed Left Socialists. Yoshida managed to form a new cabinet – his fifth – and in November 1953 his position was strengthened by Hatoyama's return to the Jiyuto.

The boost which Yoshida received from Hatoyama's abandonment of open opposition was soon counterbalanced by the discovery by procurators in 1954 that in the previous year, when two laws were passed giving the shipping companies government financial aid, Jiyuto politicians had received large sums of money from an agent of the industry. This 'Shipbuilding Scandal' attracted great public attention and became even more sensational in April 1954 when the procurator-general's request for the arrest of Sato Eisaku, the Jiyuto Secretary-General, was countermanded by the Justice Minister, Inukai Takeru (Ken). Inukai's action was forced upon him by Yoshida, but the Prime Minister's political as well as moral judgement came into question when Inukai resigned the next day. Although Sato was arrested after the end of the Diet session, and in due course acquitted, opinion polls attested to a sense of public indignation which undoubtedly contributed to the growing disenchantment with Yoshida and encouraged his rivals.

The more his adversaries manoeuvred to undermine him, however, the more stubbornly Yoshida clung to power. Even hints from such close supporters as Ikeda Hayato that he should consider resignation were ignored. In resisting as he did, Yoshida may have found justification in the conviction that he was preventing the dismantling of the policies to which he was attached – particularly the blocking of premature large-scale rearmament, the issue on which he had withstood pressure from Dulles in 1951. With Ikeda's help he again resisted American demands for rearmament in 1953 during the negotiation of a Mutual Security Assistance Pact; and although the Safety Force (as the Police Reserve had been renamed in 1952) was upgraded into a Self-Defence Force (*Jieitai*) in 1954, with a separate air force and an expanded size of 152,115 men, this was less than half of what the Eisenhower administration was seeking. It was also less than Yoshida's opponents favoured, and since Hatoyama had in 1952 told the American ambassador that Japan's defence expenditure should be doubled to a quarter of the national budget, Yoshida's continuing reluctance to have Japan shoulder what the American government deemed a fair share of the military burden must have been particularly galling to the latter. Nor was Yoshida's agreement to limited rearmament unconditional, for the United States had to pay the price of a further package of military and economic aid.

In order to remain in power Yoshida had to give ground. During the Mutual Security Pact negotiations, he moved closer to the Kaishinto's position by issuing a joint communiqué with Shigemitsu in September 1953 which accepted the aim of a gradual expansion of self-defence power; and in November 1953 he conceded Hatoyama's demand – part of the latter's terms for rejoining the Jiyuto – for the establishment of an internal party commission under Kishi to investigate the desirability of revising the constitution. These concessions only gave him a brief respite, however. By March it was evident that he had lost the support of Ogata Taketora, his most prominent ally within the Jiyuto; and in November, while Yoshida was in Washington in what proved to be a fruitless pursuit of a diplomatic triumph, Hatoyama again, together with thirty-two other members of the House of Representatives, defected from the Jiyuto, this time to merge with the Kaishinto and form the Nihon Minshuto (Japan Democratic Party). Faced with the prospect of another no-confidence motion in the Diet, two-thirds of the remaining Jiyuto Diet members now signed a petition calling for the cabinet's resignation. Yoshida still remained defiant, however, urging dissolution and another House of Representatives' election rather than resignation, even when Ogata threatened to follow Hatoyama out of the party on 7 December. Only when some ministers, at a noisy cabinet meeting the same day, refused to sign the dissolution order did Yoshida step down, whereupon Hatoyama was elected Prime Minister unopposed by the Diet. Even the Socialists gave their support when Hatoyama promised to hold a new election.

Socialist merger and the formation of the Liberal Democratic Party

In that election, which was duly held in February 1955, Hatoyama was able to strengthen his position within the conservative camp. His new party increased its representation to 185 seats, while the Jiyuto plummeted to 112. Ominously, however, not only did the government fail to gain an overall majority but the most striking gains were made by the two socialist parties. The Marxist-oriented Left Socialists, in particular, reaped the benefit of the quite widespread mood of opposition to the conservative agenda (which Yoshida had espoused almost as openly as his rivals) of undoing, or further reversing, the early Occupation reforms. They jumped sharply to eighty-nine seats, outstripping the Right Socialists who rose only to sixty-seven seats, and even making inroads into some rural constituencies. These results were the more worrying to the conservatives because there was a growing expectation that the Socialists would soon join together again. The prospect of reunification – despite the serious personal and ideological division within the Socialist camp – had been spoken of more frequently in 1954, and had even been advocated by British Labour politician, Aneurin Bevan, when he visited Japan in that year. What made the idea seem more compelling to the Socialists in 1955 was the fear that the new Prime Minister, encouraged by the upsurge of popularity – the 'Hatoyama boom' – which followed his election, might embark upon a major rearmament programme unless there was solid and effective opposition. In 1954 the Socialists had been unable to block the completion of police recentralisation and the spectre of a possible revival of militarism still loomed as a real threat in the minds of those who had suffered oppression by the Japanese imperial state. The result was that both the Left and Right Socialists declared their intention in January 1955 of combining again, and they followed this up by adopting virtually identical platforms in the February election. Full reunification was realised in October 1955.

Parallel to the movement for reconciliation on the Left, there were persistent efforts to bring about a single party on the Right. Initially they were connected with the attempt to replace Yoshida, but they were also a response to the promptings of the *zaikai* (as organised business was collectively known). *Zaikai* concern about the weakness of cabinets without a Diet majority was evident in an

Above Some of the claimed half-million participants, many desperately hungry, at the 1946 May Day rally in the once sacrosanct Imperial Plaza. *Left* Ii Yashiro, chief coordinator of the planned general strike of February 1947, disconsolate after being forced to announce its cancellation on the radio.

Above Some of the 39 women – still a record – who won seats in the House of Representatives in the 1946 election after the granting of universal suffrage. *Below* The Emperor and Empress attending a popular celebration in Tokyo of the promulgation of the new constitution later that year.

日本國憲法公布記念祝賀都民大會

Above Ex-diplomats and political rivals Ashida Hitoshi (left), who headed a coalition cabinet including socialists in 1948, and Yoshida Shigeru, who was Prime Minister four times between 1946 and 1954. *Below* Founding ceremony of the Liberal Democratic Party (15 November 1955), which reduced the in-fighting within the conservative camp.

Top left Prime Minister Hatoyama Ichiro and USSR Premier Marshal Bulganin signing the agreement normalising Russo-Japanese relations in 1956. *Centre left* Prime Minister Tanaka Kakuei with Zhou Enlai on his visit to China in 1972 to normalise Sino-Japanese relations. *Bottom left* Prime Minister Kishi Nobusuke signing the revised security treaty with the USA in 1960 under the gaze of President Eisenhower. *Above* Prime Minister Sato Eisaku discussing the reversion of Okinawa with President Nixon. *Bottom right* Ohira Masayoshi, Prime Minister 1978-80, who died in office. *Centre right* Suzuki Zenko, Prime Minister 1980-2, with President Reagan.

Above The first meeting of the second Nakasone cabinet in 1984 (second from left is Education Minister Mori Yoshiro, who became Prime Minister in 2000). *Below* Prime Minister Nakasone Yasuhiro after the LDP's landslide in 1986, painting in the eye of a *daruma,* an act which traditionally symbolises election victory (on the right is Kanemaru Shin).

Above Takeshita Noboru (right) and his successor as Prime Minister, Foreign Minister Uno Sosuke, at a conference in 1988. *Below* Kaifu Toshiki, who became one of Japan's youngest Prime Ministers in 1989 when he succeeded Uno following the Recruit scandal.

Prime Minister Miyazawa Kiichi (*above*) answering questions about the controversial Peacekeeping Operations bill at a Diet committee meeting in 1991; and (*below*) being presented with proposals for Japan to play a more active international role by Ozawa Ichiro, not long before the latter's defection brought down Miyazawa's cabinet in 1993 and ended the era of unbroken LDP rule which had lasted since the party's foundation.

April 1953 joint recommendation by the four main business associations that 'Since a strong and stable government is needed to
cope with the present crisis, the political parties should, inasmuch
as there are no great differences between them in their basic policies and objectives, forget past differences, eschew emotion, discuss
issues frankly, and cooperate in bringing about a stable political
situation.'[2] It is worthy of note that this advice was directed not
just towards the conservative parties but also to the Right Socialists. By 1955, however, the latter were being regarded as part of a
more serious Leftist threat.

The road to merger was not entirely smooth, for by no means
were all conservative politicians enamoured of the idea. Yoshida
and his henchmen, just like Wakatsuki Reijiro in 1931 and Suzuki
Kisaburo in 1933-4, were justifiably suspicious of a combination
which could threaten their position and policies; while in the
Kaishinto there was resistance from Miki Takeo, Matsumura Kenzo
and their followers, who tended to be more liberal and saw that a
merger would block off the possibility of coalition with the Right
Socialists along the lines of the Katayama and Ashida cabinets of
1947-8. These opponents of unification were easily outnumbered,
however, by those conservative politicians who, having survived
the perils and costs of three elections in four years, could appreciate
the advantages of a political reorganisation which might reduce
competition in their constituencies and would almost certainly not
expose them to such frequent election campaigns in the future.
Nevertheless, the lack of good personal relations between the leading figures in both parties impeded negotiations, and it needed
the commitment of two veteran politicians, Miki Bukichi of the
Nihon Minshuto and Ono Banboku of the Jiyuto, to bring about
direct talks between Hatoyama and Jiyuto President Ogata and
to agree on a party programme between July and September. The
one serious obstacle that then remained was the question of who
should become the new party's head. As the strength of both existing parties in the Diet as a whole was almost equal, this was not an
easy matter to resolve. Eventually a compromise was reached whereby
a formal decision was deferred until 1956 and in the meantime the
leadership functions would be carried out by a committee made up
of Hatoyama, Ogata, Miki and Ono. As a result of this agreement

[2] Cited by Masumi, *Postwar Politics in Japan*, p.295.

the inauguration of the new Jiyu Minshuto (Liberal Democratic Party, usually shortened to LDP) was able to go ahead on 15 November 1955, and what came to be known as the '1955 system' was set in place. Yoshida remained defiant by being one of the handful of Jiyuto members who declined to join (until 1957, when his arch-enemy Hatoyama had ceased to be party leader).

The Hatoyama cabinet and the reaction against the Occupation

The chief architects of the merger had originally anticipated that Hatoyama would become the first President of the LDP in early 1956 but would step down in Ogata's favour before long. Ogata's sudden death in January meant that this informal understanding could not be fully implemented, but did not prevent Hatoyama from being elected without significant opposition on 1 April. He quickly set about realising his long-cherished desire to change the course of Japanese policy, the first of his objectives being the achievement of a peace treaty with the Soviet Union. This was sought partly because it would facilitate a fisheries agreement, but much more for its political advantages. Most notably, it would represent a beginning to the process of emancipating Japan from its almost complete subservience to the United States and restoring the country's international independence. A peace treaty could also boost Hatoyama's reputation, if it were to lead to the return of the four small islands to the north of Hokkaido which the Soviet Union had seized in 1945 and which it claimed on the basis of both the 1945 Yalta agreement between Roosevelt and Stalin and (despite the fact that the Russians had not signed it) the San Francisco peace treaty. Since the Socialists, too, favoured a treaty with Russia, such a settlement could also ease the government's relations with the Left.

Negotiations with the Russians were not easy, however, even though the Soviet Union was eager for an agreement and was ready to hand back two of the disputed islands if a peace treaty were signed. Part of the difficulty arose from the Japanese Foreign Office's distinct lack of enthusiasm, but the main obstacles were the obstructiveness of other conservative politicians and the deep suspicion of the American government. Knowing that the *zaikai* were doubtful about Hatoyama's move and that there was a danger of jeopardising American economic support, the LDP Executive

Committee insisted on making return of all four islands a condition of agreement. Its stance was given formidable backing by Secretary of State Dulles when he stated in August 1956 that if the Japanese government agreed to the Soviet Union's retention of some of the northern islands, then the United States would feel entitled to take permanent possession of the Bonin Islands and the Ryukyus (Okinawa). His warning stemmed from American concern with Japan's 'tendency to drift away ... due to the decreasing economic, military and diplomatic dependence on the United States and to the growth of national pride and spirit of independence'.[3] The result was that Hatoyama gave up the bid for a peace treaty and settled in October 1956 for a normalisation of relations which, if less than he had hoped for, at least removed the Russian veto on Japan's admission to the United Nations the same year.

Hatoyama's second major objective was the removal of the Occupation-imposed constraints on Japanese sovereignty, and particularly those which impeded rearmament. Here too he fell well short of complete success. While able to continue the expansion of Japan's Self-Defence Forces, he was forced to backtrack in February 1956 after criticising the constitution for not permitting Japan to possess armaments and then suggesting that defensive necessity could justify an attack on an enemy base. Moreover, the Constitutional Research Commission which he persuaded the Diet to set up in 1956 proved a damp squib: no appointments to the committee were made until 1957 (after Hatoyama had ceased to be Prime Minister), and its recommendation that Article Nine and the provisions dealing with the status of the Emperor be revised was not forthcoming until 1964, by which time most LDP politicians no longer thought the issue worth a major confrontation with the opposition.

Even by mid-1956 the prospect of achieving constitutional revision had been effectively removed from the immediate political agenda. In that year the LDP won only sixty-one of the 126 seats which were up for election in the House of Councillors, and thus it could not hope to secure the requisite two-thirds support necessary for any proposed change in the constitution to go forward to a referendum. A month earlier an even more serious setback – described by Hatoyama as his cabinet's greatest defeat – was

---

[3] LaFeber, *op. cit.*, p.314, citing a secret report to the National Security Council.

suffered when a bill to change the House of Representatives' electoral system to one based on single-member constituencies failed to become law. Had it been passed, it could have had a major impact on post-war Japanese politics, for it would have given the LDP, as by far the biggest party, an excellent chance of winning a much larger majority of seats than it already possessed and then of going ahead with the first stage of constitutional revision. Beyond that, it also offered the prospect of cutting back the disturbing growth of Socialist representation in the Diet and preventing it from being able to mount the challenge which appeared to some commentators to be the natural consequence of Japan's ever-increasing industrialisation and urbanisation. The electoral revision bill incurred widespread criticism, however, not only because it was intended to make the LDP's majority permanent but also because the redrawing of the proposed new constituency boundaries was excessively favourable to the LDP. Even when this attempt at electoral manipulation (for which the term 'Hatomander' was coined) was given up, and a more balanced constituency division plan got through the House of Representatives, many politicians belonging to the LDP itself continued to feel ambivalent about a change which while strengthening their party was also bound to break up the bases of support which they had built up in the existing large electoral districts. Lack of enthusiasm was especially evident among the ex-Jiyuto factions within the LDP. Against this background the bill failed to pass through its committee stage in the House of Councillors and was abandoned.

Not all of the Hatoyama cabinet's attempts to reverse what it considered Occupation excesses failed. Most significantly it secured the replacement of elected school boards in 1956 by bodies appointed by local governments. But Hatoyama was unable to pursue his revisionist course much longer. Apart from health problems, he had to contend with continuing resentment from Yoshida's erstwhile supporters. His policy towards Russia had alienated them still further; and there was a real possibility that they might seek to block even the limited normalisation of relations. Only by publicly confirming his intention to step down as Prime Minister was Hatoyama able to ensure that his agreement with the Soviet Union was approved.

Kishi's rise to power

Hatoyama's retirement, on 23 December 1956, opened the way for the first contested election for the LDP leadership, and it proved to have some surprising twists. One of the three contestants, Kishi Nobusuke, secured what appeared to be a commanding lead in the first ballot with 223 votes, compared with the 151 for Ishibashi Tanzan and 137 for Ishii Mitsujiro (a one-time bureaucrat who had then become a newspaper executive) but in the run-off he was overhauled, losing to Ishibashi by 258 to 251. Kishi supposedly dispensed 100 million yen – against Ishibashi's 600,000 and Ishii's 400,000 yen – in trying to win over the LDP's Diet members and the delegates representing the party's prefectural branches, but, in contrast to what was subsequently to become normal in such elections, the man who allegedly spent most money did not win.

Party members may have had reservations about Kishi's bureaucratic background and his war-time association with Tojo, and he was not helped by his lack of both a common touch and a capacity for camaraderie. Ishibashi, on the other hand, possessed an exceptional record as a pre-war liberal, had the additional merit of having been unfairly purged at American behest, and was well known for his willingness to take risks with inflation in the cause of reviving the economy. His aim of improving Japan's relations with Communist China was also popular since the recognition, at American insistence, of the Kuomintang regime in Taiwan as the government of China (which meant that trade with mainland China was limited by having to be conducted through unofficial agreements) was widely seen as unnatural. Ishibashi was not, however, to have the opportunity to develop his own policy, for pneumonia forced him to resign after only two months in office. All that he could achieve in that short time was to encourage the extension of Japan's very limited social welfare system and preside over a decision to expand the economy by cutting taxes and increasing consumption.

Ishibashi's resignation left the way clear for Kishi to become Prime Minister, for neither Ishii nor any other faction leader chose to stand against him. Initially he retained the existing cabinet virtually without change, but in June he reshaped it to reduce the influence of the Ikeda faction and that led jointly by Miki Takeo and Matsumura Kenzo, which had been main supporters of

Ishibashi. Subsequently he went further by trying to persuade all the faction leaders to give up their separate organisations so that the LDP could become a more united and disciplined party. Like the LDP merger two years earlier, this move was backed by *zaikai* leaders who felt that the division of the LDP into factions could be a cause of instability. Less obviously, factionalism could also reduce the influence of the *zaikai* as a whole, since the factions did not receive funding (as the LDP and, to a much lesser extent, some of the other parties did) from the organisation which the *zaikai* had set up in 1955 to make the funding of political organisations by big business less direct.

The amounts received by faction leaders, mainly through personal contacts with particular companies or businessmen, were certainly large enough to give them considerable autonomy. In the 1958 House of Representatives election, for instance, the Ikeda faction alone, according to official statistics, received 127 million yen, compared with the LDP's 910 million. Clearly, companies saw advantage in a close relationship with particular party leaders; while politicians who aspired to become party president realised, especially after the 1956 LDP presidential election, that they needed solid factional backing. For their part, prospective Diet members were mostly only too ready to join factions since these could help them to achieve their initial election success and also provide the additional funds which most politicians required to consolidate their local position. Moreover, their membership of factions gave added weight to any requests they made (usually with the same political motive) for government help or public works in their own constituency. In consequence, faction leaders either dissolved their factions in name only or, in the case of Ikeda and Sato, declined to comply outright; and before long all the factions had resumed normal operation This was to be the fate of all subsequent attempts by later Prime Ministers to eradicate factionalism in the LDP.

Kishi had more cause to be satisfied with the House of Representatives election in May 1958, the first since the conservative and reformist camps had been represented by united parties. The JSP superficially seemed to fare better, since it increased its representation to 166 (from 156 for the two socialist parties in the previous election), whereas the LDP, with 287 wins, secured fewer seats than conservatives had gained in 1955 and came nowhere near to securing the two-to-one majority necessary to initiate the process of constitutional revision. Nevertheless, it was the JSP which had greater cause for disappointment, since it now seemed to be peaking after its impressive surge over the previous three elections. One reason for the slowdown in its growth may have been that since the last election conservative governments had increased social security, health insurance, and old age pensions, albeit to only a limited extent. The LDP could feel secure enough to end the relatively recent arrangement whereby some Diet committees were chaired by JSP members.

Kishi and Security Treaty revision

Election success also meant that Kishi could proceed with his major objective – the placing of Japan's relationship with the United States on a more equal footing by revising the 1951 Security Treaty. This was not a new idea. It had been broached by Foreign Minister Shigemitsu Mamoru in 1955, but was quickly shelved when his overture met with a cold reception from Dulles. Kishi was much more committed to its achievement. He prepared the way by continuing Japan's rearmament, so that the Self-Defence Forces had 210,000 personnel by 1959, thus allowing most American ground troops to be removed from Japan proper. He also went some way towards meeting American wishes that Japan play a less passive international role by himself visiting various South-East Asian countries in 1957 and by suggesting, in March 1958, that Japanese armed forces might be sent overseas. He certainly succeeded in convincing Washington that he was a strong, pro-American leader who should be encouraged, not rebuffed.

Kishi's American diplomacy got off to a good start when he was well received by President Eisenhower in Washington in July 1957. Concrete negotiations did not begin until July 1958, but by September expectations of success had been aroused. It was at this point, however, that Kishi's domestic political position began to come under serious attack, firstly in a veiled form from within the LDP and then, overtly, from the Left. Hitherto, the idea of Security Treaty revision had met with relatively little opposition, even though the radical Left mostly favoured a neutral foreign policy for Japan, for although in some ways a treaty signed freely was in principle more deplorable than one which had been accepted as the price for ending the Occupation, socialists could hardly feel enthusiastic about calling for retention of an agreement which they had opposed in 1951. The atmosphere changed, however, when a highly controversial revision of the Police Duties Bill was introduced in October 1958. Kishi's desire to turn the clock back politically had already become an issue when the government dismissed union leaders in government service after a number of strikes in the spring of 1957; and suspicion and hostility were further provoked by the prohibition on union membership by some categories of civil servants, by the institution of an 'efficiency-rating system' for teachers which was perceived as an attempt to undermine the highly active Japan Teachers Union, and also by the re-introduction of ethics classes in schools. But the revived Police Duties Bill created a great deal more concern – not just on the Left – by giving the police, in the name of public safety and order, greater power to interrogate, search and arrest, thus reawakening fears of a revival of the unchecked brutality which had often characterised the treatment of suspected dissidents before 1945. The JSP hoped to prevent it from becoming law by blocking it until the end of the current Diet session on 7 November, but on 4 November the LDP pushed through, by a dubious procedure, a surprise thirty-day extension. This move backfired. It was condemned by most newspapers and provoked not only a JSP walk-out from the Diet but also an immediate national strike by 4 million people and a huge demonstration outside the Diet. Conceivably the government could have weathered the storm, but within the LDP ranks strong criticism was expressed by Miki, Matsumura, and other anti-mainstream elements, while former Prime Ministers Yoshida, Ashida, Hatoyama and Ishibashi all urged concessions. On 22 November the bill was shelved, and following this Ikeda, Miki and another cabinet minister resigned to form a Reform Deliberation Council.

The Police Duties Bill episode not only aroused hostility, but also new expectations of what might be achieved by strong resistance and mass action. It led directly to a campaign against security treaty revision, for the various left-wing groups who had formed a People's Council to oppose revision of the Police Duties Law agreed to continue it with the new objective of opposing Kishi's plan. The JSP initiated the move, and the Japan Communist Party soon joined in (as, in all, did 134 bodies) but it was Sohyo which did most to bring about, in March 1959, an enlarged People's Council to Prevent Revision of the Security Treaty. This umbrella organisation was able to stimulate considerable hostility towards treaty revision, even before the terms of the new treaty were revealed in early 1960. In doing so it was able to build on the enormous mass of Marxist and anti-Establishment writings published since the end of the Pacific War. The fact that many areas of Japanese intellectual life, and especially the universities and the serious monthly and weekly journals, were at least partly under the sway of left-wing ideas meant that substantial sections of Japanese opinion could be convinced that monopoly capitalism in both Japan and America – the Communists were out of line in emphasising mainly the latter – was the force behind treaty revision, and that its objective was the revival of Japanese militarism as a partner of American imperialism. At a time of renewed international tension this could seem alarming, and it became even more so when a American spy-plane was brought down over Russia and the Soviet leader, Khrushchev, threatened to attack the bases (some of which were in Japan) from which such planes flew. To encourage action by Japanese citizens, the Security Treaty was likened by one radical historian to the unequal treaties of a hundred years earlier, which, it was dubiously argued, had been ended by mass demonstrations. This was a message which was particularly attractive to students, and the participation in the campaign of the 300,000-strong, Trotskyite-led, Zengakuren (National Union of Students) was to give it extraordinary vitality and a high degree of militancy when the process of treaty revision was approaching its conclusion in 1960.

The anti-revision campaign was by no means united or harmonious. In particular, there was no love lost between the Communists and the mainstream faction in Zengakuren. More significantly , right-wing socialists were deeply uneasy at being yoked together with the Communists – something they had managed to avoid in the campaign against the Police Bill – even though the latter had moderated their stance since their extremist phase in the early 1950s. Some right-wing Socialists, notably Nishio Suehiro, had long had doubts about the JSP's hostility to Japan's rearmament and about the party's espousal of neutralism, and they were more equivocal towards the security treaty and its revision than most of their fellow party-members. The JSP's involvement in a joint campaign with extreme radicals was not the only cause of tension within the party but it did much to bring differences to a head during 1959. The disagreements culminated in an attack by younger left-wing members on Nishio, which was then followed by his faction's departure, together with some other sympathisers, from the JSP in October. The depth of the rift became evident in January 1960, when the splinter group converted itself into the Democratic Socialist Party (Minshu Shakaito). The new party was backed by Zenro Kaigi, the federation of labour unions based mainly on the private sector (in contrast to the larger and more militant Sohyo, which consisted mostly of public-sector unions), but it aspired to be a broad party rather than one which just represented these workers. In rejecting revolutionary Marxism in favour of a gradual progress towards socialism it also favoured the use of parliamentary methods rather than mass action. Its defection meant that the balance within the JSP tilted significantly towards the Left, strengthening the existing emphasis on ideology – and arguably contributing to its eventual decline.

If the opponents of Security Treaty revision were less than harmonious, so too was the government party. Few other leading politicians fully shared Kishi's sense of urgency about the issue, and some of them suspected that he hoped, by achieving a major foreign policy triumph, to cling on to power. Even if they had known that he had secretly promised in January 1959 to hand over the party leadership to Ono Banboku after a new treaty had been signed, they might reasonably have doubted whether he would honour it. The LDP's strong showing in the House of Councillors election of June 1959, when it secured seventy-one seats, while the Socialists won only thirty-eight, greatly strengthened Kishi's position. He went ahead with another cabinet reshuffle, reaching an agreement with Ikeda which allowed him to face down Kono, when this hitherto staunch ally, seeking to place himself in line for the succession, tried to insist on the post of LDP Secretary-General. In the following months the disgruntled Kono objected to some of the new treaty provisions, but by 26 October they had been published, approved by the party's executive council, and rubber-stamped by the general body of LDP Diet members. From 28 October through December they underwent a preliminary scrutiny in a special Diet session, and in January Kishi went to Washington for a joint signing in anticipation of ratification.

It has been argued that at this point Kishi should have sought a renewal of his mandate by holding an election. In 1962 Kishi himself stated in an interview:

'I now know that I should have dissolved the Diet immediately after my return from Washington and sought the nation's opinion in February. The LDP would have been returned to power and there would have been no trouble with the passage of the Treaty.'[4]

He did not do so, he claimed, because the party's mood was opposed to an election. In support of this argument it can be noted that the new treaty, while not changing the US-Japan relationship fundamentally, contained provisions which would have been generally regarded as improvements. The United States was now committed to act if Japan were attacked and to consult the Japanese government on any deployment of the forces it maintained in Japan; and the treaty could be terminated by Japan after ten years. Admittedly the government was open to the criticism that it was aligning itself more closely with the United States and that Japan might be involved in American military action to defend 'international peace and security in the Far East'. But in the light of the subsequent convincing LDP election success in November, it could be maintained that these negative factors would not have weighed heavily in most voters' minds.

This reasoning cannot be dismissed lightly. Nevertheless, like many arguments from hindsight, it is not wholly compelling. The November election was won after Kishi had stepped down; if it had been held early in 1960 while he was still in office, the LDP might not have fared quite so well. Anything less than a substantial victory would have been discounted by the opposition and (with some justification given the LDP's built-in electoral advantages) been represented as a vote of no confidence in Kishi by the nation. Even if such a victory had been won, it would have been almost impossible to repress the militant students, once they had experienced the exhilaration of solidarity in action, as thousands of them had when they stormed into the Diet compound on 27 November 1959. In 1960 they were inspired by the feeling that, for the first time since the formal institution of democracy, the Establishment could be made to listen to the voice of the Japanese people – as interpreted and expressed by themselves. In this heady atmosphere, which was sustained not only by unflagging press coverage and an unprecedented degree of television exposure but also by the

[4] Cited by G. Packard, *Protest in Tokyo*, p.191.

contemporary struggle by unions to prevent large-scale redundancies at Mitsui's Miike coal mine, Kishi's use of dubious parliamentary procedures (not always with complete LDP support) in response to the opposition's delaying tactics aroused fierce indignation. The idea that Kishi was entitled to override opposition objections because the LDP could win any vote in the Diet was condemned as 'the tyranny of the majority', a more telling phrase in Japan, where consensus was seen as the ideal, than in Western democracies.

Eventually Kishi did succeed in pushing the treaty through, but he achieved this only by bringing the police into the Diet on 19 May to remove the opposition members who were attempting, by blockading the Speaker in his office and mounting a mass sit-down in the Chamber, to prevent a vote to extend the session. This meant that the treaty could also be approved and that it would automatically become law one month later. Kishi's forceful action was too much even for some LDP members – Ishibashi, Miki, Kono and twenty-four others declined to vote for the treaty – and it had an electrifying effect on public opinion, turning many who had hitherto been passive or neutral into active campaigners. The days of united action held on 4 and 15 June mobilised an estimated 5.6 and 5.8 million strikers respectively, while the demonstrations held around the Diet building on 15 and 18 June involved, it was claimed, 150,000 and 330,000. There were many violent clashes with the police and with right-wing nationalists. Only one person died, but casualties might well have been much heavier if the Director-General of the Defence Agency, Akagi Munenori, had not resisted pressure to deploy troops and if the head of the National Public Safety Commission had not expressed a lack of confidence in the police and urged caution. Kishi remained determined to cap the passing of the new security treaty with the long-planned visit by Eisenhower, but it became evident that the latter's safety could not be guaranteed and the Prime Minister eventually had to accept the cancellation of what would have been the first occasion when a serving American President set foot on Japanese soil. The atmosphere was certainly conducive to violence. Kishi himself was stabbed in July – though by a Rightist fanatic – as was the JSP chairman, Asanuma Inejiro, who had been most heavily involved in the protest movement, in October. Unlike the JSP leader, however, Kishi survived.

Political conciliation and economic growth under Ikeda

He did not, though, survive as Prime Minister. By 15 July he had been replaced by Ikeda Hayato, who defeated Ishii Mitsujiro and Fujiyama Aiichiro by 242 to 196 and forty-nine votes respectively in the first round of the LDP Presidential election, and then won against Ishii by 302 to 194 in the run-off. In the contest for the succession Kishi backed Ikeda, who had given him vital support during the Security Treaty crisis, and this may have influenced Sato Eisaku, Kishi's brother, to place his faction behind Ikeda, even though the two men were rivals, both having attended the same school in Kumamoto and pursued a career in the Finance Ministry before being brought into politics by Yoshida. The support offered by Kishi and Sato was important, for Ikeda had to contend with a widespread feeling among the four factions within the LDP which were led or dominated by men who could be regarded as career politicians (Ono, Kono, Ishii, and Miki/Matsumura) that the next party president should not be another ex-bureaucrat. In the end, money may have made the crucial difference. It was rumoured that as much as 1 billion yen was deployed on Ikeda's behalf, with Ikeda's protégé, Ohira Masayoshi, playing a key role, aided by Tanaka Kakuei, a member of Sato's faction.

Ikeda's Prime Ministership marked a change in the general approach of the LDP. This was hardly surprising, given the fact that Kishi's determination to pursue a controversial policy had provoked public protests on a scale comparable to those of 1905, 1912-14 and 1946, while in terms of the involvement of intellectuals and media coverage the Security Treaty crisis surpassed any previous incident and aroused the spectre of a greater level of political consciousness and an accentuated polarisation of attitudes. It was logical, therefore, if not entirely predictable in the light of Ikeda's strong character, that the new Prime Minister should adopt a conciliatory stance. 'The government party and the party not in power must come together in both foreign and domestic affairs', he told a surprised reporter, adding 'It is necessary therefore for us in the majority party to extend our hand in a humble spirit and treat the other side with forbearance'.[5] It was in this spirit that Ikeda hastened to defuse tension by encouraging a compromise which brought the Miike strike to an end after ten months in

[5] Cited by Uchida Kenzo, *Sengo Nihon no Hoshu Seiji*, p.166.

October. Beyond that Ikeda took a personal lead in trying to establish a new national consensus by proclaiming, as he had previously done as Minister for International Trade and Industry (MITI) in 1959, the aim of doubling national income in the next ten years. This objective was to be more than achieved. It was actually less ambitious than it seemed in that since 1953 Japan had, thanks partly to MITI's encouragement of exports and industries with high potential for expansion, already been averaging real growth rates of over 10 per cent, and these were to continue almost unbroken until 1973.

Focusing on economic success not only stimulated a 'feel good' atmosphere, but also provided a nationally and internationally acceptable outlet for Japanese nationalism. This was in marked contrast to Kishi's pursuit of security treaty revision, which was based on a nationalistic desire to restore Japan's international position but which had run up against the Left's advocacy of neutralism – itself partly inspired not just by the conviction that the United States was the chief threat to world peace but also by an underlying anti-Americanism which dated back to the perceived abandonment of democratisation during the Occupation, if not earlier. Anti-Americanism would still manifest itself in later years, especially during the Vietnam War, but it was never again as politically volatile as it had been in 1960, and subsequent extensions of the new treaty passed with surprisingly little disturbance. Moreover, although the JSP continued to take a resolutely anti-rearmament line, the tendency of the Left before 1960 to portray Japan's pre-war history as almost wholly bad – a mixture of militarism, imperialism, authoritarianism and other 'feudal survivals' – was modified by the emergence of a new People's History school, which was inspired by the crisis to seek, in a more positive fashion, examples of popular protest in Japanese history which could serve as evidence that democracy in Japan could be based on the national heritage and would not have to be seen as an American import.

Ikeda's concentration on economic growth was aided by another effect of the 1960 crisis. The forced cancellation of Eisenhower's visit brought home to the US government that there was a real danger of pushing Japan into neutralism or even friendship with China or the USSR if the Japanese government was pressed too strongly to accept the full obligations of an American ally. It seemed safer instead to leave Japan to play the economic role in the Cold

War which some Americans had envisaged for it before the Korean War. With the demand from the United States for rearmament largely in abeyance, Japanese defence expenditure grew much more slowly, declining as a proportion of GNP to less than 1 per cent and making Japanese national budgets hugely different from those of most other countries. The decline in the relative level of military expenditure opened the way to a gradual expansion of overseas aid, notably to Asian countries, but also to increased support for both regional and industrial development and agricultural prices.

To re-establish political stability Ikeda also had to deal with divisions within the LDP. The party was too young for previous rivalries to have been forgotten, and during the security treaty revision crisis there had been tentative discussions between the Kono faction and some socialist politicians about their possible creation of a new group. A similar idea was mooted in August 1960, when the Kono faction found itself in the anti-mainstream, with no representation in the new Ikeda cabinet.[6] The House of Representatives election in November, however, caused a closing of ranks; and in the subsequent cabinet reshuffle all the factions bar Ishii's were rewarded, and a better balance achieved. In the election itself the LDP increased its representation to 300 (after four successful unendorsed candidates were counted) while the JSP, with 145, and the DSP, with a much-reduced seventeen, together secured four seats fewer than the JSP had won in 1958. The victory consolidated Ikeda's position, although the conservatives' success may have owed less to the Prime Minister's personal popularity than to a backlash against the disturbances of the early summer and to the lavish use of election funds: arrests for election offences rose by 50 per cent to 16,416 and it was estimated that candidates needed to spend 20 million yen to win.

The election did not end the LDP's intra-party conflict. Indeed, at the local level that was at its most intense during elections, since the system of three-, four-, or five-member electoral districts inevitably pitted candidates from different factions against each other, and their internecine warfare was generally extremely bitter. In fact, one LDP Diet member in 1963 spoke of 'blood feuds' between conservative candidates in the same constituency and complained: 'we don't fight the socialists. We are always too busy

[6] This was the first Japanese cabinet to include a woman: Nakayama Masa, as Welfare Minister.

fighting among ourselves'.[7] At the top level, factional rivalry was as endemic as the struggle for influence among *daimyo* in the sixteenth century. Even when faction leaders were personally willing to accept the status quo, they were likely to be subjected to pressure from below from faction members eager to gain greater access to power; and there were usually ambitious sub-leaders (most of whom had, or were developing, their own fund-raising organisations) jockeying for position either to become heir-apparent to the faction leader or force him into retirement. In 1964, after Ikeda had placed Miki Takeo in charge of an investigation committee, the factions were nominally dissolved, but this move was essentially cosmetic and, just as in 1958, they were soon operating openly again.

Among the major bones of contention between factions under the Ikeda cabinet was the location of the areas to be nominated for special government treatment under the May 1962 Law to Promote the Construction of New Industrial Cities, one of the means by which the national income doubling plan was to be implemented. After much pressure and lobbying the friction was eased by the government's expanding the number of designated areas. Such a compromise proved more difficult to find on the other main cause of party disharmony, the manoeuvring to become the next Prime Minister. Sato Eisaku, whose support for Ikeda had been important in the 1960 contest for the party presidency, became anxious because Kono Ichiro was favoured in cabinet reshuffles in 1961 and 1962 and because the Kono faction increased its Diet strength in the House of Representatives election of November 1963, even though the LDP as a whole lost ground slightly. The new factional balance that had developed made Ikeda less dependent on Sato, but the latter was encouraged to seek the mantle of leadership by the man to whom both he and Ikeda owed their political careers, Yoshida Shigeru. Although living in retirement, Yoshida remained influential; indeed, his position has sometimes been compared to that which the *genro* enjoyed in the early years of the century or even that of a retired Shogun. In practice, however, it was more limited, as became evident when Ikeda ignored his hints and insisted on standing for re-election to the party presidency not only in 1962 (when he was unopposed), but also in 1964. That he should do so was not unjustified in terms of his general popularity – public

[7] Cited by N. Thayer, *How the Conservatives Rule Japan*, p.166.

opinion polls showed that this only dropped by 1 per cent over his whole term and that, uniquely among Japanese Prime Ministers between 1946 and 1974, he enjoyed more public support than opposition at its end. This did not, however, carry much weight with his impatient rivals. After a hard-fought campaign, however, in which some LDP Diet members apparently ignored their faction's wishes, the Prime Minister managed an outright win on the first ballot, with 242 votes against Sato's 160 and Fujiyama Aiichiro's seventy-nine.

The Sato cabinet and political change in the 1960s

Ikeda's triumph proved short-lived, for three months later, in November, he was forced to resign as a result of throat cancer. He was, however, able to exert greater influence over the choice of the next Prime Minister than any of his post-war predecessors had enjoyed, because a consensus emerged that there should not be another election for the party presidency so soon after the last, and in the ensuing consultation process Ikeda's voice appears to have been decisive. His choice lay between his recent challenger, Sato Eisaku, and Kono Ichiro. The latter was a forthright politician who had proved a staunch supporter for the previous four years, whereas the ultra-serious, even taciturn Sato had more support in the LDP, was trusted as a fellow ex-bureaucrat, and enjoyed the confidence of big business. In the end Ikeda came down in favour of Sato, but not before the latter had agreed to retain the existing cabinet and to state publicly that he intended to continue Ikeda's policies.

Sato apparently resented the imposition of conditions, though not because he had any plan to strike out in a new direction. In particular, economic growth remained a high priority. Before long, however, the government was forced to take the costs of growth more seriously, as protests arose against various alarming effects of industrial pollution and local residents began to object to the establishment of large-scale chemical plants in their areas. Large companies were reluctant to accept restrictions, but the constant focus on pollution by the media compelled the LDP to enact anti-pollution legislation. Although the government lagged behind most prefectural governments, it had passed no fewer than fourteen measures by early 1971.

The LDP's slowness to act may well have been an important factor in the series of opposition successes in elections for prefectural and metropolitan governors in the late 1960s and early '70s. The most notable of these were the triumphs of Minobe Ryokichi (Minobe Tatsukichi's son) in the 1967 and 1971 contests for mayor of Tokyo, following the JSP's first place in the Tokyo metropolitan assembly elections of 1965. Many gubernatorial victories, including the repeated wins of Ninagawa Torazo in Kyoto from 1950 to 1978, resulted from alliances of all or several of the opposition parties. Such cooperation, however, was hardly possible in Diet elections; and in these the LDP maintained its superiority. Its success in stemming its long-term decline in popular support (which, in the view of many commentators, would inevitably be eroded by industrialisation, urbanisation, and the weakening of traditional attitudes) can be explained partly by the improvement in living standards experienced by most sectors of society. Account also needs to be taken of the LDP's near-maximisation of its electoral potential by the steady reduction in the number of candidates it endorsed. Although this meant that the party's overall share of the vote went down to some extent (since every candidate enjoyed some purely personal or local support), it ensured that fewer votes were wasted: in a typical case, the LDP was less likely to run three candidates – and run the risk of winning only one seat – in constituencies where it might hope to return three members but where a more realistic target was two. Thus, whereas (ignoring party members who stood, and sometimes won, without official endorsement) the LDP had won 287 seats in 1958 by running 413 candidates, in 1960 it returned 296 out of 399, in 1963 283 out of 359, and in 1967 277 out of 342, while in 1969 its ratio improved to 288 successful candidates out of only 328. By contrast, the JSP, which in 1960 succeeded in winning 145 seats with only 186 candidates, calculated less well thereafter: in 1963 it ran 198 candidates but secured only 144 victories, while in 1967 it scored only 140 successes out of the 209 who stood for election. (In 1969 it did cut back the number of endorsed candidates to 183, but suffered from an electoral aberration, returning only ninety members).

Even more important than control of candidate numbers as a cause of LDP resilience was the strengthening by its Diet members of their local bases by their development of *koenkai* (support organisations). Other parties also did so to some extent, but the greater resources on which conservative politicians could draw, together with the not unrelated fact that the LDP was the party in power, gave them a significant advantage. It was natural for local economic interests and local politicians to invoke the aid of their local Diet member (and most LDP Diet members were associated especially closely with a particular geographical area within a large constituency) if they wanted funding, subsidies, or other favours from central government; and in return for such services (which were more likely to be forthcoming if the Diet member belonged to a powerful faction, and even more so if the relevant minister were a prominent member of the same faction) it was not difficult to recruit the supplicant as an influential supporter who would contribute financially or in other ways to the Diet member's political cause. Together with other fund-raising methods, such as backing from family members, old school friends and the faction leader, such aid not only allowed LDP politicians to fight increasingly expensive election campaigns but also to set up groups on whose support they could rely (and which they could, on retirement, often pass on to their chosen successor).

In some ways the position of LDP politicians resembled that of samurai when they possessed semi-independent fiefs, and their relationship with their faction leader had something in it of the mutual dependence which characterised the vassal-*daimyo* relationship. They were mostly engaged in incessant struggle for, in order to withstand competition from other Diet members in their constituency and to resist the challenge of up-and-coming prefectural assemblymen, they needed to draw more and more voters into their *koenkai*; and by means of various inducements, including occasional presents, sponsored trips, and assistance through their well-staffed political offices, they had by the mid-1960s, according to responses to independent surveys, enlisted at least 5 per cent of the electorate, including women and younger voters, into their support organisations. By the 1980s the figure was close to 20 per cent. Some faction leaders, such as Ono Banboku and Tanaka Kakuei, were able, because of their reputations, to expand their *koenkai* to much larger proportions – in Tanaka's case to 98,000 members – and even to make inroads into groups which had socialist connections. But everywhere there was a tendency on the part of local organisations, local businessmen, and grass-roots leaders to perceive the advantages of belonging to a network of

influence. Their readiness consistently to vote for their chosen political representative, and to mobilise other voters on his (or, in rare
cases, her) behalf, did much to eliminate the electoral volatility that
might have been expected of a rapidly urbanising mass society.
This was a major reason why the LDP vote remained basically firm
in both the 1967 election, despite the tarnishing of the party's
image by some well-publicised instances of corruption, and the
1969 election, when the problem of pollution was constantly in
the headlines.

The fact that the LDP position remained strong enough in the
1969 election for the party to actually recover lost ground almost
certainly owed something to a special factor. Just as in 1960 there
had been massive public disturbances, so in 1969 Japan witnessed
unusual disorder. This time it was confined mainly to the universities, where students, no doubt resentful of the pressure they had
undergone in order to get through the long-notorious 'exam-hell',
matched their counterparts in Europe and America in their militant challenge to the established order. In some cases, radical activists
seized control of university buildings and harangued faculty members and administrators, occasionally echoing the intimidating
manner of the Cultural Revolution in contemporary China. Their
battles with the police, especially for the clock tower at Tokyo
University, featured prominently on television. The public was more
alienated than sympathetic, and the JSP may well have suffered
from a backlash against their perceived excesses.

There was also a long-term development which significantly
affected the 1967 and all subsequent elections: the entry onto the
political stage of the Komeito (Clean Government Party). Sponsored – or, according to some of its opponents, controlled – by
the major new religious sect, Soka Gakkai, (an offshoot of Nichiren
Buddhism) which advanced rapidly in the post-war period, attracting adherents particularly among migrants to the cities who worked
in non-unionised jobs, Komeito scored nine and eleven successes
(as the Komei Political League) in the 1962 and 1965 House of
Councillors elections respectively. It first made a big impression in
1967, however, when it put up thirty-two candidates for the House
of Representatives and secured twenty-five seats. Two years later
it ran seventy-six candidates and returned forty-seven of them,
overtaking the Democratic Socialist Party (which increased its representation by only one – to thirty-one) and easily outdistancing

the Japan Communist Party, despite the latter's improvement to fourteen seats. Komeito's anti-establishment approach at this stage meant that its appeal was likely to be more to those who felt alienated from society and had no liking for big business. It undoubtedly drew a good many voters from the LDP, but its impact on the JSP, which had a smaller and a more urban support base, may well have been more significant. Certainly Komeito's near-doubling of its House of Representatives strength in 1969 mirrored the JSP's alarming drop from 140 to ninety members. If the proposals for the replacement of an emphasis on class struggle by the adoption of a more moderate approach (as put forward by the anti-mainstream faction leader, Eda Saburo, and his associates from the early 1960s) had been accepted, the JSP might have been better able to withstand the Komeito challenge, but Eda's advocacy of 'structural reform' failed to gain the backing of the JSP's main factions, and the party remained dominated by Sohyo and the public service unions and strongly influenced by Marxist-oriented ideologues, a fact which probably limited its public appeal.

Sato Eisaku could congratulate himself not only on presiding over the LDP's survival as the clear majority party but also on his retention of its presidency and the Prime Ministership. This was hardly predictable when he assumed office, for none of his predecessors had been able to maintain such a hold on the reins of power. Not even Yoshida had enjoyed the top position without a break for as long as Sato by the time he resigned in 1972. The latter's durability can be partly explained by the strength of his faction, which by 1971, with sixty members in the House of Representatives and forty-four in the House of Councillors, had become easily the largest in the LDP, outstripping both the sixty-nine-strong faction headed by Ohira Masayoshi (who had, after an interlude of leadership by Maeo Shigesaburo, succeeded Ikeda) and the Miki Takeo faction, with its fifty-two members. The other large faction, that of Fukuda Takeo, was firmly in the LDP mainstream and could be relied upon by Sato. This strong position did not exclude the possibility of challenge, but in the biennial elections which the party constitution allowed, Sato defeated his opponents by large margins. In 1966 he received 289 votes against Fujiyama's eighty-nine and Maeo's forty-seven, in 1968 he scored 249 to Miki's 107 and Maeo's ninety-five, and in 1970 he triumphed over Miki by 353 to 111. His position would have been less secure if Kono Ichiro had remained a contender; but the latter's death in 1965, following Ono's the year before, left the party with no other faction leader of sufficient standing and seniority to mount a real challenge.

Sato's period as Prime Minister was not marked by a radical agenda. Some of his government's measures, such as the provision of limited compensation for landlords for what they had lost in the 1946 land reform and the acceptance in the same year of the International Labour Organisation's Convention No. 87 (at the cost of having to ease some legal restrictions on Japanese labour unions) put into effect decisions which had in essence already been reached. Other measures tended to be either responses to unforeseen developments, as with the anti-pollution legislation, or reactions to pressure, most notably from foreign countries which objected to Japan's tariff barriers at a time when Japan was exporting on a much larger scale and could not so easily claim to be still catching up. The chief example of such pressure was the textiles wrangle with the United States from 1969 to 1971, when the Sato government found itself caught between, on the one hand, the demands of the Nixon administration for a cutback in Japanese exports which would fulfil the President's 1968 election promise to American textile manufacturers and, on the other, the interests of a Japanese industry which had considerable political clout. Sato's attempt to fudge the conflict of interests by vague promises, the implementation of which Japanese synthetic textile producers then resisted, led only to further friction. Not until 1971, when Minister of International Trade and Industry Tanaka Kakuei secured the agreement of Japanese manufacturers to voluntary export restrictions in return for a major package of special aid, was the problem resolved.

The retrocession of Okinawa

The textile dispute was the more damaging to Japanese-American relations because Japanese concession was seen by Nixon as part of a quid pro quo. What Sato was effectively being asked to pay for by export restraint was American acquiescence in his one major policy initiative – the reversion of Okinawa from American to Japanese control. His public reference to this aim when he was seeking the party presidency in 1964 had surprised the Foreign Ministry and seemed ambitious in view of the great strategic importance of the Ryukyus to the US Defence Department; and when the escalation of the Vietnam conflict resulted in an increasing number of bombing raids on Vietnam from US bases on Okinawa, it seemed unrealistic. It also raised political problems in Japan. Although nobody opposed the return of Okinawa in principle, it was felt by some LDP politicians, notably Foreign Minister Miki, that the immediate priorities were to improve relations with China and, more generally, to ease tension between the capitalist and communist powers. It was further anticipated that the price Japan would be likely to have to pay for Okinawa – a strengthening of Japanese support for America, especially its policy towards Vietnam – would be counter-productive. LDP leaders could not be insensitive, either, to the fact that if Sato's initiative were successful, his personal political standing would be enhanced.

The reservations felt within the LDP were more than shared by the opposition parties and by intellectuals. In criticising Sato's efforts they directed their fire on two points in particular: whether nuclear weapons would still be allowed on Okinawa after reversion, and whether the requirement of prior consultation before the United States made use of its installations in Japan proper would be extended to apply to the Americans' much more important Ryukyuan island bases. Initially it seemed as though Sato would, in order to secure his prize, allow the American forces to operate freely in Okinawa, but during 1968 opposition to such a special regime gathered strength. It was stimulated partly by the Left's concern about the government's publicity campaign to inculcate a wider sense of the need for national security, a campaign which was accompanied by an Education Ministry proposal to revise textbooks to ensure that children secured a more favourable view of Japanese history and by an LDP policy document advocating the revival of traditional values, including patriotism. On top of this, public feeling was stirred up when Japanese ports were visited by an American ship alleged to be carrying nuclear weapons. The intense speculation prompted by American refusal to confirm or deny the allegation (which was effectively acknowledged to be valid over a decade later by ex-Ambassador Reischauer) was the more embarrassing to the Japanese government in that Sato had only recently, in December 1967, pledged that Japan would not manufacture, possess, or permit the entry of nuclear weapons. LDP opinion consequently began to shift and in March 1969 Sato publicly stated that he would seek to negotiate Okinawa's return without any difference of status between the bases there and those already covered by the security treaty.

This decision made it more difficult to secure an agreement with the new Nixon administration, but the latter recognised that it was important to keep pro-American leaders in power. Furthermore, its acceptance of Reischauer's argument that the value of the bases would be undermined if Japanese opinion were alienated, together with its hope that Japan would be likely to take on the responsibilities of an ally more positively, meant that the earlier vague encouragement by Johnson was quite quickly converted into a firm commitment in November 1969. The wording of the communiqué issued at the time of the final agreement of June 1971, however, was not made perfectly clear. Nixon's national security adviser, Henry Kissinger, took care to include, with Sato's connivance, a phrase which could be interpreted as allowing nuclear weapons to be brought into Okinawa for use in case an emergency threatened Japan's existence. Moreover, the reference in the agreement itself to the importance of South Korea and Taiwan to Japanese security left little room for Japan to use the prior consultation provision to object to American military operations being launched from Okinawa into those areas.

There was no chance that an arrangement which allowed such loopholes would escape criticism. So alert was the Japanese Left to the danger it perceived of Japanese military imperialism being revived and directed towards American ends that a protest movement calling for the renegotiation of the agreement was rapidly organised. Especially in Okinawa itself, it expanded to a level which for a time matched the demonstrations against security treaty revision a decade earlier. Neither this, however, nor vehement opposition in the Diet swayed the cabinet from its purpose.

Relations with China and the end of the Sato cabinet

The formal return of Okinawa on 15 May 1972 was arguably the major achievement of the Sato government. Nevertheless, his foreign policy had never found favour with those in the LDP who wanted to make Japan more independent. The latter included not only the minority which wanted Japan to have nuclear weapons but also the much larger number who wished to recognise the Beijing regime and expand trade with the mainland. In October

1970 a League for the Restoration of Ties with China was founded, and within two months no fewer that ninety-five LDP Diet members had joined it, together with 284 other Diet members from all parties. As long as the Prime Minister retained American favour, however, he was able to resist such pressure.

This situation changed in mid-1971, when the United States suddenly abandoned two long-standing policies without consulting the Sato cabinet, even though both were of cardinal importance to Japan. In July Nixon abruptly announced that he would visit China, thus foreshadowing the ending of the non-recognition policy towards Beijing; and in August the American government not only imposed a levy on imports but went off the gold standard, a move which destabilised the Tokyo foreign exchange market and by December had led to a worrying upward valuation of the yen. These 'Nixon shocks' revealed that Sato had lost credibility as a result of his failure to deliver what the President believed him to have offered in the textile discussions and that he no longer enjoyed the latter's trust. His public standing plummeted. In January 1971 a poll had shown support for his cabinet running at 37 per cent, not much below its average level since 1964, but one year later the figure was only 23.4 per cent, and it fell further to 17.3 per cent by June 1972. Even this might not have proved fatal to Sato. Nixon's policy change on China, however, had made him a liability. His association with the previous non-recognition line and his contacts with Taiwan – he even went against party advice in supporting Taiwan's continuing membership of the United Nations – meant that without a change of cabinet it would be very difficult for Japan to follow the United States in normalising relations with Beijing and in taking advantage of the commercial opportunities which could now be expected. Advised to retire even by Hori Shigeru, a trusted henchman, Sato eventually bowed to the inevitable on 17 June.

The China factor not only forced Sato to resign, it also had a significant bearing on the question of who would succeed him. Initially the outcome seemed more uncertain than in any party election since 1960. Sato himself favoured Fukuda Takeo, an ex-Finance Ministry bureaucrat who had become the leader in 1962 of what had been Kishi's faction and who had held the key positions of Finance Minister and LDP Secretary-General. Those positions, however, had also been filled by a formidable rival,

Tanaka Kakuei, and the latter had the further advantages of being an exceptional fund-raiser, a very effective organiser, and a political operator worthy of comparison with Hara Takashi. He had left school after only six years and his public image as a warm-hearted man of the people contrasted sharply with that of the far less outgoing, Tokyo University-educated, Fukuda. Tanaka was young in Japanese political terms (at 54 he was Fukuda's junior by 14 years) and was not regarded as a suitable successor by the outgoing Prime Minister, who cannot have been pleased when his chief lieutenant began to form his own faction in the spring of 1971, eventually taking away eighty-one of Sato's 102 followers (the rest being in due course led by Hori into the Fukuda faction). However, Sato's influence had slumped: when he appealed to Hashimoto Ryutaro and Obuchi Keizo, two members of his old faction who would both become Prime Ministers themselves in due course, they bluntly told him that they were adults and would make their own decisions. Their views were typical of many younger LDP members whose seats in the Diet were not as secure as their elders' and who thought that Tanaka's election would improve their own chances of being re-elected. Despite his age, Tanaka had enormous experience, having been elected to the Diet at the age of twenty-eight and having first held ministerial office at thirty-eight, and he was quick off the mark in mounting his campaign for the party leadership, not only seeking to win over members of other factions but also publishing, a month before the election, a book, *Nihon Retto Kaizo Ron* (Remodelling the Japanese Archipelago), which set out his vision of Japan's future development and soon became became a best-seller.

Ohira and Miki also decided to stand for the LDP presidency, but significantly they reached an understanding with Tanaka which ensured that he would receive their support in the second round of voting. Hence, although in the initial ballot his 156 votes were only six more that Fukuda received (with Ohira and Miki trailing with 101 and sixty-nine respectively), in the run-off he defeated his rival by 282 to 190. Money may well have played a part in Tanaka's victory – he was alleged to have spent 8 billion yen, most of it contributed by construction companies – but he was also able to secure Ohira's and Miki's support because they, like many others in the LDP, shared his view that normalisation of relations with China should be a priority. On this issue Fukuda was on shaky ground, for the Chinese made it clear that, having been associated, as Foreign Minister, with Sato's anti-Beijing stance, he was an obstacle to a new policy.

The Tanaka cabinet's aims and setbacks

Tanaka was closer to being a charismatic politician than any of his predecessors, and this was reflected in the very high initial popularity rating of his cabinet. His reputation was based largely on his proven ability. He was the first Prime Minister who had been a successful businessman, having made a great deal of money during and after the war in the construction industry. He had performed effectively in the party and governmental positions he had held and had acquired the respect of bureaucrats as a man who could get things done, a quality which many politicians, handicapped by the habitually short stints in office which the frequent cabinet reshuffles produced, did not display. Better than any other post-war politician, he had learned how the political system worked or could be made to work.

Initially Tanaka seemed capable of living up to his reputation. With the help of Ohira, the new Foreign Minister, and the even more important cooperation of various politicians (including the Komeito leader, Takeiri Yoshikatsu) who had good connections with Beijing, he visited China in September 1972 and secured a normalisation of relations without having to make humiliating concessions which would have aroused opposition among pro-Taiwan LDP elements. This, however, proved to be his only major triumph. It was soon followed by a setback in the House of Representatives election of December 1972, which Tanaka's high standing in the opinion polls (over 60 per cent) encouraged him to call. Not only did the LDP fail to capitalise on his China success but it lost seats, ending up with only 284 members (including thirteen who ran without party endorsement). It was little consolation that Komeito's apparently inexorable progress was reversed with its reduction from forty-seven to twenty-nine seats, probably in part as a result of the bad publicity which its sponsor, Soka Gakkai, had received for trying to suppress a book which criticised the sect. The losses which Komeito suffered were matched by the Democratic Socialists' fall from thirty-one to nineteen seats, and the parties which gained were the main opposition party, the Japan Socialist

Party, which recovered from its disastrous 1969 performance to a more respectable 118 seats, and the even more anti-government Japan Communist Party. The latter jumped sharply up from fourteen to thirty-eight representatives, its reward for its continued move away, under Miyamoto Kenji's leadership, from its 1950s' emphasis on ideology and revolution towards a strategy of, on the one hand, offering help and advice to ordinary citizens, especially in the big cities, and on the other, cultivating small businessmen through the Democratic Commerce and Industry Association, which it promoted as a rival to the LDP-oriented Japan Chamber of Commerce and Industry and which by 1971 had 175,000 members (about one-sixth of all small business operators). Its tactic of selecting a number of relatively young lawyers and doctors as candidates also paid dividends.

The LDP may have made a tactical mistake in the election by endorsing ten more candidates than in 1969, but the main cause of its reverse appears to have been the growing dissatisfaction with the effects of government policy. Although anti-pollution measures were being put into effect, and an environmental agency was set up in 1971 (eventually to become a ministry in 1999), public concern remained high; and during the election campaign, the opposition parties damagingly claimed that Tanaka's plan to re-model Japan by dispersing industry to the less developed regions would spread pollution. The disturbing rate of inflation could also be blamed on the government because in its concern to offset the effects of the rise in the value of the yen against the dollar the cabinet had sought both to cushion smaller companies by increasing subsidies and to expand the domestic market by increasing the money supply and lowering the interest rate. This policy was not the responsibility of the Tanaka cabinet alone, for under its predecessor the Ministry of Finance had favoured an inflationary line as a way of maintaining a degree of undervaluation of the yen; but its extension and continuation after 1972, when prices were already rising quite sharply, proved short-sighted.

The election rebuff did not divert the Tanaka cabinet from its expansionary policies, although it did stimulate it to improve social welfare. This was an area which the Japanese state had hitherto preferred to encourage families, local communities, and companies to cope with, although many prefectural governments, both progressive and conservative, had moved towards a more positive role.

With the introduction of children's allowances, free medical care for the elderly, and substantial increases in pensions, which were also index-linked to the inflation rate, the proportion of welfare spending in the national budget increased from 13.2 per cent in 1972 to 19 per cent in 1974. Unfortunately for Tanaka the benefits of these policies were outweighed by the effects of the economic distortions which occurred during his period in office. Already by early 1973 his cabinet's popularity had fallen to 27 per cent, but worse was to come with the first major 'oil shock' which accompanied the Arab-Israeli war later that year. Not only was there a rapid quadrupling of the price of oil – which had become Japan's main source of energy by far – but exports to Japan were restricted by the Organisation of Petroleum Exporting Countries, a major concern for a country which depended so heavily on supplies from the Middle East. On top of this, shortages of other commodities also developed, leading to public apprehension and occasionally panic. To combat the high level of inflation Tanaka was forced to agree to the much tighter budget which Fukuda, his reluctant choice as Finance Minister in the crisis atmosphere of late 1973, insisted on, but what the LDP gained thereby in fiscal credibility it lost through the resulting reduction of purchasing power and through the cutbacks in production (which were responsible, in 1974, for Japan's first experience of negative growth since 1946). Tanaka's plans for remodelling the Japanese archipelago were now in complete disarray.

The economic difficulties, and the resulting loss of popular support, were almost inevitably accompanied by political setbacks. The first blow came when the cabinet tried, in the aftermath of the 1972 election, to do what Kishi had attempted: replace the existing large House of Representatives electoral districts with a predominantly single-member constituency system that would favour the major party. Although an element of proportional representation was also proposed, the scheme naturally met with wholehearted opposition by the other parties; and fear of Diet disruption, together with lack of support from Ohira, Nakasone (the leader of the former Kono faction) and Miki, meant that the bill was shelved in May 1973.

Even if electoral reform had been achieved in 1973, it would not have affected the outcome of the House of Councillors election in July 1974, in which the LDP suffered further disappointment, losing seven seats (while the JCP gained nine) and ending up with only a narrow majority in the chamber (129 out of 250). The reverse was the more damaging because of the exceptional effort which the LDP put into its campaign. Not only did it spend a huge amount of money (an estimated 50-100 billion yen), but Tanaka himself worked unstintingly making speeches in every prefecture but one. In addition, celebrities were enlisted as candidates in the national constituency, and, in an even more notable innovation – but in this case one which was not to be repeated – large companies were persuaded to sponsor and mobilise support for particular LDP candidates.

Had the LDP been more successful in the 1974 election, Tanaka might have survived longer as Prime Minister. As it was, his standing was further damaged by it not only because of the loss of seats but also because he seemed to be going beyond accepted limits. Criticism of big business involvement by the opposition parties was predictable, but unease about the heavy reliance on money politics was also expressed within the LDP, and this was one reason for Miki's resignation as Environment Agency chief in July. Miki was also motivated, however, by indignation at the deselection of a candidate from his faction for his own prefecture; and his resentment was shared by other faction leaders, whose influence was threatened by Tanaka's unprecedented gifts of substantial sums of money in July to members of their factions as well as his own. Miki's resignation was quickly followed by that of Fukuda; and to make matters worse for the LDP the most prominent business federation, Keidanren, announced that it would cease to support the party financially until its factions were dissolved.

It was against this background that Tanaka suffered a further blow in October, when a mainstream monthly journal, *Bungei Shunju*, published two detailed articles which raised serious doubts about the propriety and legality of Tanaka's financial dealings. This was not the first time that he had faced accusations of corruption. Indeed, he had been sentenced to imprisonment in 1950, only to see the sentence quashed in 1951. In 1974, however, the extent of his operations was far greater, and the revelation of his underhand methods came at a time when the government seemed to have lost its way and the public was less inclined to turn a blind eye to such irregularities. It cannot have helped Tanaka that at a rally in May he had adopted the stance of an admirer of traditional morality by proclaiming five essentials for education – 'To cherish people, to cherish nature, to cherish time, to cherish things, and to cherish your country and society' – and ten subjects for reflection, among which were 'Have I kept my promises?', 'Have I listened to the advice of others, such as my parents and teachers?', 'Have I been a nuisance to others?', and 'Have I acted courageously in what I believed to be right?'[8] When, two days after the *Bungei Shunju* articles appeared, Tanaka was grilled by foreign reporters (who may have been encouraged to look for a scandal by President Nixon's resignation over the Watergate affair two months earlier), the political situation rapidly worsened for the Prime Minister. Criticised by his enemies, lacking solid Establishment support, advised by his allies, including Ohira, that he should take personal responsibility, and aware that an opinion poll had registered the lowest-ever level of support for a Prime Minister (12 per cent), Tanaka, exhausted and dispirited, resigned on 26 November.

The Tanaka cabinet may have come to an ignominious end, but in its defence it could be argued that it was in office at an exceptionally difficult time. The international situation in the early 1970s had become more volatile, and, in contrast to the mainly beneficial effects of the Korean and Vietnam wars, Japan now found itself buffeted by external developments. Domestically, too, changes were occurring which made the political system more difficult to control than had been the case in the 1960s. The anti-pollution campaigns had both stimulated and reflected a higher level of political consciousness, and although one result of this was increased disillusionment with political parties in general, another was to encourage citizen's movements and stimulate a radicalism which was more concerned with the practical effects of government policies than with ideology. This, in turn, gave more weight to the media, which, for all the criticism of reporters for accepting too cosy a relationship with the particular politicians to whom they were assigned, were by no means in the government's pocket.

The Miki cabinet and the obstacles to political reform

The power of the media to eradicate structural corruption, however, was limited, as the experience of the next cabinet was to prove. The next Prime Minister was Miki Takeo, a Diet member

[8] *Japan Weekly Times*, 8 June 1974.

since 1937, who was generally perceived as the LDP faction leader with the most genuine concern for political ideals and the greatest interest in political reform. He was also noted for his frequent media appearances, speeches and interviews, but his position as head of government was basically weak, for his own faction was not one of the largest in the LDP and he had become LDP president not through election but as a result of manoeuvring among the party leaders. Essentially his selection was due, on the one hand, to the problems which would arise from a contest between the equally matched Fukuda and Ohira and, on the other, to the need to improve the LDP's reputation by installing someone regarded as 'clean'. From the ruling party's point of view, he was a stop-gap president, and once he became dispensable or overstepped the mark, he was likely to be eased out of office.

Miki's tenuous position did not preclude him from pursuing the cause of reform. It did, however, mean that any reform was likely to be largely cosmetic. This was evident when he sought to rectify the electoral distortions produced by demographic change: the increase in the number of urban seats was limited to twenty and still left a clear imbalance between less populous rural areas (where the LDP was particularly strong) and the relatively under-represented cities. Still stronger opposition met his attempt to reduce the importance of money politics by imposing significant restrictions on political funding. Only after the scheme had been watered down was it passed by the Diet in January 1976, and the loopholes which were left ensured that factions and individual politicians remained able to raise large amounts legally (even discounting the more dubious methods which were also practised). A further proposal to reform the procedure for electing the LDP president by extending voting rights to all the party's members was blocked; and although it finally received approval in January 1978, after Miki had ceased to be Prime Minister, it failed to achieve the objective of changing the nature of the LDP. Many new members were indeed registered, but they already belonged, for the most part, to existing *koenkai*, and their party dues were mostly paid by Diet members with the ulterior motive of being able to deploy their votes in future contests for the party leadership.

Miki's reformist tendencies were not confined to politics. He also responded to popular feeling by trying to tighten up the Anti-Monopoly Law, which had been largely disregarded since the

Occupation period but had become the focus of renewed attention because many suspected that the alarming price increases experienced since 1972 were partly caused by cartels. Needless to say, this idea was anathema to big business, and the proposed bill was emasculated during the usual LDP consultation process. Miki took the exceptional course of action of seeking opposition party cooperation to put teeth back into the measure and even got it through the House of Representatives. Before it could secure the House of Councillors' approval, however, it had to be diluted again. Miki's defeat on this issue was a replay of an earlier setback in late 1975, when he was forced by other LDP leaders not only to abandon the idea of abrogating the 1948 ban on strikes by public employees (although in practice they had been defying the law for a decade) but also to seek through the courts heavy damages after a federation of public service unions had resorted to strike action to secure this right.

The confrontation over the right to strike was not a typical feature of the 1970s. In general (though Sohyo was a big exception) labour responded to the first (and, after 1979, the second) oil shock by accepting wage restraint, placing job preservation above keeping up with inflation and, from a Western viewpoint surprisingly, seeking a later age of retirement in return for a reduction in overtime. Labour moderation was reflected in the regular meetings which representatives of sixteen industrial unions held with LDP and government officials after they formed a Council for Policy Promotion in October 1976; and by the end of the decade their cooperative attitude was publicly acknowledged by the *zaikai*. This tendency towards collaboration with capitalism was to some extent echoed on the political left. The JSP's rhetoric steadily became less ideological, and the party increasingly joined not only with other opposition parties in sponsoring gubernatorial candidates but even, on occasion, with the LDP. Its speed of adjustment was, nevertheless, insufficient to satisfy Eda Saburo, who in 1977, after more than a decade and a half of struggle with Marxist elements, especially Sakisaka Itsuro and the Socialist League, finally left to form what soon became the Shaminren (Social Democratic League). Eda's death the same year, however, reduced the new party's prospects, and it never won more than a handful of seats in the Diet.

By the time the Shaminren was formed, the possibility that the opposition might be able to challenge the LDP's dominance seemed greater than it had since the late 1950s, for in the December 1976 general election the ruling party suffered its worst result since its foundation. Even though the total number of House of Representatives seats had been increased to 511, the LDP won only 249, and although its tally was increased by eleven when the candidates who had run successfully without party endorsement were added, its majority was now wafer-thin. One important factor in its poor showing was the defection, six months before the election, of five LDP Diet members under the leadership of Kono Yohei (the son of Kono Ichiro). All of them represented constituencies in and around Tokyo, and in the election the party they formed (the New Liberal Club) did particularly well in this major conurbation, gaining seventeen victories. Although not far apart from the LDP on policy, they emphasised their disenchantment with the way their former party operated, and their support in the Diet could by no means be counted on.

Because the New Liberal Club had particular appeal in the capital, it may have affected the JCP even more than the LDP, since Communists tended to be elected as the lowest-scoring winners in constituencies in the major cities. They also were usually in competition with Komeito and the Democratic Socialists, and the latter parties' resurgence to fifty-six and twenty-nine seats respectively was probably even more responsible for the JCP's striking drop to seventeen. The JCP's loss of appeal may also have been related to the bad publicity it had been receiving. It had been criticised for the abortive agreement it had entered into in 1975 with the Soka Gakkai leader, Ikeda Daisaku – an agreement which Komeito had then rejected – and its attempt to improve its image by removing the terms 'dictatorship of the proletariat' and 'Marxist-Leninism' from its party programme and replacing them with 'workers' power' and 'scientific socialism' was attacked as insincere in the press, while at the same time it provoked friction within the party. The JSP, for its part, remained the clear second party, but with only five more seats than in the previous smaller House of Representatives.

The Lockheed scandal and the Fukuda cabinet

Disappointing though the 1976 election was for the ruling party, an even worse result might have been anticipated, for the previous lavish *zaikai* funding had not yet been fully restored and the LDP's image had been further tainted by corruption. Again it was Tanaka on whom the accusations were focused, but this time they had the novel feature that they involved a foreign company -Lockheed – and were based on the public admission by its vice-president in the United States that bribes to the value of 22 million dollars had been dispensed to ensure the sale of its planes to All Nippon Airways. After Miki had pressed the US government to cooperate in the investigation by Japanese procurators, evidence was forthcoming that Tanaka was among the politicians, bureaucrats, and businessmen who had profited – in the ex-Prime Minister's case to the tune of 500 million yen – and although he denied any culpability, he was arrested in July and indicted (and eventually found guilty, though not until 1983). This 'Lockheed Scandal' initially benefited Miki by nipping in the bud Tanaka's thoughts of making a comeback, but it soon added to his difficulties in that it led the powerful Tanaka faction to press for Miki's replacement. Tanaka was even prepared to accept Fukuda – for whom he had earlier expressed contempt – as Prime Minister. Since Ohira, whose faction ranked second to Tanaka's, also indicated his willingness to give precedence to Fukuda (on the tacit understanding that he would stand down in Ohira's favour after two years) the end of the Miki cabinet was all but inevitable. The poor election result meant that Miki no longer tried to resist party pressure, and before the end of December Fukuda had replaced him, having become party president without a contest.

Public expectations of Fukuda were not high. He was not seen as a reformer or a man of vision, and initial support for his cabinet was unprecedentedly low at 19.4 per cent. With Japan's return to relatively high (over 5 per cent) economic growth, however, this figure gradually rose. The improvement also reflected the partial restoration of the LDP's image. No fresh scandals were revealed, and the almost equal balance of power in the Diet encouraged a greater show of party unity. The fact that the LDP felt obliged to concede some Diet committee chairmanships to other parties went some way towards meeting the overwhelming demand, as measured by public opinion polls, for a coalition government; and the enactment of some measures for which the opposition had been pressing (such as greater protection for small businesses against what was claimed to be unfair competition from much larger companies) together with the acceptance of opposition demands for tax cuts, ensured that the cabinet encountered relatively few difficulties in the Diet. Even electorally the LDP recovered some ground, for although the other political parties generally managed to agree over parliamentary tactics, they failed to cooperate in the House of Councillors' election in July 1977. As a result the LDP was able to boost its morale by winning just over half of the 126 seats contested.

Fukuda's own image was improved by successes in foreign policy. In contrast to the less than warm response to Tanaka's tour of South East Asia three years earlier, the new Prime Minister was well received when he visited the region in August 1977 and offered one billion dollars' worth of financial aid as a token of Japan's partnership with the newly-created Association of South East Asian Nations (ASEAN). His accompanying assurance that Japan would never again become a military power may have been slightly disingenuous in that the Self-Defence Forces had been steadily improved over the previous two decades, but the Miki cabinet's decision in November 1976 that defence expenditure should be kept below 1 per cent of GNP (despite American pressure to bear a larger share of the defence burden) meant that there was even less cause for anxiety about a revival of Japanese militarism. Surprisingly, in view of his association with anti-Communism and Taiwan, it was Fukuda's cabinet which was responsible for a further improvement of relations with Beijing. Trade, especially oil imports from China, had seen a five-fold increase since 1972, and a new commercial agreement, paving the way for Japanese investment in the new post-Marxist era of economic reform, was signed in February 1978, to be followed in August by a Treaty of Peace and Friendship. The latter's terms included a declaration of opposition to any country seeking to establish hegemony – a thinly-disguised reference to the Soviet Union – but after obtaining the insertion of a clause stating that relations with third powers were not affected, the Japanese government overcame its hesitation. Fukuda himself played a much less active role in securing the treaty than Foreign Minister Sonoda, but his acquiescence in it did much to neutralise hostility within the LDP.

LDP factional conflict and the Ohira cabinet's loss of a Diet majority

Fukuda's achievements and increased popularity did not ensure his longevity as Prime Minister. Ohira had had as strong a claim to replace Miki in 1976 and, as LDP Secretary-General since then, had made a major contribution to the party's recovery. During 1978 he reminded Fukuda of his unwritten agreement to step down after two years, but the Prime Minister prevaricated. By July, however, a contest for the LDP presidency had become unavoidable, since not only Ohira but also Nakasone and Miki's political heir, Komoto Toshio, had put themselves forward. Fukuda himself evidently had mixed feelings, for although he too entered, he apologised to Ohira for doing so, telling him: 'I cannot control things inside the faction and have no choice but to declare my candidacy'.[9] Under the new rules the first stage of the election, held in November, took the form of a vote by all party members and associated 'party friends', and thanks to Tanaka's support, Ohira secured 550,891 votes against Fukuda's 472,502, Nakasone's 197,957 and Komoto's 88,917. In theory the LDP Diet members should then have made a choice between the two leaders, but a run-off was made unnecessary by Fukuda's withdrawal.

Ohira was an ex-Ministry of Finance bureaucrat like his predecessor, but he had come from a peasant background in Shikoku and had become a Christian in his youth. Although well accustomed to wheeling and dealing from the time he entered politics as a protégé of Ikeda, he had a philosophical bent and a taste for writing, as well as reading books. In contrast to Fukuda, Ohira projected the image of a man who appreciated the need for more fundamental change, and, even more than his predecessors, he sought the advice of academics and outside experts, establishing a number of groups to chart the future and plan Japan's place in it. He was also noted for his powers of persuasion and his willingness to be flexible. As LDP Secretary-General he had publicly acknowledged that 'It is no longer possible for one political force to do everything by itself' and had adjusted to the new balance of power in the Diet by entering into serious negotiations with other parties.[10]

[9] Cited by J. Masumi, *Contemporary Politics in Japan*, p.191.
[10] See M. Mochizuki, 'Managing and Influencing the Japanese Legislative Process: The Role of Parties and the National Diet', Ph.D. thesis, Harvard University, 1982, p.246.

With such a background Ohira might have been expected to be one of the LDP's more successful leaders. Moreover, opinion polls suggested that there was a good prospect of the government securing a more substantial majority in a new election. With this expectation Ohira brushed aside the objections of the Fukuda, Miki, and Nakasone factions and arranged for the House of Representatives to be dissolved a year early. The gamble did not pay off. Indeed, the LDP won only 248 seats (253 including unendorsed candidates), even though the party actually increased its overall share of votes cast from 41.8 per cent (in the 1976 election) to 44.5 per cent. One reason for the setback was Ohira's suggestion (which he quickly withdrew) that it would be necessary to introduce a new indirect tax to counter the growing deficit in government finances. Another was the achievement of electoral cooperation between Komeito and the DSP, as a result of which DSP representation increased by six seats to thirty-five, while Komeito rose by two to fifty-seven seats. The biggest gains, however, were made by the JCP, which reversed its 1976 setback, more than doubling its seats from seventeen to thirty-nine, largely at the expense of the JSP, which, despite being led since 1977 by the popular ex-mayor of Yokohama, Asukata Ichio, was cut down from 123 to 107 seats. The biggest disappointment, however, was experienced by the New Liberal Club, which had lost its novelty and slumped from seventeen to four seats.

The 1979 election results provided useful ammunition for further attacks on Ohira by his critics. Indeed, he was immediately faced with a leadership challenge by Fukuda which at one point degenerated into physical conflict between their supporters in the Diet − behaviour reminiscent of the confrontations between government and opposition parties which had marked the 1950s and '60s. Ohira managed to remain in office, but only by narrowly defeating Fukuda in the House of Representatives vote for Prime Minister − the first time two LDP men had carried their rivalry to that point. He continued, however, to be harassed from within his party by the Fukuda, Nakasone and Miki factions, which, together with a small new faction under Nakagawa Ichiro, formed an 'Association to Improve the LDP'. In response Ohira spoke openly of a coalition with the moderate opposition parties. While LDP internecine warfare did not lead to a formal rupture, the rift between mainstream and anti-mainstream factions became wider than at almost any time in the past, and it culminated in an unprecedented defeat for the government on a no-confidence motion in May 1980 as a result of the absence of many dissident members.

The conservative revival

The passing of the no-confidence motion was the result not only of LDP internal dissension but also of closer cooperation among the opposition parties, based on the hope that they might soon be able to form a coalition government, especially if there were a further split in the ruling party. The outcome, however, was not what they had anticipated. Instead of resigning, the cabinet opted to go to the country again, and it was vindicated by winning a substantial majority. In its best performance since 1969, the LDP increased its share of the vote to 47.9 per cent and secured 284 seats (not including unendorsed candidates). The sudden calling of the election made it difficult for the opposition parties to cooperate, and while the JSP remained constant at 107, the DSP dropped to thirty-two, the JCP fell to twenty-nine, and Komeito plummeted to thirty-two. Only the New Liberal Club bucked the trend by trebling its representation to twelve. In the simultaneous House of Councillors election the LDP was almost as successful, securing sixty-nine seats (an increase of seven over 1974).

The 1980 elections marked a significant turn-around in LDP fortunes. Admittedly a very short-term factor came into play when Prime Minister Ohira died from heart failure in the middle of the election campaign, and the LDP received an exceptional boost from sympathy-votes. In addition, better weather meant that substantially more of the less committed, but frequently pro-LDP, voters in big cities turned out than in 1979. But leaving aside such accidental factors, there were also signs of an underlying shift towards the ruling party. In 1978 an LDP-backed candidate had won the governorship of Kyoto after the left-wing ex-professor, Ninagawa Torazo, had held it for twenty-eight years, and in 1979 the party secured a similar success in Tokyo, after the socialist Minobe Ryokichi decided not to stand again. Opinion polls registered an increase in support for the LDP among Japanese in their twenties, normally the least conservative age-group, and in 1979 one poll revealed that no fewer than 61 per cent of the population regarded themselves as belonging to the middle stratum of the middle class.

This was no surprise, since for over a decade an increasing majority of respondents (rising to as high as 90 per cent) had identified themselves broadly with the middle-class, thus leading commentators to develop the idea of 'an age of new middle mass politics' in which increasingly urban/metropolitan electorates might be more volatile than before but would tend to favour the LDP.[11]

The expectation that the LDP would gain from the growth of middle-class consciousness was not based entirely on the assumption that there was an automatic correlation between being middle-class and being conservative. More important, perhaps, there was a sense that the ruling party, for all its faults, had adapted to changing conditions and could be trusted to govern more effectively than any combination of opposition parties. Over the past two decades it had become less confrontational and less overtly eager to revise the constitution or advocate large-scale rearmament. Meanwhile, the waning appeal of the once-dominant left-wing intellectuals and the ever-increasing appearance in the media of right-wing ideas deprived the JSP and JCP of one of their special advantages, while the generally condemned Soviet military intervention in Afghanistan in 1979 further reduced the appeal of the Left. At a different level, the LDP had also learned from the initiatives by reformist local governments that measures to improve social welfare, just like moves to prevent or limit pollution, would improve its image; and its introduction of better pensions and free, or cheaper, medical care almost certainly contributed significantly to the revival in its support. So too, probably, did its willingness to provide aid (through wage subsidies, retraining allowances, relocating expenses, and help in organising cartels) to ease the difficulties of depressed industries such as shipbuilding. Moreover, the revival of economic growth, while unemployment remained below the Western level, not only provided reassurance about the LDP's governing ability but also contributed to the increased sense of superiority in comparison with foreigners (53 per cent in 1983 compared with 20 per cent in 1953) which the polls also registered. The context of restored national pride may explain, in part, the decision of Miki, when Prime Minister, to visit the Yasukuni Shrine (which commemorated Japan's war dead) on the anniversary of the country's World War II surrender, as well as the relatively subdued condemnation by the

---

[11] See, especially, Murakami Yasusuke, 'The Age of New Middle Mass Politics: The Case of Japan', *Journal of Japanese Studies,* vol.8, no.1 (winter 1982).

opposition of both his visit and the subsequent ones by Prime Minister Fukuda and virtually the whole cabinet in 1981 and 1982. The political climate, however, did not change sufficiently to enable the LDP to pass a bill providing for the government to reassume responsibility for the Yasukuni Shrine.

The Suzuki cabinet and administrative reform

The marked improvement in the LDP's position after the 1980 election gave it greater latitude in dealing with the opposition than it had enjoyed since 1976 and made possible a change of course. If the party was contemplating a rightward shift, however, its choice of the sixty-eight-year-old Suzuki Zenko as Ohira's successor was hardly an obvious one, even though, as Ohira's senior lieutenant and LDP Secretary-General, he had become acting Prime Minister. His background made him an unlikely leader for the right, since he had originally been elected to the Diet during the Occupation as a JSP candidate, switching to Yoshida Shigeru's Jiyuto in 1949 in order better to represent the fishing cooperatives in the northern prefecture of Iwate where his family had long provided local leadership. Though respected as a hard-working man of sense within the LDP, he was little known to the public and he had no desire to be Prime Minister. His selection, however, prevented an untimely struggle between Nakasone and Komoto, and also suited Tanaka who, with his faction expanding still further, could expect to wield influence behind the scenes. When he accepted his new responsibility, he proclaimed that he would pursue a 'politics of harmony' and made no reference to policy initiatives.

Despite Suzuki's lack of credentials for dynamic leadership, the mood both within the LDP and outside, especially among big business leaders, made it impossible to continue in exactly the same direction. There was, though, no move to revise the constitution and only a limited increase in armaments, even though the calls for both from the Right were louder than in the recent past. Indeed, Suzuki repudiated Justice Minister Okuno in no uncertain fashion when the latter publicly advocated the adoption of a genuinely Japanese constitution. Rather than these longer-standing objectives, the focus of attention was directed towards the new target of administrative reform. Not that it was entirely new. Under the same slogan there had been an attempt to cut back the size of the bureaucracy between 1962 and 1964. But this had proved a complete failure and had not been pursued. In 1980 it was seen as a much more important priority as a result of Japan's changed economic and financial situation. The unbalanced budgets of the 1970s had created a huge burden of public debt, and the impact of the second 'oil shock' in 1979-80, although less severe than the first, reinforced the sense of urgency. Nor were the policy-makers uninfluenced by the parallel calls for a change of approach in Britain and America as the Thatcher and Reagan administrations assumed power.

The call for administrative reform was of broader scope than the term might suggest. It certainly had at its base the belief that the bureaucracy was too large (even though international comparisons suggested the opposite) and that public employees, especially in local government, were excessively remunerated – not least by more generous pensions. It also favoured, on the grounds of efficiency and cost-cutting, at least partial privatisation of some government-run enterprises. Beyond this, however, lay the perception that the size of the bureaucracy was partly due to the uncontrolled growth of the subsidies which it administered; and this in turn was linked to an awareness that bureaucrats had a vested interest in building up obligations through the distribution of subsidies to local governments, public corporations, organised business, and agricultural cooperatives, since on retirement from their ministries or agencies (usually between forty-nine and fifty-five and significantly referred to as *amakudari* – 'descent from heaven'), bureaucrats looked for comfortable and lucrative positions in these 'client' organisations (or, in some cases, used their support to run as LDP Diet candidates). On top of this, administrative reform also included the intention of partially reversing some of the 1970s' welfare measures, which were causing particular concern because the increasing (and world-leading) longevity of Japanese made it difficult to see how the more generous national pensions and health benefits could be afforded in the not too distant future.

To achieve administrative reform a high-level commission (usually known from its abbreviated Japanese title as Rincho) was set up under the prestigious chairmanship of Doko Toshio, the ex-President of Keidanren; and the appointment of the forceful Nakasone Yasuhiro as head of the Administrative Management Agency provided Rincho with vigorous support. Even so, and despite general agreement on the broad outlines of reform, its implementation proved difficult. A measure to end free medical treatment for the over-seventies by introducing limited charges was passed in 1982, but pensions were not tampered with until 1985 and it was only in that year that the privatisation of Nippon Telephone and Telegraph (NTT) was accomplished, while subsidies to rice producers only began to be reduced in the late 1980s. Moreover, cutting back on the bureaucracy and the budget ran into strong opposition from vested interests, not least the numerous LDP Diet members (usually known as *zoku giin*) who had connections with particular ministries and were, accustomed to making use of their influence to benefit their supporters, but also from public-service unions and their supporters in the JSP. Only in 1987 did the budget deficit (which in 1974 had been 21.6 billion yen) drop to below 100 billion yen from its peak of 141.7 billion yen in 1980, and not much of this improvement came from cutting down the bureaucracy.

Suzuki came in for a good deal of criticism for the slow pace and uneven success of administrative reform. Less predictably he also received a bad press for his handling of two problems relating to foreign countries. The first arose when, in the communiqué which followed his talks with President Reagan in May 1981, he was condemned by the *Asahi Shimbun* and other newspapers for allowing the American-Japanese relationship to be referred to as an alliance, thus implying a greater military commitment than was acceptable to many Japanese, even two decades after the Security Treaty crisis. When Suzuki then criticised the communiqué and allowed Foreign Minister Ito Masayoshi to take the responsibility by resigning, he was further blamed by some papers for weak leadership and at the same time attacked from the right for sending the wrong signals to the United States.

The cabinet was also embarrassed by press criticism in June 1982 that the Ministry of Education had compelled school textbook publishers and authors to alter the wording of their coverage of sensitive aspects of Japanese pre-1945 history, notably by replacing 'invasion of North China' with 'advance into North China'. Although the allegations were later found to be exaggerated, they gave the Chinese government the opportunity to protest and demand textbook revision. The Chinese position was supported by the South Korean government, and also by the Japanese Foreign

Ministry and some businesses involved in East Asian trade, but there was strong resistance from the Ministry of Education itself and from the LDP politicians (the 'education *zoku*') closely associated with it. They principally objected that it was unacceptable to be dictated to by another country, but behind this lay the fact that for years they had been seeking to re-instill a spirit of patriotism through education and had indeed been attempting to persuade publishers to make exactly the changes (and more) that were now being complained of. Moreover, the Education Ministry was still contesting the case brought against it in the 1960s by the distinguished historian, Ienaga Saburo, for not authorising a textbook written by him unless he toned down his condemnation of Japan's war-time treatment of Asian peoples. A compromise on the general issue which would be acceptable to both ministries concerned was not easily forthcoming, and in the end the issue was only resolved after the Prime Minister, who was scheduled to visit China, implied publicly in August that the authorisation process would be revised to make textbooks more acceptable to the countries which Japan had wronged.

The textbook controversy may have further diminished Suzuki's taste for office (already lessened by criticism of his cabinet's failure to hold down rice price increases), for a few months later he decided not to stand again for the LDP presidency, even though he was not expected to face a serious challenge. Four faction leaders competed for the succession, and the victor was Nakasone Yasuhiro who secured 559,673 votes in the LDP primary election in October 1982, more than the combined total for Komoto Toshio, Abe Shintaro (Fukuda's heir-apparent), and Nakagawa Ichiro (who had earlier, in 1974, been prominent in the formation of the Seirankai, a right-wing group which cut across factions – and who was to commit suicide soon after his election defeat). As in 1978 there was no need for a final decision by the party's Diet members. Had a run-off been held, the factor which had produced Nakasone's large majority – the support of the Tanaka and Suzuki factions – would have led to an equally convincing result, and the particular importance of the former was acknowledged by the new Prime Minister's inclusion of six of Tanaka's adherents in his cabinet. Tanaka had now expanded his faction to a level unmatched in the party's history, making effective use of his various means of influence, especially in the Construction Ministry and the Ministry of Posts and Telecommunications, to amass the funds necessary to attract new followers and support them in their electoral campaigns. His dominance was to continue even after he was found guilty in October 1983 in the Lockheed bribery trial and sentenced to four years' imprisonment, a penalty never implemented because of his appeal (which was still unsettled when he died in 1993).

Nakasone's new approach

Although Nakasone came to power as a result of Tanaka's and Suzuki's support, he had no intention of being a puppet. In character he was almost the opposite of the unassertive Suzuki, and he had long been noted for his provocative statements, especially on the desirability of Japanese re-armament. For him it was time for Japan to emerge from the 'post-war era' and become an 'international state', no longer constrained by the memory of defeat and shackled by Occupation impositions. He was by no means anti-American, though. Indeed, his desire to make Japan a more significant military power was fully in line with long-term (but hitherto mainly unsatisfied) American demands that Japan bear a heavier share of the responsibility for its defence; and Nakasone's unprecedentedly friendly and informal relationship with President Reagan – indicated by their well-publicised use of a shortened form of each other's personal name – was due in no small part to the Japanese Prime Minister's declaration in Washington likening Japan to a large (mistranslated as 'unsinkable') aircraft carrier. It reflected also Nakasone's willingness to make a more serious effort than his predecessors to solve the problem of trade friction (which had intensified since 1980 as a result of the rapid increase in Japanese exports to the United States) by making changes on the Japanese side rather than calling for the Americans to mend their ways and become more efficient.

Nakasone regarded administrative reform as a means of bringing about desired changes, and he was less concerned than most of his party about its effect on pork-barrel politics and the rural constituencies because he saw LDP support in the future being based on the urban middle classes. When Rincho was established he spoke of achieving results comparable to those of the Meiji renovation. His sense of mission was made clear in a speech in the Diet on 24 January 1983:

'I feel that Japan is standing at a great turning-point in post-war history. ... I think that confronting the violent change of the age we must accept the need to reconsider with fresh eyes, and without setting up taboos, our existing basic institutions and plans.'[12]

Nakasone had little opportunity to put his reforming zeal into practice in 1983. Apart from the fact that initially he gave priority to international affairs, he also had to lead the LDP in two elections that year. The first, in June, was the regular House of Councillors election, the procedure for which had been changed in 1982 so that in the 100-member national constituency (but not in the pre-fectural contests) individual candidates were replaced by party lists, with the number of Councillors from each party determined by the total number of votes received. This partial adoption of proportional representation made surprisingly little difference. The LDP returned sixty-eight members, one fewer than in 1980, but two more than in 1977, while there was little change in the positions of its rivals. In contrast, the House of Representatives election in December produced a much less favourable result for the LDP. The election was called not because the time seemed propitious but because the opposition parties boycotted the Diet proceedings, following the refusal of the government to pass a resolution enforcing Tanaka's resignation after his conviction in October. All the opposition parties focused on the Tanaka case in the campaign, and they were justified by its outcome. The JSP gained six extra seats, the DSP secured seven more, and the Komeito rose from thirty-three to fifty-nine (although the JCP lost two seats and the Shaminren remained stuck on three). Most sig-nificantly, the LDP dropped to 250, and only secured a flimsy working majority when it was joined by nine unendorsed winners and when it reached a cooperation agreement with the New Lib-eral Club (which itself had dropped from twelve to eight Diet members). The LDP may also have suffered from some voters' unease about Nakasone's intentions (which were believed to have been the main factor in his loss of popularity – from 37 to 29 per cent – between December 1982 and February 1983) and from run-ning more candidates – 339 – than it had for over a decade; and the fact that the turnout of 67.9 per cent equalled the record low lends support to the argument that the cold weather may have put off a significant number of the marginal voters on whom the ruling party

[12] Cited by Yamada Hiroshi *et al.*, *Sengo Seiji no Ayumi*, p.225.

now depended more heavily. In the election's aftermath, however, Nakasone accepted that the LDP had been reprimanded by the people. Conceding that 'one of the causes for the setback suffered by the Liberal Democratic party was that the problem of political ethics was not handled in a manner fully satisfactory to the people', he promised thorough reform.[13]

Such a promise was not convincing. Tanaka himself, far from being repudiated by his constituency, had scored his most overwhelming personal victory, and his faction had suffered fewer losses than any of its rivals. Even though Nakasone announced that he would 'eliminate all so-called political influence coming from Mr Tanaka',[14] the latter's support remained essential to him, as its continued strong representation in the new cabinet again demonstrated. With pressure to resign from Miki and Fukuda, and with a party presidential election due in late 1984, the Prime Minister could certainly not afford to alienate the 'Tanaka brigade': indeed, not only did he not encourage any moves against Tanaka, but the latter was re-admitted to party membership. However, during 1984 cracks in the Tanaka faction began to appear, when one of his lieutenants, Nikaido Susumu, took it upon himself to challenge Nakasone. He was supported not only by Fukuda but also by Suzuki, while Komeito and the DSP, hoping for an LDP split and a coalition under Nikaido, offered further encouragement. In the event Nikaido was dissuaded by Tanaka and by Kanemaru Shin, an influential sub-leader in the faction, and Nakasone was re-elected without a contest; but Nikaido's move, although abortive, foreshadowed a more successful attempt to take over from Tanaka as faction leader. This time the bid came from Takeshita Noboru (currently the Finance Minister). With the backing of Kanemaru (whose son had married his daughter) the sixty-year-old Takeshita set up a new group (the Soseikai) within the faction, and despite Tanaka's disapproval, a large majority of faction members joined it. When Tanaka suffered a stroke the following month all but a handful of the remainder went over to Takeshita and Kanemaru.

---

[13] *Liberal Star*, vol.13, no.144 (January 1984).
[14] Cited by C. Johnson, 'Tanaka Kakuei, Structural Corrupton and the Advent of Machine Politics in Japan', *Journal of Japanese Studies*, vol.12, no.1 (winter 1986), p.18.

Nakasone's position may not have been strengthened by the 1983 election but he still aspired to a more presidential style of political leadership than his predecessors had attempted. In pursuing this course he was bound to run up against factional opposition and bureaucratic obstructionism, and to overcome these obstacles he resorted to the aid of outside experts, whose recommendations would carry weight and whose reputations would be likely to ensure greater public support. Like Ohira Masayoshi, but to an even greater extent, he established, or encouraged government ministries to establish, commissions composed of academics, businessmen, and bureaucrats to investigate a variety of current problems and possible future trends and developments. One of the most important was the Special Commission on Educational Reform (Rinkyoshin), which was set up in August 1984 in the face of opposition from the Education Ministry and members of the LDP who belonged to the education *zoku*. The question of educational reform had become topical as a result of the publicity given to the increasing number of serious bullying cases in schools, but Nakasone and his advisers saw the opportunity of achieving much broader educational objectives.

Not all of these objectives were unwelcome to the Education Ministry. Nakasone's concern that education should provide a basis for national pride, for instance, was a cause which had long pitted the ministry's bureaucrats and LDP politicians against the teachers' union, Nikkyoso, itself a bastion of the JSP and an opponent of the re-introduction of traditional-style moral teaching and the old national flag and anthem. Nor did educational conservatives oppose Nakasone's emphasis on internationalisation, since the idea of opening up Japanese schools to foreign influences (notably through the increased employment of foreign teachers and assistants) was presented as important in preparing Japan to play a leading position in the world, and was accompanied by the aim of improving foreign understanding of the Japanese and their culture. The liberalisation of education, however, was another matter. Nakasone and his circle wished to move away from an emphasis on conformity, rote-learning, and examinations, and to encourage the greater diversity, flexibility and individualism which would be needed if Japan were to become a leading innovator in the anticipated 'information society'. This, however, meant reducing standardisation and challenging the exceptionally tight control exercised by the Education Ministry. In the face of the latter's opposition, Nakasone's proposals for encouraging more private schools and increasing competition among schools, like his attempts to relax the textbook approval procedure and reduce the importance of examinations, were given a low priority, and little was done to implement them after the Commission's final report in 1987, when Nakasone's period of office was close to its end. Nevertheless, it has since been argued that his efforts did pave the way for a greater degree of liberalisation in the 1990s.

The combination of liberalisation and nationalism which characterised Nakasone's approach to educational reform was also evident in two of his cabinet's most notable moves in 1985. The liberal aspect was reflected in the Equal Employment Opportunities Law, which (relying on moral exhortation rather than legal enforcement) made some attempt to eliminate the obstacles which women who wished to pursue a career faced. The nationalist side appeared on 15 August, when Nakasone acting not, as Miki and Fukuda had done, as a private individual but in his capacity as Prime Minister, led the cabinet and 172 other Diet members in a ceremony commemorating Japan's war dead at the Yasukuni Shrine. This action incurred Chinese and Korean as well as domestic criticism, however, and was not repeated (although in October 1999 the Obuchi cabinet announced that the resumption of the official ceremony would be reconsidered). There was a further hint of a return to the past in 1985 in the LDP's proposed law to protect national secrets on the ground that Japan was a paradise for spies, but after being strongly criticised this was shelved.

Nakasone had hoped that 1985 would also see the abandonment of the convention that defence spending should not exceed 1 per cent of GNP. The opposition to this of Fukuda and Suzuki proved too strong to overcome at the first attempt, but in 1986 the 1 per cent limit was breached, albeit by only a tiny fraction. Significantly, criticism of the government's action was far less vociferous than it would have been in previous decades, a reflection both of the growing levels of support for the Self-Defence Forces shown by opinion polls and of the fact that in early 1984 the JSP, now led by Ishibashi Masashi, had moderated its previous attitude of outright rejection by accepting that, although unconstitutional, the Self-Defence Forces were not illegal.

The increase in military spending went only some way towards meeting American demands that Japan shoulder more of the defence burden. Behind such demands lay an ever-increasing tension as concern over Japan's still-growing trade surplus was exacerbated by fears that American companies were being driven out of their own home market by Japanese competition. American complaints resulted, as they occasionally but less frequently had in previous decades, in 'voluntary' export restriction agreements on those Japanese products which seemed particularly threatening. The most important consequence, however, was Japan's acceptance in September 1985 of a very substantial revaluation of the yen. This was eventually to contribute significantly to financial and economic destabilisation in Japan and, indirectly, to the undermining of the 1955 political system.

It was partly in response to the rise of 'Japan-bashing' in America that Nakasone set up in the autumn a seventeen-strong Advisory Group on Economic Structural Adjustment for International Harmony under the chairmanship of a former governor of the Bank of Japan, Maekawa Haruo. Nakasone involved himself closely in the group's deliberations, and the conclusion, in its April 1986 report, that 'The time has come for Japan to make a historical transformation in its traditional lifestyle' echoed his own speeches. Its primary recommendation that in order to eliminate trade surpluses Japan should expand domestic demand marked a shift away from the return to financial orthodoxy which had characterised the earlier stages of administrative reform. In practice, however, Nakasone had neither the time nor the political power to go very far in implementing the report.

The Liberal Democratic Party's 1986 election success

Had LDP rules been followed, the Prime Minister would have had even less time, for they laid down that party presidents could serve no more than two terms of two years each, and Nakasone's second term would end in October 1986. Such political rules have rarely been regarded as sacrosanct, however, and in September 1986 they were bent to allow the LDP leader to continue in office for a further year. One reason why he was allowed an extension was that no other faction leader was in a position to mount a strong challenge. Takeshita had not yet consolidated his hold over the largest faction, and his relationship with Nikaido was delicate; Suzuki and Fukuda were in the process of stepping down in favour of Miyazawa Kiichi and Abe Shintaro respectively; and Komoto Toshio's faction was much smaller than the others. More importantly, in July Nakasone had led the LDP to an unexpectedly impressive success in the elections for both Diet chambers. In the House of Councillors election it secured seventy-two seats, its highest ever total, with Komeito suffering the most significant setback; and in the House of Representatives election the LDP scored a similar triumph, returning 300 members (304 including its unendorsed candidates), four more even than in 1960 (albeit out of a larger total). In this case the losses which matched the LDP's success were mostly borne by the JSP, which saw its representation collapse to eighty-five, leaving it with only twenty-nine more members than Komeito.

Nakasone's personal standing and campaigning style clearly played a part in the LDP victory. A reporter who accompanied him, in explaining the enthusiasm which his speeches aroused, wrote that 'the secret of Nakasone's appeal lies in his ability to stir latent national pride and patriotism',[15] but other factors also played their part. The holding of both elections at the same time encouraged a larger turnout – this time 71.5 per cent – so more of the LDP's less committed supporters went to the polls; while the cutback in the number of endorsed candidates (to 322) ensured that there was less internecine competition within the LDP. Furthermore, in anticipation of a contest for the party presidency before the next general election, the so-called 'New Leaders' of the main party factions made special efforts to strengthen their position by having as many of their followers as possible become Diet members. The weakness of the opposition, though, also cannot be ignored. The JSP's criticisms of Japanese capitalism seemed unconvincing when the rest of the world seemed to be in awe of Japanese economic power, and despite the party's jettisoning of some of its radical rhetoric, it did not look capable of governing. Significantly, it improved its image after the election by replacing Ishibashi with the first woman leader of a major Japanese political party, Doi Takako, a former professor of constitutional law. For their part, Komeito and the DSP had suffered a setback in 1983 when

[15] Cited by K. Pyle, 'In Pursuit of a Grand Design: Nakasone Betwixt the Past and Future', *Journal of Japanese Studies*, vol.13, no.2 (summer 1987), p.267.

their putative partner, the New Liberal Club, had resumed partnership with the LDP (a partnership which became a complete reunion after the 1986 election). By 1986 it was evident that they were now thinking in terms of power-sharing with a weakened LDP. Even more clearly it was obvious that the JCP was no longer advancing and could no longer hope for an alliance with the JSP.

The result of the 1986 election was even worse for the JSP than was immediately apparent, for the boost to Nakasone's standing enabled him to push ahead with one of the key targets of administrative reform: the semi-privatisation and splitting up of the loss-making Japan National Railways (JNR). Although the government retained ultimate control by holding a majority of the shares, the splitting up of the JNR into several companies paved the way for job cuts and for the weakening of the main JNR union, which had hitherto been one of the main bases of JSP support. Coming on top of the plan to undermine the Japan Teachers' Union by the introduction of a system of supervision of new teachers by non-unionised seniors, this was a significant blow for a party which had always depended heavily on unionised public employees.

Introduction of the consumption tax

The 1986 election paved the way for a significant change of course by the government. In the light of the hostile reaction to Ohira's VAT suggestion in 1979, Suzuki had promised not bring in new taxes. The Ministry of Finance, however, had long sought to establish a broader revenue base, and the expectation that by 2020 over one in five Japanese would be sixty-five years old or more made it seem the more desirable to depend less on income and corporation tax, instead expanding taxes on the sale of commodities and services. Although such a change was bound to arouse opposition, especially since Nakasone had promised during the election that a large indirect tax would not be introduced, it might appeal to the electorally important salaried workers, who were known to feel aggrieved that they could not avoid tax on their incomes in the way that farmers and the self-employed could. In December 1986 the government decided to go ahead, although not with the manufacturer's sales tax for which Nakasone pressed but with a 5 per cent VAT which LDP leaders and the Keidanren favoured. Even before the type of tax was decided, however, there was a wave of protest from the Japan Chamber of Commerce and from the various retailers' associations, while within the LDP itself there was opposition from Diet members who were concerned not to lose vital small business support. Their message was strengthened by public opinion polls and by unexpected and serious prefectural and gubernatorial election defeats. Nakasone was clearly reluctant to give up, but with a visit to the United States in the offing, he needed to secure the early passage of the budget, which included some of the measures to stimulate imports which the US government had been calling for, and he soon accepted that it would be unwise to persist.

This setback did not, however, end the plans for tax reform. Nakasone's attention now turned to making room for cuts in direct taxation by eliminating the tax-free status of the very numerous postal savings accounts. In this he was successful, but the achievement owed much to the efforts made to win over the opposition parties by Takeshita, who by the time the bill passed the Diet in September was about to become the next party president. Takeshita had become the strongest contender to succeed Nakasone, for in June he had finally emerged from his struggle with Nikaido as the leader of the largest faction, with 113 followers. Abe and Miyazawa, his main rivals (with factional strengths of eighty-five and eighty-nine respectively), could only have mounted an effective challenge if one of them had agreed to support the other, but neither was prepared to stand down. Instead of deciding the issue by a party election, though, the three men agreed in July to allow Nakasone to choose between them, and the outgoing Prime Minister opted for Takeshita.

The new LDP leader was a much more typically Japanese politician than his predecessor, being far less inclined to assert his personality and seek popularity, although he did present himself as having a special concern for rural communities, many of which were suffering from depopulation, and he was responsible for every village being given 100 million yen to spend as it wished. At heart, though, he shared Nakasone's concern to proceed with tax reform and showed a better understanding of how to secure it. Learning from the abortive attempt of 1986-7, he sought to gain acceptance by mounting a campaign to convince the public of the case for what was now described as a 'consumption' tax, by consulting at length with LDP Diet members, and by negotiating with the two opposition parties, Komeito and the DSP, which were not so adamantly opposed as the JSP and JCP. By agreeing (against the Ministry of Finance's wishes) to modify the proposed measure so as to reduce its impact on small businesses and farmers and by yielding to Komeito demands for additional welfare spending, he succeeded in getting a 3 per cent consumption tax into law inDecember 1988.

This success marked the apogee of the LDP. It had, in the 1980s, recovered from its decline in the previous decade and its control of the Diet seemed assured. Even if its level of electoral support was slightly lower than in the late 1950s and early '60s, it no longer needed to worry about a radical threat from the Left. In 1989, however, the year which also saw the death of the Showa emperor and the inauguration of the Heisei (Achieving Peace) era under the new Emperor (Akihito), the LDP's position began to crumble.

The Recruit scandal and the collapse of the Takeshita and Uno cabinets

The most obvious cause of the LDP's decline was the revelation of how big an influence money had on government and to what lengths Japanese politicians were prepared to go to secure funding. Awareness of this already existed to some extent, but whereas the Lockheed affair and other murky episodes had tended to focus on a single politician or a small group, the Recruit scandal, which first hit the headlines in 1988 but was more fully exposed during the following year, implicated well over 100 politicians (mostly from the LDP) as well as a number of bureaucrats and public figures. Among those most heavily involved were Nakasone, Takeshita and Abe, all of whom were discovered to have received at least 100 million yen in donations or other benefits from Ezoe Hiromasa, the founder of the Recruit company. That the vast sums disbursed had been worthwhile was evident from the company's extraordinary expansion in the 1980s, notably into the fields of data communications and property development.

Most of what Ezoe had done was not technically illegal, but when press reports that politicians had been able to make large gains through effectively risk-free transactions in the shares of Recruit Cosmos, Ezoe's property company, began to appear in the summer of 1988 and were then followed by increasingly detailed revelations resulting from investigations by the public prosecutor's office, they proved highly embarrassing to all concerned. Beginning with Miyazawa, the current Finance Minister, on 9 December 1988, several ministers felt obliged to resign; while in due course Nakasone was forced not only, like Tanaka earlier, to give up membership of the LDP but also to yield his factional position to a successor not of his choice, Watanabe Michio. The biggest casualty, however, was Takeshita, who stepped down as Prime Minister and party leader in May 1989, a month after one of his secretaries had committed suicide. By then his popularity had fallen to an extraordinary 3.9 per cent, while support for the LDP had slumped to 27 per cent, only 1 per cent ahead of the JSP. So abnormal was the political atmosphere that to replace Takeshita the party decision-makers exceptionally chose not one of the faction leaders but a senior member of the Nakasone faction, the sixty-six-year-old current Foreign Minister Uno Sosuke, who had not been considered important enough to merit a bribe (and even now was only turned to after a more highly respected veteran, Ito Masayoshi, had declined to be drafted because his demand for political reform was unacceptable).

As a means of repairing the LDP's reputation Uno's selection proved a serious mistake. He may have been untainted by corruption, but he had kept mistresses and although this was a common enough practice among leading politicians to be considered unworthy of comment, it attracted considerable public attention and criticism when two of the women with whom he had had long-term liaisons complained to the press that he had treated them ungenerously and unfeelingly. The publicity was the more damaging because it coincided with the House of Councillors election, and it ensured that Uno was made the scapegoat for the disastrous defeat which the LDP suffered in that contest. His resignation came after only two months in office, and he was succeeded in August by another second-line politician, the fifty-eight-year-old Kaifu Toshiki from the minor Komoto faction. This time the existence of two other candidates, one of whom, Ishihara Shintaro, was an ex-novelist and well-known right-winger, necessitated a party election, but the support of the Takeshita faction ensured a comfortable victory for Kaifu.

The new Prime Minister faced a daunting task for although only two (lower-ranking) politicians were eventually brought to trial by the investigators of the Recruit scandal, the LDP for the first time had lost control of the Diet. Even though House of Councillors elections involved only half the seats, the governing party's performance was so bad that it ended up with a mere 109, well short of the majority it had previously enjoyed, and only thirty-six more than the JSP, which unprecedentedly gained more victories than the LDP (forty-six to thirty-six). The swing to the left was even more marked when account is taken of the success of the newly-formed labour union federation, Rengo (which embraced most of the moderate Domei labour federation and a good many of the now more realistic Sohyo unions) in returning eleven of its twelve candidates. Opinion polls suggested that the main reason for the outcome was the unpopularity of the consumption tax rather than revulsion at the extent of high-level corruption, but tactical cooperation among most of the other parties also played a part. In addition to these factors the extraordinary decline in LDP support in rural prefectures indicated that many farmers had decided to punish the government for giving in to American demands by opening up the Japanese market to beef and citrus imports and for substantially cutting the price it paid to producers of rice in 1989 (after two years of resisting the customary pressure for annual increases). These developments showed that the government's proclamations of its belief in internationalisation and deregulation were more than cosmetic, and that faced with strong foreign pressure (with which Japanese exporting companies had some sympathy) the LDP was now prepared to alienate its own grass-roots supporters.

The shock of the 1989 election reverse led the LDP to make further attempts to improve its image. As well as bringing in a more presentable face as Prime Minister, the cabinet was reshaped to include, for the first time, two women, one of whom, Moriyama Mayumi, was appointed to the politically central position of Chief Cabinet Secretary. In addition, the prospect was held out that the consumption tax might be revised. These gestures seem to have had some effect, for in the more important House of Representatives election in February 1990 the LDP staged a notable comeback, yet again winning a clear majority with 275 seats (286, including unendorsed candidates). Significant losses were suffered by the smaller parties, with Komeito slipping back from fifty-seven to forty-five seats, the JCP dropping from twenty-six to sixteen, and the DSP seeing its representation almost halved (from twenty-seven to fourteen). The JSP, by contrast, continued its revival under Doi, adding fifty seats to its previous eighty-six; and it might have fared even better if it had broken further with tradition and increased the number of its female candidates substantially, as its leader wished, rather than marginally. Ironically, its failure to seize this opportunity to present itself in a fresher light was matched after the election by the LDP, which in the customary reshuffle returned to an all-male cabinet.

For a brief period the LDP could hope that it had surmounted its crises. The public appeared to have decided that one warning was enough, and with communism collapsing in Europe, the international climate was becoming more favourable for political parties which were identified with capitalism. In reality, however, the party was about to enter a period of even greater challenge. At the same time, however, the decline of the ideological threat from the Left made party cohesion less imperative. Still more important, the LDP found itself confronting new scandals and problems with which it could not cope.

The collapse of the 'bubble economy' and the impact of the Gulf Crisis

The most fundamental of the new problems was the crisis which resulted from the bursting of the so-called 'bubble economy'. Its origins lay in the overvaluation of the dollar in the early 1980s and more particularly in the over-successful attempts by Japan, and other countries, following the Plaza Accord in late 1985, to drive it down so that the United States would import less and see its huge trade deficit reduced to a more acceptable level. To counter the adverse effects on Japanese exporters which were anticipated from the corresponding rise in the value of the yen the Japanese government decided to stimulate domestic demand by lowering interest rates and increasing the money supply. It did not anticipate that, despite a 15.9 per cent drop in exports in 1986, the trade surplus would persist, and it therefore failed to perceive that its counter-measures would produce excessive capital fluidity. Some of this was eased by heavy Japanese purchases of American government bonds and by an expansion of direct foreign investment by Japanese companies (which to some extent was intended to overcome existing or potential tariff barriers but also meant the export of jobs). A good deal of the excess also went into buying shares and land, however, and in the over-confident atmosphere encouraged by the return to GNP growth rates (of about 5 per cent) which other advanced countries could not match, the stock exchange index and the price of land rose astronomically to a level which could not realistically be justified. A large amount of money was also lent to inefficient companies with overvalued land as security.

When the Ministry of Finance and the Bank of Japan finally recognised the danger and burst the bubble by raising the interest rate, the treatment not only proved painful but ushered in a period of economic stagnation which lasted longer than ever before in Japan's modern history. As the growth rate remained depressingly low (or even, in 1993 and 1997-8, marginally negative) throughout the next decade, Japan's vaunted image as economic world leader was replaced by that of a country which, except in a number of export industries which were involved in international competition, was riddled with inefficiency. Within Japan itself some politicians and businessmen accepted the diagnosis of many foreign economists that deregulation was needed to shake up inefficient sectors of the economy, including banks. Such a shake-up, however, would adversely affect, or even jeopardise the existence of many of the small and medium-sized companies from which most LDP politicians derived much of their financial support. Under strong international pressure to open up the whole of the economy to foreign companies the Kaifu administration did, in 1992, reach an agreement – the so-called Strategic Impediments Initiative – to remove non-tariff barriers, but the LDP contained powerful elements which clung to protectionism. In consequence its (and the bureaucracy's) reputation for managing the economy effectively suffered badly, even though it undoubtedly retained a good deal of electoral support as a result of its resistance to full deregulation.

The other major new problem faced by the Kaifu cabinet was the Gulf Crisis resulting from Iraq's invasion of Kuwait in 1990. The 1946 constitution made Japan's participation in the American-led military retaliation inconceivable, but Western leaders nonetheless felt that the Kaifu government was not offering all the support which they were entitled to expect, even though Japan was quick to ban imports of oil from Iraq. President Bush, in particular, was displeased when his direct request to Kaifu for Japan to pay a significant part of the cost of driving Iraqi forces out of Kuwait was blocked by the Finance Ministry. Eventually the Japanese cabinet – or, perhaps more accurately, the Finance Ministry – did raise its somewhat reluctant initial offer of one billion dollars to a massive 13 billion (part of which, at Komeito insistence, was taken from the Self Defence Forces budget) but it received little international credit for doing so. Domestically, too, its response satisfied neither those who favoured more decisive action nor those who regarded Western demands as unreasonable or who resented their hectoring tone, familiar from decades of trade disputes but even more pronounced. The existence of a substantial pacifist sentiment, albeit not on the scale of earlier decades, was also a relevant factor, as became evident in October when the cabinet, with LDP Secretary-General Ozawa Ichiro taking the lead, introduced a bill allowing members of the SDF to be seconded to a new Peace Cooperation Corps and sent to trouble-spots overseas (although their assistance was not to include fighting). The proposal was opposed by 54 per cent and supported by only 30 per cent in an opinion poll, and this public non-acceptance was reflected in the Diet, even among LDP members. As a result the government had to withdraw its proposal.

In June 1992 a broadly similar Peace-keeping Operations (PKO) bill did become law. Its passage was less strongly opposed by public opinion, probably because the Japanese had become more aware that their country's hesitation and lack of wholehearted commitment had damaged its international standing (and thus its chance of securing a permanent seat on the United Nations Security Council). Only a small minority (15 per cent) positively favoured the bill, but its opponents (39 per cent) were outnumbered by those who were resigned to its inevitability (40 per cent). Its subsequent implementation, with the sending of contingents to Cambodia, Mozambique, Zaire and the Golan Heights, helped to reduce concern that peace-keeping forces would be used to re-establish Japan as an active military power, and later polls indicated a much more favourable attitude.

In dealing with the Gulf crisis and the economic difficulties Kaifu, even more than previous prime ministers in comparable situations, did not have a free hand. From the outset he had been obliged to defer to Takeshita and Kanemaru, the men who had placed him in high office, and it always seemed unlikely that he would be allowed to remain Prime Minister for long. Possibly in the hope of strengthening his position by achieving an important success he threw his weight behind the cause of electoral reform. It seemed to be highly relevant in that it was thought to be the most effective way of reducing the influence of money; but, like Kishi and Tanaka in previous decades, LDP leaders also saw it as likely to improve their party's electoral prospects. Because of its obvious advantages Kaifu was able to push through the party in June 1991 a scheme which combined 300 single-member constituencies with a proportional representation system which would produce a further 171 members. Many senior LDP Diet men, however, were concerned about the probable break-up of their *koenkai*, and the factions headed by Miyazawa, Watanabe, and Mitsuzuka Hiroshi (who had taken over most of Abe's followers when the latter died in 1991) were anxious to see Kaifu make way for their own leader, so even if the other parties had been less opposed, it would have been difficult to secure the bill's passage. Kaifu apparently considered appealing to the country, but opposition within the LDP solidified, and in November 1991 he bowed to the inevitable and resigned.

The Sagawa scandal and the Liberal Democratic Party's fall from power

The new party president was elected under revised rules whereby, in addition to each LDP Diet member, each prefectural branch had from one to four votes (depending on their size), all of which went to the candidate who came first in the prefectural ballot; and the winner was the seventy-two-year-old Miyazawa Kiichi, whose tally of 285 gave him an outright majority over Watanabe (120) and Mitsuzuka (eighty-seven). A far more senior figure than his predecessor, he too nevertheless owed his elevation in large part to the backing of Kanemaru and Takeshita, although differences of personality and background – Miyazawa was a graduate of Tokyo University, an ex-Finance Ministry bureaucrat, and an internationalist of the Yoshida school – had contributed to ill feeling between them in the past. Unlike Kaifu, however, Miyazawa had little reforming ardour, and although he oversaw the passing of the PKO bill, under his Prime Ministership the LDP seemed to be returning to business as usual, including additional government spending on public works. Admittedly, it did set up another commission to examine political reform, and it did, in December 1992, pass laws which reapportioned Diet seats to take some account of population movement and extended formal restrictions on political contributions, but major electoral reform of the kind attempted by Kaifu was effectively deferred. Miyazawa may have been encouraged to think that normality was being reestablished by the result of the 1992 House of Councillors election, in which his party won no fewer than seventy seats (including twenty-five out of twenty-six in the single-member constituencies), while Rengo this time failed to make any impression, returning none of its twenty-two candidates. The LDP's tally was more than three times higher than that of the Social Democratic Party of Japan (SDPJ), as the former JSP decided to call itself in English in 1991. By this time the main opposition party was no longer being led by a woman, Doi Takako having been replaced in 1991 by the veteran Tanabe Makoto.

Any thought that Japanese politics was resuming its normal course, however, was to prove very much mistaken, for in September 1992 a new scandal, which would have even greater repercussions than the Recruit affair, began to unfold. It involved payments of billions of yen by another upstart company, Sagawa Kyubin, to at least 200 politicians over more than two decades, but its particular significance was that it exposed the fact that Kanemaru, the current LDP Vice-President and the power behind the Prime Minister, had acquired a huge fortune which could only, it was assumed, have been accumulated by diverting political contributions from construction and telecommunications companies to his personal account. The revelation on television of this wealth – some of it in gold bars – when his house was searched by the police, made a striking impact. That he was also shown to have connections with *yakuza*, the Japanese equivalent of the mafia, discredited him even further, and he was forced to resign his Diet seat. His disgrace undermined the position of his main protégé, Ozawa Ichiro, who lost out in a struggle with Obuchi Keizo and Hashimoto Ryutaro for leadership of the faction which Kanemaru had dominated after Takeshita's fall; and this defeat led directly to Ozawa's organising his own group within the LDP (together with another ex-member of the same faction, Hata Tsutomu) and calling for reform. When, in June 1993, the opposition parties introduced a motion of no-confidence in the government, condemning its abandonment of its electoral proposals, Ozawa and his supporters unexpectedly resisted the LDP leadership's blandishments and ensured the government's defeat. They may have anticipated that Miyazawa would be replaced by a more reform-minded LDP leader, with whom they could cooperate, but if so, they miscalculated. Instead of resigning, the Prime Minister dissolved the Diet, thus making the breach in the party irreparable. The Ozawa faction formally defected to set up the Renewal Party (Shinseito), being quickly followed by another, albeit smaller, group of disgruntled Diet members led by Takemura Masayoshi who adopted the name Sakigake (Harbinger, or Vanguard). Thus weakened, the LDP had much less chance of winning the ensuing House of Representatives election.

The July 1993 election proved to be a turning-point in Japanese politics even though the turnout of 67.1 per cent – a record low for the House of Representatives – suggested that public apathy, or disenchantment, was growing. Despite the fact that the LDP remained the largest single party with 223 Representatives (more than it had held immediately before the election), it finally lost power. Its ousting from government was not inevitable, for it was prepared to work with the centre parties, and a formal sharing of power with Komeito (which had made a partial comeback with fifty-one seats) and the DSP (which was almost unchanged with fifteen) was by no means impossible. The LDP leadership was slow off the mark, however, since Miyazawa was initially undecided as to whether to resign as LDP President, and by the time he did, all the other parties (except the JCP, which had only fifteen seats) had come together in a broad coalition.

Their choice as Prime Minister, Hosokawa Morihiro, emphasised the novelty of the situation, for he, although the grandson of a prime minister (Konoe) and an ex-member of the House of Councillors, was identified, as a governor of Kumamoto prefecture, more with local than national politics; and the party which he had formed, the Japan New Party (Nihon Shinto), mainly consisted of political newcomers. It had nevertheless won, in some cases by very large majorities, thirty-five seats, which gave it half the strength of the coalition's largest element, the SDPJ. Hosokawa's image – at fifty-five he was the second youngest Prime Minister since his grandfather and was described as eloquent, candid, handsome, stylish and even as 'a renaissance man' – was a major asset. Had he not been so attractive to the general public, it would have been difficult for the leaders of the other coalition parties to agree on who to rally behind as an alternative Prime Minister to the popular Kono Yohei, the one-time renegade whom the LDP now found it opportune to elect as its President. Behind Hosokawa, however, lurked the enigmatic and much less popular Ozawa. He now called for a new politics based not so much on a new breed of idealistic reformers, as some of his allies advocated, but on a new system, in which parties would emphasise policy and assert themselves against the bureaucracy and in which, after the removal to the political fringe of the JCP and ideologically-oriented elements of the JSP, there would be genuine competition for power between reorganised conservative and reformist forces.[16] Whether his success in shaking up Japanese politics in 1993 would lead to a more permanent reshaping of the system was to be one of the big questions during the rest of the decade.

The reasons for the LDP's long dominance

The loss of power by the LDP in 1993 leads one to the question how the party maintained its dominance, without a break, for such a long period. One answer, ironically, points to the factor which played so large a part in the LDP's fall – money. Its importance was crucial in two related ways. Firstly, the LDP, either as a party or through its factions and Diet members, acquired enormous funds – far beyond the amounts which rival parties could raise – notably from big business, the construction industry, and numerous small businesses which owed gratitude to LDP politicians or sought their aid. These funds generally increased as Japan grew richer and government expenditure accelerated, and most of them were used to good effect by politicians in building and consolidating their personal support organisations and winning elections. Just how much money was dispensed in this way is too sensitive a question to be answered with statistical exactitude, but on the basis of occasional revelations or indiscretions by politicians

[16] For his views, see I. Ozawa, 'My Commitment to Political Reform', *Japan Echo*, vol. 20, no.1 (spring 1993)

it has confidently been estimated that in the 1980s between 40 million yen (for a well-established Diet member) and 200 million yen (for a newcomer) was needed to ensure election to the House of Representatives; and that by 1992 an LDP Diet member would require 140 million yen for routine activities in a non-election year.[17] The cost of establishing and mobilising a support association was only one part of the financial equation, however. At a much broader level, it has been persuasively argued,[18] the LDP safeguarded its position, especially when it seemed to be in danger, by adopting policies – in areas such as health, pensions, and support for agriculture, small businesses, declining industries and deprived regions – which won the party favour. The fact that they incurred disturbingly high government expenditure seemed secondary to the need to preserve the governing party's majority, at least until the turn towards administrative reform in the early 1980s. As a result, a good deal of the wealth engendered by the most advanced sectors of the economy was redistributed, thus helping to make Japan less unequal in terms of income differentials than most other industrialised societies – and than it was in the 1950s.[19] This trend may partly explain the exceptionally high middle-class self-identification which has been assumed to be associated with support of the LDP.

The LDP also probably owed its survival as the party of government to its restraint while in power. Perhaps because of a traditional preference for consensus, perhaps because of fear of a return to authoritarianism, many Japanese in the post-war decades were uneasy about the government pushing through legislation against the strong opposition of the other parties; and the extent of public sympathy with the campaign against revision of the security treaty with the United States in 1960 gave the LDP a powerful reminder of this fact. Hence, rather than present its opponents with the opportunity to invoke the cry of 'tyranny of the majority', it often preferred to compromise. No fewer than 23 per cent of the bills which it submitted to the Diet between 1950 and 1990 were withdrawn or postponed because of opposition, while 15 per cent

---

[17] See R. Hrebenar, *The Japanese Party System*, p.62, and T. Pempel, *Regime Shift*, p.184.

[18] Notably by K. Calder, *Crisis and Compensation*.

[19] See, for example, K. Kato, 'Towards a New National Vision', *Japan Echo*, vol. 24, no. 2 (June 1997), p. 28.

were amended. More significantly still, the party even refrained from introducing legislation to revise the constitution, the cause which lay closest to the heart of many of its members.

The LDP's restraint was not due just to the opposition, actual or anticipated, of other parties; it was also a consequence of its own divisions. These partly derived from different conservative attitudes towards the American occupation and in particular revolved around whether Japan should continue to accept a low-posture foreign policy, focusing on economic diplomacy, along the lines laid down by Yoshida Shigeru and continued by most LDP Prime Ministers down to Suzuki, or whether it should play a more normal role, assuming a greater degree of responsibility for its defence, participating more fully in United Nations activities, and being generally less reluctant to assert its views. Any attempt to achieve a significant change of policy, however, was likely to run up against factional opposition within the LDP; and the ever-present threat that anti-mainstream factions might ignore the claims of party solidarity and act in conjunction with opposition parties militated against any turning away from the established course.

While avoidance of controversial policies played a part in keeping the LDP in office, it was not so important a factor as the weakness and disunity of the opposition parties. One opposition weakness was the very fact that the LDP's long monopoly of power deprived its rivals of experience of national administration, thus preventing them from demonstrating that they were capable of governing the country, however well they might perform at the local level. A still more important consequence was that they had far less influence on the national policy-making process and the bureaucracy than the LDP, and therefore were far less attractive to local business interests or to the very large number of independent local politicians whose main preoccupation was to secure benefits for their own area.

The appeal of the main opposition parties was also limited by the fact that they were perceived as representing particular interests. This was most marked in the case of Komeito, which remained identified with the Soka Gakkai sect, even after the party gave up or played down its purely religious objectives and replaced its slogan of 'Buddhist Democracy' in 1970 with terms such as 'humanitarian socialism' and 'middle-of-the-road reformism'. To a lesser extent the JSP was tarnished by its close association – reflected in its choice of candidates – with the public-service unions, and the DSP by its links with private-sector unions; and although both parties obviously derived important benefits from their union ties, the support of union members was far from solid. It was also a declining asset: whereas in 1950 no fewer than 50 per cent of the labour force belonged to unions, by 1992 just under 25 per cent did.

Much less obvious as an obstacle to opposition cooperation was the existence, as noted in opinion surveys in 1973, of significant differences among the various parties with regard to their members' basic attitudes and backgrounds. These were particularly marked between Komeito and the JCP, with far more university graduates supporting the latter than the former, and with 83 per cent of Komeito supporters having a religious belief compared with only 9 per cent of JCP supporters.[20] Similarly, though less markedly, 47 per cent of JCP supporters wanted to lead 'a life congenial to one's taste' against only 31 per cent on the Komeito side. Almost as significantly, 50 per cent of JCP members put individual rights above the public interest, as against 29 per cent of DSP supporters. Considerably more Komeito supporters (30 per cent) were prepared to leave matters to politicians than were DSP supporters (14 per cent), but 59 per cent of the former thought it reasonable to campaign against removal of houses for school construction compared with only 40 per cent of the latter. On the basis of such figures it has been suggested that a significant proportion of electors would have found it difficult not to feel some degree of alienation from the supporters of other parties, and thus would have looked on cooperation between their party and other parties with disfavour.

In contrast to the fact that there were obstacles to cooperation between opposition parties, the tendency within private-sector unions to avoid confrontation with management, which was especially marked after the first 'oil shock' in the early 1970s, led the DSP to be more receptive to the idea of a working arrangement with the LDP. By the 1980s this had drawn the moderate

---

[20] These, and the following figures, are taken from an intriguing article by C. Hayashi, 'Japanese Attitudes and Party Preferences', *Japan Echo*, vol. 5 (special issue, 1978). The article first appeared in Japanese in *Nihonjin Kenkyu*, no.2, July 1975.

socialists away from the scheme of a broad opposition coalition, even though the latter had begun to seem more attainable when the LDP's fortunes took a downturn in the latter half of the 1970s. Both the DSP and Komeito, it should be noted, had always been disinclined to enter into a pact with the JCP; and their distaste was shared by the JSP right-wing factions, not only because of the JCP's Marxist ideology, but also because associating with it might incur some of the unpopularity and distrust from which the JCP, more than any other party, suffered. In contrast, the left wing of the JSP shared the JCP's Marxist orientation – indeed, its continuing emphasis on ideology and general condemnation of capitalism in the 1960s and '70s, when such an approach was increasingly failing to evoke a sympathetic response from the public, was frequently blamed for the party's declining electoral performance. Nevertheless, it too was divided ideologically from the JCP because the JSP adhered to the *Rono* school of thought, which emphasised the development of Japanese monopoly capitalism, whereas the JCP followed the Kozaha line, which saw American capitalism and imperialism as the principal enemy. This division went back to the 1920s, and its deep roots had always militated against unity on the Left.

Opposition unity might conceivably have been achieved if the LDP had provoked fears of a return to the 1930s by rearming more quickly and by adopting a more assertive foreign policy. Instead, however, it maintained a low international posture and, by means of economic aid and investment, gradually dispelled much of the animosity and suspicion left by Japan's war-time imposition of its 'Great East Asia Co-Prosperity Sphere'. That LDP governments avoided the temptation to reassert Japanese power was partly due to their awareness of the outcry which would be provoked overseas. It helped too, naturally, that there was little perception among the Japanese of an external threat during the post-war era: if any country was seen as a danger, it was the Soviet Union, but only 6 per cent perceived it as such in 1966. Ultimately, though, the avoidance of a more assertive defence and foreign policy which might have reactivated nationalism as a central political force owed most to the memories of Japan's devastating war experience and to the constitutional obstacle of Article Nine. As a result, it was possible for LDP governments to resist American pressure to rearm by resorting to the argument (which carried particular weight after the 1960 Security Treaty crisis) that to do so could lead the Japanese public to turn to anti-American parties.

The avoidance, for the most part, of major controversy over foreign policy was undoubtedly important in depriving the opposition of an effective means of demonising the LDP. It also removed a potential cause of internal division within the LDP itself, but this alone does not fully explain why there was, with the partial exception of Kono Yohei's defection to form the New Liberal Club in 1976, no serious split in the party until 1993. Account needs to be taken of the willingness of LDP leaders to compromise, albeit sometimes reluctantly, and to distribute governmental and party positions in a way which was considered broadly fair in terms of factional balance. Beyond this, the nature of government under the LDP allowed its Diet members a degree of influence not only over the allocation of government expenditure but also, through a re-markably elaborate consultation process within investigative committees, a limited, but not insignificant, share in the formulation of policy. To some extent, opinions from other parties and from outside the party system were involved too. By 'binding the roots' in this way, the LDP mostly avoided the pitfalls of introducing hasty, ill-considered measures and of alienating its own supporters. This may have meant that the system was slow-moving by comparison with other countries, but the political advantages should not be underestimated.

In one crucial respect Japanese government in the period of LDP dominance did not appear to be inefficient. Whether the main cause of the high economic growth rates which marked the 1950s and '60s, and to a lesser extent the 1970s and '80s, was effective planning and guidance by MITI, the rejuvenation of Japanese capitalism after the Occupation reforms, the advantages of still being a nation 'catching-up', or any of the many other factors which have been put forward, the LDP was able, at the least, to claim credit for providing stability and not restricting economic vitality; and although it could be criticised, often with good cause, for turning a blind eye to the degradation of the environment and other adverse effects of industrialisation, it inevitably reaped the advantage of presiding over the new prosperity which most Japanese experienced. This, perhaps more than anything else, explains the LDP's success in winning more support than any of the opposition parties in every age-group and at all educational and occupational levels.[21] Over the post-war years, therefore, the LDP established an image as a party which was basically safe and competent. Crime and drug use remained relatively low, as did divorce rates, thus allowing the Japanese to feel that their society was still quite stable despite its very high level of urbanisation. Even though the extreme right occasionally attacked critics of the Emperor or made life uncomfortable for left-wing organisations like the Japan Teachers Union, criticism of the government was more openly and frequently expressed in Japan than in many countries, and the unrestrained circulation of ideas through magazines and other media made it difficult to argue that Japanese society did not enjoy a high degree of intellectual freedom and diversity. Corruption and economic mismanagement may have tarnished the LDP's image sufficiently to cause the party's fall from power in 1993, but its record over the previous four decades contained much that was positive, while its rivals had yet to prove themselves. It could not yet, therefore, be assumed that LDP dominance had ended for ever.

[21] Editorial comment in *Japan Echo*, vol. 5 (special issue, 1978), p.44.

9

THE SHAKE-UP OF JAPANESE
POLITICS, 1993-2000

The Hosokawa coalition and its reform measures

The 1993 House of Representatives election brought to an end
the long era of LDP rule, but it did not produce a shift to the Left
in Japanese politics. Rather, the reverse was true. The JCP remained very much a minority party, and until 1999 its influence
was further limited by its unwillingness to cooperate with most
other groups (as well as by the fact that all other parties sought to
distance themselves from the Communists). Much more significantly, the SDPJ saw over half its candidates defeated and lost
half its representation, a catastrophe which its participation in
government for the first time since 1948 only partially obscured.
Admittedly its seventy seats in the House of Representatives made
it the largest of the eight coalition partners, but it had a less central
role in the new government than Ozawa's Renewal Party, which,
with fifty-five successful candidates out of sixty-nine, had become
a more formidable force. It was the Renewal Party which most
clearly embraced the mood for change demonstrated not only by
the election result but also by the record level of popularity (71 per
cent) initially enjoyed by the Hosokawa cabinet (which had the
novelty of not only being a coalition and excluding the LDP but
also including three women). At the same time, however, opinion
polls suggested that not many Japanese expected that a coalition
of parties with such diverse traditions, policies, and sources of support would hold together long enough to achieve much more
than some measure of political reform which might preclude a
return to the discredited style of LDP rule.

One of the problems the Hosokawa cabinet was expected
to encounter was how to deal with a bureaucracy which had for
decades existed in a virtually symbiotic relationship with LDP

politicians and which had policy preferences of its own on some issues, notably administrative reform. Although Ozawa had been at the political centre as LDP Secretary-General and Hata had been a Minister of Finance, most of the new cabinet members had virtually no experience of national government, and a poll of bureaucrats indicated that a majority thought that the balance of power had shifted towards them with the change of administration.[1] Despite their inexperience, incoming ministers did, in a few cases, make their mark, sometimes imposing their wishes on the bureaucracy. The new Minister of International Trade and Industry, for instance, dismissed a top departmental official, while Hosokawa himself went well beyond previous Prime Ministers in publicly describing Japan's invasion of China and South East Asia a half-century earlier as an aggressive war and in apologising for Japan's colonisation of Korea. Nevertheless, it did not take the Ministry of Finance long to push Hosokawa into agreeing to increase the consumption tax from 3 to 7 per cent. Although the tax had become less unpopular, however, and the rise was to be counter-balanced by a cut in income tax, this move was not generally supported by most of the coalition partners. Indeed, it met with strong objections from Komeito (initially), Sakigake, the JNP, the DSP, and especially the SDPJ, many of whose Diet members had campaigned against the tax originally. Despite being urged on by Ozawa, Hosokawa was eventually forced to back down in February 1994, when the SDPJ threatened to withdraw from the government. In this case bureaucratic pressure was frustrated, at least temporarily. Whether it would have proved possible, however, to secure bureaucratic cooperation in carrying out deregulation and in reducing the number of civil servants, the two issues on which the movement for administrative reform had come to focus, seems doubtful. Some progress was made, through a special commission, in setting up machinery to promote and monitor administrative reform, but the fact that the SDPJ was again out of line, this time in being unsympathetic towards actions which might adversely affect the interests of the public service unions, suggests that bureaucrats might have found allies in taming the reformist ardour of the coalition had the latter not fallen in April 1994.

[1] See F. Schwartz, *Advice and Consent: The Politics of Consultation in Japan*, Cambridge University Press, 1998, p.25.

Even though the Hosokawa cabinet survived for less than a year, it did succeed in making two important changes. One was to allow, after many years of foreign pressure, imports of foreign rice into Japan after 1993. These imports were admittedly to be restricted to four per cent initially and to 8 per cent after five years, but they were supposedly due to lead to more far-reaching liberalisation after 1999; and in view of the legendary political clout of farmers, the decision was by no means easy, even though by this time sixty-two per cent of Japanese, according to one poll, had come to support the opening of the rice market.

It was even more difficult for the coalition to carry out the political reform which was its main *raison d'être*. There was a general acceptance that a single-member constituency system could reduce corruption by eliminating the costly intra-party competition (mainly within the LDP) which characterised larger election districts, and that it might encourage electors to cast their votes on the basis of parties and policies rather than what a particular politician could do for his constituents. In theory, it was also supposed to make it easier for unpopular governments to be voted out of office. Very few politicians wanted to go over to such a system completely, however, and only after intense bargaining did the SDPJ and the smaller coalition partners (which had no realistic hope of winning any single-member seats) persuade the Renewal Party and Komeito to reduce their proposed 300 small constituencies to 250 and to increase the number of members elected by proportional representation on a party ticket from 200 to 250 (with voters casting a separate ballot for each category). To avoid provoking too determined a resistance from the LDP (which was itself divided but officially advocated 300 single seats and 171 proportional representation seats) this compromise was subsequently changed to provide for a 274:226 division, but although a bill incorporating the revised ratio squeezed through the House of Representatives, it was rejected in the House of Councillors in January 1994 as a result of opposition not only from the LDP and JCP but also some SDPJ members. Instead of killing the bill, however, the rebel SDPJ councillors' strategy backfired: to ensure that electoral reform was achieved, the government reverted to the 300:200 arrangement and this time the LDP did not block the legislation.

The Hosokawa cabinet's political reform was not confined to electoral reorganisation. It also took advantage of the current popular enthusiasm for cleaning up politics to pass laws which provided for substantial public subsidies to be paid to political parties,[2] while the (generally ignored) restrictions on private contributions to individual politicians were to be more strictly monitored by limiting to one the number of organisations through which political funds could be channelled to each Diet member. From 2000, it was further stipulated, donations to politicians from companies were to be outlawed altogether. If strictly applied, the latter provision, in particular, would alter the character of Japanese politics, and in late 1999 LDP politicians were to show their distaste for it by seeking to delay its implementation. In 1994, however, when condemnation of political corruption remained widespread and the position of the LDP seemed parlous, they did not dare to defy public opinion.

The passage of political reform legislation was almost the last act of the coalition cabinet, for in April 1994 Hosokawa abruptly resigned as Prime Minister following public allegations by the LDP that he too had received secret financial favours from the Sagawa company in the 1980s. It is possible that even without this unwelcome reminder of how inseparably politics and money had become intertwined, the administration might not have continued much longer, for both the SDPJ and Sakigake had found some of the coalition's policies unpalatable and resented the dominant influence which Ozawa, drawing support from the relationship which he had developed with Komeito since 1991, had established. The SDPJ, in particular, had reason to suspect that Ozawa aimed to eliminate it as a significant force by luring away its moderate elements; and this danger seemed imminent when, directly after Hosokawa's resignation, the Renewal Party, the Japan New Party, and the Democratic Socialist Party, together with some of the smaller groups, formed a new parliamentary association called Kaishin (Renovation). In response the SDPJ joined Sakigake in declining to join in a new coalition.

Despite the defection of these two significant elements, the main anti-LDP grouping succeeded in holding on to office by securing the election as Prime Minister of Hata Tsutomu, the nominal leader of the Renewal Party. Although lacking Hosokawa's strong public

---

[2] In 1999 these subsidies amounted to nearly 34 billion yen, of which the LDP received almost 15 billion. The JCP, incidentally, declined to participate in the scheme and received no subsidy.

appeal, Hata was both more popular and more presentable than Ozawa, who was frequently accused of being taciturn, high-handed and arrogant.[3] Like Ozawa, Hata was the son of a Diet member, but he had worked for a bus company (among other duties, collecting fares) for ten years before entering politics, and he had acquired the reputation of being a genuine reformer. As Prime Minister of what was now a minority government, however, his chances of overseeing any further reform were slight; faced, after scarcely two months, with a no-confidence motion, he resigned.

The conservative-Social Democratic coalition, 1994-6

Hata's resignation did not necessarily mean that there would be a return to an LDP administration. Ozawa hoped that Watanabe Michio, who had lost to Kono Yohei in the LDP presidential election after Miyazawa's resignation, might be induced to defect by the lure of heading a coalition government, but the antipathy of Watanabe's faction members towards Ozawa and Soka Gakkai (still a crucial part of Komeito's support but also a rival of the various religious sects which were loosely associated with the LDP) frustrated this plan. The alternative was to bring the SDPJ back into the coalition, but instead of resuming cooperation, the SDPJ responded to the overtures of the LDP. So anxious was the latter to return to power and thus reduce the danger of further disintegration that it was prepared to allow the new SDPJ leader, Murayama Tomiichi, to become Prime Minister, even though he was associated with his party's left wing. Not all LDP Diet members were happy about such an unholy alliance; and ex-Prime Minister Kaifu even stood against Murayama in the Diet election in June, gaining support both from LDP rebels and some of the anti-LDP parties. With support from Sakigake as well as most of the LDP, however, the seventy-year-old Murayama emerged as Japan's first socialist Prime Minister since Katayama Tetsu in 1947-8.

Whether Murayama could still be regarded as a socialist when he stepped down in January 1996 is much less clear, for by that time he had presided over the scrapping of policies to which his party had clung for decades. Admittedly some of the groundwork had been done by the revision of the JSP programme in 1986; and

[3] See, for example, the comments in K. Obuchi, 'My Commitment to Political Reform', *Japan Echo*, vol. 20, no.1 (spring 1993), p. 14.

more recently Murayama's immediate predecessor, Yamahana Sadao, had advocated the 'creative development' of the constitution, a concept which, although vague, seemed to allow the possibility of constitutional revision. Under Murayama the SDPJ went further by accepting both the Self-Defence Forces and the security treaty with the United States, by approving closer ties with South Korea and the defence of the sea lanes around Japan, by ceasing to criticise ministerial visits to the Yasukuni shrine, and by ending its campaign against the use of the national anthem and flag in schools. It further reversed its former stance by supporting an increase in the consumption tax, albeit to 5 rather than 7 per cent and with the proviso that some of the increased revenue was allocated to local government and welfare programmes.

The SDPJ leadership may well have calculated that participation in a coalition with the LDP, rather than with reformers who wanted to break up the existing system, would be more likely to keep the party together, and perhaps even give it a new lease of life. Similarly, the abandonment of left-wing policies may have been intended to prevent defections by Rightist elements in the party. If such hopes existed, they were to be disappointed. Although Murayama himself continued to enjoy considerable respect and was subjected to surprisingly little criticism, his party fared badly in the 1995 House of Councillors election. Because it had done so well in 1989, the SDPJ was bound to lose some of the forty-one seats it had won then, but its haul of sixteen was disappointing, the more so since the LDP recovered some lost ground by gaining forty-six seats, while the junior coalition partner, Sakigake, returned three members instead of the previous one. Such an electoral setback made it more likely that there would be a recurrence of the 1994 attempt by Yamahana, under cover of a new policy group named the New Democratic League, to form a separate party made up of centre-right members of the SDPJ who were unhappy about being embraced by the LDP. That earlier move had proved abortive, but this was partly due to the fact that Yamahana's planned break with the SDPJ had coincided with a major earthquake – Japan's biggest since 1923 – in the Kobe region in January 1995. That a split had only been deferred was to be proved in September 1996, when a significant number of SDPJ right-wingers joined the newly formed Democratic Party (Minshuto).

The New Frontier Party and the 1996 election

The coalition with the SDPJ and Sakigake restored the LDP to power, but Ozawa did not abandon his bid to change the character of Japanese politics. Pursuing his attempt to create a system in which the LDP was faced by another party not just capable of governing but also, as Ozawa envisaged, of providing the sort of decisive leadership which Japan had enjoyed at the time of the Meiji Renovation, he masterminded the amalgamation of the Renewal Party, the DSP, most of the Japan New Party, and several smaller groups into the New Frontier Party (Shinshinto) in December 1994. Komeito, too, was an important participant, although it did not commit itself fully. Its caution was not surprising in view of the lack of any overwhelming popular enthusiasm for the new party and the considerable uncertainty about its future success and survival. That uncertainty remained even after the 1995 House of Councillors election, when the New Frontier Party, thanks mainly to the support of Soka Gakkai, won a highly respectable forty seats – but on a record low turnout of 44.5 per cent. Its real test was to come in the next House of Representatives election.

When that election was held in October 1996, the New Frontier Party had a different leader. Its first had been Kaifu, who had left the LDP after his failure to block the Murayama cabinet and had then won the contest for the new party's presidency against Hata and the DSP leader. Ozawa became its Secretary-General, but in December 1995, when it seemed that he might be manoeuvred out of that position following Kaifu's resignation, he successfully challenged Hata for the top position. The change of leadership was soon matched by a change of prime minister. Never eager to hold office, Murayama stood down in January and was replaced by Hashimoto Ryutaro, the recently elected LDP president. Hashimoto had earlier been considered a possible successor to Miyazawa but had been wrongfooted when Mitsuzuka Hiroshi, a major faction leader, had seized the initiative and successfully promoted the candidacy of Kono Yohei, a member of the same (Obuchi) faction as Hashimoto. In September 1995, when Kono's two-year term as LDP president ended, Hashimoto defeated Koizumi Junichiro, another rising politician. He was noted for his sharp mind, was regarded as more telegenic than most senior LDP politicians, and had more solid support within the party than the ex-renegade Kono; and he took up the prime ministership with every appearance of confidence.

There were, however, grounds for thinking that the LDP's position did not justify too much confidence. It had to share with its coalition partners some of the responsibility for the inept handling of the aftermath of the Kobe earthquake (even if much of the blame was attributed to the bureaucracy) and it could not wholly escape criticism for the failure of the police to clamp down on Aum Shinrikyo before this extreme sect launched a murderous poison-gas attack on underground travellers in Tokyo in March 1995. Moreover, notwithstanding a return to economic growth in 1995-6 – although only to 1 per cent and at the cost of large government expenditure on (often extravagant) public works – the problem of unrecoverable debts still haunted Japanese banks in particular and business in general; and the LDP's 1996 budget plan to bail out the bankrupt housing-loan companies (*jusen*) was condemned by both the public and opposition parties, not least because farm cooperatives, traditionally staunch supporters of the LDP, stood to benefit. Nor, despite the fact that the Clinton administration's call for a new framework of economic relations was less strident than its predecessor's demands, did external pressure for deregulation and fairer trade competition disappear. Moreover, relations with the United States were complicated by Japanese outrage at the rape of a Japanese schoolgirl by US servicemen in Okinawa in 1995, and by the ensuing demand for a reduction in the American military presence on the island.

It was against this general background that the House of Representatives election was held in October 1996. Much hung on the result, for in contrast to previous elections the main opposition party put up enough candidates – 361, six more than the LDP – to have a chance of winning a majority. Had that happened, the LDP might have suffered a major split, for there were elements within it, such as Kajiyama Seiroku, another senior member of the Obuchi faction and currently Chief Cabinet Secretary, who inclined towards cooperation with Ozawa, while others – notably LDP Secretary-General Kato Koichi of the Miyazawa faction and Yamasaki Taku, the LDP Policy Affairs Research Council chairman – were disposed to work with social democrats and regarded Ozawa with suspicion and distaste. The electorate did not, however, choose to punish the LDP. Instead, it was the New Frontier Party which found its existence called into question. Having entered the election with 160 incumbents, it dropped to 156 (admittedly in a House reduced by eleven), whereas the LDP increased its membership from 211 to 239. Of the 300 single-member constituencies the LDP won 169, almost double New Frontier's ninety-six. Apart from these two parties a significant impact was made only by the newly-formed Democratic Party, which included, in addition to its core of former right-wing SDPJ members, politicians who had belonged to Sakigake or, in a few cases, New Frontier. Of the Democratic Party's fifty-two seats (the same as its pre-election strength), seventeen came from the small constituencies and thirty-five from the eleven large proportional representation districts, a much more impressive result than than secured by the SDPJ, which saw its worst fears realised by return-ing no more than four members for single-seat constituencies and only fifteen in all (eleven less than the JCP).

Even more than most Japanese elections, that of 1996 was closely scrutinised by journalists and academics. Those who had hoped for major changes in electoral behaviour were disappointed, albeit not totally discouraged. One analysis found that 'although it was impossible to entirely sweep away deep-rooted habits among voters backing individual candidates rather than parties, the local organisations did succeed to some extent in redirecting support to the party level'.[4] The importance of *koenkai*, however, seemed not to have diminished, even though there was apparently a tendency for them to be, on the one hand, more organised and less personally linked to the candidate and, on the other hand, more neighbourhood-oriented. Nor, despite the tighter anti-corruption measures adopted in 1994, did electioneering appear to have become less costly overall, although this may have been due to the necessity of reorganising *koenkai* as a result of the change in constituency boundaries. That old-style attitudes and consider-ations survived was further indicated by the post-election observa-tion that toward the end of the campaign some companies and organisations had decided to back the LDP when forecasts

---

[4] M. Kataoka and M.Yamada, 'Anatomy of the 1996 Lower House Election' in H. Otake (ed.), *How Election Reform Boomeranged*, Japan Center for International Exchange, 1998, p.157. Most of this paragraph is drawn from that book.

suggested that it would win.[5] Perhaps most significantly, the anticipation that reform would lead to something closer to the British
style of politics seemed not have been justified, since 'neither
policy debate as the core of party-based electioneering nor campaigning in which a party leader's image played an important
role ... materialised scarcely at all'.[6]

The fact that most of the parties did not emphasis their policy
differences – where they existed – may have been partly responsible for the unprecedentedly low turnout by voters of 59.7 per
cent, a statistic which contrasts strikingly with the exceptional
number of candidates – 1503 (higher than in any election since
1947). Critics of the new system, such as LDP Secretary-General
Kato Koichi, complained that the need to gain a higher proportion
of the votes to win in single-member constituencies forced candidates towards the middle ground. Where one of the main parties
took a distinctive position on a central issue, as the New Frontier
Party did when calling for a further income tax cut and a freeze
on the consumption tax (rather than the scheduled raise to 5 per
cent), it opened itself to the charge of irresponsibility. The New
Frontier Party's image may also have suffered before the election
campaign from its behaviour in the Diet, for its sit-in – a vain
attempt to block the bail-out of the housing-loan companies –
would have reminded the public of the tactics of the Left in past
decades and, just like the JSP's obstructive tactics during the passage of the Peacekeeping Operations bill in 1992, appeared futile
and old-fashioned.

Had the New Frontier Party won the 1996 election – or at least
done well enough to prevent the LDP from remaining in power –
it might have survived, and the future shape of Japanese politics
might have included the possibility of alternation of power between the two parties. Electoral failure, however, meant that the
divergent elements within the NFP, and the widespread resentment of Ozawa's domineering style, could not be hidden. Virtually
as soon as the results had come in, there was talk of the party
breaking up, and by December 1996 two groups, one of them led
by Hata, had departed. They were followed by Hosokawa in June
1997 and by a number of individual defections to the LDP, which

[5] S. Kitaoka, 'The Changing Dynamics of Party Politics', *Japan Echo*, vol. 24,
no.1 (spring 1997), p.16.
[6] M. Kataoka and M.Yamada, *op. cit.*, p.165.

by September 1997 had regained its majority in the House of Representatives (although it still found SDPJ and Sakigake support valuable in that House and essential in the House of Councillors).

One of the causes of dissatisfaction with Ozawa was that he appeared to be abandoning the strategy of challenging the LDP directly and, presumably with an eye to regaining influence, turning towards the idea of 'conservative-conservative' cooperation which some senior LDP figures favoured. It was consistent with such a strategy that in December 1997, shortly after winning another contest for the New Frontier Party presidency, he suddenly dissolved what remained of the motley party and, reverting to a name – Liberal Party (Jiyuto) – which evoked the past rather than the future, formed yet another new one. He presumably hoped that this would be both a substantial force and a more acceptable partner for the LDP. If so, he largely miscalculated. More Diet members abandoned his cause than he could have predicted, and over the next several months a good many ended up joining the DPJ, making it significantly larger than the Liberal Party. Moreover, the continuation of SDPJ and Sakigake support for (though not membership of) the Hashimoto cabinet until June 1998 (despite the misgivings of Doi Takako, who had again become the SDPJ leader after Murayama stepped down in 1996) meant that the LDP, for the time being at any rate, had no great incentive for partnership with so controversial and disruptive a politician as Ozawa, even if it welcomed the Liberal Party's more accommodating attitude in the Diet.

The Hashimoto cabinet and the LDP setback in 1998

The New Frontier Party may have promised only to deceive, and disappeared without much trace after its brief three years' existence. Nevertheless, its challenge probably pushed the LDP in the direction of change a little faster than it would otherwise have gone. In particular, Hashimoto's first cabinet had, in 1996, taken up the cause of administrative reform partly because other political parties had focused on it and because the LDP feared that the New Frontier Party might gain a significant advantage from advocating it. Having proclaimed his belief in it during the election campaign, Hashimoto could hardly have subsequently abandoned the call for substantial change in the administrative, financial and social security systems, as well as the economic and fiscal structures. Moreover, the persistence of slow economic growth, the ever-looming spectre of an aging society, higher unemployment, popular disenchantment with politicians and bureaucrats, and foreign pressure for further deregulation and liberalisation, all constituted good reasons for making more radical adjustments to cope with Japan's straitened circumstances. Such change, however, would be painful both for bureaucrats and for those sectors of the Japanese economy which required protection either from foreign competition or from the effects of past mistakes. It would also indirectly hurt many politicians who continued to rely on financial support from those same economic organisations which, as participants in the governmental process, they themselves helped to protect or subsidise. Hence, the reforms devised by Hashimoto and his team tended to be gradual – as in the case of the planned liberalisation of the Tokyo financial market – or deferred – as with the decision to reduce the number of government ministries and agencies from twenty-two to twelve and to strengthen the Prime Minister's office. Such a timetable obviously left open the possibility that the plans would be modified or emasculated, as had quickly happened to some other proposals – notably post office privatisation – which encroached upon vested interests.

Among the aims proclaimed by Hashimoto was one which echoed the call in the first phase of administrative reform for a return to sound public finance by moving back to a more balanced budget. To this end the administration went ahead with the consumption tax increase, reduced the special tax cut which was due to accompany it, and increased health insurance contributions. A Fiscal Structure Reform Law in 1997 further laid down as the government's target the ending of new issues of deficit bonds by 2003. This tougher fiscal policy took too little account, however, of the fragility of consumer demand in a country where rising unemployment was undermining confidence; nor was it foreseen how seriously Japanese production would suffer from the developing Asian recession. By the end of 1997 there was growing evidence (most strikingly from the bankruptcies of Yamaichi Securities and the Hokkaido Takushoku Bank, both of which would previously have been considered too important to be allowed to fail) that the economy had not been restored to health: and the balance of opinion within the LDP shifted away from those, such as Hashimoto and Kato Koichi, who emphasised fiscal restraint, towards the advocates of a fresh attempt at pump-priming. With remarkable speed the government executed a partial about-turn by introducing a large emergency package of government expenditure, with a heavy emphasis on public works. Neither this nor the further financial relief measures taken in early 1998, though, succeeded in countering the effects of the tighter fiscal policy, and the slump in economic growth made the government appear incompetent as well as unsure of itself.

The Hashimoto cabinet was to pay the price for its economic misjudgment in the House of Councillors election in July 1998. Because it had done exceptionally well in 1992, the LDP could not hope to increase its representation and achieve an absolute majority, but it did not anticipate that it would win only forty-five seats, nor that it would suffer the humiliation of failing to return a single candidate in Tokyo, Osaka and several other major urban districts. What made the scale of the defeat even more damaging was the fact that, encouraged by an extension of polling hours, there was a significant increase – to 58.8 per cent – in the number of voters who turned out. Of the other parties, the Democratic Party did best. It had an unusually attractive leader in Kan Naoto, an ex-citizens movement activist who had, as a Sakigake member, served as Health Minister in 1996 and won acclaim for not accepting a cover-up of a bureaucratic scandal relating to HIV-contaminated blood supplies. By gaining twenty-seven seats the DPJ emphatically confirmed its position as the main opposition party. In contrast, the SDPJ continued its downward decline by securing only five seats. Ozawa's Liberal Party did only slightly better with six, while the nine seats gained by Komeito failed to match the JCP's fifteen. Reflecting the disruption of the party system following the disintegration of the New Frontier Party, no fewer than nineteen seats were claimed by politicians running as independents (only two of whom were LDP members).

The Obuchi cabinet and the LDP-Liberal Party-Komeito coalition

There was no way for Hashimoto to avoid taking responsibility for the LDP's election débâcle. Even before July he had been subjected to criticism from within the party, and he did not now delay his resignation. Some observers expected that he would be replaced by one of those critics, Kajiyama Seiroku, but the latter found himself in competition with his faction leader, Obuchi Keizo; and although Obuchi was noted much more for his lack of enemies than for his charisma – in the election campaign he acquired the nickname 'cold pizza' to add to the previous 'Mr. Pleasant' – he won by the surprisingly large margin of 225 votes to 102, with Koizumi Junichiro (heir-apparent of the Mitsuzuka faction) trailing with eighty-four. Significantly, most of the LDP factions showed a lack of solidarity by failing to provide unanimous support for the faction's favoured candidate.

Obuchi's success did not meet with much favour outside Japan, since he was seen as the least reform-minded of the candidates and the least likely to be a decisive leader. He had for many years been only the third-placed LDP candidate (behind Fukuda Takeo and Nakasone Yasuhiro) in his Gumma prefecture constituency; and he himself contrasted his gentle approach with the tougher style of Ozawa Ichiro.[7] His further observation that he was the type of person who was willing to work long and hard to win people over to his point of view indicated that he possessed a quality which was appreciated in Japanese politics; and he was not blind to the fact that the LDP had become stale and set in its ways during its long period of domination. He even went so far, in criticising the fact that so many Diet members were the sons of politicians, or ex-bureaucrats, or former union officials, as to suggest a resemblance between the LDP and the old Soviet leadership; and his appointment of a thirty-seven-year–old woman, Noda Seiko, as Minister of Posts and Telecommunications showed that he was capable of making unconventional decisions. In view of his cabinet's low initial public approval rating of 20 per cent, however, and in view of the lack of an LDP majority in either Diet House since the termination of the coalition with the SDPJ and Sakigake (neither of which could, in any case, now have provided significant support), Obuchi's prospects did not look good.

The pessimistic prognostications which accompanied the cabinet's birth were nevertheless not fulfilled, for Obuchi not only managed to avoid a forced dissolution but was still Prime Minister at the beginning of the twenty-first century. That he

---

[7] K. Obuchi, *loc. cit.*

survived as LDP leader until then was not due to any marked
resurgence in the Japanese economy, for despite Obuchi's insistence on reappointing Miyazawa as Finance Minister once
more, and notwithstanding the continued large-scale issuing of
deficit bonds, the growth rate remained sluggish and public confidence low. At the end of 1999, after growing slowly throughout
the year, the stock exchange index had only recovered to half its
level a decade earlier. Even such notable developments as the
restructuring of the banking industry, through various amalgamations of hitherto rival institutions, and the reorganisation of
Nissan under foreign direction after its merger with Renault,
seem to have been regarded as indications of the seriousness of
Japan's problems more than as guarantees that those problems
would be tackled effectively. At the political level, however, Obuchi
enjoyed considerable success, overseeing an increase in his
cabinet's popularity (despite his own lacklustre performances in
the special Diet sessions, initiated in 1999, in which he faced
questions from the other party leaders) and a definite, albeit not
necessarily a permanent, strengthening of the LDP's position.

One reason why the Obuchi cabinet managed to overcome its
shaky start was the absence of a coordinated opposition. The
other parties seem to have been more inclined to enter into partnership with the LDP than to work for its downfall. Even the
LDP's new main rival, the Democratic Party, tended to pull its
punches when attacking the government, at least until September
1999, when Kan lost (by 182 votes to 130) in a party leadership
election to Hatoyama Yukio. The fifty-two-year-old new leader –
one of two brothers who were grandsons of ex-Prime Minister
Hatoyama Ichiro and who had both risen quickly in the LDP before deserting it – had been known, ever since he played a major
role in the founding of the Democratic Party, for his advocacy of
a more forthright anti-government stance; and in late 1999, with
a House of Representatives election in the offing, his party was
becoming more obstructive in the Diet.

The Liberal Party and Komeito took a more cooperative line
towards the Obuchi cabinet virtually from the outset, and by late
1999 both had entered into formal alliance with the LDP and
both had one member in the cabinet. Not surprisingly, in view
of Ozawa's change of strategy since 1997, the Liberal Party was the
first to enter the fold. The rapprochement was urged by two LDP

elder statesmen, Nakasone and Takeshita, in August 1998, but the negotiations were principally conducted by the Chief Cabinet Secretary, Nonaka Hiromu, and despite the latter's notorious dislike of Ozawa, the new coalition materialised in January 1999. In view of the fact that partnership with the Liberal Party could not give the government a majority in the House of Councillors, and that the Liberal Party would be in danger of elimination if it entered the next election without a mutual support agreement with the LDP, Ozawa achieved a better deal than might have been expected. Not only did one Liberal Party member enter the cabinet, but the LDP agreed to reduce the size of the House of Representatives to 450 members, cut the number of ministries by two, and add a parliamentary vice-minister to each government department. The latter provision was closely connected with a further, and even more important, agreement that bureaucrats would not be allowed to answer questions on a minister's behalf in Diet sessions. Together these changes would, it was hoped, reduce the influence of bureaucrats by forcing their political superiors to take more responsibility. This implied that they, and their parliamentary vice-ministers, needed to remain in their posts considerably longer than the typical duration of less than a year.

The coalition with the Liberal Party was not welcomed by all LDP Diet members. In particular it was regarded with disfavour by two emerging leaders whose support had been important in Obuchi's LDP presidential victory, Kato Koichi and Yamasaki Taku, both of whom had good contacts with other parties and were thought to prefer a coalition with the Democratic Party now that the SDPJ had become a negligible quantity. The agreement with the Liberal Party therefore constituted a political setback for Kato and Yamasaki, and neither of them were happy about the moves during 1999 towards close cooperation with Komeito. Both of them challenged Obuchi for the LDP presidency when his first term of office ended in September, but the Prime Minister won a comfortable victory with 350 votes (253 from Diet members and ninety-seven from party branches on the basis of one vote per 10,000 members) against Kato's 113 (eighty-five from Diet members) and Yamasaki's fifty-one (thirty-one from Diet members).

Following his re-election Obuchi gave his opponents (none of whose factions were represented in his reshuffled cabinet) further cause for dissatisfaction by securing the inclusion of Komeito in the ruling coalition. This time no conditions seem to have been attached, but Komeito had a major interest in gaining access to government decision-making because it feared that the promised cut in the House of Representatives membership would be in the proportional representation section, where Komeito was more likely, it now recognised, to be successful. In its concern not to lose electoral ground it was prepared to overlook the campaign which the LDP had mounted against Soka Gakkai in 1995. For his part Obuchi needed a deal with Komeito because it could deliver a majority in both Houses and thus made the LDP less dependent on the Liberal Party. It was nevertheless a gamble, for it ran the risk, on the one hand, of pushing Kato and Yamasaki into defecting and, on the other, of undermining the existing relationship with the Liberal Party by making concessions to Komeito over Diet membership. Luckily for Obuchi, the first of these dangers did not materialise, at least in the immediate aftermath of the agreement. The second, however, brought the coalition close to breaking-point in December 1999, when the government's failure to get a compromise bill providing for the elimination of twenty proportional representation seats through the Diet before the end of the session prompted Ozawa to threaten to leave the coalition. Whether he would have been prepared to go so far must be doubtful, given the precariousness of his party's position. He was not, however, forced to make that difficult choice, for in January 2000 the seat reduction was given top priority and pushed through the Diet in spite of a boycott of parliamentary proceedings by the opposition parties – a move which was to no avail since it was patently motivated by the hope of disrupting the governing coalition rather than by any principled objection to the measure itself or even, as was alleged, to the government's procedures. Having gained little public sympathy, the Democratic Party quickly abandoned its out-of-date tactic, a retreat soon followed by the JCP and SDPJ.

The Japanese political situation at the beginning of the twenty-first century

As the Diet session of early 2000 proceeded, the LDP appeared to be in a stronger position than could reasonably have been expected in 1993. Indeed, in one respect it had never seemed so strong, even at the height of its dominance in the 1960s; whereas then it had a respectable, if distant, challenger in terms of general popularity in the shape of the JSP, by the turn of the century its main opponent, the Democratic Party, was supported by well under one in ten members of the public, according to NHK (Japan Broadcasting Corporation) surveys. Although the LDP's own support was significantly lower than it had been in earlier decades, it was still, with 30.3 per cent in mid-April 2000, far ahead of the Democratic Party (7.9 per cent), while the JCP (2.9 per cent), Komeito (3.1 per cent), the SDPJ (2.6 per cent), and the Liberal Party (1.5 per cent) lagged well behind. The Liberal Party had suffered a particular setback in early April, when about half of its Diet members defected to form the Hoshuto (New Conservative Party) rather than join their leader, Ozawa Ichiro, in withdrawing from the governing coalition. The one cause for uncertainty in these opinion surveys was that over half the respondents expressed no party preference, but given past voting patterns there seemed little reason for the LDP to fear that it would not gain a majority in the House of Representatives election due later in the year.[8]

That election took place on 25 June and confirmed the LDP's dominant position. On a 62.5 per cent turnout it won 233 of the 480 seats (a slightly better performance than its 239 out of 500 in 1996), while the Democratic Party gained 127. The thirty-one Komeito and seven Hoshuto members of the new House ensured that the coalition government retained a clear majority. Its victory undoubtedly owed much to traditional methods of winning elections – it seems significant that many of the top LDP politicians won their single-seat contest by enormous margins – but may also have been due in part to the renewed signs of marginal economic revival (and to lack of confidence in the opposition parties' ability to maintain this). The opposition parties were clearly not at one during the election campaign, with the Democratic Party's call for taxation of lower incomes finding no favour with

---

[8] It is significant that in July 1996, three months before the LDP's success in the House of Representatives election, an *Asahi Shimbun* poll found that only 26 per cent put party first in their choice of which candidate to vote for, compared with 65 per cent who emphasised personality. See S. Sato, 'LDP Redivivus: The Failure of Electoral Reform', *Japan Echo*, vol.24, no.1 (spring 1997), p.21. A *Yomiuri Shimbun* poll in 1993 showed 41 per cent voting on the basis of the party and 49 per cent the candidate.

other anti-government forces, and although they managed to achieve electoral cooperation in eighty of the 300 single-member constituencies, this did not include the JCP and it did not compare with the success of the coalition partners in nominating a single agreed candidate in almost every district. Moreover, the Democratic Party leader, Hatoyama Yukio, explicitly ruled out the idea of a coalition government involving the JCP, while mooting the possibilty of participating in one led by the LDP's Kato Koichi. In the circumstances it was not surprising that the JCP's representation dropped to 20, while the Liberal Party and SDPJ, with twenty-two and nineteen seats, remained almost static.

Despite its retention of power, however, the LDP's performance in the 2000 election was not as good as it might reasonably have hoped before April. Because it had gained additional Diet members after the break-up of the New Frontier Party, it had entered the election with rather more than the 233 candidates it returned, and among its losses were several ex-ministers. It secured fewer seats in Tokyo, Osaka and some other major conurbations than the Democratic Party, and its support seems to have come significantly less from younger voters than from the over-fifties. This was not an entirely new phenomenon, but it was more pronounced in 2000. One reason for this may have been the fact that the coalition, and especially the inclusion in it of Komeito, was unpopular: polls consistently showed that fewer than one in four respondents favoured it and that more than twice that proportion disapproved. Another factor was almost certainly the change in the LDP leadership. Immediately following the personal confrontation on 2 April that led to Ozawa's abandonment of the coalition, prime minister Obuchi suffered a stroke and went into a coma from which he did not recover before his death in May. With an election and a G-8 leaders' meeting in Okinawa both fairly imminent, LDP leaders decided with remarkable speed to avoid a presidential contest and unite in support of Mori Yoshiro, a faction leader who was currently at the centre of party affairs as its Secretary-General.

In the short term, at least, Mori's elevation to the prime ministership appeared questionable. He belonged to the education *zoku* and his traditionalist leanings were made rather too evident in May when, in a speech to Shinto priests, he stated that 'Japan is a divine country (or 'country of *kami*') with the Emperor at its centre.' He was widely criticised for using language which Japan's prewar experience had discredited, and even Komeito and other LDP leaders distanced themselves from him. The situation was not improved when soon afterwards, in an attack on the JCP, he referred to the *kokutai*, another term closely associated with prewar authoritarianism and racist thinking. Had it not been for the impending election and summit, the temptation for other LDP leaders to engineer the removal of an apparently accident-prone prime minister would have been strong. The election result was not as bad as some had feared, however, and because the coalition remained firm despite some Komeito feeling that its members' backing of LDP candidates had not been fully reciprocated, talk of Mori's replacement subsided. Much, though, seemed likely to depend on the attitude of Hashimoto Ryutaro, who in July reemerged to become head of the old Obuchi faction, the LDP's largest, and who, following the death in June of Takeshita Noboru, was in a position to exercise stronger influence. A possible danger also lurked in the form of yet another scandal, this time involving serious allegations of financial impropriety against a recent Construction Minister.

It has been suggested that the LDP owed its recovery partly to the public's impatience (the so-called 'new-party fatigue') with the kaleidoscopic way in which the opposition parties (apart from the JCP) changed their names and images during the 1990s. Even if this was so and the LDP benefited from being reassuringly familiar, it should not be overlooked that the major party too altered in some ways. In particular, its factions appeared to have undergone a change in character, with the leader becoming someone who served the faction, rather than enjoying personal dominance.[9] One explanation for this development would be that Diet members were raising more of the funds they needed by their own efforts, making them less dependent on their faction leader or his lieutenants. In fact, already in 1989, according to an *Asahi* survey, only nine per cent of an average LDP Diet member's annual income came from his faction (compared with 39 per cent from corporate contributions).[10]

Change is also inevitable, of course, in the years to come. Historians are not renowned for their ability to predict future develop-

---

[9] See Kitaoka, *op. cit.*, p.14.
[10] See A. Rothacher, *The Japanese Power Elite*, Macmillan, 1993, p.60.

ments, but one which seems increasingly probable is constitutional revision. Committees were established in both Diet Houses in 1999 to consider this issue, and deliberations began early in the following year. It was immediately evident that significant differences over whether and how the 1946 constitution should be changed still remained, and that such differences existed within most parties, including the LDP, as well as between them. Consequently, the possibility of the revision process stalling could not be ruled out. Nevertheless, public feeling seemed by the end of the twentieth century to have moved towards acceptance of change,[11] and although the constitution could to some extent be regarded as a product of American-Japanese collaboration, the continuing perception that it had been imposed on the Shidehara cabinet made the idea of rewriting it attractive, if only as a means of asserting Japan's autonomy. Such a move seemed to be in tune with the fact that from late 1997 Japanese newspapers and magazines had been calling for greater independence and distance from the United States.[12] On the other hand, the constitutional issue could conceivably polarise opinion and lead to major political conflict, especially if mismanaged by the protagonists of revision. However, the fact that not even Ozawa's Liberal Party was pushing for rapid action made it seem unlikely that there would be a major crisis. Nor was it generally anticipated that the legalisation of Japan's armed forces by the revision or replacement of Article Nine would herald a major change in Japanese defence policy or Japan's attitude towards its neighbours. In this last respect it was reassuring that, according to an *Asahi* survey, 72 per cent of Japanese approved of Prime Minister Hosokawa's 1993 declaration of contrition for Japan's wartime behaviour.

The other issue over which the possibility of a major political rift could not be discounted was economic policy, since a basic division existed as to whether to give priority to revival, as the government basically favoured, or to restructuring, which the opposition mostly advocated. In view of the speeches implicitly critical of the current policy which the anti-mainstream LDP faction

---

[11] Polls taken by the *Yomiuri Shinbun* found 50 per cent of respondents in favour of constitutional revision in 1993, compared with 23 per cent in 1986 and 33 per cent in 1991.

[12] See T. Kawachi, 'A New Backlash against American Influence', *Japan Echo*, vol. 25, no. 2 (April 1998), p. 44.

leader, Kato Koichi, made during the winter of 1999–2000, it was conceivable that he might base another leadership challenge on this issue, and that if he were again to lose, he might try to take his faction out of the party. Opinions differed, however, as to whether the LDP had become more or less vulnerable to the possibility of such a defection. One academic commentator suggested that just because the LDP appeared stronger than ever, it was less cohesive and faced a higher risk of sudden split or collapse.[13] Against this it could be argued that factional rivalry was less intense than it had once been, and that LDP politicians, having had a taste of opposition, would not again jeopardise their hold on power.

Perhaps the strongest indication that political change may be forthcoming is the fact that after the collapse of the 'bubble economy' traditional attitudes and patterns of economic and social behaviour, including the vaunted 'lifetime employment' system, have been coming under challenge. The resulting tendency to introduce new ways of working and living, which is further encouraged by the ever-increasing Japanese awareness of how things are done in other countries, appears likely to lead to closer scrutiny of political institutions too, particularly if the current plan to move the seat of government out of Tokyo to a much less populated area should actually go ahead. But even if significant change should occur, it seems safe to predict that continuity with the past will remain strong and that the Japanese political system will not, at least for a very long time, lose its distinctive character.

---

[13] Sato, *op. cit.*, p. 25.

BIBLIOGRAPHY

For readers who wish to see modern Japanese political development in longer historical perspective, J. W. Hall, *Japan from Prehistory to Modern Times*, London: Weidenfeld and Nicolson, 1970, and W. G. Beasley, *The Japanese Experience*, University of California Press, 1999, are excellent introductions. On pre-modern Japanese history Sir G. Sansom's *Japan: A Short Cultural History*, London: Barrie and Jenkins, first published in 1931 and several times reissued, has become a classic, as has his *The Western World and Japan*, 1950, republished by Tuttle in 1977. An excellent up-to-date treatment of the Tokugawa period can be found in C. Totman, *Early Modern Japan* , University of California Press, 1993. Japanese history is placed in a broader context by an eminent historian (and ex-ambassador to Japan) in E. O. Reischauer, *The Japanese*, Harvard University Press, 1977, while the social development of modern Japan is succinctly surveyed by A. Waswo, *Modern Japanese Society, 1868-1994*, Oxford University Press, 1996.

There are several excellent general histories of modern Japan in English, notably W. G. Beasley, *The Rise of Modern Japan*, New York: St Martin's Press, 1995 (earlier editions were published by Weidenfeld and Nicolson as *The Modern History of Japan*), and H. Borton, *Japan's Modern Century*, Ronald Press, 1955, rev. edn 1970. Well-considered surveys are also to be found in E. O. Reischauer, J. K. Fairbank and A. Craig, *East Asia: The Modern Transformation*, Boston, MA: Houghton Mifflin, 1965, and M. Jansen, *Japan and China; from War to Peace, 1894-1972*, Rand McNally, 1975. Political histories of modern Japan are much less numerous and leave more to be desired. R. Scalapino, *Democracy and the Party Movement in Prewar Japan*, Berkeley: University of California Press, 1953, was long the standard account, but only deals with the pre-war period and is written with a very heavy emphasis on the flawed nature of Japanese political development. J. Halliday, *A Political History of Japanese Capitalism* (New York: Pantheon Books, 1975) provides an often stimulating Marxist critique, but is more general than its title might suggest and far less detailed in its treatment of the 1868-1945 period than in its examination of the post-war years. A provocative recent treatment which focuses on important topics or themes in modern Japanese history and is based on rational choice theory (which not all will find convincing) is J. Ramseyer and F. Rosenbluth, *The Politics of Oligarchy*, Cambridge University Press, 1995. There are many valuable insights in a soon-to-be-published (by Routledge) translation of a work on democracy and its critics in prewar Japan by Banno Junji, but although this ranges from the 1870s to the 1930s, it does not provide a full narrative. Of the other books which deal with Japanese political history over a lengthy period, R. Ward (ed.), *Poliltical Development in Modern Japan*, Princeton University Press, 1968, is a collection of loosely-connected essays, while G. Allinson, *Japanese Urbanism: Industry and Politics in Kariya, 1872-1972*, University of California Press, 1976, concentrates on one particular area and is not confined to politics. D. Brown provides a broad treatment of a dominant factor in Japanese politics in *Nationalism in Japan,* University of California Press, 1955, while the assorted essays contained in T. Najita and J. V. Koschmann (ed.), *Conflict in Modern Japanese History*, Princeton University Press, 1982, lend support to the editors' claim that compromise and harmony have been overstressed by many Western historians of Japan. A set of parallel essays which provides a basis for comparison with another non-Western country is to be found in R. Ward and D. Rustow (eds), *Political Modernization in Japan and Turkey*, Princeton University Press, 1964. The role of the state in various aspects of Japanese life is illuminated in a stimulating work by S. Garon, *Molding Japanese Minds*, Princeton University Press, 1997. More obvious methods of government control are surveyed by R. Mitchell in *Censorship in Imperial Japan*, Princeton University Press, 1983, and in *Janus-Faced Justice: Political Criminals in Japan*, Honolulu: University of Hawaii Press, 1992; and the same author has also investigated one of the least savoury sides of Japanese politics in *Political Bribery in Japan*, University of Hawaii Press, 1996. Those who suffered from being excluded from the political process are brought into prominence by M. Hane, *Peasants, Rebels and Outcastes,* New York: Pantheon, 1982.

If general political histories are lacking, monographs are abundant. On the Meiji Ishin there is the magisterial work by W. G.

Beasley, *The Meiji Restoration*, Stanford University Press, 1972, well supplemented by M. Jansen, *Sakamoto Ryoma and the Meiji Restoration*, Princeton University Press, 1961, and by A. Craig, *Choshu in the Meiji Restoration*, Harvard University Press, 1961. A more recent book on Choshu's role, which is distinctive in identifying a 'service intelligentsia' as the primary force in the Meiji Ishin but suffers from not examining the situation inside Choshu after 1867, is T. Huber, *The Revolutionary Origins of Modern Japan*, Stanford University Press, 1981. An older work, which drew on Marxist pre-war interpretations to present the first serious analysis of the Meiji Ishin is E. H. Norman, *Japan's Emergence as a Modern State*, Institute of Pacific Relations, 1940 (also included in J. Dower (ed.), *Origins of the Modern Japanese State*, New York: Pantheon, 1975). Though dated and sometimes inaccurate, it retains considerable value. More recent assessments of the crucial transformation from Tokugawa to Meiji are to be found in M. Jansen (ed), *The Cambridge History of Modern Japan,* vol.5: *The Nineteenth Century,* Cambridge University Press, 1989; M. Jansen and G. Rozman (eds), *Japan in Transition*, Princeton University Press, 1986, which contains a series of extremely useful essays on a wide range of aspects of early Meiji history; M. Umegaki, *After the Restoration*, New York University Press, 1988, and M. Nagai and M. Urrutia (eds), *Meiji Ishin: Restoration and Revolution* Tokyo: United Nations University Press, 1985. P. Akamatsu, *Meiji 1868*, London: Geo. Allen and Unwin, 1972, should also be mentioned, although its value is somewhat diminished by an unsatisfactory translation from the original French version. The institutional changes which took place in the Meiji Ishin are focused on, rather narrowly, by R. Wilson, *The Genesis of the Meiji Government in Japan, 1868-1871,* University of California Press, 1957, as are the social and political backgrounds of the early Meiji leadership in B. Silberman, *Ministers of Modernization*, University of Arizona Press, 1964. A unique insight into the day-by-day preoccupations and life-style of one of the main actors in the Ishin has been made available though the translation by S. Brown (ed.) and A. Hirota of *The Diary of Kido Takayoshi*, 3 vols, University of Tokyo Press, 1983-6.

The outstanding English-language books on Japanese political development in the Meiji period are J. Banno, *The Establishment of the Japanese Constitutional System*, London: Routledge, 1992, and G. Akita, *The Foundations of Constitutional Government in Modern*

Japan, 1868-1900, Harvard University Press, 1967. In explaining why a constitution was introduced and how its operation led both oligarchs and parties towards compromise, the latter has superseded G. Beckmann, *The Making of the Meiji Constitution,* Universtiy of Kansas Press, 1957. Unfortunately there is nothing comparable on the People's Rights movement. Some aspects of the movement are illuminated by D. Irokawa in his scintillating *The Culture of the Meiji Period,* Princeton University Press, 1985 (translated from a book first published in Japanese in 1970), and by R. Bowen in *Rebellion and Democracy in Meiji Japan,* University of California Press, 1986, a slightly idiosyncratic work which focuses on the violent political protests of the 1880s; but the most satisfactory treatment remains, arguably, N. Ike, *The Beginnings of Political Democracy in Japan,* John Hopkins University Press, 1950, which was written when the local dimensions of political activism had hardly begun to be explored. The findings of Japanese local historians are still very little reflected in Western writing on Japan, but A. Fraser was an early pioneer in this field with *A Political Profile of Tokushima Prefecture in the Early and Middle Meiji Period, 1868-1902,* Australian National University Occasional Paper, 1971, and more recently the Kawasaki area in the early Meiji period has been studied by N. Waters, *Japan's Local Pragmatists,* Harvard University Press, 1989, as has what was formerly the largest feudal domain in J. Baxter, *The Meiji Unification through the Lens of Ishikawa Prefecture,* Harvard University Press, 1994. The local dimension also looms large in R. Mason's fascinating account of *Japan's First General Election,* Cambridge University Press, 1969.

Even more neglected than local political history is, surprisingly, the study of the Diet, but insight into its formative phase is provided by A. Fraser *et al.* in *Japan's Early Parliaments, 1890-1905,* London: Routledge, 1995, and there is an overview which focuses on its changing composition during its first century in D. Ramsdell, *The Japanese Diet,* University Press of America, 1992 . A further aspect which has suffered from serious neglect is the Meiji press, but a major step towards filling that lacuna has been made by J. Huffman, *Creating a Public,* University of Hawaii Press, 1997. Something of the quality of political leadership in the Meiji period can be assessed through B. Silberman and H. Harootunian (eds), *Modern Japanese Leadership: Transition and Change,* Universtiy of Arizona Press, 1966 and through two substantial biographies –

M. Iwata, *Okubo Toshimichi: The Bismarck of Japan*, University of California Press, 1964, and R. Hackett's exhaustively researched *Yamagata Aritomo in the Rise of Modern Japan*, Harvard University Press, 1971. J. Lebra, *Okuma Shigenobu: Statesman of Modern Japan*, Australian National University Press, 1973, is unfortunately too brief to be entirely satisfactory. A case study which throws light on decision-making at the highest levels is S. Okamoto, *The Japanese Oligarchy and the Russo-Japanese War*, Columbia University Press, 1970, which also provides the closest examination of the war's political effects, including the Hibiya Park riots. Some political aspects of the earlier Sino-Japanese war, including the position of the Emperor, are considered in S. Lone's penetrating *Japan's First Modern War*, London: Macmillan, 1994. The creation of the Meiji Emperor's popular image is the subject of T. Fujitani, *Splendid Monarchy*, University of California Press, 1997. There is no comprehensive study of the Meiji Emperor's political role, but he is briefly treated, together with his two successors, in S. Large, *Emperors of the Rising Sun*, Tokyo: Kodansha, 1997.

Specialised studies of political development in the period when parties acquired a real share in power are by no means as numerous as might be expected. In particular there is a remarkable lack of books which deal with the issue of Taisho Democracy. B. Silberman and H. Harootunian (eds), *Japan in Crisis: Essays in Taisho Democracy*, Princeton University Press, 1974, does not entirely fill this gap, excellent though many of its contributions are. Two more recent studies, fortunately, deal well with significant aspects of the issue: A. Gordon, *Labor and Imperial Democracy in Prewar Japan*, University of California Press, 1991, and S. Garon, *The State and Labor in Modern Japan*, University of California Press, 1987. There is a satisfactory analysis of the rise of the Seiyukai in T. Najita, *Hara Kei in the Politics of Compromise, 1905-15*, Harvard University Press, 1967; and the emergence of something approaching a two-party system is well treated by P. Duus, *Party Rivalry and Political Change in Taisho Japan*, Harvard University Press, 1968, a book which contains perhaps the best description in English of political party behaviour and methods in pre-war Japan. Valuable light is also thrown on Japanese politics in the interwar period by S. Hastings, *Neighborhood and Nation in Tokyo, 1905-1937*, University of Pittsburgh Press, 1995. Mention should be made of T.F. Mayer-Oakes (trans. and ed.), *Fragile Victory*, Detroit: Wayne State University

Press, 1968, which gives an insider's view of the 1930 London Naval Treaty crisis in the shape of the political record kept by Baron Harada, the political secretary and go-between of Prince Saionji. The political career of the last *genro* himself is the subject of L. Connors, *The Emperor's Adviser*, London: Croom Helm/Nissan Institute, Oxford, 1987.

Compared with the mainstream parties, the Left is reasonably well served. There is a comprehensive survey by G. Totten, *The Social Democratic Movement in Pre-War Japan*, Yale University Press, 1966, and the emergence and difficulties of the legal left-wing parties are critically examined in S. Large, *Organized Workers and Socialist Politics in Interwar Japan*, Cambridge University Press, 1981. The radical student movement is thoroughly investigated by H. Smith, *Japan's First Student Radicals*, Harvard University Press, 1972, as is the extreme left in G. Beckmann and G. Okubo, *The Japanese Communist Party, 1922-45*. R. Scalapino, *The Japanese Communist Movement, 1920-1966*, University of California Press, 1969, offers a longer, less detailed view. One of the less directly political obstacles to both the left and the established political parties is explored by R.Smethurst, *A Social Basis for Pre-War Japanese Militarism: The Army and the Rural Community*, University of California Press, 1974, which focuses on the Imperial Reservist Association.

A number of books cover both the 1920s and 1930s. Among them J. Morley (ed.), *Dilemmas of Growth in Pre-War Japan*, Princeton University Press, 1971, is a valuable collection of essays, including an important one by A. Tiedemann on big business and politics. The effort of the Justice Ministry to suppress dangerous radical ideas in both decades is objectively examined by R. Mitchell, *Thought Control in Prewar Japan*, Cornell University Press, 1976. G. R. Storry, *The Double Patriots*, London: Chatto and Windus, 1957; Greenwood Press reprint, 1973, gives an overview of the growth of nationalist ideas and societies in the 1920s and their explosion in the 1930s. The radical young officers' movement, which culminated in the 1936 mutiny, is vividly described by B. Shillony, *Revolt in Japan*, Princeton University Press, 1973. A shorter treatment of the February 26 Incident by Shillony appears in G.M.Wilson (ed.), *Crisis Poliltics in Pre-War Japan*, Tokyo: Sophia University, 1970, together with three essays on other aspects of 1930s political life. Army factionalism is examined in J.B.Crowley, *Japan's Quest for Autonomy, 1930-38*, Princeton University Press,

1966, although more has been learned about military politics since it was written and some of its revisionist arguments now seem overstated. It is usefully supplemented by L. Humphreys, *The Way of the Heavenly Sword,* Stanford University Press,1995, which focuses on the army in the 1920s; by M.Peattie, *Ishiwara Kanji,* Princeton University Press, 1975, a judicious study of a remarkable soldier who had a significant impact on Japanese poliltics; and, more generally, by M. and S. Harries, *Soldiers of the Sun,* 1991. Insight into the army's influencing of public opinion is provided by L. Young, *Japan's Total Empire,* University of California Press, 1998. On the question of Japanese fascism, M.Maruyama, *Thought and Behaviour in Modern Japanese Politics,* edited by I.Morris, Oxford University Press, 1963, remains stimulating. The topic has been rather neglected by non-Japanese historians, but it is systematically treated in some detail in a comparative study by P. Brooker, *The Faces of Fraternalism,* Oxford: Clarendon Press, 1991. G. Kasza touches on it too in his *The State and the Mass Media in Japan, 1918-1945,* University of California Press, 1988, while W. Fletcher, *The Search for a New Order: Intellectuals and Fascism in Pre-War Japan,* University of North Carolina Press, 1982, throws light on one important aspect of it by examining the intellectual advocates of the New Structure movement in and before 1940-41 and the ultimate failure of their plans. The major work on the new political order, and the response of the parties to the changed atmosphere of the 1930s, is G. Berger, *Parties out of Power in Japan, 1931-41,* Princeton University Press, 1977. It concentrates more on 1937-41 than 1931-36, however. Four other valuable studies, which are particularly helpful in explaining the decision for war with the United States in 1941, are M. Barnhart, *Japan Prepares for Total War,* Cornell University Press, 1987; R. Butow, *Tojo and the Coming of War,* Stanford University Press, 1961; Y. Oka, *Konoe Fumimaro,* University of Tokyo Press, 1983, and D. Titus, *Palace and Politics in Pre-war Japan,* Columbia University Press, 1974. The two latter volumes are also relevant to an understanding of the role of the inner Establishment generally in pre-war Japan; and Titus provides the only serious study of the Court between 1868 and 1941. His book should be read, together with S. Large's balanced study, *Emperor Hirohito and Showa Japan,* London: Routledge, 1992, and P. Wetzler, *Hirohito and War,* University of Hawaii Press, 1997, by anyone who is tempted to give credence to the sensationalistic assertions of D. Bergamini,

Japan's Imperial Conspiracy: How Emperor Hirohito led Japan into War against the West, New York: Morrow; London: Heinemann, 1971. Insight into the Emperor's attitude can be acquired through the translation by M. Hane of part of the diary of the general who served as his main link with the army before and during the Minobe affair, *Emperor Hirohito and his Chief Aide de Camp: the Honjo Diary, 1933-36*, University of Tokyo Press, 1982. Japanese politics during the Pacific War have tended to be ignored by historians, but B. Shillony, *Politics and Culture in Wartime Japan*, Oxford Universtiy Press, 1981, and E. Drea, *The 1942 Japanese General Election*, University of Kansas Press, 1979, go some way towards filling this gap, and S. Ienega, *Japan's Last War*, translated by F.Baldwin, Oxford: Blackwell, 1979 (also published as *The Pacific War*, New York: Pantheon, 1978) touches on some aspects of wartime politics in the course of a trenchant survey of the 1931-45 period. There are many books on the ending of the war; the best, as far as the Japanese political process is concerned, remains R. Butow, *Japan's Decision to Surrender*, Stanford University Press, 1954.

The Occupation period has received a great deal of attention, particularly from American historians and ex-Occupationnaires. During the last two decades it has benefited from both a more objective approach and from the opening to researchers of voluminous new archival materials. Among older works, K. Kawai, *Japan's American Interlude*, University of Chicago Press, 1960, offers a good introduction, but needs to be supplemented by more recent works such as R. Ward and Y. Sakamoto (ed.), *Democratizing Japan*, University of Hawaii Press, 1987; T. Nishi, *Unconditional Democracy; Education and Politics in Occupied Japan, 1945-52*, Hoover Institution Press, 1982; M. Schaller, *The American Occupation of Japan*, Oxford University Press, 1985, and J. Dower, *Empire and Aftermath: Yoshida Shigeru and the Japanese Experience, 1878-1954*, Harvard University Press, 1979. Dower's volume provides a particularly substantial critical assessment of the Occupation, but pays relatively little attention to party politics. J.Willliams, *Japan's Political Revolution under MacArthur*, University of Georgia Press, 1979, is also disappointing in this respect (and unconvincing in its denial that there was an American 'reverse-course'), although it does have interest as a personal account by a member of SCAP's Government Section. Fortunately, a detailed treatment is now available in the form of a translation of a work by one of Japan's most productive political scientists, J.Masumi, *Post-War Politics in Japan, 1945-1955*, University of California Press, 1986; and an older book by H.Quigley and J.Turner, *The New Japan*, University of Minnesota Press, 1956, is still of value too. Yoshida Shigeru, *The Yoshida Memoirs*, Houghton Mifflin, 1962, expressed the views of the man who rose to unexpected dominance of the main conservative party. Among more specialised studies of relevance to post-war politics, R.P.Dore, *Land Reform in Japan*, Oxford University Press, 1959, and J.Moore, *Japanese Workers and the Struggle for Power, 1945-47*, University of Wisconsin Press, 1983, require particular mention, as does the detailed, and largely personal, account of labour union development and the 'reverse-course' by the one-time 'New Dealer' head of SCAP's Labour Division, T.Cohen, *Remaking Japan*, ed. by H.Passin, New York: The Free Press, 1987. In recent years new light has been thrown on the creation of the postwar constitution (and the extent and nature of Japanese influence on it) by T. Kataoka, *The Price of a Constitution*, London: Taylor and Francis, 1991; K. Inoue, *MacArthur's Japanese Constitution*, University of Chicago Press, 1991, and S. Koseki, *The Birth of Japan's Postwar Constitution*, Boulder, CO: Westview Press, 1997. This is also one of the topics covered by J. Dower in his wide-ranging and penetrating *Embracing Defeat*, London: Allen Lane, the Penguin Press, 1999.

Books on politics since the Occupation are much more numerous. Pride of place must go to another translation of a work by J. Masumi, *Contemporary Politics in Japan*, University of California Press, 1995, which provides a richly detailed political history down to the 1980s. It is usefully supplemented for the 1950s by T. Kataoka, *Creating Single-Party Democracy*, Hoover Institution Press, 1992. The Liberal Democratic Party in the 1950s and 1960s is well examined by H. Fukui, *Party in Power*, University of California Press, 1970, and N. Thayer, *How the Conservatives Rule Japan*, Princeton University Press, 1969, and its election success was illuminated by G.E.Curtis in his classic *Election Campaigning: Japanese Style*, Columbia University Press, 1971. An important study of broader scope, which combines theory, analysis and history, is K. Calder, *Crisis and Compensation: Public Policy and Political Stability in Japan, 1949-1986*, Princeton University Press, 1988, and there is also an insightful, if much shorter, treatment of political history during the second half of the twentieth century in G. Allinson, *Japan's Postwar History*, Cornell University

Press, 1997. The close links between politicians and business leaders are emphasised by C.Yanaga, *Big Business in Japanese Politics*, Yale University Press, 1968, and the contribution of government planning to Japan's economic growth is famously described and highly evaluated by C.Johnson, *MITI and the Japanese Miracle: the Growth of Industrial Policy, 1925-1975*, Stanford University Press, 1985. Among subsequent analyses D. Okimoto, *Between MITI and the Market*, Stanford University Press,1989, is noteworthy. E.Vogel (ed.), *Modern Japanese Organization and Decision Making*, University of California Press, 1975, is valuable for an understanding of how Japanese government functioned in the 1970s, while C. Johnson, *Japan: Who Governs*, New York: W.W.Norton, 1995, is a lively collection of essays which, among other things, presents a revealing picture of Tanaka Kakuei. Changes of attitude towards Japan's international position among government leaders, intellectuals and bureaucrats are examined by K. Pyle, *The Japanese Question*, AEI Press, 2nd edn, 1996. G. Packard's lively *Protest in Tokyo: the Security Treaty Crisis of 1960*, Princeton University Press, 1966, remains unsurpassed as an account of the major political crisis of post-Occupation Japan, throwing light on, among other things, the persistent divisions on the Left. These are also extensively discussed in a comprehensive analysis of the left-wing parties (down to the mid-1960s) by A. Cole, G. Totten, and C. Uyehara, *Socialist Parties in Post-War Japan*, Yale University Press, 1966. A recent study of labour unions and their political activities is I. Kume, *Disparaged Success*, Cornell University Press, 1998. All the parties are carefully assessed in R. Hrebenar *et al.*, *The Japanese Party System*, Boulder CO: Westview Press, 1986 and subsequent editions. Of the many books on the Japanese political process in general, particular mention should be made of B. Richardson and S. Flanagan, *Politics in Japan*, Boston, MA: Little, Brown, 1984, J. Stockwin, *Japan: Divided Politics in a Growth Society*, Weidenfeld and Nicolson, 1975 – extensively revised and brought up-to-date as *Governing Japan*, Oxford: Blackwell, 1999; G. Curtis, *The Japanese Way of Politics*, Columbia University Press, 1988; J. Kyogoku, *The Political Dynamics of Japan*, University of Tokyo Press, 1987; H. Abe *et al.*, *The Government and Politics of Japan*, University of Tokyo Press, 1994; B. Richardson, *Japanese Democracy*, Yale University Press, 1997, and M. Kohno, *Japan's Postwar Party Politics*, Princeton University Press, 1997.

A number of books focus on Japanese political developments in the 1990s. Particularly notable is T. Pempel, *Regime Shift*, Cornell University Press, 1998, a *tour de force* which places Japan in a comparative, as well as a broader postwar, context. Useful surveys of recent developments can also be found in P. Jain and T. Inoguchi (ed.), *Japanese Politics Today*, Basingstoke: Macmillan Education, 1997; M. Mochizuki, *Japan: Domestic Change and Foreign Policy*, Rand, 1995, and N. Narita, *Changing Japanese Politics*, Foreign Press Center/Japan, 1999. The important 1996 election is analysed in H. Otake (ed.), *How Election Reform Boomeranged*, Japan Center for International Exchange, 1998. Japanese leaders are castigated for failing to adjust to the new economic and social problems of the 1990s by R. Katz, *Japan: the System that Soured*, Armonk, NY: M.E. Sharpe, 1998, and G. McCormack, *The Emptiness of Japanese Affluence*, M.E. Sharpe, 1996. A useful survey of various aspects of contemporary Japan is P. Heenan (ed.), *The Japan Handbook*, London/Chicago: Fitzroy Dearborn, 1998.

Biography provides its own distinctive approach to Japanese political history. In addition to those already noted, there are several other biographies of significant political figures, notably C. Yates, *Saigo Takamori*, Kegan Paul International, 1995; L.R.Oates, *Populist Nationalism in Pre-War Japan: a Biography of Nakano Seigo*, London: Geo. Allen and Unwin, 1985; S.Minichiello, *Retreat from Reform* (a study of Nagai Ryutaro), University of Hawaii Press, 1984; G.M.Wilson, *Radical Nationalist in Japan: Kita Ikki, 1883-1937*, Harvard University Press, 1969; F.O.Miller, *Minobe Tatsukichi*, Universtiy of California Press, 1965; F.Notehelfer, *Kotoku Shusui*, Cambridge University Press, 1971; H.Kublin, *Asian Revolutionary: The Life of Katayama Sen*, Princeton University Press, 1964; T.Stanley, *Osugi Sakae, Anarchist in Taisho Japan*, Harvard University Press, 1982, and S. Sato *et al.*, *Postwar Politician*, Tokyo: Kodansha, 1990, a eulogistic account of Ohira Masayoshi. There are also three studies of important political journalists, which go some way to make up for the paucity of studies of the Japanese press: J.L. Huffman, *Politics of the Meiji Press: The Life of Fukuchi Genichiro*, University of Hawaii Press, 1980; J.Pierson, *Tokutomi Soho, 1863-1957*, Princeton University Press, 1980; and S.H.Nolte, *Liberalism in Modern Japan: Ishibashi Tanzan and his Teachers, 1905-1960*, University of California Press, 1986. K.Strong, *Ox Against the Storm*, Tenterden, Kent: Paul Norbury, 1977, which tells the story of Tanaka Shozo, a pioneer protester against corruption and pollution in the Meiji period, should also be mentioned. Finally, it should be noted that essays on some modern political leaders are to be found in A.Craig and D.Shively (ed.), *Personality in Japanese History*, University of California Press, 1970, and that brief studies of Ito, Okuma, Hara, Inukai and Saionji by an eminent Japanese historian are contained in Y.Oka, *Five Political Leaders of Modern Japan*, University of Tokyo Press, 1986.

Books on political ideas and ideology form a further category. A broad but penetrating analysis is provided by T.Najita, *Japan*, Englewood Cliffs, NY: Prentice-Hall, 1974. Both H. Harootunian, *Toward Restoration*, University of California Press, 1970, and J. Koschmann, *The Mito Ideology*, University of California Press, 1987, examine closely the intellectual origins of the Meiji Ishin. Political thought in the late nineteenth century is included in the comprehensive survey by M. Kosaka, *Japanese Thought in the Meiji Era*, Pan-Pacific Press, 1958, and the ideas of both the People's Rights theorists and the Meiji oligarchs are surveyed by J. Pittau, *Political Thought in Early Meiji Japan, 1868-1889*, Harvard University Press, 1967. The influence on the Meiji constitution of Ito Hirobumi's principal foreign adviser is assessed by J. Siemes, *Hermann Roesler and the Making of the Meiji State*, Tokyo: Sophia University and Tuttle, 1968. C. Gluck, *Japan's Modern Myths: Ideology in the Late Meiji Period*, Princeton University Press, 1985, is a remarkable tour de force which offers an original and stimulating examination of non-official as well as official ideas and attitudes and goes well beyond the normal bounds of intellectual history by providing an authoritative depiction of the political and social context within which the various strands of ideology were formed. The Nohonshugi tradition is the subject of T. Havens, *Farm and Nation in Modern Japan, 1870-1940*, Princeton University Press, 1974; and two even more traditional influences on modern Japanese political thinking are discussed by W.W.Smith, *Confucianism in Modern Japan*, Tokyo: Hokuseido Press, 1959, and D.C.Holtom, *Modern Japan and Shinto Nationalism*, University of Chicago Press, 1943. There is also a translation (by J.O.Gauntlet) of the 1937 official version of the ideology of Japanism in R.K.Hall (ed.), *Kokutai no Hongi: Cardinal Principles of the National Entity of Japan*, Harvard University Press, 1949, but this is not commonly available. Fortunately, extracts from it are included in the wide-ranging selection of primary texts edited by R. Tsunoda, W. de Bary and

D. Keene, *Sources of Japanese Tradition*, Columbia University Press, 1958. On the other side of politics the difficulties of assimilating Marxism are described and discussed in G. Bernstein, *Japanese Marxist: A Portrait of Kawakami Hajime*, Harvard University Press, 1976, and G. Hoston, *Marxism and the Crisis of Development in Pre-War Japan*, Princeton University Press, 1986.

For those who read Japanese there are many more books available for use. Those which have been particularly helpful in the writing of this book include:

Iwanami Shoten (ed), *Iwanami Koza Nihon Rekishi*, vols 15-23, Iwanami Shoten, 1975-6.
Hayashi Shigeru and Tsuji Kiyoaki (ed.), *Nihon Naikaku Shiroku*, vols 1-6, Dai-ichi Hoki, 1981.
Masumi Junnosuke, *Nihon Seito Shiron*, 7 vols, Tokyo Daigaku Shuppankai, 1966-80.
Hashikawa Bunzo and Matsumoto Sannosuke (ed.), *Kindai Nihon Seiji Shiso Shi*, 2 vols, Yuhikaku, 1970.
Shinobu Seizaburo, *Nihon Seiji Shi*, 4 vols, Nanso-sha, 1978.
Chuo Koronsha (ed.), *Nihon no Rekishi*, vols 21-26, Chuo Koronsha, 1966.
Fujiwara Akira *et al.* (ed.), *Kindai Nihon no Kiso Chishiki*, Yuhikaku, 1972.
Toyama Shigeki, *Meiji Ishin to Gendai*, Iwanami Shinsho, 1968.
Sakata Yoshio, *Meiji Ishin Shi*, Miraisha, 1960.
Nakamura Masanori (ed.), *Taikei Nihon Kokka Shi*, vol.4, Tokyo Daigaku Shuppankai, 1975.
Inada Masatsugu (ed.), *Meiji Kokka Keisei Katei no Kenkyu*, Ochanomizu Shobo, 1966, rev.edn, 1977.
Tamamuro Taijo, *Saigo Takamori*, Iwanami Shinsho, 1960.
Horie Hideichi and Toyama Shigeki (ed.), *Jiyuminken no Kenkyu*, vol. 1, Yuhikaku, 1959.
Emura Eiichi and Nakamura Masanori (ed.), *Kokken to Minken no Sokoku*, Sanshodo, 1974.
Umetani Noboru, *Meiji Zenki Seiji Shi no Kenkyu*, Miraisha, 1963.
Akita Kindai Shi Kenkyukai (ed.), *Kindai Akita no Rekishi to Minshu*, 1969.
Emura Eiichi, *Jiyu Minken Kakumei no Kenkyu*, Hosei Daigaku Shuppankyoku, 1984.

Miyachi Masato, *Nichi-Ro Sengo Seiji Shi no Kenkyu*, Tokyo Daigaku Shuppankai, 1967.

Mitani Taichiro, *Nihon Seito Seiji no Keisei*, Tokyo Daigaku Shuppankai, 1967.

Oka Yoshitake, *Tenkanki no Taisho*, Tokyo Daigaku Shuppankai, 1969.

Matsuo Takayoshi, *Taisho Demokurashii*, Iwanami Shoten, 1974.

Kimbara Samon, *Taisho-ki no Seito to Kokumin*, Hanawa, 1973.

Banno Junji and Miyachi Masato (ed.), *Nihon Kindai Shi ni okeru Tenkanki no Kenkyu*, Yamakawa Shuppansha, 1985.

Tokyo Daigaku Shakai Kagaku Kenkyujo (ed.), *Fascism-ki no Kokka to Shakai*, 8 vols, Tokyo Daigaku Shuppankai, 1978.

Ito Takashi, *Showa Shoki Seiji Shi no Kenkyu*, Tokyo Daigaku Shppankai, 1969.

Abe Hirozumi, *Nihon Fascism Kenkyu Josetsu*, Miraisha, 1975.

Miyake Masaki *et al.* (ed.), *Showa Shi no Gumbu to Seiji*, vols 1-4, Dai-ichi Hoki, 1983.

Yabe Teiji, *Konoe Fumimaro*, Yomiuri Shimbunsha, 1976.

Tsutsui Kiyotada, *Showa-ki Nihon no Kozo*, Yuhikaku, 1984.

Boeicho Boeikenshujo Senshishitsu (ed.), *Senshi Sosho: Daihonei Rikugunbu*, vols 1 and 2, Asagumo Shimbunsha, 1967.

Ishida Takeshi, *Hakyoku to Heiwa*, Tokyo Daigaku Shuppankai, 1968.

Masumi Junnosuke, *Sengo Seiji*, 2 vols, Tokyo Daigaku Shuppankai, 1983.

Ito Takashi, *Showa-ki no Seiji*, Yamakawa Shuppankai, 1983.

Yamada Hiroshi *et al.*, *Sengo Seiji no Ayumi*, Horitsu Bunkasha, 1990

INDEX